By the Editors of
CONSUMER GUIDE®

With assistance from the
American College of Preventive Medicine

MEDICAL BOOK OF

HEALTH HINTS & TIPS

*100*S OF PRACTICAL WAYS
TO LIVE A HEALTHIER LIFE

Publications International, Ltd.

WRITERS

Bobbie Hasselbring is former senior editor of *Medical Self-Care* and has authored five books on mental and physical health, including portions of *The Home Remedies Handbook* and *Women's Home Remedies Health Guide.* A nationally recognized health writer, she has written a health and fitness column for the *Oregonian* and *Northwest Magazine.* The American Heart Association presented her with its Award for Media Excellence in 1991 and 1992.

Heather Joslyn is a writer and editor who has worked extensively in the health field. Her work has appeared in *New Physician, McCall's, Special Report,* and in a series of health publications, including *Adult's Health Advisor, Skin Care,* and *Dental Health Advisor.*

Brianna L. Politzer is a freelance writer specializing in health, medicine, and nutrition. She has worked as a newspaper reporter and editor and has contributed to many health publications, including *Medical Tribune News Service, American Health, AIDS-Patient Care, The Home Remedies Handbook,* and *Women's Home Remedies Health Guide.*

CONSULTANTS

This publication was reviewed by the **American College of Preventive Medicine** (ACPM), the professional organization of physician specialists who practice preventive medicine. The ACPM advances the science and practice of disease prevention and health promotion, and provides leadership in research, professional education, development of public policy, and enhancement of standards for preventive medicine. The ACPM was founded in 1954. Appreciation is extended to the following members of the ACPM for their participation:

Stephen B. Corbin, D.D.S., M.P.H., Associate Director for External Relations, Division of Oral Health, National Center for Prevention Services, Centers for Disease Control and Prevention

Martha Johns, M.D., M.P.H., Medical Director, Center for Health Promotion, Sharp HealthCare; Clinical Faculty, Sharp Family Medicine Residency

Karen C. Johnson, M.D., M.P.H., Assistant Professor, Departments of Preventive Medicine and Medicine, University of Tennessee

Mark B. Johnson, M.D., M.P.H., Director, Jefferson County Department of Health and Environment

Steven Jonas, M.D., M.P.H., Professor of Preventive Medicine, School of Medicine, State University of New York at Stony Brook

Robert A. Margulies, M.D., M.P.H., Senior Attending Physician, Prehospital Emergency Medical Services, Hartford Hospital; Clinical Assistant Professor, Emergency Medicine/Surgery, University of Connecticut School of Medicine

Steven H. Woolf, M.D., M.P.H., Assistant Clinical Professor, Department of Family Practice, Medical College of Virginia

ILLUSTRATIONS

All illustrations by Lane Gregory except those on page 347 by Joanne Adams

PHOTO CREDITS

Front cover: **T.J. Florian/Rainbow:** (bottom); **FPG International:** Ron Chapple (top center); Arthur Tilley (top); **Photri:** (bottom center).

CONTENTS

CONTENTS

CONTENTS

CONTENTS

CONTENTS

FOREWORD

*M*edical Book of Health Hints & Tips offers you practical, up-to-date, accurate information in readable, bite-size chunks, without all the lofty medical terms or jargon.

Medical Book of Health Hints & Tips is meant to be a comprehensive volume, but we don't expect you to read it cover-to-cover in one sitting. The book is organized into large chapters dealing with general areas of interest, such as nutrition and medical care, and these, in turn, are broken down into more specific topics. Browse the table of contents, and make some mental notes about sections you'd like to refer to later. Then read a section every now and then, when you have a few minutes. If you have a health problem now or are interested in a specific topic, look it up in the index at the back of the book, and refer to the pages noted. Pay special attention to information marked with a square icon ❏. This symbol indicates specific steps you can take to improve your health. But use common sense when you follow the advice. Don't try every suggested treatment for a given ailment all at once, for example.

Keep in mind, too, that this book is not meant to replace your doctor's advice and treatment. We have indicated which symptoms might suggest a serious problem and warrant a trip to the doctor. And we encourage you to discuss any health concerns or questions you may have with your doctor.

We invite you to become actively involved and responsible for your own health. Don't think of your physician as being in sole charge of your health. Think of it as a partnership effort in which you have an essential role. As you participate in that partnership, refer to this book often and educate yourself about the range of factors that influence your mental, physical, and emotional health. Analyze the way you care for your body and resolve to make changes for the better. Use the book to spur discussions with your doctor. Above all, use it to be the healthiest and happiest you can be.

NUTRITION

*M*any of us received a rudimentary nutrition education in grammar school. We learned about the "four food groups" and were taught to eat moderately from each group every day. We also learned a bit about how our body uses specific vitamins and nutrients: vitamin A for eyesight, calcium for strong bones and teeth, and so on.

Times have changed.

Researchers now know the foods we eat strongly influence our health: They pave the way for us to have healthy babies, help prevent or promote diseases, may sharpen or weaken our mental acuity, and may even affect our moods. In short, we now know proper nutrition is vitally important to almost every physiological process and function.

These physiological processes may be complicated, but learning what you need to know about nutrition doesn't need to be. Just read this chapter, then think before you open your mouth.

❑   ❑   ❑

Dietary Guidelines: The Food Pyramid

There Are Now Six Food Groups Instead of Four

Many factors are involved in answering the question "What should I eat?" But one thing is certain—the days of the basic four food groups are long gone. Here are just three of the many reasons for their disappearance.

First, they weren't specific enough.

Second, no distinction was made in the value of nutrients. In other words, all the food groups were considered equally important. An apple was encouraged with the same emphasis as a steak.

Third, the recommendations did not specify preferences within each food group; for example, ice cream appeared to be as healthful as a glass of skim milk.

Enter the Dietary Guidelines for Americans created by the U.S. Department of Agriculture (USDA), and the corresponding Food Pyramid. The new recommendations were designed to answer some of the criticisms of the old basic four food groups.

The following are the official U.S. Dietary Guidelines:

- ❑ Eat a variety of foods.
- ❑ Maintain a healthy weight.
- ❑ Choose a diet low in fat, saturated fat, and cholesterol.
- ❑ Choose a diet with plenty of vegetables, fruits, and grains.
- ❑ Use sugars only in moderation.
- ❑ Use salt and sodium only in moderation.
- ❑ If you drink alcoholic beverages, do so in moderation.

The guidelines are accompanied by the Food Pyramid, which graphically illustrates the emphasis each food group should have in our diets. There are now six food groups instead of four. Fats and sugars occupy the smallest space at the top of the Pyramid, since they should be eaten less frequently than other foods. Also, small symbols throughout the Pyramid caution us to be on the alert for hidden fats and sugars within other foods.

FOOD PYRAMID

Proceeding downward, here are the recommended number of daily servings of each food group:

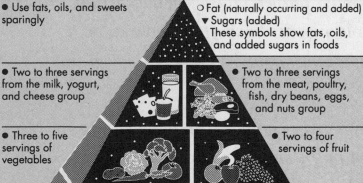

- ● Use fats, oils, and sweets sparingly

○ Fat (naturally occurring and added)
▼ Sugars (added)
These symbols show fats, oils, and added sugars in foods

- ● Two to three servings from the milk, yogurt, and cheese group
- ● Two to three servings from the meat, poultry, fish, dry beans, eggs, and nuts group
- ● Three to five servings of vegetables
- ● Two to four servings of fruit

- ● Six to 11 servings from the bread, cereal, rice, and pasta group

How Much Is a Serving?

Serving size depends on the food. Here's a quick primer. One serving equals:

- ● ½ cup cooked vegetables
- ● ½ cup raw vegetables or 1 cup raw leafy greens

- 1 piece of fruit (such as a medium-size apple, orange, or banana)
- ½ cup diced fruit, grapes, or berries
- 6 ounces of juice
- 1 slice of bread
- ½ cup cooked rice, cereal, grain, or pasta
- ½ bagel
- 1 ounce of dry cereal
- 1 cup of milk or yogurt
- 1½ ounces of cheese
- 3½ ounces of meat, fish, or chicken

According to the USDA, most people need at least the minimum number of servings of foods from each group daily. Body size and activity level may increase the number of servings needed by certain individuals. Young children, the agency states, need the same variety as adults but may eat smaller servings.

The new guidelines are a definite improvement over the old, but two primary problems remain.

First, although we are cautioned against excess intake of fats and sugars, the Food Pyramid still groups steak (a relatively high-fat, high-cholesterol, low-fiber source of protein) with beans (a low-fat, cholesterol-free, high-fiber source of protein). Cookies, cakes, and pies are grouped with bread. Spinach is grouped with french fries. In short, this guideline graphic doesn't indicate which foods in each food group are highest in nutritional value.

Second, the number of servings of certain foods may not be adequate for everyone. For example, pregnant women need higher amounts of calcium-rich dairy products and high-protein foods. (Refer to *Nutrition During Pregnancy*

and Breast-feeding, page 39, for more information.)

However, with a little extra knowledge, savvy consumers can use the guidelines as the basis for a diet that meets their nutritional needs, promotes good health, and may reduce the risk of disease. Here are some pointers to get the most out of the guidelines:

❑ **Try to select foods that are minimally processed.** Many foods lose nutrients during processing. For example, whole-wheat bread and pasta contain more essential nutrients than bread or pasta made with bleached white flour. Likewise, brown rice is better for you than white rice. The closer the food is to its original form, the more nutrients.

❑ **Don't peel fruits and vegetables.** When you can, leave the skin on. It contains many vitamins and minerals. Just be sure to wash the skins.

❑ **Ideally, choose fresh or frozen foods.** These contain the most nutrients.

❑ **Try not to boil vegetables.** Essential nutrients are boiled away into the cooking water. Instead, steam vegetables on the stove or in the microwave with only a few tablespoons of water. If you must boil vegetables, do so in the least amount of water for the shortest time possible to preserve their vitamin and mineral content.

❑ **Don't overcook vegetables.** Eat them raw or cook them only until they are tender-crisp.

❑ **Choose the foods within each food group that are lowest in salt, fat, and sugar.** Add only minimal amounts of these dietary nemeses when preparing food.

Ideally, Choose Fresh or Frozen Foods

Carbohydrates Are the Body's Principal Source of Energy

❑ **Choose milk in cardboard containers.** Or buy milk in colored plastic containers rather than translucent plastic containers when possible. Light breaks down some of the vitamins contained in the milk.

The Macronutrients

Macronutrients come in three varieties: carbohydrates, proteins, and lipids (fats and oils). The body needs all three of these macronutrients to survive. To thrive, it needs them in the proper amounts. The following sections are a short course on macronutrients—what your body uses them for, where to find them, and how much you need of each.

CARBOHYDRATES

Carbohydrates come in three varieties: simple, complex, and fibrous. All three types contain about four calories per gram. Here's a breakdown:

● Complex carbohydrates, or starches, are found in legumes (dried peas and beans), grains, vegetables, and fruits.

● Fiber is found in whole grains, legumes, vegetables, and fruits.

● Simple carbohydrates, or sugars, are found in table sugar, honey, natural fruit sugars, and molasses.

Carbohydrates are the body's principal source of energy. They fuel all bodily functions, including the digestion of other foods. While the other macronutrients can also be converted into energy, carbohydrates are the easiest fuel source for the body to process.

According to the USDA's Food Pyramid, more than half of our daily calories should come in the form of carbohydrates. Here's how to get the most nutritional bang for your buck:

❑ Consume the majority of your carbohydrate calories in the form of whole grains, beans, potatoes, fruits, and vegetables.

❑ Minimize your intake of foods made with white flour and white sugar, such as cake, cookies, and candy.

❑ Eat high-fiber carbohydrates, such as bran cereal, apples, dry beans (kidneys, pintos, and limas), peas, parsnips, and potatoes. (For more information on the benefits of dietary fiber, see *Increasing Your Fiber Intake*, page 23.)

PROTEIN

Protein, like carbohydrate, contains four calories per gram. It performs two essential functions in the body: growth and maintenance of tissues and formation of infection-fighting antibodies. Protein is found in many foods, primarily those of animal origin. High-protein foods include:

● meat
● poultry
● fish and shellfish
● eggs
● dairy products
● grain products
● dry beans and peas

While it's important to eat enough protein (especially during childhood, adolescence, and pregnancy), too much protein can put unnecessary stress on the kidneys. It may also contribute to obesity, heart disease, and possibly certain cancers when the sources of protein consumed are primarily high-fat meat and dairy products.

The recommended dietary allowance (RDA) for protein is 0.8 gram per kilogram (2.2 pounds) of ideal body weight per day. Pregnant and breast-feeding women require an additional 30 and 20 grams, respectively.

LIPIDS

Lipids are a group of fatty substances that include fats, oils, and waxes. They help the body absorb and transport fat-soluble vitamins (A, D, E, and K), act as a ready source of energy, insulate against heat loss, and act as a cushion for many tissues and organs.

The following types of lipids are found in food: triglycerides, hydrogenated or partially hydrogenated fats and oils, cholesterol, and linoleic acid.

Triglycerides: the primary form of fat found in foods. Fat is composed primarily of three types of fatty acids: saturated, polyunsaturated, or monounsaturated. The biggest distinction between saturated and unsaturated fats is that the saturated ones, such as butter or shortening, are solid at room temperature. Vegetable oil (polyunsaturated) is not. Saturated fats are implicated in raising the body's cholesterol level and in clogging the arteries.

Saturated fats are found in all animal products, as well as in coconut and palm oils. Polyunsaturated fats make up most of the fats in corn, safflower, sunflower, and soybean oils. Olive and canola oil contain mostly monounsaturated fat. Peanut oil has slightly more monounsaturated than polyunsaturated fat. In general, the less saturated fat an oil contains the more healthful it is.

THE EIGHT ESSENTIAL AMINO ACIDS

Proteins are composed of 20 organic compounds called amino acids. The body requires these amino acids to put dietary protein to work. While the body can synthesize half of these amino acids, it must get at least eight of the others from the diet. (The final two come partly from the body and partly from nutritional sources.) These eight are called the essential amino acids.

Protein sources are considered "complete" if they contain all eight of the essential amino acids. They are "incomplete" if they lack one or more of the essential eight. All animal products are complete sources of protein, but plant sources usually lack a few amino acids. They can be combined to create proteins as complete as those found in meat and dairy products (refer to *A Vegetarian Lifestyle: Is It for You?*, page 35).

❑   ❑   ❑

Hydrogenated or partially hydrogenated fats and oils: lipids processed to prolong shelf life. They are semisolid at room temperature. Hydrogenating a fat or oil creates *trans* fatty acids, which research has found to be potentially more harmful than saturated fats.

Cholesterol: a white, crystalline substance found in all animal fats and oils (refer to *Eat to Control Your Blood Cholesterol Level*, page 14).

Linoleic acid: the only "essential" polyunsaturated fatty acid. This means the body cannot synthesize this lipid and must obtain it through dietary sources.

It's well known that one step in losing excess body fat is reducing fat intake. One reason is fat contains a whopping nine calories per gram. (Remember, protein and carbohydrate have only four.) Also, the body needs to do minimal processing to store dietary fat as body fat; therefore, it processes and stores fat more readily than protein or carbohydrates. In addi-

One Step in Losing Excess Body Fat Is Reducing Fat Intake

13

tion to providing a hefty dose of calories, a high-fat diet is also associated with an increased risk of heart disease and certain types of cancer.

Most nutrition experts believe that no more than 30 percent of the calories you consume in a day should come from fat (see the next section, *Eat to Control Your Blood Cholesterol Level*).

Eat to Control Your Blood Cholesterol Level

To Reduce Your Blood Cholesterol Level, Reduce Saturated Fat in Your Diet

Whether you're among the thousands with a high blood cholesterol level or you just want to make sure your cholesterol level stays low, reducing saturated fat in your diet should be your top priority.

A few facts about cholesterol:

- **Cholesterol is essential to your body's chemistry.** But you don't have to consume any: The body is able to manufacture all the cholesterol it needs.

- **All animals produce cholesterol.** So foods from animal sources, such as egg yolks, meat, poultry, fish, and milk products, contain cholesterol. Plants do not produce cholesterol, so grains, fruits, vegetables, and nuts do not contain cholesterol.

- **Heredity determines how much cholesterol the body makes.** In other words, some people manufacture more cholesterol than other people do, depending on their genes. The upshot is that your neighbor might eat bacon burgers until they come out of his ears and have a low blood cholesterol level, while you eat nothing but sprouts and nonfat cream cheese and your cholesterol level is dangerously high.

- **Your body can adjust somewhat.** If you regularly consume foods from animal sources, your body slows down its production of cholesterol. If you eat mostly foods from plant sources, your body manufactures more cholesterol to get the amount it needs. However, saturated fat can disrupt the body's cholesterol balancing mechanism.

- **The amount of cholesterol in foods you eat is not the most important "no-no."** The amount of saturated fat consumed has the greatest dietary effect on blood cholesterol levels. Total fat intake and total calorie intake are important as well. In fact, if you cut the total amount of fat in your diet, you'll probably also cut your cholesterol intake, since most high-cholesterol foods contain a lot of fat.

- **Cholesterol is distributed throughout the body by lipoproteins.** Low-density lipoprotein (LDL), often referred to as "bad" cholesterol, carries cholesterol to the cells. The cholesterol that is not used by the cells can build up on artery walls. This build up, known as atherosclerosis, may decrease blood flow through the arteries and lead to heart attacks and strokes. High-density lipoprotein (HDL or "good" cholesterol) helps rid the body of cholesterol by carrying it to the liver where it is excreted.

- **The ratio of LDL to HDL is what counts.** In other words, a high total cholesterol level (LDL plus HDL) may not be so bad if you have a high level of HDL. Likewise, a low total cholesterol may not be as good as it seems, if the HDL is very low. Here's the straight scoop: A desirable level of LDL is below 130, and a desirable level of HDL is 35 and above. (For more information, see *Keep Tabs on Your Blood Cholesterol Level* in Chapter 8, page 293.)

Now that you know the technical details, here are the five commandments for a cholesterol-lowering diet:

- ❑ **Reduce the amount of fat in your diet.** No more than 30 percent of your overall calories should come from fat. You can reduce the percentage of fat you consume to ten percent of calories without any adverse health effects. (The exception to this rule is for babies and children, who need a higher amount of fat in their diets to grow properly. Don't give skim or low-fat milk to a child younger than aged two years.)

- ❑ **Sharply reduce your use of saturated and hydrogenated fats.** Also, avoid palm oil and coconut oil, which are solid at room temperature and have the same effect on your health as saturated fats do. (See *The Macronutrients,* page 12.) The total amount of these fats you eat should compose no more than ten percent of your daily caloric intake.

- ❑ **Substitute monounsaturated and polyunsaturated fat for saturated fat.** But remember to keep your total fat intake to no more than 30 percent of your total daily calories.

- ❑ **Limit foods high in cholesterol.** These include egg yolks, baked goods made with eggs and saturated fats, liver, dark meat poultry, and whole-milk dairy products.

- ❑ **Keep your total number of calories to a reasonable number.** Base your calorie intake on your age, your weight, and your activity level. If necessary, ask your physician for help with this. Never go below 1,200 calories per day.

Here are some specific tips to help you comply with the guidelines:

- ❑ **Figure the maximum number of fat grams you can eat per day.** Multiply the number of calories you consume in a day by 0.30, then divide the total by 9. Then budget your fat intake over the course of a day. Alternatively, figure out the percentage of fat calories in a given food: Multiply the number of fat grams by 9, divide by the total number of calories, then multiply by 100.

- ❑ **Use saturated-fat-laden meats mostly as condiments or for special occasions.** These include beef, lamb, salami, sausage, and bacon. Replace them with skinless, white-meat chicken and turkey; lean cuts of meat; fish; or vegetable sources of protein in your daily diet.

- ❑ **Replace high-fat dairy products with nonfat or low-fat versions.** These days, a wide variety of tasty low-fat and fat-free yogurt, sour cream, whipped topping, cheese, and cream cheese is available.

- ❑ **Limit your use of margarine and butter.** Remember, although margarine is not as

No More than 30 Percent of Your Daily Calories Should Come from Fat

The RDAs Serve as a Nutritional Frame of Reference

high in saturated fat as butter, it is hydrogenated. Hydrogenated fat contains *trans* fatty acids, which may be as bad or worse for you than saturated fats.

❑ **When sautéing foods, use only a small amount of olive or canola oil.** Make friends with a can of nonstick spray, and use nonstick cookware, if possible.

❑ **Lower your consumption of all meats, and increase your consumption of high-fiber foods.** Good high-fiber choices include whole grains, fruits, and vegetables. These foods fill your stomach without filling you up with fat and cholesterol. Also, high-fiber foods have a cholesterol-lowering effect.

❑ **Learn the art of making an egg-white omelet.** Accustom yourself to nonfat liquid egg substitutes. In recipes, use two egg whites for every whole egg called for.

Understanding the RDAs

We all have different nutritional needs. Infants require different amounts of nutrients and calories than adolescents. Pregnant or breast-feeding women require different amounts of nutrients than other women, and both groups may require different amounts than men. How then do we know what we as individuals need?

This is where the National Research Council in Washington steps in. This agency reviews the many nutrition studies published every year in order to establish dietary guidelines. It provides these guidelines in the form of the Recommended Dietary Allowance, or RDA.

In short, the RDAs are meant to serve as a nutritional frame of reference for most people. The RDAs attempt to specify the minimum amounts of certain nutrients the population at large needs to maintain good health. Because the RDAs are aimed at large groups, they are not meant to specify the exact amounts of nutrients you as an individual should strive to take in. Only a nutritionist, dietitian, or physician can determine what's right for you. However, if you are in good health, using the RDAs as a reference point will probably do you no harm.

VITAMINS AND MINERALS

The tables on the next two pages provide a graphic introduction to two vital nutrients: vitamins and minerals. These nutrients round out the list of essential nutrients that includes carbohydrate, lipids, and protein. (See *The Macronutrients*, page 12.) A diet that supplies all of these essential nutrients in appropriate amounts is referred to as an "adequate diet."

The first table lists the vitamins your body craves, some of the effects of deficiency of each, some foods that contain them, and the RDAs for each nutrient. **Fat-soluble vitamins** dissolve and are stored in fat. If too much of these vitamins is stored in the body, the effects can be harmful (see the sidebar, *Warning: Vitamin Toxicity*, page 19). The first four vitamins listed—A, D, E, and K—are fat-soluble. The remaining vitamins are

VITAMINS: THEIR FUNCTIONS, YOUR BODY'S REQUIREMENTS

Substance	Deficiency	Food Sources	RDA
A (retinol)	Night blindness, dry skin, susceptibility to infectious diseases	Green, yellow, and orange vegetables; yellow fruits; butter; whole milk	Men: 1,000 mcg Women, PG: 800 mcg BF: 1,300 mcg
D (calciferol)	Rickets (weakened, malformed bones)	Fish liver oils, fortified milk, egg yolk	Aged 11–24: 10 mcg Aged 25+: 5 mcg PG or BF: 10 mcg
E (tocopherol)	Liver and neurologic disorders	Vegetable oils, egg yolk, dark green, leafy vegetables	Men: 10 mg Women: 8 mg PG: 10 mg BF: 11–12 mg
K (phylloquinone, menaquinone)	Blood slow to clot	Green leafy vegetables, liver, egg yolk, meat, dairy products	Men: 70–80 mcg Women: 60–65 mcg Women 25+: 65 mcg
C (ascorbic acid)	Scurvy, blood and bone disorders, inflamed gums	Citrus fruits, tomatoes	60 mg PG: 70 mg BF: 90–95 mg
B_1 (thiamin)	Heart failure, muscle weakness, loss of appetite, nervous system disorders	Pork, liver, yeast, whole or enriched grains, legumes	Men: 1.2–1.5 mg Women: 1.0–1.1 mg PG: 1.5 mg BF: 1.6 mg
B_2 (riboflavin)	Dry skin, inflamed lips, cracked mouth corners, sensitivity to light	Milk products, meat, organ meats, enriched grains	Men: 1.4–1.7 mg Women: 1.2–1.3 mg PG: 1.6 mg BF: 1.7–1.8 mg
Niacin (nicotinic acid)	Weakness, anorexia, indigestion, dermatitis, mental deterioration	Meat, enriched or whole grains, poultry, fish, peanuts, milk products	Men: 15–19 mg Women: 13–15 mg PG: 17 mg BF: 18 mg
B_6 (pyridoxine)	Dermatitis, anemia	Meat, whole grains, poultry, fish	Men: 2 mg Women: 1.6 mg PG: 2.2 mg BF: 2.1 mg
Folacin (folate, folic acid)	Digestive problems, blood disorders, weight loss	Liver, greens, mushrooms, whole grains, legumes	Men: 200 mcg Women: 180 mcg PG: 400 mcg BF: 260–280 mcg
B_{12} (cyanocobalamin)	Blood, digestive tract, and nervous system disorders	Meats, milk, eggs	2 mcg PG: 2.2 mcg BF: 2.6 mcg
Biotin	Anorexia, depression, dermatitis, hair loss	Egg yolk, organ meats, yeast, whole grains, nuts	30–100 mcg
Pantothenic acid	Burning feet, fatigue	Liver, meat, cereal, milk, legumes	4–7 mg

Key: BF = breast-feeding women, mcg = micrograms, mg = milligrams, PG = pregnant women, PM = postmenopausal women

17

MINERALS: IMPORTANT DIETARY COMPONENTS

Mineral Name	Main Function	RDA	Food Sources
Calcium	Bone and tooth development	Aged 11–24: 1,200 mg Aged 25+: 800 mg PG, BF, PM: 1,200 mg	Dairy products, green leafy vegetables
Chromium*	Glucose metabolism	0.05–0.2 mg	Whole grains, meats, cheese
Copper*	Iron absorption and use	1.5–3 mg	Shellfish, nuts, liver, legumes, fruits and vegetables
Fluoride*	Bone and tooth development	1.5–4 mg	Fluoridated water, fluoride tablets
Iodine	A component of thyroid hormones	150 mcg PG: 175 mcg BF: 200 mcg	Iodized salt, some baked goods
Iron	A component of red blood cells	Men: 10 mg Women: 15 mg PG: 30 mg	Liver, meat, whole grains, green leafy vegetables, shellfish, nuts
Magnesium	A component of teeth and bones; aids protein synthesis and energy release	Men: 350 mg Women: 280 mg PG: 320 mg BF: 340–355 mg	Nuts, legumes, whole grains, soybeans, seafood, dark green vegetables
Manganese*	Bone formation	2–5 mg	Whole grains, legumes, nuts
Phosphorous	Bone and tooth formation; energy storage and release	Aged 19–24: 1,200 mg Aged 25+: 800 mg PG or BF: 1,200 mg	All animal products, soft drinks
Potassium*	Helps maintain water balance and metabolism of protein and carbohydrates	2,000 mg	Meat, milk, potatoes, bananas, oranges, legumes
Selenium	Helps prevent cell damage and heart problems	Men: 70 mcg Women: 55 mcg PG: 65 mcg BF: 75 mcg	Liver, kidney, meat, seafood
Sodium*	Regulates water balance	500 mg	Table salt, processed foods
Zinc	A component of bones; helps metabolize carbohydrate, fat, and protein	Men: 15 mg Women: 12 mg PG: 30 mg BF: 15 mg	Oysters, meat, eggs, whole-grain bread, poultry, liver

Key: BF = breast-feeding women, mcg = micrograms, mg = milligrams, PG = pregnant women, PM = postmenopausal women
* These minerals do not have RDAs. The figures provided are estimates of safe and adequate daily dietary intake.

water-soluble: vitamins C, B$_1$, B$_2$, B$_6$, and B$_{12}$, niacin, folacin, biotin, and pantothenic acid.

While extra amounts of water-soluble vitamins are excreted in the urine, large quantities of vitamin C and some of the B vitamins have been known to produce side effects.

Your body also needs minerals to function properly. The table on page 18 lists the RDAs for minerals, food sources, and how your body puts minerals to work.

Both the vitamin and mineral table provide the RDAs for all adults, unless otherwise specified (see key at bottom of charts). The ages given are in years.

Antioxidants: The Answer to Heart Disease?

The antioxidant beta-carotene (a form of vitamin A) and vitamin E have made a lot of headlines lately. That's because these nutrients have been found to actually reduce cell damage (oxidation), with some very dramatic results. Here's the lowdown on some of the latest research findings.

- In a study of 87,245 female nurses 34 to 59 years of age, those who took vitamin E supplements for more than two years had a risk of heart disease that was 34 percent lower than that of women who did not take vitamin E. Women who took the supplements for less than two years showed no apparent benefit.

- A study of 39,910 male health professionals between 40 and 75 years of age found that the men who took at least 100 IU (international units) of vitamin E per day for at least two years had a risk of developing heart disease that was 37 percent lower than the men who did not take a supplement. Beta-

WARNING: VITAMIN TOXICITY

It's true you can sometimes get too much of a good thing. When taken in large doses, some vitamins can be harmful. Some of the possible effects appear below.

Vitamin A: Hair loss, joint and muscle soreness, irritability, drowsiness

Vitamin D: Elevated calcium levels, kidney stones, diarrhea, nausea, headache

Vitamin E: Delayed blood clotting

Vitamin K: Bleeding; in pregnant women and infants, possible red blood cell breakdown, jaundice, brain damage

Vitamin C: No known toxic effects (However, excess amounts may cause diarrhea, red blood cell breakdown, and scurvy when use ceases.)

Niacin: No known toxic effects (However, large doses may cause headache, skin flushing and tingling, and indigestion.)

Vitamin B$_6$: No known toxic effects (However, large doses may cause diarrhea.)

❑   ❑   ❑

carotene, the study found, lowered the risk of heart disease by 70 percent among smokers and by 40 percent among former smokers.

- A European study found that high levels of beta-carotene in the body were associated with a lower risk of heart attacks. The study authors also concurred with the results of earli-

Get the Bulk of Your Nutrients from Food Sources

er studies linking supplemental vitamin E with lowered heart disease risk. The researchers advocated eating more foods rich in beta-carotene, such as carrots and green, leafy vegetables.

- In contrast, a Finnish study found no decrease in heart disease or cancer risk from supplemental vitamin E and a slight *increase* in cancer risk from supplemental beta-carotene in smokers, thus highlighting the need for more research before solid supplement recommendations can be made.

Should You Take Supplements?

Looking at the RDAs for all the different nutrients may seem daunting. You may worry about getting enough of the nutrients you need. Should you take a vitamin or mineral supplement?

The answer is not clear-cut. Most dietitians and nutritionists advocate getting the bulk of your nutrients from food sources. If you rely on supplements, you may miss out on the other potentially health-enhancing substances in foods. Also, if supplements contain too much of a certain nutrient, they may deplete other nutrient supplies in your body.

There are exceptions to these recommendations, however:

- Women of childbearing age and pregnant women are usually advised by their physician to take a supplement containing iron, calcium, and folic acid—all of which the develop-

ing fetus needs in large amounts. Women are often advised to continue taking the supplements throughout breast-feeding. (If you are pregnant or breast-feeding, consult your doctor before taking any supplements.)

- There is a growing belief that women should take calcium supplements throughout adolescence and adulthood to prevent osteoporosis.

Steer Clear of Miracles and Megadoses

You walk into the health-food store and face shelves upon towering shelves of little bottles. Signs adorn the place, claiming weight-loss miracles and sure cures for PMS. Are these claims fact or fancy?

Probably fancy.

The truth is, many vitamin- and herbal-supplement manufacturers often make promises they can't keep. But because many products are not subject to approval by the Food and Drug Administration (FDA), these wild claims are not regulated. (The FDA is addressing the lack of regulation, so this may be changing.)

Likewise, supplements often contain amounts of vitamins and minerals that are many times the RDA. These excess doses can be toxic, even fatal.

For example, many manufacturers sell beta-carotene supplements containing 25,000 IU (international units) of the vitamin—an amount that can cause side effects ranging from headaches and nausea to birth defects in a pregnant woman's developing fetus.

If you do choose to take a supplement, stick with the RDAs or seek a physician's advice.

Why Popeye Eats His Spinach

"An apple a day keeps the doctor away," the old adage goes. The saying may be old, but the information couldn't be more timely. The truth is, new findings are prompting researchers to believe a high intake of fruits and vegetables can reduce the risk of many types of illness—from heart disease to cancer.

The USDA has launched a campaign called "Five a day for better health," which, as the phrase suggests, encourages consumers to eat a total of at least five servings of fruits and vegetables every day. Here are the main reasons:

- Whole fruits and vegetables contain high amounts of fiber, a nutrient that helps the digestive system stay regular and lowers cholesterol levels. Fiber can also help prevent or reduce the risk of hemorrhoids, diverticulosis, and colon cancer.

- Fruits and vegetables are excellent sources of vitamins, especially the disease-fighting antioxidants beta-carotene and vitamin C.

Including a variety of fruits and vegetables in your daily diet ensures that you get adequate amounts of the different types of nutrients and fiber they contain.

Five a Day: Fruits and Vegetables

You understand you should eat at least five servings of fruits and vegetables every day. And you understand you should choose a variety of these foods so you're sure to get all the nutrients you need. So, where do you begin?

The USDA recommends that you select from five major groups: fresh fruits, cooked vegetables, fruit juices, fresh leafy vegetables, and dried fruits. Include at least one fruit or vegetable each day that is rich in vitamin A, one that is rich in vitamin C, and one that is high in fiber.

Feeling overwhelmed? The chart on page 22 should help. It lists fruits and vegetables rich in fiber and vitamins A and C. Serving sizes are specified. The foods listed also provide many other essential nutrients; see *Vitamins: Their Functions, Your Body's Requirements* on page 17 and *Minerals: Important Dietary Components* on page 18.

Choosing Fresh Fruits and Vegetables

Shopping for produce doesn't have to be a daunting task. With a little bit of knowledge and practice, you can make sure you come home with fresh vegetables and ripe fruits every time. Here are some pointers:

A High Intake of Fruits and Vegetables Can Reduce the Risk of Illness

FRUITS & VEGETABLES

MAIN FOOD	NUTRITIONAL VALUE
FRUITS	
1 apple	fiber
3 apricots	vitamin A, fiber
10 dried apricots	vitamin A, fiber
2 plums	fiber
4 prunes	fiber
1 banana	fiber
2 figs	fiber
1 kiwifruit	vitamin C, fiber
½ cup blueberries	fiber
10 strawberries	vitamin C, fiber
½ papaya	vitamins A, C
½ grapefruit	vitamin C, fiber
1 orange	vitamin C, fiber
6 oz tomato or orange juice	vitamin C
1 peach	fiber
½ mango	vitamins A, C
¼ cup raisins	fiber
1 tomato	fiber
1 cup cherries	fiber
1 cup grapes	fiber
⅓ cantaloupe	vitamins A, C, fiber
¼ cup dried dates	fiber
VEGETABLES	
5–7 green beans	fiber
½ cup winter squash	vitamin A, fiber
5 zucchini sticks	fiber
½ large baked potato	vitamin C, fiber
5 broccoli florets	vitamin C, fiber
1 cup fresh spinach	vitamin A, fiber
5–7 snow peas	vitamin C, fiber
1 cup romaine lettuce	vitamin A
¼ cup fresh chili peppers	vitamins A, C
½ cup cooked asparagus	fiber
½ cup red or green pepper	vitamin C
½ cup cooked corn	fiber
½ cup cooked lentils	fiber
½ cup cooked carrots	vitamin A, fiber
1 raw carrot	vitamin A, fiber
½ cup cooked peas	fiber

❑ **Look for fruits and vegetables with skins intact.** Select items with the fewest dents, bruises, cuts, insect holes, and brown spots. If you can't find an item in good condition, skip it. Choose a frozen version or shop someplace else.

❑ **Select broccoli that is green and firm.** Limp stalks and yellow florets mean the vegetable is past its prime. (A trace of purple on the florets is OK.)

❑ **Choose bell peppers that are firm all over.** If they are a bit soft but you plan to use them the day you buy them, then go ahead.

❑ **Look for zucchini with deep green, intact, smooth skin.** Wrinkling or a green-black color is a sign of age. Many people believe the smaller specimens are the most flavorful.

❑ **Select asparagus with heads that are dry and purple, not wet or brown.** Asparagus is very tasty no matter what its thickness, but the thicker stalks can sometimes be a bit tough.

❑ **Examine pints of berries for mold.** It sometimes hides underneath the plastic wrapper.

❑ **To tell if a cantaloupe is ripe, smell it.** If you smell a sweet melon fragrance, it's ripe.

❑ **Press the top end of honeydew melons.** They are ripe when the brown circle at the top is tender and yields a bit when you press firmly with your thumb.

❑ **Shake a coconut and listen for its milk sloshing.** If you can't hear this sound, pass the coconut by.

❑ **Buy produce in season.** Out-of-season fruits and vegetables may be less flavorful—and may also be more expensive.

Follow these guidelines to ensure fruits and vegetables are as nutritious when you serve them as when they were harvested:

❏ **Avoid peeling fruits and vegetables whenever possible.** The skin contains many nutrients.

❏ **Eat as many raw fruits and vegetables as you can.** Nutrients are lost in cooking.

❏ **Grill, stew, broil, sauté, bake, and steam vegetables.** Avoid boiling, since nutrients are boiled away into the cooking water.

❏ **Scrub vegetables well.** Use water (not soap) to remove pesticide residues before eating.

Increasing Your Fiber Intake

Fiber is a veritable household word these days. It seems every third commercial on television promotes one or another product containing this wonder substance and promises benefits ranging from bowel regularity to weight loss. So what's the scoop on the fiber mystique? Does fiber do what it is purported to do? What's the best form to consume it in? How much should you be getting?

Fiber, a form of carbohydrate, has several health benefits.

• Fiber promotes bowel regularity, which helps prevent hemorrhoids.

• It may reduce the risk of colon and rectal cancers.

THE IMPORTANCE OF INCREASING FIBER INTAKE SLOWLY

You know how much fiber you should be eating and which foods contain it. However, resist the urge to make up for lost time by boosting your fiber intake to the recommended level overnight. Otherwise, you may be in for an uncomfortable gastric surprise, including gas, bloating, constipation, or diarrhea. Instead, increase your fiber intake gradually, going up to recommended levels over the course of a couple of weeks, even a month, and be sure to increase your fluid intake at the same time.

❏   ❏   ❏

• Fiber reduces the risk of diverticulosis, a condition characterized by small pouches (diverticula) on the colon wall, and diverticulitis, inflammation of the diverticula.

• Fiber lowers cholesterol.

Dietary fiber is found only in plant foods, not in animal products. Since it is not digested, the body absorbs no calories from fiber. Because of this, and because it gives the stomach a feeling of fullness, fiber is an excellent weight-control aid (when consumed in suggested amounts). There are two main types of fiber: insoluble and soluble.

• Insoluble fiber speeds up the movement of food through the intestines and promotes bowel regularity. Cellulose, hemicellulose, and lignin are all types of insoluble fibers. They can be found in foods such as asparagus, peas, kidney and pinto beans, and the wheat bran found in whole-wheat breads and cereals.

• Soluble fibers slow down the movement of food through the intestines. They also appear to be effective at lowering blood cholesterol. Pectin, gum, and

Fiber Lowers Cholesterol

Fiber Contains No Calories

mucilage are examples of soluble fibers in the diet. Oat bran is a source of soluble fiber, as are rolled oats, broccoli, brussels sprouts, grapefruit, apples, and pinto and navy beans.

The typical American takes in 10 to 20 grams of dietary fiber a day. Although there is no RDA for fiber, several groups recommend an intake of fiber of 20 to 35 grams of fiber per day. Here are some examples of the amounts of fiber contained in common foods:

Food	Amount	
½ cup bran cereal	10.0	grams
3 cups popcorn	2.8	grams
1 slice whole-grain bread	2.7	grams
½ cup whole oats	1.6	grams
½ cup brown rice	1.3	grams
1 slice white bread	0.8	gram
½ cup white rice	0.5	gram
1 small apple	3.8	grams
1 small pear	2.5	grams
½ cup blackberries	3.7	grams
½ grapefruit	1.3	grams
10 grapes	0.4	gram
½ cup kidney beans	4.5	grams
½ cup pinto beans	3.0	grams
½ cup peas	5.2	grams
1 small potato	3.8	grams
½ cup broccoli	2.6	grams
½ cup iceburg lettuce	0.5	gram

Should You Take a Fiber Supplement?

Many types of fiber supplements are available: powders to mix with water or juice, tablets, capsules, even cookies. These products may be helpful for those who eat a low-fiber diet or who have chronic problems with constipation.

However, as with vitamins and minerals, most nutrition experts recommend getting as much fiber as you can from food sources. Supplements, they argue, should not be necessary with a balanced, high-fiber diet.

Discuss fiber supplements with your doctor. Should you choose to take a supplement, build up to the recommended dosage over a couple of weeks or a month to avoid gastrointestinal distress.

Eat More, Be Healthier, and Weigh Less

Eating a high-fiber diet need not be a chore. On the contrary, if you cut your fat intake, you can boost the amount of high-fiber carbohydrates you eat without increasing your calorie intake. The result? Not only will you be healthier and trimmer, but you'll be able to eat a significantly higher volume of food. If it sounds too good to be true, just take a look at the facts:

- One gram of fat contains about nine calories; a gram of carbohydrate, only about four (although one gram of alcohol contains seven calories). Fiber, since it is not digested by the body, contains no calories.

- Fiber fills you up and helps you feel full longer.

• The body tends to use carbohydrates as energy, rather than storing them as fat. Fat, on the other hand, more easily ends up on your hips and thighs.

To put it another way, which would you rather have—two tablespoons of olive oil on your salad or a white meat turkey sandwich on whole-wheat bread with lettuce, tomato, onion, and mustard? The former contains 28 grams of fat and 240 calories; the latter about the same number of calories, but only about four grams of fat. Another example: You can have one ounce of potato chips (about 10) if you're willing to consume more than 150 calories and nine grams of fat. Or you can choose one ounce of pretzels (about 10 large twists or 50 stick pretzels) for 110 calories and less than *one gram* of fat. It's simple: Cut the fat, and you can eat more.

The Importance of Reading Food Labels

If you're serious about eating healthfully, you'll have to master an important skill: reading the nutrition labels on food packages.

You may have noticed food labels look a little different these days. These new food labels have many advantages: First and foremost, they're designed to help consumers compare food products. For example, nutrition information is uniform. Labels must list the same nutrients—those most important to your health—such as total fat, cholesterol, sodium, and total carbohydrate. Serving sizes

FIGURING FAT INTAKE

Food labels provide the number of grams of total and saturated fat per serving along with the Percent Daily Value (%DV) based on a 2,000-calorie diet. But your caloric intake may be different. Remember, whether you need to lose weight, gain weight, or just control your present weight, you should still consume no more than 30 percent of your calories from fat. And no more than one-third of this percentage should be from saturated fat.

Based on your caloric intake, this chart lets you see at a glance how many grams (g) of fat you can consume to stay within the recommendation of 30 percent of total calories. The chart also displays the number of grams of saturated fat (Sat Fat) you should limit yourself to. (Numbers are rounded off.)

CALORIES	FAT (g)	SAT FAT (g)
1,200	40	13
1,400	47	16
1,500	50	17
1,600	53	18
1,800	60	20
2,000	67	22
2,200	73	24
2,300	77	26
2,400	80	27
2,500	83	28
2,600	87	29
2,800	93	31
3,000	100	33
3,200	107	36
3,500	117	39

have been standardized: Because they're based on the average amount of the food usually eaten at one sitting, you can easily compare the nutritional value of similar products. Another new feature is the Percent Daily Values. These numbers show how these foods fit in a 2,000-calorie-a-day diet.

Take a look at the food label on page 26. You can easily spot the new labels with their **Nutrition Facts** boldly displayed. Serving size is listed first.

Incidentally, when you assess calories and nutrients, be honest with yourself. If the serving size indicated on the label of your

NUTRITION FACTS

Serving size ½ cup (114g)	Servings per Container 4
Amount Per Serving	
Calories 90	**Calories from Fat** 30
	% Daily Value*
Total Fat 3g	5%
Saturated Fat 0g	0%
Cholesterol 0mg	0%
Sodium 300mg	13%
Total Carbohydrate 13g	4%
Dietary Fiber 3g	12%
Sugars 3g	
Protein 3g	
Vitamin A 80%	Vitamin C 60%
Calcium 4%	Iron 4%

* Percent Daily Values are based on a 2,000 calorie diet. Your daily values may be higher or lower depending on your calorie needs.

	Calories:	2,000	2,500
Total Fat	Less than	65g	80g
Sat Fat	Less than	20g	25g
Cholesterol	Less than	300mg	300mg
Sodium	Less than	2,400mg	2,400mg
Total Carbohydrate		300mg	375g
Fiber		25g	30g

Calories per gram:
Fat 9 • Carbohydrate 4 • Protein 4

favorite ice cream is one-half cup, but you usually fill your bowl to the brim, you need to figure your calories based on the amount you actually consume—not just the standard serving size. Notice also that the label provides the total calories and the number of calories from fat.

The Percent Daily Values appear next. The government has set these values based on current nutrition recommendations, such as the suggested limitation on calories from all sources of fat (**Total Fat** on the label) to no more than 30 percent of total calories. This recommendation is represented on the lower part of the label by the **Less than 65g** entry for Total Fat in a 2,000 calorie diet.

This simply means that in a diet consisting of 2,000 calories, no more than 65 grams (which is equivalent to about 30 percent of total calories) should come from total fat. The 3 grams of fat in the sample food label constitutes about 5 percent of the maximum of 65 grams allowed for one day. This is a small amount of fat, leaving you plenty of room to consume a variety of foods before reaching the maximum fat consumption for the day.

This same information is given for cholesterol, sodium, carbohydrate, and protein.

Percent Daily Values are also supplied for vitamins A and C, calcium, and iron.

Food Labels at a Glance

Keep these tips in mind when selecting foods that are low in fat, cholesterol, and sodium, but high in dietary fiber, vitamins, and iron. Your goal should be to consume no more than 30 percent of your calories from fat, but to consume 100 percent of the daily value for total carbohydrate, dietary fiber, vitamins, and minerals.

Remember, too, three types of carbohydrates combine to give the total carbohydrates: simple (sugars), complex, and fibrous (dietary fiber). To select a healthy food, look for:

- a large difference between the number of calories and calories from fat
- a low number of total fat grams
- an even lower number of grams of saturated fat
- a low cholesterol value
- a low sodium value
- a high value for total carbohydrates *along with* a low value for sugars, indicating that the total comprises mostly complex and fibrous carbohydrates
- a 10 percent or more value for vitamins and minerals

A Label Lexicon

Here are some other words you frequently see on labels along with their definitions. The amounts indicated are per serving.

Calorie free: less than 5 calories

Low calorie: 40 calories or less

Reduced calorie: at least 25 percent less calories per serving compared with original product

Light or Lite: one-third less calories or 50 percent less fat—additionally, if more than half the calories are from fat, fat content must be reduced by 50 percent or more from original product

Fat free: less than ½ gram of fat

Low fat: 3 grams of fat or less

Reduced fat: at least 25 percent less saturated fat per serving compared with original product

High fiber: 5 grams or more of fiber

Lean: less than 10 grams of fat, 4 grams of saturated fat, and 95 milligrams of cholesterol

Extra lean: less than 5 grams of fat, 2 grams of saturated fat, and 95 milligrams of cholesterol

Cholesterol free: less than 2 milligrams of cholesterol and 2 grams or less of saturated fat

Low cholesterol: 20 milligrams or less of cholesterol and 2 grams or less of saturated fat

Sodium free: less than 5 milligrams of sodium

Very low sodium: 35 milligrams of sodium or less

Low sodium: 140 milligrams or less of sodium

When perusing the list of ingredients, check for the following items:

- **Ingredients high in fat or cholesterol, such as:**
  - Saturated fats
  - Palm oil or coconut oil
  - Hydrogenated oils
  - Eggs
  - Cheese
- **Sugar near the top of the list** (the ingredients are ranked in order of their amounts)
- **Salt near the top of the list**
- **Nitrates and nitrites** (substances found in sausages and hot dogs that have been linked to adverse health effects)
- **Any ingredients you may be allergic to**

Do You Know the Difference Between Fat Free and Lite?

Reducing the Fat in Food Doesn't Mean Reducing Taste

The Creation of a Recipe Makeover

You, like many people, may be under the impression that reducing the fat in food also reduces its good taste. This does not have to be so. You can still eat most of the foods you love—if you modify them to meet your new dietary goals.

This section shows you how to make over your favorite recipes—transforming them into foods that will please your waistline and your doctor, as well as your palate.

To start, here's a list of easy substitutions that work well in most recipes:

❏ Replace whole milk with one percent, skim, or nonfat dry milk.

❏ Replace half-and-half or cream with evaporated skim milk (except in recipes calling for whipped cream).

❏ Replace regular sour cream with low- or nonfat sour cream or nonfat yogurt.

❏ Replace regular mayonnaise with low-fat or nonfat versions.

❏ Replace regular yogurt with low-fat or nonfat yogurt.

❏ Replace whole eggs with double the number of egg whites or with a fat-free egg substitute.

❏ Thicken soups with a couple of tablespoons of flour or cornstarch mixed with the same amount of cold water instead of relying on heavy cream to thicken.

❏ Reduce the amount of fat in recipes by half or more.

(Experiment with lower and lower amounts until you find out how little fat the recipe can contain without affecting the way the food turns out.)

❏ In some recipes for baked goods, try replacing fat with the equivalent amount of applesauce. This may not work for all recipes, however, so do some experimenting.

❏ Instead of frying in oil, sauté in chicken broth, and use non-stick pans coated with nonstick spray.

❏ Replace regular cheese with reduced-fat cheese; in recipes use less cheese, adding flavor with herbs and spices.

❏ Use low-fat or nonfat mayonnaise, margarine, or salad dressing as sandwich spreads instead of regular margarine or mayonnaise.

❏ Use low-fat or nonfat creamers instead of half-and-half in coffee and tea.

❏ Choose low-fat, nondairy whipped toppings, yogurt, or nonfat sour cream (sweetened with sugar or artificial sweetener, if desired), instead of whipped cream topping.

❏ Instead of starting white sauces with a "roux" of flour and butter, start by whisking a tablespoon of flour into a cup of skim milk; heat slowly, stirring, to thicken. Add more flour if necessary (whisk into cold milk separately before adding to sauce). Add one-half teaspoon of chicken bouillon to replace butter flavor.

❏ Use low- and nonfat margarine wherever possible. (Keep in mind, though, that some of the lowest-fat margarine may not be appropriate for cooking and baking.)

- Instead of using pan drippings, make gravy by adding flour (whisked into cold water) to meat or poultry stocks; heat slowly, stirring to thicken. Add bouillon for extra flavor.
- Reduce the amount of meat and nuts in recipes.

Here is an example of how significantly you can alter a recipe's fat and calorie content, with a little imagination. And the makeover is guaranteed to satisfy your craving for creamy, cheesy sauce.

The original:

Sauce for Classic Fettucine Alfredo

6 T unsalted butter

⅔ cup heavy cream

½ tsp salt

Generous dash ground white pepper

Generous dash ground nutmeg

1 cup freshly grated Parmesan cheese (about 3 oz)

2 T chopped fresh parsley

Place butter and cream in large, heavy skillet over medium-low heat. Cook and stir until butter melts and mixture bubbles. Cook and stir two minutes more. Stir in salt, pepper, and nutmeg. Remove from heat. Gradually stir in cheese until thoroughly blended and smooth. If necessary, return briefly to heat to completely blend cheese. Do not let sauce bubble or cheese will become lumpy and tough.

Pour sauce over cooked fettucine and stir and toss over low heat until sauce is thickened and fettucine is evenly coated. Sprinkle with parsley. Serve immediately.

(Makes 4 servings)

Fat content per serving: 38 grams
Calories per serving: 400

The low-fat makeover:

Low-fat Sauce for Fettucine Alfredo

1 15-oz can of evaporated skim milk

½ cup fat-free grated Parmesan cheese

1 tsp chicken bouillon granules

Generous dash ground white pepper

Generous dash ground nutmeg

2 T white cooking wine or dry chardonnay, if desired

2 T chopped fresh parsley

Combine milk and cheese; slowly bring to a boil over medium heat, stirring often. Add bouillon, pepper, nutmeg, and optional wine. Simmer until mixture reaches desired thickness. Toss with fettucine; sprinkle with parsley.

(Makes 4 servings)

Fat content per serving: ½ gram
Calories per serving: 123

CHOOSING AND PREPARING MEAT AND POULTRY

- Choose light-meat poultry instead of dark meat.
- Remove skin from poultry—before or after cooking.
- Choose loin and round cuts of beef, which are leaner: These include eye of round, top round, top loin, sirloin, and tenderloin.
- Choose loin and leg cuts of pork, lamb, and veal, including tenderloin, center loin chops, and shank portions.
- Be alert to grades of meat: Prime has the most fat, while Select has the least amount of fat. Choice grade falls in between.
- Trim all visible fat from meats.
- Bake, broil, or roast instead of frying meat and poultry.

29

There Are Important Reasons to Watch Your Sodium Intake

How Much Water Do You Need?

Commercial diets are notorious for insisting you drink eight glasses of water a day. Correctly, they often claim water helps flush excess fluids out of your body. Quite incorrectly, they often also allege that water can perform miracles, such as making you lose weight faster, plumping up wrinkled skin, adding years to your life, and so on.

So what's the truth about water? There are a few truths.

There's no argument about the fact the body needs water more than any other substance, with the exception of oxygen. The adult body is composed of approximately 55 to 65 percent water. It is necessary for almost all physical processes.

It is also true if you drink a lot of water, you retain less water. The numbers on the scale may make you think you are losing weight, but you may just be losing water weight. That means eating a dill pickle or a salty Chinese meal may add those pounds right back.

❑ **Listen to your body.** Drink when you are thirsty.

❑ **Know when you *need* to drink water.** In some circumstances you need to take extra care to drink enough water, even if you don't feel thirsty. These times include when you sweat a lot (because of a fever, in hot weather, or when you exercise) and when you are vomiting or have diarrhea.

Sodium: Friend or Foe?

Labels touting "reduced sodium," "no salt added," or "sodium-free," appear on all kinds of products these days. What's the big deal about sodium? Is it dangerous to your health? Should you try to eliminate it from your diet?

Even if you wanted to, you probably couldn't eliminate all sodium from your diet. The mineral is found in almost everything, from the water we drink to the fruits and vegetables we eat (albeit, in small amounts). And sodium is important to your health: Without enough of it for a long enough period of time, you would become quite ill. However, there are important reasons to watch your sodium intake.

First, sodium controls water retention. A high intake of sodium causes the body to retain excess water, resulting in bloating, swelling of the limbs, excess water weight, even headaches.

Second, a high sodium intake has been linked to elevated blood pressure (an excess of the mineral increases blood volume) in people who are sodium sensitive. Unfortunately, no test will tell you whether you are sodium sensitive. But about one-third of those who suffer from hypertension find a reduction in sodium intake helps lower their blood pressure.

How much sodium do you need? At a minimum, probably about 500 milligrams per day. Experts vary in their opinions of the upper limit, with estimates ranging from three to five grams per day. One teaspoon of table salt (sodium chloride) contains about two grams of sodium. But remember—hidden sources of sodium lurk everywhere, so read food labels in addition to keeping the salt shaker off of the table.

Here are some tips to help you reduce your sodium intake:

❑ **Don't salt foods while cooking.** Instead, sprinkle salt on—lightly—at the table if desired. You'll taste the salt more, but use less. But be sure to *try* the food first. You may find it tastes just fine without the added salt.

❑ **Avoid pickled foods.** Also avoid those processed in brine. So go easy on the dill pickles, sauerkraut, and olives.

❑ **Buy reduced-sodium or no-salt-added snacks and canned soups and vegetables.**

❑ **Avoid salted and smoked meats and fish.** Choose tuna fish packed in water or rinse oil-packed tuna with water.

❑ **Limit your intake of salty condiments.** These include ketchup, mustard, soy sauce, barbecue sauce, broths, and Worcestershire sauce.

❑ **Learn to spice up your foods with herbs and spices instead of salt.**

❑ **Use commercial salt-free herbal blends instead of salt.**

❑ **If you cook with wine, choose table wine.** Cooking wine is much higher in salt.

Many people trying to reduce their sodium intake find their taste for salt is an acquired habit—one that can be unlearned. If you gradually reduce your salt intake over a period of time, you'll probably find your taste buds adjust by becoming more sensitive to smaller amounts of salt in food.

Ensuring Food Safety

Eating the right foods is important, but so is making sure the food you eat is fresh and wholesome. Food prepared or stored improperly can be dangerous, even lethal. While some principles of food safety are common sense (such as not eating food that is clearly spoiled or growing mold), others may not be so obvious.

There are 6.5 million cases of food poisoning and 9,000 food-poisoning deaths every year in this country. Those most susceptible to food-related illnesses are children, the elderly, and those whose immune systems are compromised by other illnesses. Here are some pointers to help ensure you and your loved ones don't become statistics. (For information on specific types of food-borne illnesses, see *You Can Foil Food Poisoning* in Chapter 7, page 215.)

❑ **Keep cold food cold and hot food hot.** Bacteria tend to grow in temperatures between 40°F and 140°F.

❑ **Pay special attention to foods containing eggs, milk, and other dairy products.** If these products are not kept refrigerated, they spoil rapidly. At picnics or barbecues, keep these foods in a cooler at all times. This rule goes double for salads and spreads, such as chicken or tuna. Commercial mayonnaise contains an acid that retards spoilage, but the ratio of acid to other ingredients may not be enough to

There Are 6.5 Million Cases of Food Poisoning Every Year

prevent dangerous bacteria from growing.

❏ **Try to avoid raw eggs.** Certain foods, such as Caesar salad dressing and homemade egg nog, are made with raw egg. If you're not sure if a food contains raw eggs, skip it. Also, don't sample the cookie dough.

❏ **Keep your refrigerator as cold as possible—40°F or below.** Use a thermometer to accurately gauge the temperature.

CHOP ON WOOD?

In 1992, researchers at the University of Wisconsin sent cooks reeling. They published the results of a study that found bacteria that can lead to food poisoning more likely to be present on plastic cutting boards than on wood. This study challenged long-held beliefs that plastic cutting boards are safer than wooden cutting surfaces because they are easier to clean and less likely to have cracks and grooves that harbor bacteria.

So what type of board is best? Based on additional studies conducted by the Food and Drug Administration (FDA) and the U.S. Department of Agriculture (USDA), the USDA's Meat and Poultry Hotline still recommends use of cutting boards with easy-to-clean, nonporous surfaces made of plastic, marble, or glass. In separate studies, investigators from the FDA and USDA found wood surfaces more likely to absorb bacteria into cracks, while thorough cleansing of plastic cutting boards removed all traces of bacteria.

Callers to the Meat and Poultry Hotline are also advised that if they do use wood cutting boards, they should reserve their use for cutting meats and poultry. Cooking these foods kills any food-contaminating bacteria present. Foods that will not be cooked, such as vegetables, fruits, and bread, should be chopped on a different, preferably plastic, cutting board.

Whichever type of board you choose, wash it thoroughly with hot soapy water after each use. Frequently sanitize boards with a solution of 2 teaspoons of chlorine bleach and 1 quart water, allowing the solution to penetrate the board. Finally, replace any boards with grooves or cuts, which may harbor bacteria.

❏   ❏   ❏

❏ **Keep meat, poultry, and fish refrigerated or frozen.** Thaw them only in the refrigerator or the microwave. Never leave meat products on the counter to defrost, since bacteria may multiply.

❏ **Keep raw meat, poultry, and fish well wrapped in the refrigerator.** Drippings from these products can transfer bacteria to other foods.

❏ **Keep raw meat, poultry, and fish separate from other foods.** Rinse these foods under cold water before cutting and cooking.

❏ **Wash working surfaces, utensils, and hands in hot, soapy water immediately before and after preparing raw meat, poultry, or fish.** Never cut anything else with an unwashed knife that has been used to cut raw animal flesh.

❏ **Cut meats, fish, and poultry on nonporous surfaces.** Plastic cutting boards, for example, tend to be easier to clean well. (See sidebar, *Chop on Wood?*)

❏ **Cook beef, pork, and poultry to an internal temperature of at least 160°F.** There should be no trace of pink inside any of these foods, and juices should run clear.

❏ **Refrigerate or freeze all leftovers as soon as possible, even if still hot.** Store foods in small, shallow containers to speed up cooling.

❏ **Don't stuff poultry before cooking.** Instead, prepare stuffing or dressing separately.

❏ **Avoid eating raw fish, such as sushi.** If you do choose to eat sushi, make sure you go to a reputable restaurant and choose mostly cooked seafood, such as shrimp or crab. Never eat raw poultry, beef, or pork.

FOOD STORAGE GUIDELINES

According to the USDA, all foods can be safely frozen. But freezing may affect the quality and eventually the taste of certain foods. The following chart gives you a good idea of how long some foods retain their quality in the refrigerator or freezer when properly wrapped.

PRODUCT	REFRIGERATOR (40°F)	FREEZER (0°F)
Eggs		
Fresh, in shell	3 weeks	Do not freeze
Raw yolks, whites	2–4 days	1 year
Hard cooked	1 week	Do not freeze
Frozen foods		
TV dinners, frozen casseroles	Keep frozen until ready to heat	3–4 months
Deli and vacuum-packed foods		
Store-bought or homemade salads (egg, chicken, tuna, ham, or pasta)	3–5 days	Do not freeze
Store-cooked convenience meals	1–2 days	Do not freeze
Hot dogs (opened package)	1 week	2 months
Hot dogs (unopened package)	2 weeks	2 months
Luncheon meats (opened)	3–5 days	2 months
Luncheon meats (unopened)	2 weeks	2 months
Meats		
Beef steaks	3–5 days	1 year
Chops, pork	3–5 days	6 months
lamb	3–5 days	9 months
Roasts, beef	3–5 days	1 year
lamb	3–5 days	9 months
pork or veal	3–5 days	6 months
Stuffed pork and lamb chops	1 day	Several months but quality may be affected
Hamburger and stew meats	1–2 days	4 months
Cooked meat and meat dishes	3–4 days	3 months
Meat cooked in gravy or broth	1–2 days	3 months
Corned beef (in pouch with pickling juices)	5–7 days	1 month (drained, wrapped)
Ham (canned)	6–9 months	Do not freeze
Ham (cooked, whole)	7 days	2 months
Ham (cooked—half or slices)	3–5 days	2 months
Bacon and smoked breakfast links or patties	1 week	2 months
Sausage (raw from pork, beef, or turkey)	1–2 days	4 months
Hard sausage (pepperoni, jerky)	2–3 weeks	4 months
Poultry		
Chicken or turkey, whole	1–2 days	1 year
pieces	1–2 days	9 months
ground	1–2 days	4 months
Stuffed chicken breasts	1 day	Several months but quality may be affected
Fried chicken, other chicken dishes	3–4 days	3 months
Pieces in broth or gravy	1–2 days	3 months

Lactose Intolerance Is the Inability to Digest Milk Products Properly

Coping with Lactose Intolerance

Milk products are found in all sorts of delicious foods, ranging from appetizers to desserts. Foods made with milk products are also important dietary sources of calcium. However, some people have problems digesting milk.

The culprit is lactose, a sugar found in milk. In those who cannot digest it properly (because they lack sufficient amounts of an enzyme called lactase), lactose may cause stomach cramps, bloating, gas, and diarrhea.

If you're among the ranks of the lactose intolerant (and if you are, you're probably aware of it), do not despair. There are many ways you can enjoy the foods you love, without suffering the uncomfortable aftereffects.

Here are some tips to help you cope with lactose intolerance:

❑ **Use trial and error to learn how much lactose you can take in without a problem.** Everyone has a different degree of lactose intolerance. And dairy products contain differing amounts of lactose. With a bit of experimenting, you may find you can drink one glass of milk with no problem, but more than that, and you develop symptoms. Start by eliminating all dairy products and lactose from your diet for a few weeks. Then, add back small quantities of milk or cheese. Keep a journal to monitor symptoms. You may find you must eliminate some foods entirely, but you can tolerate small portions of others.

❑ **Read labels—between the lines.** Lactose can turn up in unexpected places, such as in medications, where it is often used as a binder. Sometimes, however, the labels don't specify "lactose." To be extra sure, look for the following buzzwords: whey, curds, milk by-products, dry-milk solids, non-fat dry-milk powder, casein, galactose, skim-milk powder, milk sugar, or whey-protein concentrate. Hidden sources of lactose may include bread, cereals, pancakes, chocolate, soups, puddings, salad dressings, sherbet, instant cocoa mix, candies, frozen dinners, cookie mixes, hot dogs, and—yes—even birth control pills. While the amounts of lactose in these products may be small, people who are very sensitive may develop symptoms.

❑ **Eat dairy products only as part of a larger meal or a snack, never alone.** This practice buffers the effects of lactose on your system. Having other foods in your stomach at the same time slows the digestive process and may help you avoid symptoms.

❑ **Try using lactose-free or lactose-reduced milk products.** These are readily available in most supermarkets (two common brands are Dairy-Ease and Lactaid). However, be aware that most of these products still contain some lactose and may cause problems for the severely lactose-intolerant.

❑ **Try lactase-enzyme drops.** If even lactose-reduced milk causes you problems, you can remove even more lactose from it by adding these drops (complete instructions are on the package). Lactase-enzyme drops are available in most supermarkets and drugstores.

❑ **Consider taking lactase tablets.** If you can't live without cheese, ice cream, or other dairy products, try taking these supplements with the first bite of lactose-containing foods. You can vary the dosage to meet your needs (read package directions). Lactase tablets are also sold in supermarkets and drugstores.

❑ **Eat only yogurt containing active cultures.** These are generally well tolerated by lactose-intolerant people. Usually the ingredients list specifies whether the yogurt contains these cultures. If your supermarket doesn't carry these yogurts, try your local health-food store.

❑ **Try hard cheese.** You may be able to tolerate the harder cheeses, such as cheddar and Swiss, which contain less lactose than the creamier, softer cheeses, such as Brie.

A Vegetarian Lifestyle: Is It for You?

Thousands of Americans refrain from eating meat (and sometimes other animal products, too) for myriad religious, moral, or health reasons. Whatever the motivation, a plant-based diet can be a healthy choice—if it is undertaken with a sound knowledge of nutrition.

Avoiding meat or dairy products can be a great way to cut down on your intake of fat, saturated fat, and cholesterol. It can also help you save money, since these products, on average, cost more than most vegetable and grain products.

But there are pitfalls to a meatless diet:

• Meat, fish, poultry, eggs, and milk are the only sources of complete protein, meaning they contain all eight of the essential amino acids (see sidebar, *The Eight Essential Amino Acids*, page 13). To obtain the high-quality protein your body needs, you need to learn how to combine plant-based protein sources (more on this later).

• Dairy products are the best sources of calcium available. It can be difficult to obtain enough calcium from a plant-based diet—especially for children and for women with a high calcium requirement, such as women who are pregnant, breast-feeding, or menopausal.

• Many of the nonmeat sources of protein—whole dairy products and nuts, in particular—are very high in fat. Some vegetarians make the mistake of thinking they are cutting fat by avoiding meat, when, in fact, they are still getting an excessively high percentage of their calories from fat.

• A vegetarian diet may not be the best choice for children, who need high amounts of protein and calcium for proper growth. Parents who desire their children to be vegetarians should consult a physician, nutritionist, or dietitian for guidance.

Here are some guidelines for a healthy vegetarian diet:

A Plant-Based Diet Can Be a Healthy Choice

Vegetarians Must Be Sure to Get Enough Protein and Calcium

1. Learn how to combine proteins. As mentioned above, grains, beans, and nuts all contain some protein. However, all lack a few of the eight essential amino acids that compose a complete protein.

To ensure your protein intake is adequate, you'll have to learn to mix and match complementary proteins in each day's diet—although you don't need to consume them at exactly the same time. The following is a list of nonanimal, complementary protein combinations:

Nutritional yeast + rice, wheat, or oats

Legumes (beans or peas) + rice, wheat, corn, or oats

Soybeans + peanuts + sesame

If you do choose to add dairy products to your diet, you can rely on them as protein sources—as long as they don't contain too much fat. You can also include smaller amounts of dairy products in your diet as a complement to the proteins in grains, beans, and nuts. Here are some complete protein combinations:

Beans + milk

Peanuts + milk

Rice, wheat, or oats + milk

Corn + soy + milk

2. Keep tabs on your calcium intake. Calcium is an important mineral, particularly for growing children and women (pregnant and breast-feeding women have especially high calcium requirements). But most vegetables and grains are relatively low in calcium. The following guidelines will help you make sure you're getting enough calcium:

❑ **Familiarize yourself with good sources of calcium.** Some of the best plant-based sources of the chalky mineral are tofu (if made with calcium sulfate), broccoli, spinach, kale, and turnip greens. One-half cup of tofu contains between 25 and 39 percent of the U.S. RDA for adults. (Refer to the table, *Minerals: Important Dietary Components*, page 18, to check your calcium requirement.) The same amount of cooked broccoli, spinach, or turnip greens contains between 10 and 24 percent of the U.S. RDA. Some orange juices are fortified with calcium, as are many enriched bread and cereal products.

❑ **Take advantage of milk-based products if you can.** One cup of milk contains between 25 and 39 percent of the U.S. RDA for calcium. Eight ounces of low- or nonfat plain yogurt contain more than 40 percent of the U.S. RDA. Many cheeses—especially cottage cheese—are also high in calcium. (Choose the low-fat variety.)

3. Don't lose track of fat. It's very easy to eat a high-calorie, high-fat vegetarian diet. Here are some tips to help you avoid this pitfall:

❑ **Use nuts and seeds sparingly.** One cup of cashews contains 63 grams of fat; a cup of macadamia nuts, 103 grams—more fat than most people should eat in a day!

❑ **Read labels.** Check the fat content of packaged foods.

❑ **Limit your use of oil, margarine, and butter in cooking and baking.** One tablespoon of each contains about 14 grams of fat.

❑ **Use only low- and nonfat dairy products.** They contain the same amount of protein as the high-fat versions.

4. Eat a balanced diet. Variety is the key to a diet rich in all the nutrients your body needs. Make sure to eat plenty of different types of fruits, vegetables, and grains every day.

Eating to Prevent Osteoporosis

You've heard a lot about osteoporosis lately. You probably know it is a disease that primarily affects postmenopausal women. You're probably also aware that it degrades the density of the bones, causing them to become porous and brittle.

You may not know osteoporosis is almost completely preventable and—to some degree—reversible. Three major factors impact women's bone density:

- Estrogen (the production of which decreases after menopause)
- Exercise (primarily the weight-bearing sort, such as running and walking)
- Calcium intake (especially the amount during pregnancy and breast-feeding)

If you are going through menopause, you can talk to your doctor about estrogen-replacement therapy and how it might help you. Also, read the profiles related to osteoporosis, pages 300–302. As far as exercise goes, refer to Chapter 2, *Fitness*, for tips on bone-healthy workouts. Meanwhile, make sure to fight losses in bone density by increasing your calcium intake. The following pointers may help:

❑ **Drink your milk.** Many women (and men, too) left milk at the wayside with their school books and saddle shoes. However, aside from containing high amounts of protein, milk is one of the most important sources of calcium. And whole milk's high fat content need not get in your way: Skim milk actually contains more calcium than high-fat milk. If you are lactose intolerant, try one of the low-fat, lactose-reduced milks on the market, such as Dairy Ease or Lactaid (see *Coping with Lactose Intolerance*, page 34). Some of these products are fortified with extra calcium to help you get more of the mineral for your buck. Cheese and yogurt are also great sources of calcium. And some orange juices are now fortified with additional calcium.

❑ **Eat your spinach.** Spinach, turnip greens, kale, and broccoli are among the best nondairy sources of calcium. Although it's difficult to eat enough of these foods to meet your daily requirement, they can help you go a long way toward it.

❑ **If you take an antacid, choose one that is calcium-rich.** Many antacids contain significant amounts of calcium carbonate. If you find yourself in need of one of these medications, go for the ones that give you the added benefit of a calcium boost.

❑ **Consider a calcium supplement.** A supplement can be a dietary boon for those with a high calcium requirement. While experts feel it is better to obtain the bulk of your nutri-

Osteoporosis Is Almost Completely Preventable

ents from food, women who are pregnant or breast-feeding may want the extra insurance a supplement can provide. Talk to your doctor about the right dosage for you.

However, if you do decide to take a supplement, beware: Recent studies have discovered high amounts of lead in certain types of calcium supplements, including natural oyster-shell calcium. Surprisingly, the synthetic calcium used in antacids was found to contain the least amount of lead.

Eating for Peak Athletic Performance

Athletes May Need to Modify Their Diets

No special nutrition standards have been developed for serious exercisers and athletes. However, these persons, who place high energy demands on their bodies and expect top performance, may also need to modify their diets accordingly.

Many food and supplement manufacturers would have you believe their pills, shakes, power bars, and sports drinks are a must for athletic performance. However, there's no reason those who participate in heavy physical exercise can't derive the nutrients they need from their daily diets.

If you participate in high-endurance or competitive sports or serious bodybuilding, the following nutrition tips may help to keep you energized and ready to work out.

❑ **Stay hydrated.** Replacing fluids lost to sweat is the number one rule for any exerciser, from the two-day-a-week aerobicizer to the elite athlete. And, contrary to what advertisers would have you believe, drinking plain water is the best way to put back fluids you've lost if you exercise for less than two hours.

Don't worry that you've lost too much sodium or other minerals during athletic events or profuse sweating. Perspiration contains only one gram of sodium per liter. (Can you imagine sweating a liter?) You can usually replace this amount through your normal dietary intake of sodium.

If you have lost more than eight pounds of body weight due to fluid loss, you can mix up your own sports drink by adding one-fifth teaspoon of salt to a quart of water, with perhaps a bit of juice added for palatability.

In general, drink plenty of water before, during, and after heavy exercise.

❑ **Carbo-load.** Many athletes find eating a high-carbohydrate diet, particularly for several days before competition, gives them extra physical endurance. While this connection has not been scientifically proved or disproved, it is known that carbohydrates, because they are easily digested, are the body's preferred source of energy.

When you consume carbohydrates, the body stores them as glycogen, a form of glucose used for quick fuel. Since the body can store large amounts of glycogen for future use, it is conceivable you could build up a reserve for an anticipated athletic event.

In any case, eating plenty of low-fat complex carbohydrates

(whole grains, pasta, and rice are your best bets) can't hurt you, so there's no harm in trying.

❑ **Keep your fat intake low.** It's well known that excess body weight can impede athletic performance, especially in weight-bearing exercises, such as running. (If you don't believe ten pounds can make a difference, try running around the block with a ten-pound weight in a knapsack on your back.) However, since exercise burns up calories at a rapid rate, you must also make sure you provide your body with the fuel necessary to see you through your workout or athletic event. (You wouldn't expect your car to run without gas, right?)

So fuel up with lots of nutritious, low-fat foods, such as whole grains, pasta, fruits, and vegetables, and low-fat protein sources (mentioned below). Studies have shown that fat intake—not caloric intake—is most closely related to the amount of body fat you carry.

❑ **Get adequate protein.** Next to water, muscles are composed mostly of protein. But since most of us already consume more than enough protein, you needn't go on a protein binge to build muscle. If you're trying to build muscle (for bodybuilding, for aesthetics, or to improve your athletic performance), you can get the protein you need from these low-fat sources: fish; skinless, white-meat poultry; some lean cuts of pork and beef; low- and nonfat dairy products; egg whites; and combinations of beans or peas and grains.

Nutrition During Pregnancy and Breast-feeding

Pregnancy and breast-feeding place special demands on your body. Not only must you eat and drink to nourish yourself, but you must also provide sustenance for your growing baby.

Trying to design your diet by looking at the RDAs may be a bit overwhelming, especially when your baby's health hangs in the balance. But it's easy to get the nutrients you and your baby require if you think of your daily diet in terms of food portions. The guidelines that follow help you do just that. You're likely to need an additional 300 calories per day while you're pregnant, 400 to 500 while you're nursing. Before making any changes in your diet, however, discuss them with your doctor.

Calcium
This mineral is especially important during pregnancy and breast-feeding. During pregnancy, it is used to supplement the fetus' developing bones and teeth; during breast-feeding to make milk. If you do not consume enough calcium, your body pulls it from your bones, possibly predisposing you to osteoporosis later in life. On the other hand, your body stores calcium very well during this time. Consuming enough may help ward off future losses in bone density. For extra insurance, ask your doctor about taking a calcium supplement.

During pregnancy, shoot for four servings of calcium-rich foods every day. During breast-feeding, you'll need five servings, plus one

You're Likely to Need an Additional 300 Calories per Day While You're Pregnant

Whole Grains Supply Your Body with Needed Energy

extra serving per additional baby if you are nursing twins, triplets, or more. One serving equals:

- 8 ounces milk
- 1 cup nonfat or low-fat yogurt
- 1¼–1½ ounces hard cheese; ¼ cup Parmesan cheese
- ⅓ cup nonfat dry milk
- 1¾ cups low-fat cottage cheese
- 1½ cups broccoli, turnip greens, kale, or spinach
- 3 tablespoons black strap molasses
- 9 ounces tofu prepared with calcium sulfate

Protein
The amino acids that make up protein are the building blocks of the body, so your growing baby needs plenty! Also, be aware that a high consumption of protein during pregnancy has been associated with a lower incidence of pregnancy-related high blood pressure and lower rates of certain birth defects.

Pregnant and breast-feeding mothers alike should choose at least three protein servings from the following list (or substitute with similar foods in similar amounts):

- 3 glasses low-fat or skim milk
- 1¾ cups low-fat yogurt
- ¾ cup low-fat cottage cheese
- 3 ounces Swiss cheese
- 2 large eggs plus two whites
- 5 egg whites
- 3 ounces meat, fish, or poultry
- 5–6 ounces tofu
- 5–6 tablespoons peanut butter
- Protein combination of beans or peas and grains (about ¾ cup beans to 1½ cups brown rice, for example)

Grains
Whole grains supply your body with needed energy. If you don't take in enough carbohydrates, your body begins to burn protein for energy, robbing you and your baby of this important macronutrient. Grains also supply fiber that can help relieve the constipation that is a common discomfort of pregnancy. While you are pregnant or nursing, you need six or more servings per day:

- ½ cup cooked barley, bulgur, brown rice, wild rice, oats, or millet
- 1 slice whole-grain or enriched bread
- 1 corn tortilla
- 1 corn or bran muffin
- 2 rice cakes
- ¼ cup wheat germ
- ½ bagel
- ½ cup pasta
- ½ cup beans (such as kidney or navy)
- ½ cup peas
- 6 crackers
- 2 cups popcorn

Yellow and Orange Fruits and Vegetables
These are important sources of beta-carotene. You should eat five servings a week if you're pregnant or nursing:

- ½ cup dried apricots or 7 fresh apricots
- ½ cantaloupe
- ½ cup cooked carrots or 1 raw carrot
- 1 mango
- 3 nectarines
- 1½ papayas
- ½ cup canned pumpkin

- 1 sweet potato or yam
- 3 slices watermelon
- ¾ cup winter squash

Citrus and Vitamin C Foods

Vitamin C is important for the body's ability to manufacture collagen, the substance that holds tissue together. It also helps iron absorption and may help fight infection. Pregnant or nursing, you should consume one to two servings per day:

- 1 cup raw cabbage
- 1 cup cooked cauliflower
- ½ medium cantaloupe
- ½ grapefruit or ⅔ cup grapefruit juice
- 1 lemon, lime, or orange or ½ cup juice
- ½ cup papaya
- 1 red or green pepper
- 2 small potatoes, with skin
- ½ cup strawberries
- 2 tangerines
- 1 large tomato, 1 cup tomato juice, or ⅔ cup tomato purée

Greens

Dark green vegetables are rich in vitamins and minerals, particularly A and B-complex, which help your body use the protein in other foods. Two servings a day is adequate for pregnant and nursing mothers:

- 1 cup cooked broccoli
- 1 cup brussels sprouts
- ⅔ cup of raw spinach, endive, watercress, asparagus, or sprouts
- ⅔ cup cooked kale, or collard, turnip, or beet greens
- ½ cup lettuce (except iceberg, which contains few nutrients)

Iron-Rich Foods

Most obstetricians suggest that their pregnant and nursing patients take an iron supplement to prevent anemia. You can also boost your intake by consuming iron-rich foods, such as beef, black strap molasses, carob, chick-peas and other dried legumes, dried fruit, Jerusalem artichokes, cooked oysters, sardines, spinach, and liver. Iron is also found in wheat germ, whole grains, and iron-fortified cereals.

Getting Enough Fluids while Pregnant or Breast-feeding

Dehydration can cause special problems for pregnant or nursing women, among them, premature labor or a diminished milk supply.

In most cases, you can trust your natural thirst to tell you how much fluid to drink. However, the following circumstances require you to take extra care to stay hydrated:

- Hot weather
- Vigorous exercise
- Vomiting (Curse that first trimester!)
- Diarrhea
- During labor, when your physician may decide to give you fluids intravenously
- During breast-feeding, especially when trying to build up your milk supply (try drinking a glass of water, milk, or juice at each feeding)

You Can Take an Iron Supplement to Prevent Anemia

Most Obstetricians Believe You Should Not Restrict Your Salt Intake During Pregnancy

Your Salt Intake During Pregnancy

Physicians used to believe a high salt intake was the primary cause of high blood pressure during pregnancy. Now, however, most believe a more important cause is an inadequate intake of protein and calcium.

Sodium is now recognized for its importance in assisting the necessary increase in blood and fluid volume that occurs during pregnancy. Sodium deficiency during pregnancy has been linked to the following symptoms:

- Arm and leg cramps
- Fatigue
- Weakness
- Headaches
- Dizziness
- Low amniotic-fluid volume
- Low blood pressure

These days, most obstetricians believe you should not restrict your salt intake during pregnancy. But don't go out of your way to add salt to foods either.

Freezer Cuisine for Busy Cooks

So, you're determined to start a new healthy-eating regimen for yourself and your family. But your schedule keeps you so busy you're sure you'll be eating take-out food again by next week. What can you do?

Set aside time to cook on weekends or days that aren't quite so hectic. Then, freeze the fruits (and vegetables, grains, and meats) of your labor to eat during the next week. Most frozen foods keep quite well for weeks, even months, when stored properly (see the table, *Food Storage Guidelines,* on page 33).

Some foods lose flavor and become mushy when cooked after being frozen. Others, especially soups and stews, keep very well in the freezer. Trial and error will help you determine which of the recipes in your repertoire are good candidates for freezing.

Here are some freezing tips:

- **Anticipate how you'll use the food.** For example, if you'd like to use a stew for two separate meals, freeze it in two separate containers. Individual portions of many foods can be frozen in resealable plastic freezer bags. If you plan to defrost food in the microwave, freeze it in a microwave-safe container. That way, it can go right from the freezer into the microwave oven.

- **Package food properly.** Use an air-tight plastic container with a lid (leaving one-half inch of space at the top to allow for expansion), or freeze in resealable plastic freezer bags, taking care to squeeze out air before closing. You can also wrap food first in plastic wrap, then in aluminum foil, again, pressing out as much air as possible.

- **Freeze foods while they are still fresh.** The fresher they are when they're frozen, the better they'll taste when defrosted and reheated. Also, set your freezer as cold as possible (0°F or below), so foods freeze as quickly as possible. Since freezer thermostat dials may be incorrect, leave a weather thermometer inside to check the temperature.

❏ **Label your foods with freezer or masking tape.** Foods often are indistinguishable when frozen. Also, jot the date down on the label so you'll know if foods are past their prime.

❏ **Reheat foods properly.** The microwave can be a tremendous boon for heating or defrosting frozen foods. If you heat on the stove top, keep the flame low and stir frequently to prevent burning.

A Lifetime of Healthy Eating

You can't expect to change years of bad eating habits overnight. However, you can learn to set realistic goals and take small steps toward them every day.

Likewise, your family may balk if you suddenly change the foods you cook from macaroni and cheese and fried chicken to broiled chicken and pasta salad. Making changes slowly and gradually helps them adjust to a healthier lifestyle as well.

Lastly, if, with a dramatic flourish, you throw out every high-fat, high-sugar food in your refrigerator tonight, you're likely to be bingeing on chocolate bars by next week. Changes that last a lifetime start with an attitude that leaves room for small indulgences, not with Spartan strictness. There are two steps you can take to slowly improve your diet, for a lifetime of good health: Analyze your diet and create a plan of action.

Analyze Your Present Diet

For one week, write down everything you eat. "Everything" means meals, snacks, and—yes—even surreptitious bites snatched off your spouse's plate or off the cutting board while you're preparing a meal. Every morsel that passes between your lips counts.

At the end of the week, analyze what you've written, as follows:

❏ **Total the amount of calories, fat, sodium, and fiber you consume.** Use food labels to gather your numbers.

❏ **Survey your numbers.** Are you eating too much fat or salt?

❏ **Look at the total number of calories.** Are a high proportion (more than ten percent) of your calories coming from sugar?

❏ **Check out your average fiber consumption.** Is it high enough? Where can you add fiber to your diet?

❏ **Identify the foods that contain the most fat, salt, and sugar and the least fiber.** Can you modify your recipes for these foods to make them healthier?

❏ **Analyze your intake of the different food groups.** Are you meeting the recommended number of servings? Does your diet contain sufficient variety?

Once you've identified the problem spots in your diet, move on to the next step.

Write a Plan of Action

Making a plan for slowly modifying your diet ensures you don't go overboard by making too many changes at once. It also gives you realistic goals to strive for (achieving even small goals helps you

Slowly Improve Your Diet for a Lifetime of Good Health

Acquiring New Eating Habits Takes Lots of Practice

stay motivated and avoid burning out on your new regimen). Here are some tips to create a plan you can stick to:

❑ **Let your food analysis be your guide.** You know where your problem spots are. Now, create strategies for fixing them, one by one. Say, for example, one significant source of fat in your diet is the extra creamy, double fudge nut ice cream you indulge in every night after the kids go to bed. Don't swear off the creamy stuff forever. Instead, perhaps, set a goal of limiting yourself to eating it once a week—Saturday night, for example. If you must have something cold and sweet during the rest of the week, substitute nonfat frozen yogurt. Similar goals might be to switch from white to whole-wheat bread, or from whole milk to two percent milk and eventually to skim.

❑ **Write down your list of goals, then schedule them for implementation.** Don't try to do too much at once; choose one goal a week and stick to it. This way, you won't end up feeling deprived.

❑ **Don't magnify failure.** Acquiring new eating habits is like any other activity—it takes lots of practice before you get really good at it. Expect that you may experience setbacks. Say, for example, you down the entire quart of ice cream— don't beat yourself up over it. Recognize that eating that whole quart is a *temporary* setback, not a reason to give up and revert to your old ways of eating. Make a list of all the ways you've stuck to a healthy eating regimen to see all the times you've succeeded.

❑ **Don't excuse yourself.** If it happened once, it can happen again, so don't just dismiss a setback. Think about what may have led to it so you can avoid a recurrence. Perhaps the kids were particularly rambunctious that day and you sought solace in the quart of ice cream. Be prepared with other ways of pampering yourself next time the kids act up. Take a long bath. Rent a movie. Or top a small bowl of that ice cream with mounds of fruit—bananas, peaches, blueberries, and so on—to fill your bowl to the brim without the added fat.

❑ **Reward yourself at regular intervals for adhering to your plan.** Take yourself to a movie, buy yourself a new pair of shoes, or spend a day out of town. Positive reinforcement may help keep your motivation going strong.

W E I G H T

C O N T R O L

*Y*ou got off the scale, adjusted the dial, then stepped back on again. The reading just couldn't be right—couldn't. But up, up the numbers went, settling on a trio of digits you thought you'd never see between your own two feet.

Berating yourself for your lack of self-control at all those extra-heavy holiday dinners, you step off the scale. You feel miserable. Depressed. Angry at yourself.

If you're upset over your weight—take heart. You are not alone. According to the latest figures from the American Heart Association, 47 million American adults are 20 percent or more over their desirable weight. That's one chubby problem.

If you're tired of battling your weight and are ready to get a head start on shedding those pounds once and for all, read on.

❏   ❏   ❏

Americans Spend Upwards of $32 Billion a Year on Diet Products and Services

The Weighty Facts

Almost one-fifth of the population of the United States is overweight. However, a great many more people are concerned with weight control—so much so that the focus on weight has reached the proportions of a national obsession. Consider the following statistics:

- Americans spend upwards of $32 billion a year on diet products and services.

- Up to 78 percent of women in the United States consider themselves overweight. However, this statistic is not supported by reality. In fact, 45 percent of American women are *underweight*. Clearly, the problem for many women is one of perception not pounds.

- Of 3,000 adolescents surveyed in a University of Vermont study, 66 percent of the girls aged 13 to 18 years were trying to lose weight, although they were already at a normal weight.

- In 1990, liposuction (the surgical removal of fat deposits) was the number one cosmetic-surgery procedure performed in this country.

- There has been a sharp rise in reports of eating disorders in the United States, especially among young women. Researchers have found that a high percentage of these cases began with a weight-loss diet.

A Longing to Be Lean

The facts and figures only emphasize what most of us already know: Americans have an intense desire to be thin. So why are so many of us still overweight? And when we do manage to lose weight, why do most of us regain it within two to five years?

It's time to put an end to the obsession and get a jump-start on success. The rest of this chapter is designed to help you get a good idea of how much weight you really need to lose (if any). It brings you up to date on the latest medical research on weight control, and shows you how to set a realistic goal weight and shed your pounds slowly, safely, and permanently. Finally, it helps you trace the emotional origins of your weight problem and develop a healthy body image.

Do You Need to Lose Weight?

Although your mirrored reflection might prompt you to automatically answer "Yes," there may be more to this question than meets the eye.

While your secret (or not-so-secret) fantasy may be to look as thin as the new breed of waif-like models or to be as wiry as a basketball player, many factors should influence your weight-loss goals. Consider the following:

NOT JUST A MATTER OF SCALE

Perhaps more important than a number on a scale in determining whether you need to lose weight is the affect your current weight has on your quality of life—your confidence, your self-image, your relationships. Take a few moments to respond to the questions in the table below.

BECAUSE OF MY WEIGHT . . .	ALWAYS TRUE	SOMETIMES TRUE	NEVER TRUE
I feel physically uncomfortable.	❏	❏	❏
I feel socially unacceptable.	❏	❏	❏
I am self-conscious in social situations.	❏	❏	❏
I am afraid of being rejected.	❏	❏	❏
I am less productive than I could be at work.	❏	❏	❏
I am afraid to go on job interviews.	❏	❏	❏
I feel clumsy and awkward.	❏	❏	❏
I avoid recreational or social activities that involve physical activity.	❏	❏	❏
I feel unsure of myself.	❏	❏	❏
I am very moody.	❏	❏	❏
I have difficulty being assertive.	❏	❏	❏
I don't like myself.	❏	❏	❏
I feel out of control.	❏	❏	❏
I spend a lot of time worrying about my weight.	❏	❏	❏
I do not feel sexually attractive.	❏	❏	❏
I have little or no sexual desire.	❏	❏	❏
I don't want anyone to see me undressed.	❏	❏	❏
I do not enjoy sexual activity.	❏	❏	❏
I have difficulty finding clothes to fit me.	❏	❏	❏
I avoid activities where wearing a bathing suit or shorts is expected.	❏	❏	❏

If you answered "sometimes true" or "always true" to more than four of these questions, your weight negatively impacts your quality of life. If you answered "sometimes true" or "always true" to ten or more questions, your quality of life may be dramatically diminished by your weight.

ARE YOU AN APPLE OR A PEAR?

Another factor that should influence your decision to lose weight is where the fat is located on your body. Studies have shown that an apple-shaped body (in which the fat is located primarily around the abdomen) is more unhealthy than a pear-shaped body (in which the fat clusters mostly around the thighs and buttocks). If you have a "pear" body type and are at the higher end of what is considered healthy, you probably need be less concerned with your weight than those with "apple" shapes.

See *Setting a Realistic Goal Weight* for help developing a sensible goal weight.

❑　❑　❑

For Most Women, Looking Like a Model Is Not a Realistic Goal

Fact: Although the models who grace the pages of fashion magazines are supposed to represent the "average" woman, only one out of 40,000 women actually has a model's proportions. In other words, for most women, looking like a model is not a realistic goal.

Fact: Although it is true that obesity is associated with many health problems (including heart disease, diabetes, and high blood pressure), ultra-thinness is not always synonymous with good health. For example, many female athletes, dancers, and models stop menstruating. This *amenorrhea*, as it is called, is associated with a loss of bone density, which can increase the risk of osteoporosis, or "porous" bones, down the road.

Fact: Quick weight losses are not usually maintained, often leading to a cycle of loss and regain, called "yo-yo dieting." Yo-yo dieting has been linked to many adverse health effects, including gall bladder problems, an increase in the risk of heart disease, and a slower rate of metabolism (making the weight harder to lose in subsequent dieting attempts).

Fact: When weight is lost through restricting calories (especially when the diet is not accompanied by aerobic and strength-training exercise), muscle mass is lost along with fat. Muscle burns more calories than fat, even while the body is at rest. Thus, the loss of muscle mass leads to a slowing of metabolism, among other things. So if weight is regained—as it usually is—and the pounds come back as fat—as they usually do—the result is a gradual, unhealthy increase in body fat.

Fact: As mentioned previously, research has shown that most cases of eating disorders are preceded by a weight-loss diet.

Fact: Heredity greatly influences body composition. In other words, if you come from a stocky family, your natural predisposition might be toward a heavier-than-average build. That doesn't mean you should resign yourself to being dangerously overweight; it simply means that ultra-thinness is not a realistic goal.

What have researchers gleaned from these facts? A few things:

- **Losing weight is serious business.** Since it can lead to yo-yo dieting and even eating disorders, attempts at weight loss should only be undertaken if it is really necessary.

- **A realistic weight goal is important.** Most average people cannot achieve model thinness. Trying to lose more weight than is realistic for your build and your genes may lead to weight regain and yo-yo dieting (not to mention persistent feelings of frustration and failure).

- **Weight loss should be approached slowly and sensibly.** Quick weight loss often leads to quick weight regain. Losing weight should be approached through permanent behavior changes, not through short-term diets.

Now that you know the facts, try to answer the question again: Do you need to lose weight? If your weight is within the healthy ranges established by the Metropolitan Height-Weight Table (see page 50) and if you have a healthy proportion of fat to lean tissue (see *The Importance of Body Composition,* page 51), the answer should probably be "No."

Setting a Realistic Goal Weight

So, you've determined you really do need to lose weight, but, intelligently, you've thrown out the image of your face on top of Cindy Crawford's (or Michael Jordan's) body with your old size 2 (or 28-inch waist) jeans. Where do you go from here?

According to obesity researchers John P. Foreyt, Ph.D., and G. Ken Goodrick, Ph.D., a "goal weight" is very different than an "ideal weight." The two experts, who wrote the book *Living Without Dieting,* see ideal weight as "a fantasy which corresponds to the socially acceptable weight in a society obsessed with thinness." This ideal is usually defined by the low end of the range specified by the Metropolitan Height-Weight Table (see page 50). Foreyt and Goodrick emphasize that *a number on the scale is less important than*

being healthy and feeling well physically and mentally.

Incidentally, one of the researchers' suggestions for setting a realistic goal weight is that your goal weight should be no lower than the lowest weight you have been able to maintain for at least a year since you were 21 years old.

METROPOLITAN HEIGHT-WEIGHT TABLES

The following are the widely used weight tables published by the Metropolitan Life Insurance Company. They are to be used by people aged 25 to 59 years, in shoes (with two-inch heels, for women), and wearing five pounds of indoor clothing for men and three pounds for women. The weights given are a factor of height and frame size.

DETERMINING YOUR FRAME SIZE

Start by measuring the circumference of your right-hand wrist in front of the wrist bone. Then divide your height (in inches) by your wrist measurement:

$$\text{Height} \div \text{Wrist Circumference} = X.$$

Use the following guidelines to determine your frame size.

FEMALE	MALE	FRAME SIZE
X > 11.0	X > 10.4	Small
X = 10.1–11.0	X = 9.6–10.4	Medium
X < 10.1	X < 9.6	Large

Example: If you are a woman 5 feet 5 inches tall, and your wrist measures 5½ inches, your equation would look like this:

$$65 \div 5.5 = 11.8.$$

Your frame size is small, so you should refer to that column in the Metropolitan Height-Weight Table.

(Formula reprinted with permission from *PMS: What It Is and What You Can Do About It* by S. Snead and J. McIlhaney. Courtesy of Baker Book House Company, copyright 1989.)

METROPOLITAN HEIGHT-WEIGHT TABLES

MEN

Height	Small	Medium	Large
5'2"	128–134	131–141	138–150
5'3"	130–136	133–143	140–153
5'4"	132–138	135–145	142–156
5'5"	134–140	137–148	144–160
5'6"	136–142	139–151	146–164
5'7"	138–145	142–154	149–168
5'8"	140–148	145–157	152–172
5'9"	142–151	148–160	155–176
5'10"	144–154	151–163	158–180
5'11"	146–157	154–166	161–184
6'0"	149–160	157–170	164–188
6'1"	152–164	160–174	168–192
6'2"	155–168	164–178	172–197
6'3"	158–172	167–182	176–202
6'4"	162–176	171–187	181–207

WOMEN

Height	Small	Medium	Large
4'10"	102–111	109–121	118–131
4'11"	103–113	111–123	120–134
5'0"	104–115	113–126	122–137
5'1"	106–118	115–129	125–140
5'2"	108–121	118–132	128–143
5'3"	111–124	121–135	131–147
5'4"	114–127	124–138	134–151
5'5"	117–130	127–141	137–155
5'6"	120–133	130–144	140–159
5'7"	123–136	133–147	143–163
5'8"	126–139	136–150	146–167
5'9"	129–142	139–153	149–170
5'10"	132–145	142–156	152–173
5'11"	135–148	145–159	155–176

Before you proceed: Don't assume you know your frame size. See the sidebar, *Determining Your Frame Size,* page 49; you might be surprised at the results!

The Importance of Body Composition

Many obesity experts believe you're probably better off focusing your attention on improving your body composition (the ratio of muscle to fat) rather than on improving the numbers on the scale. There are many reasons for this:

- **Muscle weighs more than fat, and the scale cannot reflect this.** In other words, when you have a high proportion of muscle to fat, you may weigh more, but you will probably also look better and be healthier than when you weighed less.

- **Fat takes up five times more space than muscle per unit of weight.** So the higher the proportion of fat you have to muscle, the larger you'll be.

- **The more muscle mass you have, the more calories you burn, even when your body is at rest.** That's because fat-free body mass (which includes muscle) is the prime determinant of the metabolic rate. If you are a person with a slow metabolism (for whom every morsel of food seems to turn to fat), building muscle may turn you into a lean, mean, fat-burning machine. Your rate of metabolism will increase along with your muscles.

On the other hand, if you lose weight without building muscle, you will lose lean muscle tissue along with the fat, leaving your rate of metabolism depressed and making you more likely to gain the weight back.

- **Most people agree that a sleek, muscular form is more attractive than a thin, flabby one.** If you focus just on losing weight without building muscle, the latter is what you are likely to end up with.

Unfortunately, muscle mass is more difficult to measure than body weight. There are three main ways it's done:

Hydrostatic (underwater) weighing, which is done by trained personnel at some health clubs. This is thought to be the most accurate method of body-fat measurement.

Skinfold-caliper testing, which relies on a device that pinches and measures the amount of fat directly below the skin. This method is most accurate when conducted by trained personnel. (You can, however, purchase a caliper and instruction booklet from a sporting goods store or mail order through a fitness magazine for use at home.)

Bioelectric impedance analysis, which uses a device that estimates the total amount of water in the body and, from there, gives an estimate of the percentage of body fat. Of the three methods, this is thought to be the least precise.

A desirable amount of body fat is between 8 and 15 percent for men and between 15 and 22 percent for women. Above 24 percent for men and above 33 percent for women is considered overly fat.

The More Muscle Mass You Have, the More Calories You Burn

Weight-Loss Strategies

The Best Way to Lose Weight Is to Adopt a Healthier Lifestyle

Health experts agree. The best way to lose weight and maintain that weight loss is not by means of a "diet," but by adopting a healthier *lifestyle.* Do your darndest to forget the idea that if you diet for a few weeks or months, you'll see a new you. You might, in fact, see a trimmer you, but will you see a *better* you? A *healthier* you? Will you see that trimmer you a year down the line? Not likely, unless you change your eating and health behaviors.

So how do you start? First, you probably need to learn new lifestyle habits. Don't let that statement scare you off. There's lots of help available to guide you through the process of shedding potentially unhealthy food and exercise habits and replacing them with habits that promote health.

There are three basic routes you can take on the road to weight control and better health:

- Join a commercial program (such as Weight Watchers, Jenny Craig, The Diet Center, or Nutri-System).
- Follow a published diet plan.
- Design your own plan (with or without the aid of a physician, dietitian, or nutritionist).

Some people choose a formal program in part because they feel they can't go it alone. Studies have shown that ongoing monitoring and support is a factor in weight-loss success. But not all programs are equal. While some do offer members a weight-control plan that includes education on eating and exercising properly, the methods of other programs may be less than safe. And the fact of the matter is, most programs have poor long-term success rates: Most people gain the weight back within a few years of leaving the program.

Following a published diet can also jump-start your efforts—if you can find a plan that is safe and effective and does more than give you low-calorie meal plans.

Designing your own weight-loss plan has several advantages:

- **What works for others may not work for you.** If you're a busy parent who works late, you may not have time to painstakingly plan out the meals specified in a rigid diet plan. Likewise, if you work on a construction site, a microwaveable meal isn't going to fit into the middle of your day.

- **A plan you devise on your own costs much less than commercial diet programs.** This is especially true for the programs that require you to purchase their food.

- **You can set your own pace.** You can alter your eating style to comply with a commercial program or published diet, but those kinds of changes are unlikely to stick. Tailoring your own gradual program—one that provides for your individual preferences and eating style—increases your chances for long-term success. And, together with the information in this book (also see Chapter 1, *Nutrition,* and Chapter 3, *Fitness*) and advice from a health professional, you'll know your plan is safe.

- **You can design a plan for your whole family.** Even if you're trying to lose weight, you needn't eat foods that are "different" than what the rest of your family is eating. Weight control doesn't have to be an experience of sacrifice and denial. A low-fat, well-balanced diet is something your whole family can enjoy. Learning to cook foods more healthfully, and choosing leaner cuts of meat, lower-fat snacks, carbohydrates over sweets—these are the components of a successful weight control plan. The healthful behaviors you adopt can pave the way for a healthy lifetime for every member of your family.

The next several sections will help you design your own weight-loss and maintenance program—one you *and* your family can happily live with for the rest of your lives.

If you do choose to join a commercial weight-loss program or search for a published diet, refer to *Evaluating Diet Plans,* on page 66.

Assessing Your Behaviors

Before you can make a plan to change your lifestyle, you've got to take a good, hard look at what you're doing now. To start, consider keeping a food and exercise diary for at least a week, preferably two. Analyzing this diary will help you get a handle on many factors contributing to your weight prob-lem, from your fat intake to the connection between what you eat and your emotional state.

Here's what to include:

❏ **Whenever a morsel of food passes your lips, write it down.** Include the amount, even if it's just a bite or two.

❏ **Note your mood when you eat.** If possible, also note the circumstances immediately preceding your eating.

❏ **Write down the times you eat.** It is particularly important to note the times of unplanned snacks so you can see if a pattern develops.

❏ **Keep track of the exercise you do.** Make a note of what activities you engage in and for how long. Also rate on a scale from 1 to 10 how hard you feel you worked out.

❏ **Comment on your self-image.** Has your progress made you feel better about yourself?

With the aid of food labels or, if necessary, a book that lists nutritional values of food (you can pick one up at any bookstore or library), conduct a formal dietary analysis. Add up each day's calories, grams of fat, and grams of fiber. Write down the number of servings of grains, fruits, vegetables, dairy products, and protein-rich foods.

A sample food and excercise diary appears on page 70.

The next section outlines the behaviors you'll need to adopt if you want to lose weight. Read through them, then proceed to *Putting Words into Action* (page 55) for tips on how to use your food diary to help you integrate what you have learned into your everyday life.

A Low-Fat, Balanced Diet Is Something Your Whole Family Can Enjoy

Understanding the Principles of Weight Loss

If You Want to Lose Weight— Eat

The old school of weight management was a nice, tidy equation: Eat fewer calories than your body requires and you'll lose weight. Unfortunately, as the knowledge of obesity has increased, so has the complexity of that simple formula. Fortunately, you don't need a Ph.D. to figure out how to lose weight. Instead, take a look at the following list of principles, all drawn from the most up-to-date scientific research.

1. **If you want to lose weight— eat.** New research shows that the old starvation school of dieting can actually contribute to your weight problem. Here's why:

-   The more you go hungry, the more likely you are to later lose control and overeat.

-   Drastically cutting calories causes the body to slow down its metabolic processes in an effort to hold onto its energy stores (fat). In this way, very-low-calorie diets can actually turn a normal metabolism into a sluggish one.

-   Strategies for quick weight loss often employ unsafe practices, such as cutting out an entire food group (such as carbohydrates). This can compromise your health and deprive you of essential nutrients.

-   It is virtually impossible to cover your nutritional bases on a diet of less than about 1,200 calories a day. If you doubt this, consider the following: The USDA's dietary guidelines (see page 10), recommend you get *at least* five servings of fruit and vegetables, two servings of lean meat or other protein-rich food, two servings of dairy products, and six servings of grains— every day. Even if you ate only the lowest-fat, lowest-calorie sources of these food groups, you would still be getting about 1,200 calories per day.

2. **Count fat, not calories.** It turns out that not all calories are created equal. New research has proved that the body tends to burn protein and carbohydrate calories at about the same rate that you take them in. The more you eat, the more the body burns. In simpler terms—it is almost impossible for the body to store protein and carbohydrate as fat.

On the other hand, the body stores about 95 percent of the fat calories you take in if they are in excess of your energy needs. The reason is the burning of fat, unlike the burning of protein and carbohydrate, is not driven by your intake. The body only burns fat for energy when it runs out of protein and carbohydrate calories. The upshot? You'll end up wearing about 95 percent of every tablespoon of butter you smear on your toast.

Another reason to count fat instead of counting calories is fat is more calorie-dense than the other two macronutrients. Whereas protein and carbohydrate only have about four calories per gram, fat has about nine. If you trim the fat from your diet, you'll also be cutting a significant amount of calories (allowing the body to take the fat it needs from your fat stores).

How much fat should you eat? For good health, not more than 30 percent of your daily calories should come from fat. Some people get half their calories from fat. For them, dropping that to 30 percent would be enough to help them obtain an acceptable weight. To lose weight, you might need to cut that number even further—possibly to 20 percent of calories (never go below 10 percent, since this may have adverse health effects). As a general guideline, women should eat somewhere between 20 and 40 grams of fat per day; men, 30 to 60 grams.

3. Bolster your fiber intake. Fiber is indigestible—meaning it passes through the body without adding any calories. And because it is bulky, it makes you feel full. If you increase your fiber intake, you end up feeling fuller while eating fewer calories.

Also, a high-fiber diet is associated with many health benefits, ranging from reducing the risk of colon cancer and diverticulosis to promoting bowel regularity.

Government research suggests you should get 20 to 35 grams of fiber a day.

4. Hold onto your fat-free mass. As mentioned previously, your body's fat-free mass—which is composed primarily of muscle, bone, and water—is the primary determinant of your metabolic rate. The more lean tissue your body has, the faster it burns up calories, even while it is at rest. But when you lose weight quickly, you can also lose this beneficial lean tissue, slowing your metabolism down and making it harder for you to maintain your weight loss without permanently lowering your caloric intake.

If you preserve your body's fat-free mass, you can lose weight without causing an undesirable slowing of the metabolism. Here's a four-step formula for doing just that:

❑ Lose weight slowly and gradually.

❑ Perform regular aerobic exercise (see *Exercise as Part of the Weight-Loss Equation,* page 61, as well as the *Fitness* chapter, beginning on page 71).

❑ Consider starting a program of strength training, working up to use of moderately heavy weights, to build up your muscle mass.

❑ Make sure you get at least the minimum number of daily food servings specified by the USDA's dietary guidelines.

Putting Words into Action

Now you know what you have to do to lose weight. But how do you integrate these principles into your daily life? Here's a blueprint for designing your own weight-loss plan:

1. Go back to your food diary and start a list of improvements you need to make.

❑ **Look at the number of fat grams you normally eat in a day.** Chances are, it's higher than it should be. On your list, write down "Cut fat intake to 30 percent." Figure out what the main sources of fat are in your diet and write those down, too.

❑ **Check out how much fiber you are eating.** If it comes up short (less than 20 to 35 grams

Not More than 30 Percent of Your Daily Calories Should Come from Fat

Commit Yourself to Losing No More than One Pound per Week

per day), make a note to boost your fiber intake. Also write down where you could increase fiber in your diet (for example, substituting whole-grain bread for white bread; see *Increasing Your Fiber Intake*, page 23).

❏ **Look at the number of servings of food you generally eat.** If you are eating fewer than the minimum, write that down on your list.

❏ **Look at the total number of calories you eat on an average day.** Is it enough? (Check food labels to help you determine this.)

❏ **Are you eating high amounts of sugary foods?** If so, write it down.

❏ **Check your activity level.** Are you doing strength-training exercise to preserve your lean muscle mass? If not, write it down. Are you performing some sort of aerobic exercise for at least 20 minutes, three times a week? If not, jot that down, too. (See *Exercise as Part of the Weight-Loss Equation*, page 61, for more information.)

2. **Make a realistic plan for gradually implementing your list of goals.** Here's how:

❏ **Commit yourself to losing no more than one pound per week.** This is thought to be a safe rate for weight loss.

❏ **Make lifestyle changes slowly.** Changes you make gradually are more likely to stick.

Start by looking at your list. Break down each needed improvement into small, achievable goals and schedule them for implementation. For example: One week, decide to substitute your normal ration of butter on your toast with fruit-only jam. If you normally eat

about one-half tablespoon of butter every morning, this small change could add up to a savings of 49 fat grams and 441 calories per week—no small potatoes! The next week, you might plan to start walking to the corner store instead of driving, or to switch from whole milk to skim milk.

Make sure you allow for indulgences you know you cannot realistically give up. If your goal is to cut down to 40 grams of fat per day, and you know your morning would feel hollow without half-and-half in your coffee, budget that into your fat allowance.

Plan to gradually phase in your changes over a period of six months to a year.

3. **Reward your successes.** Promise yourself that for every week you take at least three 30-minute walks, you will put $5 in a jar. When you've saved up enough money, buy yourself something you've wanted for a long time, such as a massage or tickets to a sporting event.

4. **Don't punish yourself for failure.** It took you a lifetime to develop your bad habits, and it's going to take many months (or years!) to break them. If you accept from the beginning that you cannot execute your new plan perfectly (or instantly!), you may be more likely to get back on the wagon when you fall off. (Remember, the more restrictive you are, the more likely you are to rebel and overeat or underexercise.)

And all you chocoholics out there? It's not realistic to swear off chocolate forever. If you allow yourself to indulge once in a while, it may be easier to pass it by the rest of the time.

5. **Never say "diet."** The word "diet" suggests a temporary eating plan—something you follow for

weeks or months. You, however, are devising a slow, gradual plan to permanently change your behaviors. This is the reason you can afford to make mistakes. A piece of birthday cake can ruin a diet. Over the course of a lifetime of healthy eating, however, it means very little. If you follow your plan 80 percent of the time, you'll still be making large strides toward meeting your goals.

The "Out-of-Sight, Out-of-Mind" Theory

You're sitting on your sofa, innocently watching television, not even *thinking* about food when you are suddenly confronted by the image of a giant ice cream sundae, smothered in whipped cream and dripping with chocolate sauce. Two seconds later, you're scuttling toward the icebox, practically foaming at the mouth.

How about this one: You get home from work two hours later than usual, and you're starving. You open the refrigerator door and begin to scan its contents. Your eyes light upon the piece of cheesecake left over from last night's dinner party (the salad ingredients are well hidden in the vegetable bin below). Soon, you're standing at the kitchen counter, nibbling away at the creamy white confection.

Sound familiar?

Don't feel guilty—it's human nature. Researchers have found that even the sight and smell of food can stimulate the production

BAD HABITS AND BETTER SUBSTITUTIONS

Here is a chart of satisfying substitutions you can make for common dietary pitfalls:

WHEN YOU'RE CRAVING . . .	TRY . . .
Chocolate	❏ Fat-free chocolate mousse, frozen yogurt with low-fat hot fudge topping (1 gram of fat per 2 tablespoons) ❏ Fat-free brownies ❏ Fat-free hot cocoa
Potato chips	❏ Fat–free potato chips (available in many grocery and health-food stores) ❏ Air-popped popcorn
Tortilla chips	❏ No-oil tortilla chips ❏ Corn tortillas cut into wedges and baked in the oven until crisp
Creamy cheese sauce	❏ Low-fat cheese sauce made with evaporated skim milk and low- or nonfat cheese, thickened with flour
Cookies	❏ Fat-free, fructose-sweetened cookies
Bread and butter	❏ Bread with fat-free margarine
An entire pizza with the works	❏ A few slices of veggie pizza
Apple pie with ice cream	❏ Warm apple compote with fat-free frozen yogurt
Spaghetti marinara with pork sausage	❏ Spaghetti marinara with turkey sausage

of serotonin, a substance that plays a powerful role in controlling the appetite.

Fortunately, you don't have to be a slave to the contents of your kitchen. You can take control of your eating by implementing the "out-of-sight, out-of-mind," theory. Here's how:

Don't Bring High-Fat, Sugary Foods into Your Home

❑ **Don't bring high-fat, sugary foods into your home.** If you do, you're likely to end up eating them.

❑ **Make sure you have plenty of foods on hand that are convenient, tasty, and healthful.** These foods should be from each of the food groups and include everything from main meal ingredients to snacks. Also keep a supply of flavor enhancers on hand, such as herbs, spices, flavored vinegars, and fresh lemon.

❑ **If you tend to be a nibbler, stock your kitchen with low-fat, high-carbohydrate snacks.** These include pretzels, fat-free cookies, low-fat frozen yogurt, no-oil tortilla chips, and air-popped popcorn. Such healthful alternatives will also satisfy your family's cravings for junk food.

If this doesn't keep family members happy, try bringing home only small quantities of junk food at a time (one night's dessert instead of a week's worth). If even this strategy leaves them complaining, try enlisting (or begging and pleading) for their support in your weight-loss efforts.

❑ **Divert your attention.** Wash the dishes during food commercials and avert your eyes (and your nose!) as you walk past the donut shop on the way to work.

Snack Yourself Skinny

Along with the outdated advice that you should drastically reduce calories to lose weight inevitably came the dictum: Don't eat between meals. Fortunately, this imperative has been left by the wayside along with beehive hairdos and disco fever. A more educated—and definitely more livable—perspective on snacking has come into vogue of late. Consider these arguments in favor of snacks:

❑ **Hunger is a major cause of overeating.** Makes sense, right? You were so good all day: You ate your bowl of bran cereal with skim milk for breakfast, and salad with tuna fish and melba toast around noon. You've been running around like a lunatic all afternoon, trying to meet a deadline. You finally arrive home and sit down to dinner (it's close to seven o'clock by now). You proceed to eat three helpings of everything. After dinner, you eat half a quart of ice cream.

What's happening here? You're starving, of course. You haven't eaten for seven hours!

Contemporary wisdom tells us to plan snacks into our day, heading that out-of-control hunger off at the pass. A well-planned snack (think banana, non-fat yogurt, graham crackers with jam) may fill you up enough so you're not quite so desperate when you sit down to a meal.

❑ **Eating little and often stimulates the metabolism.** This practice coaxes your metabolism into burning more calories than it does when it is faced with a large meal after fasting for hours. Some experts even recommend eating five or six planned mini-meals a day, instead of three large ones. (Notice that these should be "planned." Choosing to eat smaller meals more often does not mean you should stuff your face all day without any concern for the number of calories you're taking in.)

❑ **Snacking can be a good way to keep your energy levels high.** This is especially true if you nibble on high-carbohydrate, low-fat foods. (Being tired is another cause of overeating.)

❑ **A snack can help round out your nutritional needs, if you're not meeting your requirements at meals.**

Dining Out

*Q*uestion: How can you eat at a restaurant when you're supposed to be dining solely on microwaveable food?

Answer: You can't.

Question: How can you eat at a restaurant when you're on a sensible, lifetime weight-control program?

Answer: Easy—simply learn the right foods to eat.

Restaurants need not be battlegrounds of temptation, sin, and guilt. There is also no reason you should nibble on a dinner salad without dressing while your companions feast on prime rib. The trick is to learn what to eat and in what proportions.

The following is a list of tips for eating out without sabotaging your weight-loss efforts. Bon appetit!

❑ **Choose restaurants that give you a range of options.** A little research may turn up some surprising facts. For example, many fast-food establishments—notorious for deep-fried foods and burgers dripping with grease—are now trying to cater to customers who are committed to a low-fat lifestyle. These restaurants now offer a range of healthful foods, from salads with low-fat dressings to grilled chicken breasts and baked potatoes. Even a pizza parlor need not be off-limits. Simply order your pizza with vegetable toppings and limit the number of pieces you have. (There are roughly five grams of fat per slice of cheese or veggie pizza—not bad for such a delectable indulgence.)

❑ **Learn the key words.** The menu provides clues about how an item is prepared. "Fried," "sautéed," "breaded," "cream sauce," "scalloped," "au gratin," and "rich" are all red-light words. Instead, look for "grilled," "broiled," "steamed," and "poached."

❑ **Ask your server.** After you've picked an entrée that you've guessed is low in fat, double-check with your waiter or wait-

You Can Enjoy Dining Out Even When You're Watching Your Weight

Discover How Delicious Low-Fat Cuisine Can Be

ress. Many times, grilled and broiled entrées are basted with an unhealthy helping of butter or oil.

❑ **Have it your way.** Ask for food to be prepared to your specifications (such as grilled without butter), whenever possible. After all, you're paying for it! Most restaurants are happy to cater to customers with special dietary needs.

❑ **Order the sauce on the side.** If you absolutely can't resist ordering an entrée that comes with a rich sauce, ask your server if you can have the sauce on the side. This way, you can add a spoonful or two without drowning your food in fat. The same goes for salad dressings.

❑ **Choose white-meat, skinless poultry or fish over fatty meats.**

❑ **Eat pasta.** Pasta—when served without fatty cream sauces—can be a delicious, satisfying, low-fat meal. Marinara and other tomato-based sauces are usually low in fat, so, *mangia!*

❑ **Eat bread.** Many breads (exclusive of biscuits, hush puppies, and croissants) are low in fat. And if you choose whole-grain bread, you get fiber as an added bonus. Adding butter provides you with four grams of fat per pat, so tread lightly. (You'll be surprised how fast you can get used to eating bread plain, especially when it's fresh!)

❑ **Share dessert with a friend.** If you feel as though you will keel over dead if you don't have a taste of the tiramisu, by all means, indulge. Try limiting yourself to a few bites, however, or split it with your dinner companion. Alternatively,

choose something low fat and satisfying, such as a cappuccino (made with steamed milk, not whipped cream), sorbet, sherbet, or fresh berries (without the whipped cream).

❑ **Budget a high-fat meal into your day.** If you know you're going somewhere where you will have few or no low-fat options, simply compensate by eating extra lightly during the rest of the day and for the next day. That doesn't mean skipping meals, however. (Remember, eating regularly stimulates your metabolism.) Simply eat lower-fat fare, such as whole grains, fruits, vegetables, and lean protein sources.

Learn from the Spa Chefs

Health spas are known for serving some of the tastiest, healthiest food in the world. And no wonder: Their chefs spend hours devising ways to make low-fat, low-calorie cuisine taste delicious.

While you probably have much less time to cook than a spa chef does, you can adopt the masters' philosophy—dressing up low-fat fare to give it gourmet panache. And you don't have to spend a lot of time doing it, either. The following tips may give you a few ideas:

❑ **Experiment with flavored vinegars (and leave out the oil).** Balsamic vinegar makes a wonderful marinade for freshly sliced tomatoes (try adding a few sprigs of fresh basil and a sprinkle of coarsely ground pepper). Other vinegars that add flavor without fat include tarragon, raspberry, and sherry.

❑ **Make a little oil go a long way.** Although you're trying to cut the fat out of your cooking, four or five drops of sesame oil (a staple in Chinese cooking) can add a lot of flavor, with very little fat. Likewise, a (light) sprinkle of walnut oil can add gourmet flair to a warm salad of wilted greens.

❑ **Use sun-dried tomatoes instead of olives when cooking.** These tomatoes, which can be purchased dry instead of packed in oil and are available in many supermarkets and gourmet food stores, have a chewy texture and a strong flavor that complements many dishes (they are delicious with chicken or pasta). Before using, allow them to soak in hot water for about 30 minutes.

❑ **Use fresh herbs and spices, whenever possible.** A tomato sauce made with fresh, ripe tomatoes can be elevated to the status of nearly divine when you add chopped, fresh basil and oregano. Stir them in a few minutes before serving for peak flavor.

❑ **Go shopping for unusual salad ingredients.** Iceberg lettuce and carrots soon lose their luster, but a salad made with fresh, peppery arugula, raddicchio, and endive can add a touch of low-fat, nutrient-dense elegance to a meal. Other oft-ignored greens include watercress, escarole, and curly endive.

❑ **Be fruity.** Pears poached in zinfandel, berries with balsamic vinegar, and sliced, fresh mango all make delicious desserts. Buy them at the peak of the season and be adventurous. If your recipes are creative enough, you may forget these sweet treats are fat-free!

For additional tips on low-fat cooking, see *The Creation of a Recipe Makeover*, page 28.

Exercise as Part of the Weight-Loss Equation

As mentioned previously, exercise is a crucial part of a lifetime weight loss and maintenance program. To review, a combination of regular aerobic and strength-training exercise provides you with a variety of benefits:

- Helps preserve lean muscle mass during weight loss
- Burns extra calories
- Speeds up the metabolism
- Tones and shapes the body

Exercise for weight loss has a slightly different emphasis than exercise for general fitness. To achieve the benefits listed above, you should maximize the time spent doing aerobic activity, but work at a lower intensity level than if you were trying to improve your cardiovascular fitness. Also, because you are trying to build muscle (the cornerstone of the metabolism), during strength training you should use moderately heavy weights lifted through a few sets of repetitions. If you just want to maintain your muscle tone, use lighter weights lifted through more repetitions.

Exercise Is Crucial to a Lifetime Weight Control Program

It Takes Some Time to Get Fat Out of "Storage" in Our Bodies

AEROBIC EXERCISE

The *Fitness* chapter of this book contains a section on selecting the type of aerobic exercise that's right for you (see *Choosing an Aerobic Workout*, page 80). While most fitness organizations recommend three sessions of aerobic exercise per week to maintain cardiovascular fitness, you'll probably need to work in two or three more to really jump-start your weight loss program.

❏ **Find your appropriate target heart-rate range.** The formula for determining this range appears on pages 77 and 78 of the *Fitness* chapter. You'll want to work at the lower end of this scale (about 60 percent). This way, you'll be able to maintain the exercise for a longer period of time, while still getting your pulse up to a level that keeps you burning fat. The ability to maintain the exercise is important, because it takes some time to get fat out of "storage" in our bodies, so longer periods of more moderate activity are preferable to short bursts of intense activity.

❏ **Take it slow at first.** If you have been sedentary, walking is probably the best exercise for you to start out with (but check with your physician, especially if you have any chronic health problems). Start small, perhaps with walks of 15 or 20 minutes three or four times a week.

❏ **Make a note of your progress and try to increase your time a little bit each time you work out.** Try not to get discouraged. Since you're in this for the long haul, there's no need to rush progress. As long as you stick to your routine, you will see noticeable results, probably sooner than you imagine.

Aerobic exercise builds muscle in those who were sedentary previously. But as you continue to exercise, aerobic activities *preserve* muscle mass rather than build it. If you wish to *build* muscle, you'll need to add strength training to your exercise regimen.

STRENGTH TRAINING

In the past, fitness and weight-loss experts touted aerobic exercise as the most important type of exercise for burning fat. But new research shows that strength training also plays an important role. Here's why:

1. It is true that aerobic exercise burns more calories while it is being performed than strength training does. And aerobic exercise has an "after-burn" effect: Calories continue to burn at a higher level for several hours after the exercise is completed. But several hours after exercise, the metabolic rate returns to normal.

Strength-training exercise, on the other hand, permanently elevates the metabolic rate because it increases the amount of lean-muscle mass in the body. So the more muscle you build, the more calories you burn, even while you're sitting in front of the television, doing nothing.

2. As mentioned previously, when you lose weight by virtue of a reduced-calorie diet, you lose lean-muscle mass along with fat. Aerobic exercise helps you maintain muscle mass. But strength training *adds* lean-muscle mass. If your weight loss program includes both aerobic exercise and strength

training, you are likely to end up with a significantly improved ratio of fat to muscle—leaving you leaner, stronger, and more compact than ever before.

3. As you lose weight by dieting, your body requires less and less fuel to maintain itself. For this reason, when you stop dieting, you have to consume a permanently reduced number of calories to maintain your weight loss. However, if you have boosted your lean-muscle mass through aerobic exercise and strength training, your body requires more calories to survive. (And isn't that statement music to your ears?) You won't have to be hungry to stay thin.

The *Fitness* chapter of this book contains an entire upper- and lower-body strength-training program (see *Strengthening the Upper Body*, page 87, and *Strengthening the Lower Body*, page 90). As mentioned in that chapter, weight lifting is not for individuals with cardiovascular problems or for pregnant women. Check with your doctor regarding appropriate exercises before embarking on any new exercise regimen.

Once you've got your physician's okay, you can start working strength training into your routine.

❏ **For maximum results, train both the upper and lower body at least twice a week each.** Allow a day of rest before repeating the same workout.

❏ **Use weights light enough for you to lift for at least 3 sets of 8 repetitions,** but not so light you can perform more than 3 sets of 15 repetitions. When you can easily perform 3 sets of 15, move up to heavier weights.

HOW MANY CALORIES DOES IT TAKE?

This table shows calories burned during various activities. The estimates are calculated for a 150-pound person. Add or subtract 7% from these figures for every 10 pounds above or below 150 pounds. So if you weigh 170 pounds and you play basketball, multiply 141 calories by .14 (14%, or 7% for each 10 pounds over 150):

$$141 \times .14 = 19.7$$
$$141 + 19.7 = 161$$

You burn about 161 calories during 15 minutes of play.

ACTIVITY	CALORIES BURNED PER 15 MINUTES
Aerobic dancing	105
Badminton	99
Ballroom dancing, continuous	53
Basketball	141
Canoeing (recreational)	45
Cleaning house (steady movement)	63
Cooking dinner	47
Cycling	
5.5 mph, level ground	66
9.4 mph, level ground	102
Football	135
Gardening (raking)	56
Golf (walking, no cart)	87
Horseback riding	
walking	42
trotting, English style	113
Piano playing	41
Rowing (machine, fast pace)	105
Running	
10 min per mile	174
8 min per mile	213
6 min per mile	260
Skiing	
cross-country	146
downhill	101
Squash	216
Swimming, freestyle	143
Table tennis	69
Tennis	111
Volleyball	51
Walking	
3–4 mph, level ground	66–99
down stairs (steady pace)	50
up stairs (steady pace)	151

Does Stress Send You to the Refrigerator?

Are You an Emotional Eater?

A weight problem often represents more than a matter of eating too much or exercising too little. Many overweight (and underweight) people find they use food (or a lack of food) as a tool to help them through anger, boredom, insecurity, loneliness, exhaustion, stress, or frustration.

Emotional eating is an understandable phenomenon. After all, food is our original source of nurturing in life. In most cultures, it symbolizes comfort, love, and togetherness. (Why else would we eat so much at family gatherings?) An emotional connection to food is our social legacy.

But using food as a substitute for other needs can have several serious adverse effects. First, it can take your attention off the real problem (dissatisfaction with your job, for example), and prevent you from taking steps to right the situation (such as getting counseling). Second, it may escalate until your eating patterns are out of control and you cause yourself permanent physical or emotional damage (see *Recognizing the Symptoms of an Eating Disorder,* page 65). Third, it is very likely to interfere with your weight-loss efforts.

The following questions are designed to help make you aware of the connection between your emotions and your eating habits:

- Do you find it difficult to stop eating, even when your stomach is full?
- Do you find yourself bingeing?
- Do you often overeat before a big event (such as a presentation) you are anxious about?
- Do you eat when you are bored?
- Does stress at home or at work send you to the refrigerator?
- Do you often eat when you are not hungry?
- Do you fantasize about food?
- Do you spend much of your time focused on your weight problem?
- Does eating make you feel guilty?
- Do you overeat mostly when you are alone?

If you answered "Yes" to more than a few of the above questions, you are probably an emotional eater. There is a good probability you eat in response to feelings of stress, loneliness, frustration, worry, or anger. Instead of dealing with your problems directly, you "stuff" them down with food.

You may also spend an inordinate amount of time focused on food and weight. This may serve as another distraction, designed by your subconscious to take your attention away from what is really bothering you.

The following list of suggestions may help you begin to get familiar with your own patterns of emotional eating and put food back in its rightful place in your life. However, if your problem is severe or persistent, consider getting professional help.

❏ **Go back to the food journal described on page 53.** (Remember, you wrote down your moods and the circumstances that immediately preceded you eating?) Look for patterns, such as frequent night eating during periods of stress or while your spouse is away on a business trip. Try to figure out and write down the most common emotional reasons for your eating.

❏ **Check your emotional state before you eat.** Right before you take the first bite of a meal or snack, ask yourself how you feel. Rate your hunger on a scale from 1 to 10. Are you really hungry? If not, try to determine whether you are confusing emotion with hunger.

❏ **When you catch yourself about to eat for emotional reasons, commit yourself to postpone eating for about 20 minutes.** Use this time to try and find a better way to get your emotional needs met. Are you tired? If so, perhaps you can take a nap or set aside a few minutes for relaxation. Are you under a lot of stress? If so, a short walk or a talk with a supportive friend might help. Are you bored? If so, perhaps you can amuse yourself in a different way, such as by writing a letter or reading a book.

Recognizing the Symptoms of an Eating Disorder

Emotional eating can keep your weight at a higher level than you'd like. It can also keep you from effectively dealing with your problems. However, when eating behaviors swing wildly out of control, they may cross the line into what is known as an eating disorder.

Eating disorders can influence more than your weight. They may cause health problems ranging from amenorrhea (a cessation of menstruation) to electrolyte imbalances to tooth decay. Sometimes they are even fatal.

There are three widely recognized types of eating disorders: anorexia nervosa, bulimia nervosa, and binge eating.

Anorexia nervosa is characterized by chronic undereating to the point that body weight is reduced to an unhealthily low level.

Bulimia nervosa is usually defined as a pattern of intermittent binges (in which the person takes in very large amounts of food) followed by purges (self-induced vomiting, laxative and diuretic abuse, or excessive exercising).

Binge eating is similar to bulimia nervosa, but without the purging.

While these three eating disorders are differentiated by their symptoms, their roots are the same. All stem from:

- an excessive preoccupation with weight and shape

- an obsessive drive for thinness

- a need to sublimate feelings and problems by focusing on food and weight

If you see yourself as fitting any of these descriptions, you would be wise to seek professional help from a therapist or physician. Thousands of people have recovered from eating disorders, and so can you. On the other hand, left untreated, eating disorders can be fatal.

The following two organizations may be able to help you find your way:

Eating Disorders May Cause Serious Health Problems

Evaluate Diet Plans Thoroughly

International Association of Eating Disorders Professionals. This organization can refer you to a qualified therapist in your area. Write to 123 NW 13th Street, Suite 206, Boca Raton, FL 33432, or call 407-338-6494.

Overeaters Anonymous. This self-supporting organization offers a 12-step program based on the principles of Alcoholics Anonymous. There are meetings all over the world for persons with any type of eating disorder. There are no membership fees or dues to pay (although donations are accepted). To get information on meetings in your area, call 310-618-8835.

Evaluating Diet Plans

If you've read through this chapter and are still convinced you can't design and stick to your own weight-loss program, you may want to buy a diet book or join a weight-loss clinic. However, to avoid laying out your hard-earned cash for something that does not deliver (or, worse, that is unsafe), here is a list of questions you should get answered before you make your final selection:

- **Does the plan require you to eat fewer servings than are recommended by the USDA's dietary guidelines?** (See *Dietary Guidelines: The Food Pyramid,* page 10.) Unless the program is a doctor-supervised very-low-calorie diet, this is a sign it is not nutritionally sound.

- **Does the program recommend that you eat fewer than 1,200 calories per day?** If you are eating fewer than 1,200 calories per day, you will be hard-pressed to get your nutritional needs met. Also, you may lose lean-muscle mass along with fat, increasing the likelihood that you gain the weight back.

- **Does the plan prohibit eating from any particular food group (such as breads, grains, and cereals)?** This is not a safe method for losing weight.

- **Does the program promise weight loss at a rate faster than one pound per week?** After an initial loss of retained water, one pound a week is the recommended rate for permanent weight loss. Losing weight faster may cause you to lose lean-muscle mass and slow your metabolism.

- **Can you afford it?** What are the additional expenses, if any? Some programs charge a low initial fee, but require you to buy their prepackaged food. Others charge in advance and do not refund your money if you drop out.

- **Does the program publish any statistics on its long-term success rates?** If they cannot provide proof of their success, why should you trust them?

- **Is the program medically supervised?** This is not necessary, but it is helpful.

- **Does the program involve aerobic and strength-training exercise?** If not, you will lose lean-muscle mass along with any fat.

- **Does the program fit into your lifestyle?** If not, the changes you make are unlikely to be permanent.

- **Does the program offer any help with binge eating, if you need it?** Behavior modification is important for permanent weight loss.

- **Does the program provide maintenance support after you lose the weight?** Is the cost of the maintenance program included in the initial fee? Studies show that people who receive ongoing support are most likely to keep the weight off.

- **Will your goal weight be individualized or will it be based solely on your height and weight?** A good program takes into account your family history of obesity, your personal history, and your body composition. (See *Setting a Realistic Goal Weight* on page 49.)

- **Does the program encourage you to meet the Recommended Dietary Allowance (RDA) for vitamins and minerals, or does it recommend that you get less or more?** Exceeding or not meeting the RDAs may cause adverse health effects.

- **Does the program rely on appetite-suppressant drugs?** Appetite suppressants may help in the short term, but they do not provide a solution for permanent weight loss and maintenance.

- **Does the program provide you with group support?** Although not necessary, group support can be very motivational.

- **Will the program help you develop a healthy body image?** A healthy body image has been linked with high self-esteem. Low self-esteem and depression are likely to contribute to overeating.

- **Can the program provide any scientific papers that have been published in journals that demonstrate the effectiveness and safety of its methods?** If not, why should you place your trust in it?

- **Will the program provide you with help to steer your family toward healthier eating habits?** Permanent weight loss is easier when the whole family joins in.

- **Is the program reputable?** Ask for client references.

- **Have any complaints against the program been filed with the Better Business Bureau?** For your protection, call your local Bureau and check.

Avoiding Snake Oil

Have you heard about the new thigh cream—the one that is supposed to melt the fat right off your legs? How about the pills that are supposed to take the weight off, without requiring you to change your diet at all? And what of those low-calorie meal-replacement shakes?

The market is flooded with over-the-counter weight-loss pills, devices, and gimmicks. Each promises its own special brand of magic. Each requires you to contribute less and less effort to losing weight.

With so many fraudulent claims out there, how can you decipher fact from fiction?

Simple: You can't.

Can You Distinguish Diet Facts from Phonies?

You Cannot Fast for the Rest of Your Life

The truth of the matter is that the weight-loss industry is not very tightly controlled by the government (although this is changing fast). If you don't stand firm and refuse to be hoodwinked, it's easy to be taken in by a sleazy vendor who's out to prey on your desperate desire to be thin.

Unfortunately, a silver bullet for weight loss has yet to be discovered. If it existed, we'd all be thin by now (after all, Americans spend more than $32 billion a year on weight-loss products and services). While manufacturers may tout celebrity testimonials to the efficacy of their products, they are usually pretty quiet about their five-year success rates (the number of people who have maintained their weight loss for five years). The fact remains: Losing weight is not the hard part. Keeping it off is.

If this all sounds discouraging, take heart: You can lose weight and keep it off without spending truckloads of cash on shakes or diet pills. All you have to do is believe in yourself and follow the principles outlined in this chapter. Save your money for the new wardrobe you'll need after the weight comes off.

Drastic Measures

There are a number of methods physicians sometimes use in order to precipitate a rapid and dramatic weight loss. Among them are:

- Medically supervised fasts
- Stomach stapling
- Wiring the jaws shut

Because all of these procedures are quite drastic, they are usually reserved for the "morbidly" obese—that is, people who are so overweight their immediate health is threatened. If you are not morbidly obese but are fantasizing about one of these treatments, consider the following facts:

Fact: Medically supervised fasts do promote rapid weight loss. But as this chapter describes, rapid weight loss is not usually maintained, since it generally results in large losses of lean tissue as well as fat, and this loss of muscle actually decreases your body's fat-burning ability. In addition, medically supervised fasting is only a temporary method of achieving weight control—you cannot fast for the rest of your life. So unless you learn to alter your eating and fitness habits, you're likely to end up gaining the weight back once you stop fasting. Quick weight loss has also been associated with a number of adverse health effects. Lastly, a large, rapid weight loss may leave you with excesses of saggy, flabby skin.

Fact: Ileal bypass surgery (commonly called stomach stapling) reduces the capacity of the stomach, thereby suppressing its ability to hold much food. However, like all surgical procedures, it carries some risks. It may also cause severe gastrointestinal discomfort.

Fact: Wiring the jaws shut may work for some people, but not for those skilled at using blenders to make milk shakes. Also, when the wires come off, the weight is likely to be regained because of a slowing in metabolism and a loss of lean-muscle mass. Lastly, wires don't help you change your eating habits, and long-term deprivation can lead to bingeing and compulsive eating.

Self-Acceptance and Self-Esteem

Our culture's obsession with thinness can make things difficult for people who are overweight. Studies have shown that overweight people suffer from discrimination in school, in their jobs, and in their social lives. Self-esteem can suffer in the face of so much adversity.

However, no matter what kind of treatment you receive from the world, it remains your responsibility to be your own best advocate. No matter how you look on the outside, your well-being and happiness depend on the way you feel about yourself inside. You can counter the negative messages you receive with some positive messages of your own.

One form of therapy, called cognitive therapy, focuses on retraining your thinking to eliminate some of these negative messages and move you towards self-acceptance. You can practice these techniques to help counter the destructive "self-talk" that damages your self-esteem (and may keep you overeating). See the sidebar, *Positive Thinking*, for some sample cognitive arguments and counter arguments.

At first, your counter arguments may seem forced and artificial. However, negative thinking is no more than a bad habit, and bad habits can be broken. It's simply a matter of retraining your subconscious mind.

Another powerful tool for improving your self-image is affirmation. With this technique, you repeat positive messages to yourself in an effort to coax the subconscious mind into a new way of thinking.

Start by sitting down with a piece of paper and drafting a positive message to yourself. One or two sentences should be enough. Use the present tense and employ strong, decisive language; for example: "I am a kind, generous person. I love and accept myself exactly as I am," or "My body is beautiful, no matter what the scale says. I take good care of my body and treat it with love." Practice saying your affirmation to yourself repeatedly, several times a day.

Perhaps the most powerful tool in the battle for self-acceptance is a loving, supportive network of friends. A support group can help you see things in a new light when you are feeling down, encourage you to stay motivated, and accept you when you are having problems accepting yourself.

You can join a group or start one of your own. However, do make sure the group is nonjudgmental and accepting of its members, regardless of their weight. Make sure the other participants

Your Happiness Depends on How You Feel Inside, Not on How You Look Outside

POSITIVE THINKING

NEGATIVE THOUGHT	COUNTER ARGUMENT
My thighs are fat and lumpy.	My thighs are strong; they support me and carry me through life.
I look terrible in a bathing suit.	I am a good swimmer and I enjoy the water. How I look in my bathing suit is irrelevant.
When I meet people, I'm certain their first thought is that I am fat.	I have more to offer than my looks. People who are put off by my weight are not worth my time.

have goals similar to your own. Exchange phone numbers and encourage members to call each other in times of crisis.

Inside or outside of a group, practice treating yourself with the love and kindness you'd bestow

upon a dear friend. Self-acceptance and self-esteem will take you a long way toward meeting all of your goals, from weight loss to career success to developing a deep-rooted satisfaction that pervades your entire life.

CHART YOUR PROGRESS

Researchers in the area of fitness and weight loss have found that keeping a daily food and exercise diary can help individuals lose weight. It seems the diary helps dieters stay focused on their goals, plan meals and exercise activities, and reflect on their eating behaviors. A written record of how you stick to or deviate from your goals can be a powerful tool in behavior change.

It's equally important that you monitor your progress in other areas besides your weight. You should reward yourself not only for improvements in eating habits but for improvements in *thinking* habits. You should monitor not only inches you have lost, but negative feelings about yourself you've lost, too.

Here is a sample page from a dieter's diary. Good luck!

Date_____

FOOD LOG

Food	Amount	Fat (g)	Calories
Breakfast			
		Total	Total
Lunch			
		Total	Total
Dinner			
		Total	Total

Snacks			
Time	Food/Amount	Situation/Feelings	Calories
			Total

Daily Totals: Fat _____ Calories _____

Date_____

EXERCISE LOG

Activity	Duration	Comments
Aerobic		
Strength		
Stretching		

SELF-ACCEPTANCE LOG

How I felt about myself today:

What I did well today:

Something I did for myself today:

What I found satisfying about today:

How I can make tomorrow better:

F I T N E S S

*T*he term "fitness" may bring to mind people working out at a health club or students doing calisthenics during P.E. class. But most athletes and fitness professionals see fitness as going beyond merely physical conditioning.

According to the International Association of Fitness Professionals, "physical fitness" refers to "an enhanced physiological or functional capacity that allows for an improved quality of life.

"Quality of life," the definition continues, "implies an overall positive feeling and enthusiasm for life, without fatigue or exhaustion from routine and required activities."

Note that this definition encompasses the mind and the body. It makes no reference to skill or physical coordination. It describes a physiological state of well-being that allows an individual to participate fully and energetically in every aspect of life. If this definition intrigues you, read on.

❑   ❑   ❑

Physical Fitness Is Feeling Well Physically and Mentally

Just One Part of the Fitness Equation

This chapter is designed to help you achieve one aspect of fitness—strengthening your physical self: improving the function of your cardiovascular system, building muscle strength, enhancing body composition.

We urge you to refer to the other chapters in the *Medical Book of Health Hints & Tips* for advice on completing the fitness equation—maintaining and improving your physical and emotional health. The information contained under such headings as *Nutrition, Emotional and Mental Health, Coping with Stress, Major Medical Problems,* and *Everyday Health Problems* has been compiled to help you live fully—to help you live well, in every sense of the word.

The Five Components of Physical Fitness

Physical fitness is feeling well physically and mentally, having the energy and stamina to perform your daily tasks without becoming fatigued, and maintaining that energy throughout your life. Sounds great—but how do you get from here to there?

There are five basic components of physical fitness: muscular strength, muscular endurance, cardiovascular endurance, flexibility, and body composition. Here's a short course:

Muscular strength is the force a muscle or muscle group can exert when flexed. For example, when you pick up a shopping bag, you flex the biceps muscles and exert a force on the bag against gravity. Muscular strength is important in standing up, sitting down, lifting, carrying, and so on.

Muscular endurance is measured by the length of time you can continually exert muscular force, or by the number of contractions the muscle can withstand before becoming fatigued. Walking is a test of muscular endurance, as is standing for long periods, gardening, cleaning, writing, and so forth.

Cardiovascular endurance, also called aerobic fitness, is a measure of your heart's stamina. It is a function of the heart-lung system and that system's ability to deliver blood and oxygen to the muscles during ongoing exercise. If you have little cardiovascular endurance, walking up stairs or down the street leaves you winded. Poor cardiovascular endurance can severely impact your life, rendering you tired and immobile.

Flexibility is a measure of the joints' range of motion. Adequate flexibility allows you to touch your toes and sit cross-legged. It also gives you mobility and helps prevent injury. Lower back and hamstring (back of the leg) flexibility is particularly important, since tightness in these areas is associated with lower back pain and injury. Often overlooked, flexibility is one of the most important components of fitness.

Body composition is the ratio of lean body mass (that of muscles, bones, nerve tissue, skin, and organs) to fat. Lean tissue is metabolically active, meaning it needs significantly more fuel than does fat to maintain its activity. Fat needs little fuel to maintain its functioning. Furthermore, too much fat can literally weigh you down and interfere with your performance during exercise by putting additional stress on your muscles and joints. It also puts strain on the heart, forcing it to work harder to carry the extra load.

Because muscle weighs more than fat, it is more important to measure body composition than body weight when evaluating fitness. In other words, a 5-foot 2-inch, 175-pound male body-builder could be considered overweight if evaluated on body weight alone. However, if his muscle-to-fat ratio was considered, a different determination might be made. A desirable amount of body fat is between 8 and 15 percent for men and between 15 and 22 percent for women. Above 24 percent for men and above 33 percent for women is considered obese.

- Having more energy
- Raising the level of high-density lipoprotein (HDL) in your blood (HDL is the "good" cholesterol that is thought to protect against heart disease)
- Experiencing less chronic pain
- Losing weight
- Relieving stress
- Sleeping better
- Reducing your chances of developing osteoporosis, a significant loss of bone density

You don't have to run a marathon or become a triathlete to experience the positive side effects of being in shape. All you have to do is set small goals and work toward them every day.

Many formerly unfit people have discovered the joys of fitness and have become steadfast converts. They have found ways to make staying in shape an important daily priority. After awhile, sticking to a routine becomes not a chore but an anticipated, enjoyable part of life. When you put fitness at the top of your list, you will experience these payoffs, too.

Many Formerly Unfit People Have Discovered the Joys of Fitness

The Fringe Benefits of Fitness

Fitness provides many desirable perks. If you work to improve your muscular strength and endurance, as well as your cardiovascular endurance, flexibility, and body composition, you can expect to experience many of the following benefits:

- Feeling better
- Looking better

Evaluating Your Fitness Level

Before you begin any exercise program, it is important to evaluate your present fitness level. This way, you'll know in which areas you most need to improve. (If you are pregnant or have any chronic health problems, it is imperative to have your fitness evaluated by a physician.)

If You Have Any Health Problems, Get Your Doctor's OK Before Lifting Weights

Here are some informal tests that will give you a good idea of how fit you are:

Muscular Strength

The best way to test muscular strength is by going to a gym and—with the aid of an instructor or a knowledgeable friend—experimenting until you find the amount of weight you can comfortably lift with each successive muscle group.

❑ To avoid straining or injuring yourself, determine the amount you can lift for at least 8 consecutive repetitions. This amount will be much lighter than the amount you can lift for only 1 repetition.

❑ Write down the amount of weight you can lift with each successive muscle group. These are the amounts you'll use when you begin a strength-training regimen.

If you don't have access to a gym, but want to buy handheld dumbbells for use at home, try these two tests in the store:

Biceps curls. Stand with your knees bent, hip-distance apart. Pick up a 3-pound weight in each hand. Extend the arms down the front of the thighs, inner forearms facing outward. Slowly curl the weights up until they almost touch the shoulders, then slowly lower to the starting position. Repeat 8 times. If 3 pounds feels like a piece of cake, move up in 3- to 5-pound increments until you find the right weight.

Triceps kickbacks. From the biceps-curl position, bend the knees a little more and lean forward slightly. Using the 3-pound weights, bend the elbows and—keeping your arms very close to

your sides—position a weight at each hip. Slowly extend the arms straight out and up in back of you, then slowly lower to the starting position. (Don't move those elbows!) Repeat 8 times. Move up in 3- to 5-pound increments until you find the weight that works best for you.

Some words of caution:

❑ Lifting excessively heavy weights—especially if you're not well-versed in proper form—can cause serious injuries.

❑ Weight lifting is not for pregnant women or persons with high blood pressure or cardiovascular disease. If you have any chronic health problems, get your physician's OK before attempting to lift weights.

Muscular Endurance

A standard test of muscular endurance is the two-minute, bent-knee sit-up test.

1. Lie on your back on an exercise mat with your feet flat on the floor and your knees bent. Your heels should be 12 to 18 inches from your buttocks.

2. Fold your arms across your chest, fingertips on your shoulders. If you like, have someone hold your feet on the ground.

3. Keeping your feet on the floor, sit up and touch your left elbow to your right knee. Return your shoulders to the mat. This is one repetition.

4. Repeat, this time touching your right elbow to your left knee.

5. Repeat the exercise (counting the number of repetitions you perform) for two minutes. Evaluate your result with the scoring chart on page 75.

Flexibility

To assess your flexibility, try this simple test.

1. Stand with your knees just slightly bent; feet, hip-distance apart.

2. Slowly reach your arms down toward your feet, with the goal of putting the palms flat on the floor. Do not bounce or push the stretch any further than is comfortable.

You won't need any formal scoring system to tell you how you've done: If you can't reach lower than your knees, you're probably pretty stiff. If you can put your palms flat on the floor, you probably have adequate flexibility in your hamstrings and lower back.

Cardiovascular Endurance

A medically supervised test of cardiovascular endurance is advisable if you have been sedentary or if you have any suspected or confirmed health problems. If you are healthy, you can try the test described below.

1. Take a walk on an uninterrupted route (such as a jogging track). Your pace should be quite brisk—just below a jog. You want to walk fast enough that you can carry on a short conversation, but not so fast you are gasping for air.

2. Carry on walking at the same pace for up to 30 minutes, stopping earlier if you become exhausted.

Though this is not a standard test of cardiovascular endurance, a short walk, as described above, gives you a good idea of your cardiovascular fitness level. Ask yourself the following questions: How do I feel? Am I winded, exhausted? Did I have a hard time maintaining the pace? Did I need to

quit long before the half hour had passed?

Body Composition

To get an accurate measurement of your body fat, you should go to a gym where they perform hydrostatic weighing (done in a tank of water) or skinfold caliper tests. But there's an easier, if less accurate, way to measure:

Look in the mirror. Are there rolls of fat around your middle? Do you have a lot of fat on your thighs, your buttocks, your arms? Are you very overweight? Make an honest assessment of whether you need to reduce your body fat. (Also see *Do You Need to Lose Weight?* in Chapter 2, page 46.)

Aerobic Versus Anaerobic Exercise

Aerobic exercise is the cornerstone of cardiovascular conditioning. An aerobic exercise is a repetitive motion that elevates the pulse to a target zone and holds it there for at least 20 minutes. In so doing, the activity exercises the cardiovascular (heart-lung) system.

How Flexible Are You?

SCORING THE BENT-KNEE SIT-UP TEST

RATING	MEN	WOMEN
Outstanding	79–91	64–72
Excellent	68–78	57–63
Very Good	60–67	50–56
Average	51–59	45–49
Below Average	42–50	39–44
Poor	33–41	33–38
Very Poor	32 or fewer	32 or fewer

Aerobic Exercise Benefits You in Many Ways

Aerobic exercise benefits you in other ways besides strengthening your heart. It elevates your metabolic rate during the exercise and for hours after you perform it. That means you burn fat at an increased rate. It also can help raise your energy level and your spirits. Lastly, it can help reduce stress and improve the quality of your sleep (especially when performed about six hours before you go to bed).

The following is a list of activities that, when performed at the appropriate intensity level for 20 minutes or more, constitute an aerobic workout:

- Walking (at a brisk pace)
- Jogging
- Running
- Bicycling (stationary or moving)
- Stair climbing
- Aerobic dance
- Step aerobics
- Swimming
- Cross-country skiing
- Rowing
- Skating

The opposite of aerobic exercise is anaerobic exercise. These activities require large amounts of oxygen in quick bursts. Because of the high oxygen demand it places on the heart, anaerobic exercise is not usually sustainable for a period of 20 minutes.

The following is a list of anaerobic activities. While they do aid in improving muscle strength and body composition (see *Strength Training: An Important Component of Fitness*, page 86), they should not be confused with activities that strengthen the cardiovascular system. Also, because of the stress they place on the cardiovascular system, these anaerobic activities should not be performed by pregnant women or by people with high blood pressure, cardiovascular disease, or other chronic health problems:

- Weight training
- Push-ups
- Chin-ups (pull-ups)
- Any exercise, when performed at an intensity that leaves the participant gasping for air or unable to sustain the activity for at least 20 minutes

Determining Your Aerobic Target Heart Rate

As mentioned above, aerobic activities are those that can be sustained at a specific rate of intensity for at least 20 minutes. There are good reasons for working within this "training zone":

- It significantly raises the rate at which the muscles use oxygen, and causes the heart rate to rise so the circulation can get the oxygen to the muscles.
- It exercises the heart, without overtaxing it.
- It elevates the metabolic rate and burns fat.
- It encourages the release of endorphins, natural substances within the body that produce a pleasurable sensation, the so-called "runner's high."

The target aerobic heart rate—the zone where you can expect to experience the benefits mentioned above—is usually considered to be between 60 and 85 percent of your (theoretical) maximum pulse rate (which is roughly 220 minus your age). Beginning exercisers, pregnant women, and people with health problems should stay at the lower end of the scale; more advanced exercisers and athletes can push to the top of the zone.

The following are two easy and relatively accurate ways to determine your aerobic target heart-rate zone: the Karvonen Formula, the more scientific of the two, and the Maximum Heart-Rate Formula, the more popular.

The Karvonen Formula

1. Calculate your maximum heart rate. Maximum heart rate is the highest heart rate a person can attain during vigorous exercise. Although the only way to accurately assess maximum heart rate is a medically supervised test that monitors the heart, you can estimate your maximum heart rate by subtracting your age from 220. (This formula is based on the knowledge that a baby's maximum heart rate is approximately 220 beats per minute and it decreases by about one beat per year.)

2. Determine your resting pulse rate. Resting pulse is best measured first thing in the morning, before you get out of bed. The pulse should be taken either for 30 seconds and multiplied by two, or for a full 60 seconds (see *How to Take Your Pulse,* page 78). For the most accurate determination of resting pulse, take your pulse on three mornings, then average the readings (add them together and divide by 3).

3. Calculate your heart-rate reserve. Subtract your resting heart rate from your maximum heart rate.

KARVONEN FORMULA SAMPLE

If you're 35 years old, and your resting heart rate is 78, you would calculate your target heart rate range as follows:

$$220 - 35 = 185$$
$$185 - 78 = 107$$
$$107 \times .60 = 64 + 78 = 142$$
$$107 \times .85 = 91 + 78 = 169$$

Your target heart-rate range is 142 to 169 beats per minute.

❏ ❏ ❏

4. Determine your target heart-rate range. To establish the range, you need to complete the following formula once using the lower end of the intensity range (60 percent), and once using the higher end of the range (85 percent). This formula determines the target heart rate as a percentage of the target heart-rate reserve, plus the resting heart rate:

- Multiply the heart-rate reserve by 0.60. Add the resting heart rate. This number is the lower end of your target zone.

- Multiply the heart-rate reserve by 0.85. Add the resting heart rate. This number is the upper end of your target zone. (See the *Karvonen Formula Sample.*)

Maximum Heart-Rate Formula

1. Calculate your approximate maximum heart rate: Subtract your age from 220. (For an explanation of the source of this equation, see step 1 under *The Karvonen Formula.*)

2. Multiply your maximum heart rate by 0.60. This is the lower end of your training zone.

3. Multiply your maximum heart rate by 0.85. This is the upper level of your training zone. (See

Maximum Heart-Rate Formula Sample. Also see the table *Your Target Heart Rate.*)

The Talk Test

The Talk Test is another less scientific, but still useful, method of assessing whether you are working to the proper level of aerobic intensity. Here's how to use it.

As you exercise, check the signals your body sends you. You should be able to answer Yes to the following questions:

- Can you breathe comfortably, deeply, and rhythmically?
- Could you carry on a short conversation while exercising at this level?

If you are gasping for breath or cannot talk, you should slow down and reduce your intensity. This method is best when used in conjunction with taking your pulse.

MAXIMUM HEART-RATE FORMULA SAMPLE

If you're 35 years old, figure your training zone as follows:

Step 1. 220 - 35 = 185

Step 2. 185 x .60 = 111

Step 3. 185 x .85 = 157

Your heart rate training zone range is 111 to 157 beats per minute.

❏　❏　❏

How to Take Your Pulse

Taking your pulse is a way to monitor your intensity level during aerobic exercise. The count is based on the average number of pulses in a full minute.

But since your pulse rate drops rapidly when you stop moving, it is best to take the pulse for no longer than ten seconds, then mul-

YOUR TARGET HEART RATE

The following chart shows the target aerobic training zone as a factor of age, using the maximum heart-rate formula. To find your appropriate aerobic training zone (in pulse beats per minute), simply examine the column below your age range. At the peak of exercise, your pulse should be between the top and bottom numbers in the column, or, roughly, 60 to 85 percent of your maximum heart rate.

% OF MAX HEART RATE	AGE RANGE									
		20–25	26–30	31–35	36–40	41–45	46–50	51–55	56–60	61–65	66–70
60%	119	115	112	109	106	103	100	97	94	91
65%	128	125	122	118	115	112	109	105	103	99
70%	138	134	131	127	124	120	117	113	110	106
75%	148	144	140	137	133	129	125	122	118	114
80%	158	154	150	146	142	138	134	130	126	122
85%	168	163	159	155	150	146	142	138	133	129

tiply by the appropriate factor to approximate a full minute's pulse rate. For example, you can take your pulse for six seconds and multiply by 10, or take your pulse for ten seconds and multiply by 6. (Time under six seconds is too short to accurately count.)

Never try to take your pulse with your thumb because it has a pulse of its own. Also, when you start counting, count the first beat as "zero," not as "one."

You can take your pulse at one of the following four locations:

❑ **The wrist.** Place the index and middle finger on the radial artery of the wrist—the artery in line with the thumb. Press lightly to feel the pulse.

❑ **The temple.** Press the index and middle fingers lightly in front of the upper part of the ear, above the cheekbone.

❑ **The neck.** Gently place the index and middle finger on the carotid artery, which is located on the neck, just to the side of the throat. Never press hard at this location, since excess pressure can cause a reflex action that slows the heart rate.

❑ **The chest.** Place the heel of the right hand over the left side of the chest, fingers pointing in the direction of the left shoulder.

Consider a Low-Impact Workout

The mid-1970s gave birth to a new form of exercise: aerobic dance. With its emergence came an enthusiastic breed of participants, scantily clad in Spandex and eager to jump, kick, twist, and bounce their way to cardiovascular fitness. Aerobic dance turned out to be a refreshing new way to get the pulse up into the training zone, burn fat and calories, listen to music, and have a great time.

But the rise in popularity of aerobic dance was accompanied by a rise in the number of injuries associated with the sport. Instructors and participants alike started to develop symptoms of joint stress such as shin splints, knee problems, stress fractures, heel pain, foot pain, and twisted ankles.

Hence, low-impact aerobics was born. This new variation of aerobic dance centered around the principle of keeping one foot on the floor at all times. There would be no more (or, certainly, fewer) jumping jacks, hops, skips, bounces, and the like. To get their pulses up, participants used their arms and worked their muscles through a larger range of motion.

Although high-impact aerobics still exists, low-impact aerobics has gained popularity. And no wonder: Not only is it safer and easier on the body, but it opens the door to participants who could not easily join the high-impact classes, such as the elderly, those new to fitness, the severely overweight, and those who suffer from knee and joint problems.

Today, several new forms of low-impact aerobic exercise eliminate most of the joint stress caused by high-impact aerobic dance. Here are a few of the most common ones:

Step aerobics. In this sport, instructors lead participants through a variety of arm and leg movements while stepping up and

Low-Impact Aerobics Is Safer and Easier than the High-Impact Variety

There's an Aerobic Exercise That's Just Right for You

down on a bench of varying height.

Slide aerobics. This sport involves wearing nylon booties over athletic shoes and sliding back and forth on slick plastic.

Stair climbing. A variety of machines enables participants to raise their pulse rates by stepping, climbing, or jogging on pedals.

Cross-country ski machines. These machines—the most prominent brand is NordicTrack—give participants the low-impact, calorie-burning power of cross-country skiing.

Of course, time-honored forms of low-impact exercise still exist, including stationary cycling, walking, rowing, cross-country skiing, and swimming. All of these activities give you a range of ways to safely elevate your pulse, without placing additional stress on your joints.

Choosing an Aerobic Workout

With so many types of aerobic exercise to choose from, how do you know which one is best for you? Take this quiz to find out.

1. **Your environment:**
a. Do you have access to a gym that has cardiovascular equipment, such as rowing machines, stair climbers, exercise bikes, or treadmills?
b. Do you have access to a swimming pool?
c. Do you have access to aerobics classes (step, low-impact, cardio-funk, Jazzercise, slide, and so on)?

d. Can you run or walk outside in your neighborhood? If so, do you live in an area that has many days of good weather throughout the year?

2. **Solitary vs. group exercise:**
a. Are you more motivated by a group, or are you self-disciplined?
b. Do you want to spend time with others, or would you prefer to use your exercise time to be alone?
c. Do you have small children at home? Is it difficult for you to get out?
d. Do you enjoy loud music, or would you prefer to listen to soft music or books on tape?

3. **Your experience level:**
a. Do you need instruction, or are you an experienced exerciser?
b. Do you want to learn a new activity or sport, or do you want to continue with an activity or sport you know well?

4. **Your health:**
a. Are you pregnant or recently postpartum?
b. Do you have any chronic health problems?
c. Do you have any previous joint or muscle injuries?
d. Are you a beginning exerciser in your 50s or 60s or older?
e. Are you severely overweight?

Analyze your responses:

Question #1:
a. If you have access to a gym, you can take advantage of the many types of equipment it offers. Cross-training (alternating machines and exercises) can keep your motivation high, reduce your chances of injury, and give your body a well-rounded workout.

b,c. Access in your community to a swimming pool or aerobics classes also gives you a range of choices. Choose the activity that strikes your fancy.

d. Walking, running, in-line skating, and cycling may be viable options if you live in an area where you can spend time outside.

Question #2:

a,b. If you just can't get motivated on your own, consider joining a gym that has good instruction or taking exercise classes. If you're more of a self-motivator, consider trying outdoor activities, swimming, exercise videos, or home exercise equipment.

c. Exercise videos, walking (with a stroller perhaps), or home exercise equipment might be good choices if you have small children at home or can't often leave the house by yourself.

d. If you can't put up with the loud rock and roll, disco, or rap music used in many aerobics classes and gyms, you might be happier running, walking, in-line skating, or cycling alone with a portable stereo and headphones.

Question #3:

a. If you're new to fitness, instruction in the form of a trainer at a gym or in an exercise class helps ensure you get a safe workout. An instructor can also help you safely increase the intensity and duration of your exercise as your fitness improves.

b. If you have some experience in the sport of your choice, go to it. However, if you're primed for a change to something new, consider joining a gym that has good instructors or taking exercise classes.

Question #4:

a. Exercise during pregnancy and after giving birth can be perfectly safe and beneficial to the mother—provided appropriate types of exercise are chosen and the activities are performed correctly. If you are pregnant or have recently given birth (especially if you're new to fitness), you may be best off joining a pregnancy or postpartum exercise group. There are also several safe pregnancy and postpartum exercise videos on the market. See *Exercise During Pregnancy,* page 99, for more information.

b. If you have any chronic health problems, you should consult your physician before beginning any exercise program. After a thorough physical examination, ask the doctor about the types of exercise you can safely participate in. Also ask about types of exercise that may favorably impact your condition.

c. If you suffer from knee or joint problems, or if you have any old injuries, you'll need to choose activities that won't cause your condition to deteriorate. Low-impact exercises are probably your best bet. Ask your physician which type you can safely try.

d. If you are a beginning exerciser aged 50 or older, consult your physician before beginning an exercise program. If you get a clean bill of health, consider starting out with walking, stationary cycling, low-impact aerobics, or swimming. These activities, when performed correctly, can provide a safe, gentle cardiovascular workout.

e. If you are severely overweight, consult your physician before

Consult Your Physician Before Beginning Any Exercise Program

choosing an exercise program. When you get the green light, start out with low-impact activities. Running, jogging, and high-impact aerobics may put too much stress on your joints.

Muscle Anatomy 101

Do You Know Your "Pecs" from Your "Abs"?

Before embarking on a fitness program, familiarize yourself with the major muscle groups you'll be working. Although there are many more muscles in the body than are listed below, the following is a brief dictionary for muscles you're most likely to hear people referring to around the weight room of a health club, for example. The scientific name is listed first. The more common weight-room terms (where appropriate) are enclosed in parentheses.

Biceps brachii ("biceps"): These two muscles originate from the center of the upper arm. One goes up to the shoulder joint; the other down to the elbow.

Deltoids ("delts"): This group of muscles consists of the anterior deltoid (at the front of the shoulder), the posterior deltoid (at the back of the shoulder), and the middle deltoid (along the side of the shoulder). In the weight room, these muscles are often lumped together.

Gastrocnemius ("calf muscle"): This is the large muscle at the upper portion of the calf (at the lower portion of the calf is a little-known muscle called the soleus).

Gluteus maximus, medius, minimus ("glutes"): Known in common conversation as the buttocks, the gluteals are actually three separate muscles. All three control lateral motion of the hip joint; the gluteus maximus also controls the flexion of the hip joint when it is flexed more than 60 degrees (as it is when climbing, for example).

Hamstrings: This muscle group is made up of the biceps femoris, the semitendinosus, and the semimembranosus, all of which reside at the back of the thigh.

Latissimus dorsi ("lats"): These muscles control the sides of the trunk, above the waist.

Obliques ("waist"): These muscles make up the waist, on either side of the trunk, below the latissimus dorsi.

Pectorals ("pecs"): These three muscles run diagonally from the shoulder toward the chest, straight across from the shoulder joint toward the chest, and along the clavicle toward the chest.

Quadriceps ("quads"): The technical name for this large muscle is rectus femoris. It runs down the front of the thigh from the hip joint to just above the knee.

Rectus abdominis ("abs"): This muscle extends from the diaphragm down to the pelvis. It's also called the abdominal muscle.

Rhomboids: There are two of these muscles—the major and the minor. They are located between the shoulder blades.

Trapezius ("traps"): There are three trapezius muscles—the upper, the middle, and the lower. But when you hear the name of this muscle group tossed around in the weight room, it usually refers to the upper trapezius, which spans the area between the top of the shoulder and the side of the neck.

Triceps: These muscles are usually called by their proper name. They are opposite the biceps, originating in the center of the back of the upper arm, going up to the shoulder and down to the elbow.

Wrist flexors and extensors ("flexors and extenders"): Responsible for flexing and extending the wrist, these muscles are on the inside of the forearm.

Components of a Safe Exercise Session

Cardiovascular conditioning, strength training, and flexibility are all important parts of fitness, and this chapter gives you a good idea of where to begin with each. However, there is more to a safe and effective exercise session. The following guidelines can serve as the blueprint for a textbook-perfect workout:

1. **The Warm-up.** Start every exercise session—whether it be an aerobic workout, a strength-training workout, even a stretching routine—with a 5 to 10 minute warm-up (see *Sample Warm-up and Cool-down,* page 84). A warm-up gets the blood flowing. It also helps to warm and loosen up the

muscles before stretching. Some experts believe a warm-up can help prevent injury during athletic activities.

2. **The Stretch.** A routine that stretches all of the major muscle groups further loosens up the muscles and may help prevent injury. See *Your Stretching Routine,* page 84, for instructions on seven very effective stretches to fulfill your complete stretching routine.

3. **The Main Event.** Now you're ready for a strength-training or aerobic workout. If you plan to incorporate both types of activities into your exercise session, it's probably best to complete the aerobic portion first. This way, you'll get your pulse rate and your energy level up, then continue burning calories as you strength-train.

4. **Check of Aerobic Intensity** (for aerobic workouts). At the peak of your exercise, check your pulse to be sure it's in your target training zone (see *Determining Your Aerobic Target Heart Rate,* page 76, *How to Take Your Pulse,* page 78, and *Your Target Heart Rate,* page 78, for more information). Adjust your intensity level accordingly.

5. **The Cool-down.** The cool-down is the opposite of the warm-up. It's a chance to allow your pulse rate to return to normal and, in the case of a strength-training workout, to loosen up the muscles you've been working. It should last at least five minutes, but, ideally, you should allow 10 to 15 minutes to cool down (see *Sample Warm-up and Cool-down,* page 84).

6. **The Final Stretch.** This final stretch is believed to prevent soreness after exercising. It also gives your body a chance to cool down and ends the workout on a placid note.

Start Every Exercise Session with a Warm-up

SAMPLE WARM-UP AND COOL-DOWN

A warm-up gets you ready for more serious work. It prepares your muscles to start moving and may help prevent injury. You need to perform some sort of activity that, if it was done at a higher intensity level, would be considered aerobic. You can integrate low-intensity stationary cycling, marching, walking—whatever you like. The same activities are appropriate for a cool-down.

Here is an example:

❏ March in place for two minutes.

❏ Take four long strides forward, and four long strides back. Clap on every fourth step. Repeat for two minutes.

❏ Do two minutes of "grapevines": Take four steps to either side, crossing one leg in back of the other as you step. Repeat to the other side.

❏ Do two minutes of "Charlestons": Take a long step forward, swinging your arms in opposition. With the other leg, take a long step forward. Again, swing your arms in opposition. Step back with the first leg (keep those arms going). Finally, take a long step back with the second leg. Repeat.

❏ Finish with two more minutes of marches.

❏   ❏   ❏

Flexibility: Part of a Well-Rounded Program

The benefits of aerobic conditioning and strength training are immediately apparent—all you have to do is check your energy level and take a look in the mirror. The benefits of improving your body's flexibility, however, are a bit more elusive.

Maintaining flexibility is important for preventing injury, both during athletic and everyday activities. As such, you should make stretching a permanent part of your fitness routine.

Most fitness associations recommend you perform proper stretching exercises before and after any aerobic or strength-training workout. The following section gives you specific stretching exercises for all the major muscle groups.

Your Stretching Routine

The following stretches can be performed both before and after an aerobic or strength-training session.

As a general guideline, stretch only as far as is comfortable. Never push a stretch to the point of pain. Also, you should never bounce while stretching; "ballistic stretching," as this is called, can cause injury. One final safety tip: Pregnant women need to take extra care when stretching. During pregnancy, joints become quite lax. Stretching too far can injure muscles and connective tissue.

Perform the following stretches in sequence. Before beginning, warm up the muscles with five minutes of low-intensity marching, walking, stair climbing, or any other aerobic activity (see *Sample Warm-up and Cool-down*).

1. **Shoulder loosener.** Stand with the knees slightly bent, feet hip-distance apart. Shrug the shoulders, pulling them up towards the ears, then lowering. Repeat four times.

Slowly circle the shoulders backwards for 8 counts, then forward for 8 counts.

2. **Neck looseners.** Gently cock the head to the right. Hold for a count of 8. Repeat on the left side.

Look as far to the right as you can, while still holding your shoulders square. Hold for a count of 8. Repeat on the left side.

Gently roll the head from shoulder to shoulder, pulling the head close to the chest. Do not roll the head to the back. Repeat 8 times.

3. **Waist stretch.** Assume a wide stance, knees and shoulders relaxed. Rest your right hand on your right outer thigh and reach your left arm up and over your head. Hold for a few counts, breathe in, then exhale deeply, allowing your body to relax even further into the stretch. Hold for a slow count of 8. Repeat on the left.

4. **Standing back stretch.** Stand with your feet hip-distance apart, knees bent. Put one hand on each knee. Eyes downward, align your head with your spine. Arch your back toward the ceiling (keep your abdominal muscles tight), hold for a slow count of 4, then release, allowing your back to arch only slightly. Repeat 3 times. *Note:* If this stretch puts too much strain on your back, skip it.

5. **Modified runner's lunge.** Assume a wide stance, then turn to the right, pointing your right leg to the right and bending your right knee. Keep your left leg straight (but don't lock your knee). Place both hands on your right thigh and stretch forward, making sure your knee never juts out past your toes (you may need to move the left leg farther back). Press the left leg toward the floor, feeling the stretch in the front of your right upper thigh. Hold for a count of 8. Repeat with the left leg.

6. **Hamstring stretch.** Sit on the floor, left leg straight ahead, left toe pointing toward the ceiling. Bend the right leg so the sole of the foot rests against your left inner thigh (see Figure 3.1). Gently lower your chest toward your left thigh. Do not bounce and do not twist at the waist. Lean forward until you feel the stretch in your hamstring muscles (see Figure 3.2). Hold for a count of 4. Repeat with the right leg.

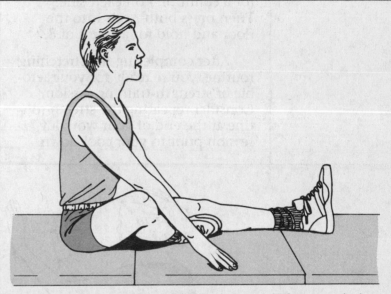

Fig. 3.1 Hamstring stretch. This exercise helps stretch the back of the thigh. Proper posture is important: Sit tall.

Fig. 3.2 Extend forward slowly without rounding the back.

7. Calf stretch. Stand slightly more than arm's length from a wall. Keeping your legs straight and your heels to the floor, place your palms on the wall. Bend your arms and slowly lean toward the wall until you feel a stretch down the back of the legs (see Figure 3.3).

Keep your back straight and your abdominal muscles tight. Press the heels into the floor, alternating between the left and right for a count of 4 on each side. Then press both heels into the floor and hold for a count of 8.

After completing the stretching routine, you're ready for your aerobic or strength-training session. Consider repeating the stretch routine at the end of your workout session prior to your cool-down.

Fig. 3.3 Calf stretch. This exercise stretches the calves and achilles tendons. Be sure to keep your heels flat on the floor.

Strength Training: An Important Component of Fitness

You have no desire to be an elite athlete or a bodybuilder. Why should you incorporate strength training into your fitness regimen?

It's easy to overlook the benefits strength training has to offer. But improving your muscle strength helps you in a variety of ways. Here's what you'll have to look forward to:

- Greater stamina in everyday activities
- A higher metabolism (muscle burns more calories than fat, even when the body is at rest)
- Decreased chance of injury during everday activities
- Possible improvement in or maintenance of bone density
- Better body composition (an improved ratio of lean tissue to fat)
- A toned, attractive physique

A common mistake is to assume that improving muscle strength means building bulky muscles. In fact, bodybuilders have to work very hard (through exercise and diet) to achieve that sinewy, rippled look! Here is the difference between a routine designed to tone the muscles and one designed to build bulk:

- A toning/strengthening routine uses lighter weights, lifted through many repetitions. As the muscles get stronger and gain stamina, more repetitions are added. Weight is increased very slowly.

- A bulk-building workout uses very heavy weights, lifted through few repetitions. The amount of weight is increased as soon as the muscle can withstand it.

While it's a valid goal to want arms like a Mr. or Ms. Universe contestant, it's also perfectly acceptable to want a lean, toned look. If that is your intention, you should design a routine that incorporates the principles mentioned above for a toning/strengthening routine.

Guidelines for Strength Training

If you've joined a gym, ask for strength-training tips from a well-credentialed instructor. But you can design a safe and effective strength-training program for use at home.

Some of the exercises in the following two sections require the use of hand held dumbbells. If you're just beginning, or if you haven't yet bought dumbbells, you can start out using small cantaloupes or large soup cans.

Here are a couple of tips to help you get started:

❑ **Before using dumbbells, figure out which weight to start with.** A general guideline is that you should be able to complete at least 2 sets of at least 8 controlled repetitions with the weight you choose. If you can't, it's too heavy. Likewise, if you can comfortably do more than 3 sets of 12 repetitions, it's time to move

up to a heavier weight. You may find you need different weights for different exercises.

❑ **Work upper body one day and lower body the next.** Always allow muscle groups one day of rest between workouts. If you want to work out every other day, you can train the whole body during each session.

❑ **Exhale as you contract the muscle or lift the weight.** Inhale as you relax the muscle or lower the weight.

The exercises in the next two sections are intended only for those who are in good health and who are not pregnant. If you have any chronic health problems, consult your doctor before starting any type of strength-training program. *Do not perform these exercises to the point of discomfort. Skip the exercise if you feel any pain.*

Strengthening the Upper Body

Before trying these exercises, read the guidelines in the previous section. Unless otherwise noted, each exercise should be performed for 2 to 3 sets of 8 to 12 repetitions.

1. **Biceps curl** *(tones the biceps)*
Sit on the edge of a stool or bench or stand with the knees slightly bent, about hip-distance apart. Hold one weight in each hand and extend the arms down the front of your thighs with the inner forearms facing outward. Without moving the upper arms, slowly lift the weights, for 4 counts, until they are almost

If You Feel Any Pain when You Exercise, Stop

touching your upper arms. At the peak of the movement, flex the biceps muscles and hold for 2 counts. Slowly lower the weights to the starting position, to the count of 4.

2. Triceps kickback *(tones the backs of the upper arms)*

Stand with your knees bent, feet about hip-distance apart. Lean slightly forward, take a weight in each hand and hold them right next to your hips. Elbows should be bent and held closely to your sides. Without moving your upper arms or your elbows, straighten the arms and extend the weights as high as you can in back of you, to the count of 4. Flex the triceps and hold for 2 counts. Slowly lower the weights to the starting position to the count of 4.

3. Front raise *(tones the anterior deltoid, or front of the shoulder)*

Stand with the knees slightly bent, feet about hip-distance apart. Hold a weight in each hand, with the arms extended down the front of the thighs, wrists facing outward. Slowly raise the weights to shoulder level, to a count of 4. Hold for 2 counts, then slowly lower to the starting position to the count of 4.

4. Side raise *(tones the middle deltoid, at the side of the shoulder)*

Hold a weight in each hand, with the arms extended down the sides of the thighs, wrists facing outward. Slowly raise the weights to shoulder level, to a count of 4. Hold for 2 counts, then slowly lower to the starting position also to the count of 4.

5. Chest fly *(tones the pectoralis major muscles)*

Lie on a weight bench or aerobics step (if you have one) or on the floor. Hold a weight in each hand, arms extended out to the sides at chest level, the insides of

the forearms facing up toward the ceiling. The arms should remain rigid throughout the exercise, although the elbows should be slightly bent (not locked). Slowly bring the weights together directly above your chest, to the count of 4. Hold for 2 counts, then slowly lower to the starting position, again, to the count of 4.

6. Abdominal crunch *(tones the upper portion of the rectus abdominis)*

Lie on your back, with your knees bent, heels on the floor, slightly closer than hip-distance apart. Lace your fingers behind your neck, holding the elbows straight out to the sides (see Figure 3.4). Keep your chin up by looking directly up toward the ceiling.

Holding this position, curl your upper body up toward the knees, ***keeping the lower back firmly pressed into the floor*** (see Figure 3.5). As you lift, simultaneously tighten the abdominal muscles and curl the pelvis up and toward the navel. Lower shoulders and pelvis to the starting position. At the peak of the crunch, the shoulders and back should form no more than about a 45-degree angle with the floor (don't come up all the way to your knees).

Perform this exercise for a slow 24 repetitions (2 counts up, 2 counts down). To increase the intensity of the workout as you gain strength, you can add repetitions.

7. Oblique crunch *(tones the oblique muscles at the sides of the waist)*

Lie on the floor in the same position as for the abdominal crunch, except rest the outside of the right ankle against the left thigh, with the right knee pointing out from the body. Keep your fingers laced behind your neck. Keeping your right shoulder on the ground, raise your left shoul-

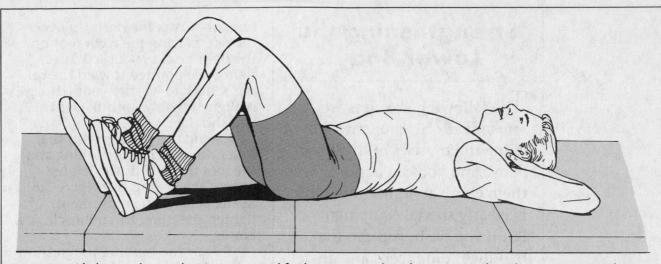

Fig. 3.4 Abdominal crunch. You can modify this exercise by placing your hands across your chest.

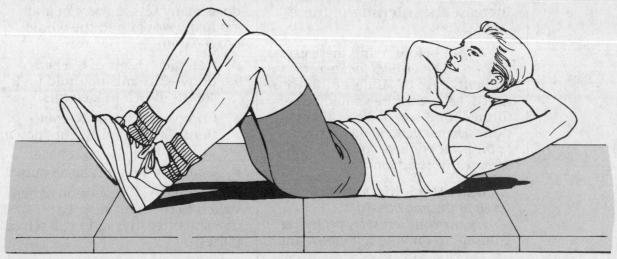

Fig. 3.5 Proper form is very important when performing abdominal crunches. Do not flex at the neck and keep your lower back on the floor at all times. Finally, move *slowly*.

der toward your knee (do not move your knee). Lower to the starting position. As with the abdominal crunches, oblique crunches can be performed for a slow 24 repetitions (2 counts up, 2 counts down). You can increase workout intensity by adding more sets or a few sets of pulses. Repeat with other side.

8. Reverse crunch *(tones the lower portion of the rectus abdominis)*

Lie on the floor, with your fingers either laced behind your neck or under your hips (the latter posi-

tion helps to support the lower back). Hold your legs up, perpendicular to your body, and cross them at the knee, allowing your feet to loosely hang. In a slow, controlled motion, lift the lower back off the floor while tightening the lower abdominal muscles. Slowly lower to the starting position. Complete as many repetitions as you can, maintaining proper form. Gradually build to 3 sets of 8 repetitions. As with the other crunches, you may add pulses to increase intensity.

Strengthening the Lower Body

The following exercises are safe and effective for strengthening the muscles of the lower body. And you can perform them easily at home. You don't need any special equipment. But if you wish, you can use handheld dumbbells and ankle weights (where appropriate) to increase the intensity of these exercises.

Again, before trying these exercises, read *Guidelines for Strength Training,* page 87. Unless otherwise noted, each exercise should be performed for 3 sets of 8 to 12 repetitions. *Do not perform these exercises to the point of discomfort. Skip the exercise if you feel any pain.*

1. Inner thigh lift *(tones and develops the inner thigh)*
Lie on your left side, propping yourself up on your left elbow and forearm. Cross the right leg over the left, placing the right foot on the floor next to your left knee, right knee pointed toward the ceiling. Check to be sure your left leg is aligned with your hip, waist, and shoulder.

Extend the left leg, with the inner thigh facing the ceiling and the foot flexed. Lift the left leg toward the ceiling (see Figure 3.6). At the peak of the movement, tighten the inner thigh muscle. Lower.

Follow the training progression below. Don't worry if you can't do the whole routine at first. Simply do as many sets as you can and gradually work up to the whole progression.

- Complete 3 sets of 8 repetitions—2 counts up, hold for 2 counts, down in 2 counts.

- Complete 2 sets of 8 repetitions—3 small pulses up, down in 1 count.

- Complete 1 set of 8 small pulses.

Complete all repetitions, then switch to the right side. To increase intensity, add extra sets of pulses.

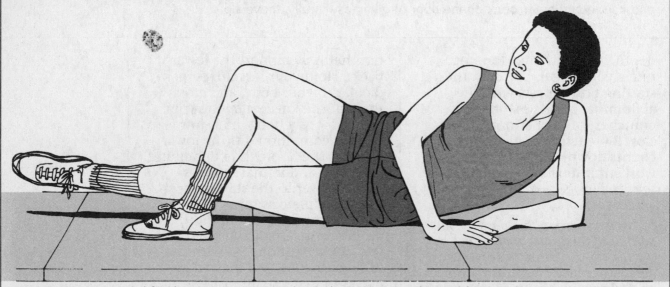

Fig. 3.6 Inner thigh lift. This exercise strengthens the groin muscles (adductors) by requiring the leg to move toward the midline of the body.

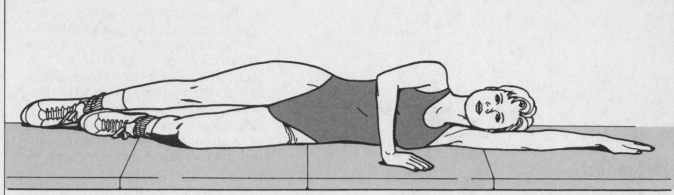

Fig. 3.7 Outer thigh lift. This exercise conditions the muscles in opposition to those in the inner thigh lift. You strengthen the hip and outer thigh by moving the leg away from the midline of the body.

Fig. 3.8 Lift the top leg to your side up and out from the hip socket. Keep your hips stacked at all times; do not allow them to rotate.

2. Outer thigh lift *(tones the outer thigh and gluteal muscles)*

Lie on your side with your head resting on your extended arm. Bend your bottom knee to increase your base of support. Make sure your hips are stacked one above the other and perpendicular to the floor (see Figure 3.7).

Lift your top leg about two feet, with your foot parallel to the ceiling and your toe pointing out (see Figure 3.8).

Follow the training progression that follows. Complete all repetitions, then switch to the other side.

- Complete 3 sets of 8 repetitions—2 counts up, hold for 2 counts, down in 2 counts.
- Complete 2 sets of 8 repetitions—3 small pulses up, down in 1 count.
- Complete 1 set of 8 small pulses.

3. Calf raise *(tones and develops the gastrocnemius muscles)*

Stand with your feet hip-distance apart. Rise onto your toes, hold for 1 count, then lower. (If necessary, place one hand against a wall for balance.) Repeat for 3 sets of 8 repetitions.

Exercise Warning: It's important to keep well hydrated whenever you exercise. Keep a water bottle next to you and take a drink every ten minutes or so, *even if you don't feel thirsty.*

Skip Any Exercise That Causes Pain

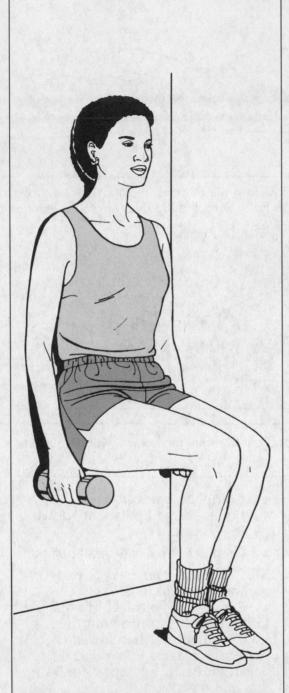

Fig. 3.9 Parallel squat. You may find it easier to squat down into sitting position if you do so against a wall. As you continue to perform this exercise, your quadriceps will lengthen, allowing you to remain in this position longer. Do not perform this exercise if you feel pain in your knees.

4. Parallel squat *(tones the quadriceps, hamstrings, and gluteal muscles)*

Take a dumbbell (or a soup can or cantaloupe) in each hand. Stand with feet a little closer than hip-distance apart, knees slightly bent. Hold the weights at your sides. Squat down by sitting back, as though you were lowering yourself into a chair. Keep your back straight. To avoid knee stress, make sure your weight is firmly in your heels.

Lower yourself until your thighs are parallel with the floor—no lower (see Figure 3.9). In addition, do not allow your knees to bend so far that they extend forward beyond your toes; keep your knees aligned above your toes. Tighten your buttocks, and press up to the starting position. Perform each repetition to a count of 8 (4 counts up, 4 counts down).

If you find it difficult to maintain your balance when performing this exercise, try leaning one palm against a wall or lower yourself into position with your back against a wall, as illustrated.

Safety tip: If you feel pain in your knees, or if they grind or click excessively, try this exercise without weights. If you still feel pain, skip this exercise altogether.

5. Wide leg squat *(tones quadriceps, hamstrings, gluteals, and inner thigh muscles)*

Assume a wide stance, with the toes pointing outward. Follow the procedure for the parallel squat, above. Again, your knees should never go beyond your toes. If you feel excessive strain in your knees, try these squats without the weights. If you still feel pain, skip this exercise altogether.

6. Butt-busters *(tones the gluteals and hamstrings)*

a. Start with your right knee bent and aligned under your hip, your left leg extended behind

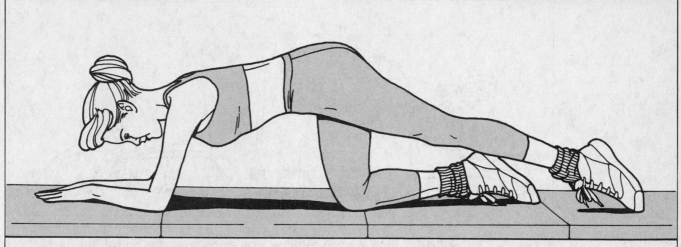

Fig. 3.10 Butt-busters. This exercise contours and strengthens the gluteals. Be sure to keep your head aligned with your spine. Look at the floor not ahead of you.

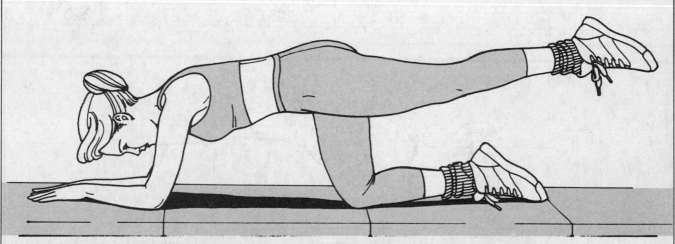

Fig. 3.11 This exercise requires extension of the hip joint by pressing the leg behind the body. When you lift your leg, keep your thigh parallel to the floor. Keep your abdominal muscles tight.

you with the toe touching the floor, and your elbows, forearms, and hands resting on the floor. Make sure your elbows are aligned under your shoulders, and, eyes downward, your head is aligned with your spine (see Figure 3.10). Slowly lift your left leg so the thigh is parallel to the floor, while simultaneously tightening the buttocks (see Figure 3.11). Do not lift any higher, or you place strain on the lower back (do not arch your back and do not lock your knee). Lower almost to the floor, without touching down. Repeat the exercise for 3 sets of 8 slow repetitions. To add intensity, follow the training sequence described for inner thigh lifts (page 90). When you have completed your repetitions, move onto step *b* with the same leg, before changing sides.

Fig. 3.12 This part of the exercise requires you to contract the hamstring and hold it while contracting the gluteals.

Fig. 3.13 Do not lift the thigh beyond the height of your hips. Contract and squeeze the gluteals during this movement.

b. Kneel on both knees, keeping your head, elbows, forearms, and hands in the same position (see Figure 3.12). Keeping the left leg bent and the bottom of your foot toward the ceiling, press the heel toward the ceiling and simultaneously tighten the buttocks (see Figure 3.13). The squeeze in the gluteal muscle makes this exercise very effective; you need only keep the movement small. As with step *a*, be sure not to arch your back. Lower to the starting position. Repeat for 3 sets of 8, following the training sequence described for inner or outer thigh lifts to add intensity. When you have completed steps *a* and *b* on the first side, repeat the sequences with the other leg.

Designing a Balanced Weekly Training Plan

You've identified your fitness goals, you've chosen your workout environment (your home, the gym, the local track, the swimming pool, and so on), you've selected the type of cardiovascular exercise that's right for you. You even know how to warm up, cool down, stretch, and monitor your intensity. Now it's time to put it all together and design an exercise schedule that helps you start working toward that state called fitness. Here's how:

❑ Assess your daily energy cycles.
❑ Make room in your schedule.
❑ Become goal-oriented.

Read on to learn more.

Assess Your Daily Energy Cycles

Are you a morning person or a night person? What time of the day are you normally most productive? Pick a time of the day when you feel your body has the most energy for exercise.

Many experts believe the best time for exercise is early through late morning. Late afternoon is thought to be one of the lowest energy periods for most people. But everyone is different. Only you know what's right for you.

If you have problems sleeping, you may want to choose a workout time that ends approximately six hours before you normally go to bed. Here's why:

- Exercise (especially aerobic exercise) raises your core body temperature and keeps it high for up to six hours after you complete it. This rise in body temperature can interfere with deep sleep, which requires a drop in body temperature.

- On the other hand, six hours after a workout, when the body temperature drops, you'll probably find that you fall asleep more easily and sleep more soundly.

Make Room in Your Schedule

One of the most convenient excuses for not exercising is not having enough time. If you have found yourself saying this to yourself over and over again as you read this chapter, ask yourself the following questions: Do I have time to shower every day? To brush my teeth? To eat? To sleep (for at least a few hours)? Unless you are a very unusual individual, the answer to all of these questions is: "Of course."

"But," the whiny voice inside your head may counter, "I *have to* do all these things. They are absolutely necessary to my daily functioning and my health."

Therein lies the rub.

The secret to making time for fitness is to change your perception of it from being a luxury to being a necessity. The truth is exercise is another way to take care of your body and is just as important as these other activities. Lack of exercise will not lead to cavities, certainly, but chances are you'll age quicker, experience more illness, feel worse, look worse, be less productive, and—possibly—die younger. When you take all that into consideration, can't you make the time?

At a minimum, all you need is one hour a day. In that period of

Make Room in Your Schedule for Exercise

Any Activity Can Improve Your Physical Fitness

time, you can warm up, stretch, complete a 30- to 45-minute cardiovascular or strength-training workout, cool down, and stretch again. You can even take a day or two off per week to reward yourself for a job well done. Now, what were those excuses again?

Become Goal-Oriented

If your goals are to burn fat or to increase or maintain your cardiovascular endurance, strength, or flexibility, you'll need to orient your workouts accordingly. That means putting the emphasis on the areas you most want to improve.

❑ **To improve your ratio of muscle to fat:** You'll want to emphasize long periods (45 minutes or so) of lower-intensity aerobic exercise and plenty of strength-training exercises to build muscle (muscle tissue elevates your metabolism, helping you burn more fat, even while your body is at rest). Plan to integrate three to five aerobic workouts and two to four strength-training sessions (with moderately heavy weights) every week.

❑ **To increase cardiovascular endurance and maintain your strength:** Factor in longer, higher-intensity aerobic workouts and moderate strength-training sessions (lift lighter weights for many repetitions).

❑ **To increase your muscle strength and maintain your cardiovascular endurance:** Do a minimum of three 20-minute aerobic sessions per week, and devote the rest of your sessions to high-intensity weight work.

❑ **To increase flexibility:** Do a minimum of three 20-minute aerobic sessions a week, and

two strength-training sessions with light weights lifted for many repetitions. Increase the time you devote to stretching. (Don't forget those warm-ups and cool-downs!)

Remember that it's important to at least do *something*—even if that something is yard work, walking the dog, riding a stationary bike, and so on. You don't have to follow a marathon runner's training schedule to increase your physical fitness. For most people, any activity helps.

Do It Right

Once you've designed your weekly training plan, consider these few final words of advice:

❑ **Write it down.** Make a weekly chart outlining your fitness plan for every day. Include the time you've set aside to work out and the activities you've planned for that time. Hang it on your refrigerator or your bathroom mirror.

❑ **Give your body time to recover.** For strength training, don't work the same muscle groups two days in row. If you work the upper body one day, work the lower body the next day. The exception is the abdominal muscles, which you can safely work every day. One good way to ensure that you don't over-stress your body is to alternate between sessions devoted to cardiovascular work and sessions devoted to strength training.

❑ **Vary your workouts.** Mixing and matching types of exercise can be a terrific way to avoid injury and stave off boredom.

Cross-training, as this is called, also helps you develop a balanced physique because you avoid over-working some muscle groups and under-working others.

❑ **Be kind to yourself.** If you are ill or extremely tired, don't push yourself. Listen to your body's signals and take it easy. Either work out at a very low intensity (take a leisurely walk, for example), devote your entire session to relaxing stretches, or take the day off. The harder you are on yourself, the more likely you are to burn out and quit.

Choosing a Health Club

If you decide to join a health club, be a wise consumer and do a little research before taking out your checkbook and making the investment. Health clubs differ in style, equipment, clientele, services, and the type and quality of instruction they provide. They also vary in the types of memberships they offer. Here are some questions you should ask before signing anything:

- Is the location convenient? Try to choose a club close to home or work. The easier it is for you to get there, the more likely you are to stick to your training schedule.
- Is the club open during the hours you'd like to attend?

- Does the club offer child care?
- Does the club offer activities you're interested in?
- Is the club coed? If so, decide if you feel comfortable working out with members of the opposite sex.
- Can you afford the membership? Does the club offer financing?
- Do you have to make a long commitment, or can you pay month by month?
- Does the club offer "freeze time?" (Freeze time is a temporary membership suspension—great for the end of a pregnancy or a long illness.)
- If you move, can you transfer your membership to another club?
- What is the nature of the club's clientele—informal and supportive of newcomers or competitive and exclusive? If you don't feel comfortable there, chances are you won't want to spend much time at the club.
- Does the club offer adequate instruction on using the equipment? Will the staff guide you, help you set goals, and monitor your progress?
- How are the classes (if applicable)? Are the instructors certified by a reputable fitness organization (such as the International Association of Fitness Professionals)?
- Will the club give you a daily pass so you can try out the facilities, equipment, and classes before joining? If so, talk to other members and ask them how they like the club. Do they regret joining? Do they feel they are getting their money's worth?

Do You Know What to Look for in a Health Club?

Always Exercise Safely

Ten Tips for a Safe Workout

No matter what kind of fitness routine you design for yourself, you should observe the following ten tips for a safe workout:

1. **Wear the right shoes.** Proper footwear is an important key to injury prevention during athletic activities. And because different sports impact your body in different ways, you need different types of shoes for each. For example, aerobic dance stresses lateral moves. For this reason, most aerobic shoes are made of leather for lateral support—not nylon or canvas—and have a relatively high top. Running, on the other hand, requires low tops and a cushy insole to protect your joints from the impact.

2. **Breathe.** It sounds like the most obvious thing in the world, but the truth is most of us don't breathe correctly, especially when we exercise. Here are some breathing tips:

❑ **For running, pace your breath rhythmically with your steps.** Breathe deeply in through your nose and out through your mouth. If you get a side stitch, slow down a bit and concentrate on deep, long inhalations. Extra oxygen usually makes the pain go away.

❑ **For aerobics, just make sure you are not holding your breath.** This can easily happen while you concentrate on following the instructor. Otherwise, no special breathing is required.

❑ **While performing abdominal crunches, exhale as you crunch upward, inhale as you lower.** This breathing technique helps you press your back into the floor and contract your abdominal muscles correctly (the crunch naturally squeezes the air out of your diaphragm).

❑ **For weight lifting, exhale as you lift the weight, inhale as you lower it.**

3. **Drink plenty of water before, during, and after your workout.** In hot weather, this is a double imperative.

4. **Check the weather.** Save your marathon outdoor workouts for reasonable temperatures. There are no extra merit points for those who run ten miles in 110 degrees Fahrenheit weather or during a snowstorm. If you absolutely must exercise outside during a heat wave, drink extra water (bring some with you!), and wear plenty of sunscreen and a hat. If even extreme cold can't keep you indoors, wear lots of layers and don't stay out too long.

5. **Foster a healthy respect for automobiles.** If at all possible, run, walk, bike, or skate in low-traffic areas. Always obey traffic laws, and never assume a driver will stop for you.

6. **Be a beacon in the darkness.** Always wear light-colored clothing and reflective gear after sundown. Sporting goods stores carry clothing with reflective strips for runners and walkers. Cyclists should be sure to have lights on both the front and rear of their bikes.

7. **Don't rile up the neighbor's dog.** Some dogs get overly excited when a cyclist or jogger passes through their territory. If you are approached by a threatening

canine, don't try to outrun it. You may only aggravate his chasing instinct. Simply freeze in your tracks, fold your arms across your chest, and wait for the dog to calm down. You can try a firm but friendly command, such as "sit," or "stay." Slowly walk away with your head down (as a submissive dog would) when you feel it's safe to do so.

8. **Take a self-defense course.** If you exercise outside, especially at night, consider educating yourself in the ways and means of self-defense. Your fitness habit need not make you a target.

9. **Wear a Medic-Alert bracelet if you have a medical condition.** This way, if you get injured or become unconscious while exercising away from home, emergency personnel will be aware of your needs.

10. **Carry identification when you exercise away from home.** Also pocket a list of phone numbers of people to call in an emergency.

Exercise During Pregnancy

There's no need to drop your fitness routine during pregnancy. In fact, appropriate types of exercise can help you stay energized, sleep better, preserve your aerobic fitness (important when you're lugging extra pounds of baby weight), reduce back pain, and prepare your body for the rigors of childbirth and new motherhood.

However, you do need to follow the safety guidelines put forth by the American College of Obstetrics and Gynecology:

❏ Exercise regularly (at least three times a week). But put competitive activities on hold until a couple of months after the baby is born.

❏ Do not exercise in hot, humid weather or when you have a fever.

❏ Avoid all forms of high-impact exercise. Exercise on a soft surface, such as a wooden or tightly carpeted floor.

❏ Avoid deep knee bends.

❏ Stretch only to the point of gentle tension. Avoid deep stretches.

❏ Warm up your muscles. Make sure to do something like five minutes of slow walking or low-intensity stationary cycling before performing vigorous exercise.

❏ Perform gentle stretches after vigorous exercise. Again, do not stretch to the point of maximum resistance.

❏ Keep close tabs on your heart rate during exercise. It should never exceed 140 beats per minute.

❏ Rise from the floor slowly and gradually to avoid large drops in blood pressure.

❏ Drink plenty of water before, during, and after exercise.

❏ If you had been sedentary before your pregnancy, only engage in low-intensity activities. Increase your activity level very slowly and gradually.

❏ Stop exercising and consult your physician if you develop any unusual symptoms.

❏ Do not exercise vigorously for more than 15 minutes at a time.

There's No Need to Drop Your Fitness Routine During Pregnancy

- After the fourth month of pregnancy, do not perform any exercise that requires you to lie on your back.
- Avoid exercises that might cause a temporary rise in blood pressure. Such exercises include push-ups, pull-ups, and lifting heavy weights. Ask your doctor's opinion about using 1- or 2-pound weights.
- Consume enough calories to make up for those you burn during your workouts.
- Do not allow your body temperature to rise above 104°F (38°C). Doing so may cause harm to the developing fetus.

INCORPORATING MORE ACTIVITY INTO YOUR DAILY ROUTINE

You can increase your body's strength, burn calories, and maintain your flexibility through your everyday activities.

Here are some tips to help you integrate more activity into your daily routine:

- Take the stairs instead of using the elevator, whenever possible.
- Park your car a few blocks from your office and walk to work.
- Walk instead of driving, whenever possible.
- Turn your housework into a workout: Put on some music to up your energy level. Sweep, dust, and mop vigorously. Stretch your muscles as you wash the windows. Mow the lawn as fast as you can (Watch your toes!).
- Do abdominal crunches and leg lifts while you watch television.
- Take the dog for an extra-long walk or a gentle jog.
- Accompany your kids to the park and challenge them to a game of tag, some one-on-one, or hopscotch.
- Take a morning walk with a friend before work.

Staying Motivated

You can learn a few tricks to help you stick to your exercise schedule. Here are a few:

- **Use the buddy system.** An exercise partner is a great way to inject fun into what could turn into a monotonous routine. If you plan a lunchtime jog with a friend, you're less likely to cop out when the burger joint beckons.
- **Participate in local athletic events.** Cycling trips, racewalks, and road races can all be ways to make exercise more exciting. And a bit of friendly competition may propel you to hit new fitness heights.
- **Keep a journal of your progress.** Each day you work out, jot down what you did, how long you did it for, how much weight you used, how high your pulse was at the peak of your session, or what your time was (for running, walking, or cycling a specific distance). If improving body composition is your goal, write down your weight and body measurements once a month. When you get discouraged, flip through this journal to remind you of how much progress you've made.
- **Commit yourself to six weeks.** If you can stick to your workout schedule for six weeks—performing at least three sessions of aerobic exercise and two strength-training workouts per week—you are virtually guaranteed to see improvement in your fitness level. This progress might be just the kick you need to keep you going back for more.

CHAPTER 4

ORAL

HEALTH

Can you smile with confidence? A bright smile with healthy teeth and gums can enhance your appearance and your self-image.

Oral health refers to the health of your mouth, but there's more to it than an attractive smile. Oral health impacts your overall health. For example, the teeth are an essential part of the body's digestive system. A healthy mouth is necessary to break up the food you eat into small pieces that can be swallowed easily and digested. The malnutrition problems older people face can be caused or made worse by oral health problems that make it unpleasant or impossible for them to eat and enjoy many foods.

The self-care strategies and regular professional dental care outlined in this chapter can help you prevent oral health problems and keep your smile bright.

❏ ❏ ❏

Most Oral Health Problems Are Preventable

What a Mouthful!

Consider the functions of your mouth: It enables you to take in nourishment and experience a world of flavors, kiss a child goodnight or a lover hello, ask for a raise or laugh with a friend, hum a melody or whistle a happy tune, play a mean saxophone or toot on a flute.

But these activities, which most of us take for granted, may be difficult or even impossible when oral health problems occur—problems such as tooth decay and gum disease. And although much progress has been made in reducing oral diseases, most of us are still at risk for oral health problems.

That's the bad news. The good news is that most oral health problems are preventable. The techniques for maintaining good oral health are simple, but they must be performed consistently and in conjunction with regular visits to a dentist. Professional care and the prevention practices this chapter describes are the keys to keeping your chompers intact. By sinking your teeth into this information, you'll be holding on to oral health.

Not Another Cavity!

Who among us hasn't cringed when, during a checkup, the dentist casually says, "You have some dental decay. We'll need to schedule another visit." What causes tooth decay, or what dentists call *dental caries?*

Dental decay is actually an infection brought on by several factors—usually, a combination of too much sweet or starchy, sticky food and too little oral hygiene. If you have lots of cavities, chances are you're eating lots of these types of foods, not brushing correctly or often enough, not receiving the benefits of fluoride, and not seeing your dentist regularly. Heredity can also play a role in your susceptibility to certain types of tooth decay since it determines the shape of your teeth and the pattern of pits and grooves that are vulnerable to decay.

Each tooth is made up of a hard, protective outer layer of enamel. Just under the enamel is a slightly less hard substance called *dentin* that surrounds the sensitive pulp, the "heart" of the tooth, which contains the nerves and blood vessels that nourish the tooth. When you chew food, a sticky combination of mucus, bacteria, and food particles forms on the tooth surfaces. If brushing and flossing don't remove this "gunk," called *plaque,* from the teeth, bacteria in the plaque begin to break down the food particles. It is this bacterial breakdown process, fueled by sugar and other simple carbohydrates, that produces acid that can erode tooth enamel and create tooth decay.

Combating Bacteria

In dental decay, bacteria is the real culprit. If the acid-forming bacteria in plaque isn't removed, the acid literally burns a small pit or "cavity" in the enamel by dissolving the enamel's calcium and phosphate. If this now-tiny cavity isn't treated, the bacteria's acid continues to destroy the enamel and the dentin beneath it. Eventually, the destruction progresses through the dentin and into the pulp where it can cause an infection (abscess) and, over time, may lead to loss of the tooth.

A critical factor in fighting dental caries is getting rid of the acid-producing bacteria. Since this bacteria is normally present in the mouth, it's impossible to eliminate it entirely. However, you *can* control it by removing as much plaque as possible with proper brushing and flossing and rinsing with antibacterial mouth washes.

Since it doesn't take long for plaque and its acid-forming bacteria to form, be sure to brush and floss at least twice a day, especially after meals.

Bring On the Fluoride

Since the 1940s, Americans have had a powerful anticavity ally—fluoride. Fluoride is a trace element found naturally in soil and water. It incorporates into tooth enamel and makes it more resistant to decay.

About 62 percent of the population served by public water supplies in the United States drinks water fortified with fluoride, and in those areas, the incidence of tooth decay is lower than in areas where water is not fluoridated. Fluoride in its various forms has been credited as the primary reason that dental caries among school-aged children has declined by half over the past 20 years. However, fluoride and the issue of fluoridated water is still controversial in many places.

Some opponents blame fluoridated water for heart, kidney, and liver disease; cancer; birth defects; allergies; and other illnesses. They insist that fluoridation of municipal water supplies constitutes medical treatment without consent. Small white spots can appear on teeth if children consume too much fluoride during their tooth development years, but research has not found any adverse health effects associated with fluoridation.

Fluoride from the Beginning

Fluoride works when ingested or applied directly to the tooth surfaces. It is especially effective in children. The National Institute of Dental Research estimates that in the United States, schoolchildren in areas with fluoridated water have on average between 18 and 25 percent less tooth decay than children who don't receive fluoridated water. Most dental experts say fluoride is particularly important for children from birth to about 16 years of age, or a year after all the permanent molars have appeared.

If your water isn't fluoridated, you can supplement fluoride for your children in the form of tablets, drops, or vitamin-fluoride combinations. Supplementation is prescribed for children starting at 6 months of age and up to 16 years of age. Correct dosage is important, so talk with your dentist about supplementation. The American Dental Association recommends the following supplementation schedule for children who live in areas without fluoridated water: The dosage is 0.25 mg per day for children 6 months to 2 years of age; 0.5 mg per day from aged 3 to 6 years; and 1. 0 mg daily from aged 6 to 16 years.

Your dentist can also topically apply fluoride to children's teeth. Many experts recommend such

Fluoride Is Especially Effective in Children

Brushing and Flossing Are the First Lines of Defense in Fighting Dental Decay

topical application every year for children younger than 13 years of age, although children who drink fluoridated water or take supplements and brush with a fluoride toothpaste may not need professional topical fluoride treatments if they don't get decay.

Since too much fluoride ingested during tooth development can cause tooth staining, young children should be taught to use only a small, pea-sized dab of toothpaste (a concentrated form of fluoride), to rinse well after brushing, and not to swallow toothpaste. Children younger than age six years shouldn't use fluoride rinses unless their dentist advises it.

Regular use of topical fluoride can improve the cavity resistance of teeth at any age. In fact, research has shown fluoride helps reduce cavities in older people, especially when gums recede with age, exposing softer root surfaces to decay. In addition to supplements, you can get fluoride in toothpastes, mouthwashes, and in fluoride gels that are professionally applied to teeth.

The Right Way to Brush and Floss

Brushing and flossing are the first lines of defense in fighting dental decay. You should brush your teeth at least twice a day, preferably after eating.

While most people brush their teeth regularly, fewer of us floss regularly. However, it's flossing—drawing a waxed or unwaxed string between the teeth—that gets out bacteria and food particles lodged in those areas. Try to floss after every meal. When you can't,

be sure to floss at least once a day, preferably before retiring. Plaque doesn't need much time to develop. So the hours you're asleep are the perfect time for bacteria to turn into plaque.

How often you brush and floss are certainly important, but how you perform these simple tasks is the key to eliminating the bacteria-producing plaque that causes cavities. Follow these tips:

BRUSHING TIPS

1. Hold the toothbrush at a 45-degree angle against the teeth (see Figure 4.1). Start at the gumline and use a gentle, circular, "scrubbing" motion. Use short strokes. Don't press too hard. Only the tips of the bristles actually clean the teeth. Using a light pressure allows the bristles to move freely and clean the teeth. (See *Is Your Toothbrush Right for You?*, page 107.)

Brush the outer surfaces of each tooth on the upper and lower jaw. Be sure to keep the bristle ends pointed against the gumline.

2. Brush the inside surfaces of the teeth with the same angled, scrubbing motion (see Figure 4.2).

3. Brush the chewing surfaces of the teeth (see Figure 4.3).

4. Clean the inside of the upper and lower front teeth by tilting the brush vertically and making several up-and-down strokes (see Figure 4.4).

5. Gently brush the tongue and the roof of the mouth, two areas where bacteria can accumulate (see Figure 4.5).

FLOSSING TIPS

Learning to floss properly takes a little practice. If you have a condition, such as arthritis, that limits your hand or finger dexterity, consider using a floss holder, a simple

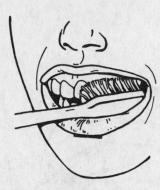

Fig. 4.1 Tilt the toothbrush so the bristles point toward the gumline. Keep the movements small, moving half a tooth at a time.

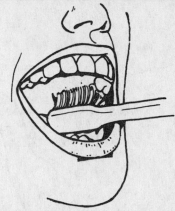

Fig. 4.2 Use the same short, circular motion to clean the inner surfaces of your teeth.

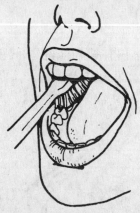

Fig. 4.3 Hold the brush flat to clean the biting surfaces.

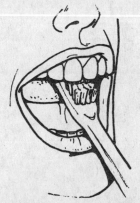

Fig. 4.4 Use gentle up-and-down strokes to clean the insides of upper and lower teeth.

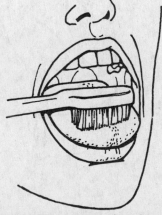

Fig. 4.5 Be sure to brush your tongue! Doing so helps freshen your breath and remove bacteria.

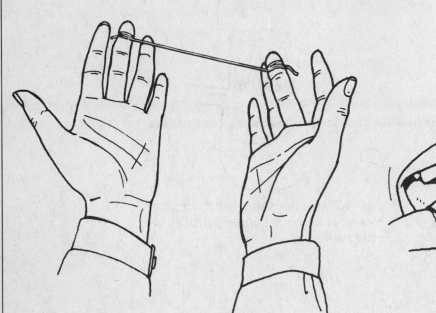

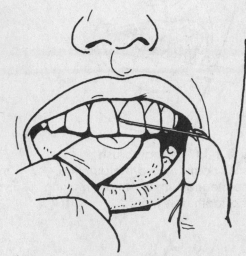

Fig. 4.6 Wind an 18-inch length of floss around your middle fingers.

Fig. 4.7 Slide the floss between teeth with a gentle sawing motion until it reaches the gumline.

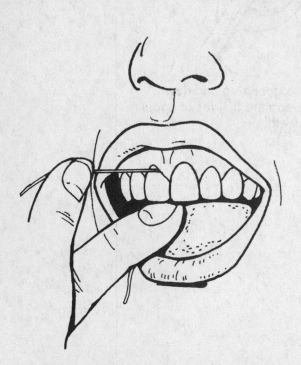

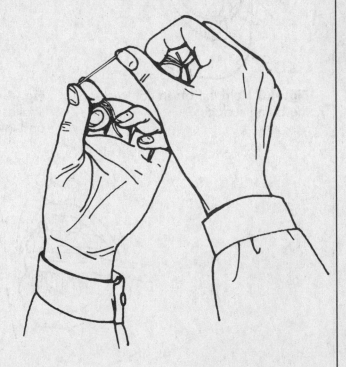

Fig. 4.8 Curve the floss around the tooth, slide it into the space between the tooth and gum, then scrape the tooth as you pull the floss (and any plaque) away from your gums.

Fig. 4.9 Unwind fresh floss as you go.

instrument prestrung with floss that makes flossing easier.

If you've never flossed your teeth before, your gums may bleed and become a little sore. The bleeding and soreness should subside within a few days. If it does not, see your dentist.

1. Cut off an 18-inch piece of waxed or unwaxed dental floss and wind it around the middle finger of each hand, wrapping most of the floss around one finger (see Figure 4.6). One finger supplies the floss; the other takes it up as you use it.

2. Using the thumb of one hand and the forefinger of the other, *gently* slide the floss back and forth between two teeth in a gentle sawing motion (see Figure 4.7).

3. At the gumline, curve the floss and pull it up and down against the surface of each tooth to remove plaque (see Figure 4.8).

4. Before moving to the next two teeth, wind the floss around the "take up" finger and release more floss from the "supply" finger to get a clean bit of floss (see Figure 4.9). This step is important to prevent introducing bacteria from the just-flossed teeth. Repeat steps 2 through 4 for all the teeth.

Fight Tooth Decay with Your Diet

In addition to improper oral hygiene, the other half of the cavity equation is sugary, sticky foods that adhere to the teeth. The acid-forming bacteria in plaque, especially *Streptococcus mutans*, love to feed on sugars

IS YOUR TOOTHBRUSH RIGHT FOR YOU?

❑ **Choose a soft brush.** Toothbrushes with too-hard bristles can actually damage gums and wear away enamel at the gumline. Also, use a brush with end-rounded or polished bristles.

❑ **Use a brush that fits.** Toothbrushes come in a variety of sizes. Select one that fits the size of your teeth and mouth.

❑ **Experiment.** Some toothbrushes come with varying angles and brush widths. Experiment and find one that allows you to reach all surfaces of your teeth.

❑ **Keep brushes current.** Too often our toothbrushes look like they're better suited for scrubbing the bathroom tile than our teeth. Toss out the old brush if it has frayed, bent, or broken bristles. Change your toothbrush at least every three or four months for effective cleaning.

❑ **Consider electric.** If you hate to brush or if you have dexterity problems, consider one of the new "rotary" electric toothbrushes. Ask your dentist to recommend a brand. Also, standard toothbrushes can be modified for those people who have difficulty gripping them.

❑ **Ask your dentist.** He or she can offer advice on the best toothbrush for you.

❑ **Never use someone else's toothbrush!**

❑   ❑   ❑

and starches. By changing your eating habits, you can reduce your risk of developing cavities.

Follow these dietary tips to fight tooth decay:

❑ **Limit between-meal snacks.** Many of us brush after eating a meal, but few of us brush after snacking. If you are in the habit of snacking between meals on sugary and starchy foods without brushing, you're providing food for the decay-causing bacteria.

❑ **Cut back on sugary snacks.** Eat them only when you are

Always Try to Brush After You Eat

able to brush after eating. When you crave munchies, choose a high-fiber food, such as popcorn, or fresh fruits, which contain natural sugars but don't stick to the teeth as much as confections.

❑ **Eat plenty of fiber-containing foods.** First, a diet high in fiber is filling and helps you cut down on the amount of sugar you eat. Second, high-fiber foods, such as fruits and vegetables, stimulate the production of saliva, which acts as a natural rinse and "neutralizer" against bacteria.

❑ **Watch out for sticky foods.** It's not only how much sugar or starch a food contains, but also how long the food clings to the teeth that plays a role in cavity formation. The stickier the food, the more apt it is to remain on the teeth where it provides nourishment for bacteria. Choose foods that are less sticky, especially when you can't brush. (See sidebar, *Watch those Sticky Foods*.)

❑ **End your meal with cheese.** In some cultures, cheese is served for dessert. This is not only a tasty way to end a meal, but the cheese neutralizes mouth acids.

❑ **Rinse out.** Always try to brush after you eat. But when you can't brush, rinse your mouth with water to help dislodge food particles and reduce the amount of bacteria present.

Try a Toothpick— But Be Careful!

Should you use a toothpick to clean your teeth? It certainly won't replace a toothbrush or floss, but most dentists say using a toothpick after eating is OK if you have food stuck between your teeth, and if you use toothpicks with caution. The hard wood of a toothpick can injure soft gums, and you risk pushing food even farther between teeth or teeth and gums. If untreated, impacted food can cause a painful infection.

A safer route is to use toothpicks with a holder, such as Perio-Aid, which allows you more control over the toothpick. Even better are toothpick-like products, such as Stim-U-Dent, which are made from soft balsa wood and are triangle-shaped to fit between teeth.

Never use toothpicks or toothpick-like products to remove plaque. Stick to brushing and flossing. If plaque isn't removed regularly, it will turn into calculus,

WATCH THOSE STICKY FOODS

Sticky foods cling to the teeth and provide food for acid-producing bacteria. Always try to brush and floss after eating sticky foods such as these.

Slightly sticky	Apples, bananas, hot fudge sundaes, milk chocolate bars
Moderately sticky	White bread, cream-filled sponge cake
Sticky	Caramels, raisins, figs (dried), jelly beans, doughnuts
Very sticky	Crackers, granola bars, oatmeal cookies, sugary cereal, potato chips, sweetened puffed oat cereal, cream sandwich cookies, peanut butter crackers

❑   ❑   ❑

hard material on tooth surfaces, which may be tooth colored or stained yellow to dark brown. Once calculus forms, it can only be removed through a professional cleaning.

brushing, flossing, the use of fluoride, and regular professional care. If you want to add a rinse to your oral hygiene program, look for Listerine, or a similar product carrying the ADA seal of acceptance.

The Rap on Rinses

Seal Your Teeth Against Cavities

You've seen the television commercials—simply rinse with antiplaque products and, voilà, no more cavities or at least fewer cavities. Do prebrushing rinses really fight plaque, the soft film that clings to teeth and causes tooth decay?

Most dental experts say their claims are questionable at best. In the early 1990s, pharmaceutical companies that marketed prebrushing rinses claimed they removed as much as "300 percent more plaque than brushing alone." However, subsequent studies haven't borne out their claims, and the Food and Drug Administration has forced these companies to stop making such assertions or to produce evidence in support of them.

One mouthwash, Listerine, has proved effective in reducing plaque and gingivitis, the beginning stages of gum disease. In 1987, Listerine provided research evidence of its effectiveness and received the American Dental Association (ADA) seal of acceptance. Several store brands now also contain Listerine's active ingredients: eucalyptol, methyl salicylate, menthol, and thymol.

Keep in mind that rinses such as Listerine can't take the place of

One of the newest and most effective weapons in the fight against tooth decay is sealants, thin plastic coatings that are applied to teeth to form a barrier between the tooth's surface and food particles and acid-forming bacteria.

First, teeth are cleaned and the enamel is slightly etched with an acid solution. Then, a clear or opaque plastic liquid resin is applied to the chewing surfaces. Sealants harden in place by means of chemical self-activation or with use of a high-intensity light.

Most dentists say sealants are most effective when applied to the permanent molars. These teeth, with their pits and fissures, are difficult to keep clean and are susceptible to decay. The sealants protect them. In children with high risk of dental caries, premolars and pits and fissures on other teeth also may benefit from sealants.

Just how effective are dental sealants? Very, say dental experts, especially for children and teenagers. In one 15-year study of children whose permanent molars were sealed, only 39 percent of the sealed teeth had cavities versus 94 percent of the unsealed teeth. The American Dental Association recommends dental sealants for all

One of the Most Effective Weapons in the Fight Against Tooth Decay Is Sealants

children who are at risk of pit and fissure decay. Sealants may also be used in primary teeth with distinct pit and fissure patterns that make them susceptible to decay.

The sealant procedure is painless, and the sealants generally last about seven years and can be easily replaced if they wear down. The price for sealing a tooth runs about $23 nationally, and some dental plans cover it. In public programs, the cost is markedly lower.

Which Toothpaste Should You Choose?

Most Toothpastes Are Very Similar

One brand of toothpaste says it contains baking soda. Another claims to control tartar. Still another says it freshens your breath and makes your teeth whiter. And most contain the cavity fighter fluoride. Is there any difference in toothpastes?

The answer is yes and no. All toothpastes contain a cleaning agent or abrasive, often silica or some other mineral. They also contain various flavoring and coloring agents, and usually a therapeutic agent such as fluoride. In that way, most toothpastes are very similar.

Baking soda is an age-old tooth-cleaning remedy that is again gaining popularity. A natural abrasive, it makes a good cleaner and polisher, but it's not so abrasive it harms enamel. Baking soda also has the advantage of neutralizing acidic bacterial wastes and deodorizing your mouth. You can simply make a paste of water and baking soda and brush with it. Or you can use baking soda tooth powders or pastes. If you want the added benefit of enamel-strengthening fluoride, you can buy baking soda toothpastes or powders with fluoride added, or use a fluoride rinse.

When the sticky, whitish plaque film isn't adequately removed from teeth, it can harden into a rough porous deposit called *tartar,* or *calculus.* It's tartar the dental hygienist chips and scrapes off your teeth during cleaning. Some dental experts believe tartar's rough surface makes removing the sticky plaque that causes tooth decay more difficult. Toothpastes that claim to control tartar contain special agents called pyrophosphates, which slow the mineralization of tartar. Research has shown tartar control toothpastes can cut the formation of new tartar deposits in half.

Which toothpaste should you use? Here are a few tips:

❏ Choose one you like and you'll consistently use.

❏ Look for a brand that has the ADA seal of acceptance, which means it has undergone rigorous testing to support its claims.

❏ Choose a toothpaste that contains fluoride even if you live in an area with fluoridated water.

❏ Opt for a baking soda toothpaste or brush with a baking soda and water paste a couple of times a week if staining or dull-looking teeth are a problem for you.

❏ Consider using a tartar control toothpaste if your dentist or dental hygienist says your teeth have a lot of tartar formation.

Help! My Gums Are Bleeding

You're brushing your teeth, and when you rinse and spit, you see a little blood. It's no big deal, right? It happens all the time. It may be a bigger deal than you think. You may have gingivitis, the first stage of gum disease. You could also have the more severe form of periodontal infection, periodontitis.

Gingivitis is the early, *reversible* first stage of gum disease. More than half of adults have it. Its symptoms include gums that look red and swollen and bleed easily.

Like cavities, gingivitis is caused by bacteria. Plaque, the sticky, whitish film that coats teeth and causes dental decay, is constantly forming and can build up on the teeth and gums. If plaque isn't removed daily with brushing and flossing, toxins produced by the bacteria irritate the gums, causing the redness and swelling. Over time, these toxins can destroy the gum tissue and cause it to separate from the teeth, forming pockets. Bacteria can then gather in these gum pockets and cause the gums to further detach. At this stage, the gum disease is destructive periodontitis. Left untreated, periodontitis destroys bone and other tissues that support the teeth and, if left untreated, can lead to tooth loss.

If you have gingivitis, several factors can make it worse:

- Hormonal imbalances caused by pregnancy, menstruation, and even adolescence
- Diseases such as diabetes

- Some medications
- Breathing through your mouth, which dries the gums and can cause an overgrowth of gum tissue
- Stress

But for most of us, gingivitis is caused by poor dental hygiene. *Don't* wait until your gingivitis progresses to more serious periodontitis to do something about it. Make an appointment with your dentist and have your teeth and gums thoroughly evaluated on a regular basis. Your dentist can tell you whether your gum disease can still be treated with self-care or if you also need some professional help.

Try these self-care tips, along with the advice of your dentist:

- **Brush your teeth after every meal.** Carry a travel toothbrush and travel-sized toothpaste with you and slip into the bathroom to brush your teeth after eating when away from home.
- **Floss daily.** No amount of brushing can get out food particles and bacteria between the teeth. If you have difficulty getting the floss between your

Gingivitis Is the First Stage of Gum Disease

SIGNS AND SYMPTOMS OF GUM DISEASE

If you notice any of these signs and symptoms, schedule an appointment with your dentist right away.

- Gums that bleed easily
- Red, swollen, or tender gums
- Gums that have pulled away from teeth
- Persistent bad breath or a bad taste in the mouth
- Pus between teeth and gums
- Loose or separating teeth
- A change in the way your teeth fit together

Most of Us Simply Don't Brush Long Enough

teeth, try using the waxed variety. If you have problems mastering flossing, use a floss holder, available at pharmacies.

❑ **Choose a tartar control toothpaste.** The demineralizing agents in these toothpastes slow the formation of tartar or hardened plaque. And don't forget the fluoride!

❑ **Brush longer.** Most of us simply don't brush long enough. If you think you're doing a good brushing job, ask your pharmacist for "disclosing tablets" that temporarily stain the plaque red. Brush and then use the tablets. You'll be surprised at how much plaque you miss. Try brushing for at least three minutes each time.

❑ **Don't miss the back teeth.** We usually do a pretty good job of cleaning the teeth that show when we smile. We're less thorough on the back teeth. That's where most dental hygienists find large deposits of tartar and plaque and where gingivitis is often the worst.

❑ **Brush more softly.** Choose a soft bristle brush and use less pressure when you brush to do a more effective job. If you apply too much pressure, the tips of the bristles, which do the cleaning, can't move properly. Too much pressure can also damage the enamel at the gumline and result in painfully sensitive teeth.

❑ **Try baking soda.** Make a paste of baking soda and water and brush your teeth with it two or three times a week. Not only will it make your teeth look whiter and feel terrific, the baking soda neutralizes bacterial acids that cause the redness, swelling, and frequent bleeding associated with gingivitis.

❑ **Have your teeth cleaned regularly.** You can clean off the soft plaque with thorough brushing and flossing, but only your dentist or dental hygienist can remove rock-hard tartar (also called calculus). Schedule appointments for professional cleanings regularly. Talk with your dentist about the schedule that is right for you.

Overcoming Dental Jitters

Most of us aren't crazy about going to the dentist, but a small percentage of people have dental phobias. The mere thought of a visit to the dentist causes them profound anxiety. Some are so fearful they refuse to see a dentist for years at a time. The health risks of these dental jitters can be serious and even deadly.

If you have a dental phobia, try these tips:

❑ Look for a dentist who is gentle and understands the problem.

❑ Ask your dentist for shorter appointments.

❑ Make treatment contracts that outline the work and methods.

❑ Agree on hand signals to indicate when you need a break.

❑ Bring a personal radio with headphones and tapes of soothing music to help distract you and drown out some of the "dental noise."

❑ Look into behavior therapy. Also called "desensitization therapy," this involves learning relaxation and visualization techniques, confronting the feared experience through slides or videos, dress rehearsals, and, finally, facing the dental appointment. Such therapy is usually effective in as few as three to five sessions.

❑ Read *How to Overcome Fear of Dentistry* by Dr. Robert F. Kroeger.

Are Dental X rays Safe?

You sit down in the dental X-ray chair and you're feeling pretty comfortable and relaxed—that is, until the technician lays the lead shield apron on you and scurries behind a protective wall before pushing the button that activates the X-ray machine. You've heard even a single dose of radiation can cause irreversible cell damage that can lead to cancer. Are dental X rays safe?

It's true that overexposure to radiation from X rays can pose health risks. But the risk from X rays obtained in the average dental exam is small. Most experts say the benefits of spotting cavities and gum problems outweigh this small risk. Still, it's a good idea to be an informed health consumer and question the need for X rays. Talk with your dentist about how often you should have dental X rays based on your dental health history and the number of annual visits. Also, be sure to let your dentist know if you have recently undergone X rays for other medical conditions. And if you are pregnant, you should postpone dental X rays.

The Mercury Filling Scare—Poison or Profit?

You've probably heard the rumor—people are becoming ill from the mercury in their fillings. They are experiencing, so the story goes, everything from insomnia to multiple sclerosis. Therefore, you should have all your silver fillings replaced—at a tremendous cost—with ceramic or gold fillings. Right? Wrong!

Billions of teeth are filled with an amalgam of metals such as silver, copper, tin, zinc, and mercury. In its most basic state, mercury is poisonous. But when combined with other metals in a filling, mercury becomes inactive. A few people are allergic to mercury, but this is apparent within hours or days of having a tooth filled.

The newer, tooth-colored ceramic and composite resins are subject to fracturing and are less resistant to wear. No one knows how long they'll last, but metal amalgams can last for many years. Gold is good but very expensive. And removing fillings can increase the teeth's sensitivity and cause structural damage that can result in the need for root canal work or extractions.

Should you have your fillings replaced? The ADA puts it this way, "removal of amalgam restorations from the nonallergic patient

The Risk from X rays Obtained in the Average Dental Exam Is Small

for the alleged purpose of removing toxic substances from the body is improper and unethical." Or, to put it another way, save your money and your teeth.

Your Dentist Can Determine the Right Checkup Schedule for You

Your Dental Checkup Schedule

For most adults, an annual dental checkup and teeth cleaning is adequate. But some people need to visit the dentist more frequently because of their risk for oral disease. Only your dentist can determine exactly the right dental checkup schedule for you. However, you can use these general guidelines to determine when you should schedule a dental examination.

Every three months if:
❏ you have more than six cavities a year, or
❏ your oral hygiene is poor.

Every six months if:
❏ you have one to two cavities per year and use adequate oral hygiene;
❏ you wear dentures and also smoke cigarettes and drink alcohol; or
❏ you're older than aged 35 and you smoke and drink alcohol.

Every 12 months if:
❏ you have minimal or no dental decay, your oral hygiene is good, and you don't smoke or drink;
❏ you wear dentures without difficulties.

Selecting the Right Dentist

Choosing the right dentist can make all the difference in how you feel about regular professional dental care. Ask friends and family for recommendations. You can also get referrals from your family physician, the local dental society, or a hospital or university with a dental school. Make sure the dentist you select meets these criteria:

● Takes a complete medical and dental history, including drug allergies and chronic illnesses.

● Employs sterile methods: Both dentist and hygienist wear a face mask and gloves, wash their hands between patients, and sterilize instruments, drills, and other equipment.

● Stresses prevention and willingly shows you how to care for your teeth and gums at home.

● Carefully explains all treatments, alternatives, and potential complications, and willingly answers all your questions.

● Provides for emergency care, even after hours and on weekends.

● Willingly discusses fees and provides written estimates and itemized bills.

● Gives gentle care and demonstrates concern for your comfort and safety.

● Has a neat, clean, orderly office.

Dictionary of Dental Specialists

Your regular dentist may recommend you see a specialist for some oral health problems. This list of specialists briefly describes their area of expertise.

Endodontist: Diagnosis and treatment of diseases and injuries involving the tooth pulp and supporting tissues.

Oral pathologist: Diagnosis of the changes caused by diseases of the mouth.

Oral and maxillofacial surgeon: Surgery for diseases, injuries, and defects of the jaw, mouth, and face.

Orthodontist: Movement of teeth or correction of malformations or misalignments between the teeth and jaws.

Pedodontist: Children's teeth.

Periodontist: Disease of the gums and tissues supporting the teeth.

Prosthodontist: Dentures, bridges, and other replacements for missing teeth.

Your Dental Dictionary

Dentists, like other medical professionals, often toss around dental terms that can be confusing or, in some cases, even a little bit frightening. Here's your guide to understanding dental lingo.

Abrasion: Abnormal wearing away of the teeth.

Bicuspids: The teeth between the pointed canines ("eyeteeth") and the rounded molars farthest back in the mouth. The term literally means having or ending in two points.

Calculus or Tartar: The hardened mineralized form of plaque. Consisting mainly of calcium, phosphorus, and bacteria, tartar accumulates around the gumline. If not professionally removed by your dentist or hygienist, tartar can irritate the gums and cause them to become puffy and inflamed and to bleed easily.

Canines: The pointed teeth between the front teeth (incisors) and the bicuspids; often called the "eyeteeth."

Crown: The visible part of the tooth. Also the name for the restoration applied by the dentist that covers the entire tooth—sometimes called a "cap."

Dental caries: The medical term for cavities. Initially, dental caries causes the tooth's enamel to decay or erode.

Dentin: The hard substance just below the enamel that surrounds the sensitive pulp.

Edentulous: The term that describes the loss of all the natural teeth.

Enamel: The hardest tissue in the human body. It is the protective outer layer of the tooth.

Gingivitis: The first and most treatable stage of gum disease. Gingivitis is caused by toxic effects from the buildup of plaque and tartar. If you have gingivitis (most children and adults have at least a mild case), your gums may be red and swollen and bleed easily, especially when you brush or floss.

Can You Talk Your Dentist's Language?

People Lose Their Teeth as They Age Because They Haven't Taken Care of Them

Gums: The soft, pink tissue surrounding the teeth, covering the bone and the part of the tooth not visible.

Incisors: The front teeth—the "cutting" teeth.

Interdental cleaning: The use of dental floss or interdental stimulators (such as Stim-U-Dent) to clean between teeth.

Molars: The largest teeth in the back of the mouth with the nearly flat, broad biting surfaces.

Occlusion: Your bite. When the dentist evaluates your occlusion, he or she is assessing how your teeth fit together when you bite down. A **malocclusion** describes poorly aligned teeth.

Periodontal ligaments: The fibers that hold the tooth in the jawbone.

Periodontitis: The more advanced and serious stage of gum disease that follows untreated gingivitis. Gums recede and pockets form where bacteria can breed. Periodontitis can cause bone that supports the teeth to erode and can result in tooth loss.

Plaque: The thin, whitish film that coats the teeth and tongue. Caused by bacteria, it uses carbohydrates, especially sugary sucrose, and creates an acid strong enough to dissolve the tooth's enamel. Bacteria in plaque, over time, are also responsible for gum disease.

Pulp: The soft, sensitive tissue that fills the inside of the tooth. Functioning as the "heart" of the tooth, the pulp contains the nerves and blood vessels that nourish the tooth.

Restoration: A filling.

Root: The part of the tooth lodged in a socket in your jawbone.

Scaling and planing: The terms used to describe professional teeth cleaning. Regular and thorough brushing and flossing can remove the majority of soft, filmy plaque from your teeth. However, only your dentist or hygienist can remove hardened tartar (calculus).

Wisdom teeth: The last teeth to erupt. If they erupt (not everyone has wisdom teeth), they are the third molars.

Debunking Dental Myths

Everyone knows brushing and flossing regularly is important, but what you don't know (or what you *think* you know) can hurt your dental health. Take a look at the following dental myths and get some wisdom for your teeth.

Myth: You can never brush or floss too much. Brushing too often or too vigorously can injure the gums and abrade tooth structure, leading to sensitive teeth or gingival injury (known as recession). Brushing two or three times a day and flossing daily is plenty for most people.

Myth: You should replace your toothbrush whenever you visit your dentist. Most people visit the dentist once or twice a year. You should replace your toothbrush at least that often. But plan on purchasing a new brush every three or four months or whenever the brush bristles appear worn, bent, or matted.

Myth: It's a fact of life that you'll lose several or all of your teeth as you grow older. Aging doesn't cause tooth loss—decay, gum and bone disease, or trauma does. The primary reason people lose their teeth as they age is they haven't taken proper care of them through proper brushing and flossing and regular professional care.

Myth: *To clean your teeth, you really need some of those high-tech appliances such as electric toothbrushes or oral irrigators.* Nothing beats old fashioned brushing and flossing. Electric toothbrushes, oral irrigators that squirt water between the teeth, floss holders, and special picks for cleaning teeth are all useful, but they don't replace regular home and professional care. If you have a dexterity problem, perhaps because of arthritis, that makes it difficult to brush or floss, some of these devices can be very helpful.

Myth: *You should undergo teeth X rays every two years.* Only your dentist can determine the correct interval for undergoing X rays of your teeth. Dental X rays do deliver a small radiation exposure and shouldn't be performed without specific cause. If you're pregnant or think you may be pregnant, delay dental X rays until after you've delivered.

Myth: *A toothache that goes away by itself means the tooth has recovered from whatever the trouble was.* Tooth pain is a sign something is wrong. Pain caused from dental decay or other problems can come and go. Don't delay in consulting your dentist.

Myth: *If you drink a lot of milk, you won't have cavities.* Milk is a good source of calcium, which the body needs to build strong teeth and bones. But drinking milk or taking calcium supplements won't prevent dental cavities or arrest their progress.

Myth: *Unwaxed floss is best.* It doesn't matter what kind of floss you use as long as you use it and it works for you. There's no evidence that unwaxed floss cleans teeth better than waxed floss. Some people find it easier to use waxed floss.

Pass the Breath Mints

Bad breath (halitosis) is caused by the same bacteria that feed on plaque and cause tooth decay. Persistent bad breath is an indication you need to see your dentist. If you have bad breath, try these freshening tips:

❑ **Brush and floss often.** After meals is best. Try to brush at least twice a day and floss daily.

❑ **Rinse often.** Rinsing your mouth with water after eating or snacking can help remove some food debris when brushing is not possible.

❑ **Use an antibacterial mouthwash.** Listerine and similar mouthwashes can decrease the amount of bacteria present.

❑ **Eat parsley.** Fresh parsley is a natural breath deodorizer.

❑ **Try sugarless breath mints or sugarfree gum.** These products promote saliva production, which helps rinse your mouth. But be sure to choose sugarless products. The sugared variety provides food for bacteria.

❑ **Don't smoke.** Odors are transmitted from the lungs.

Persistent Bad Breath Is an Indication You Need to See Your Dentist

THESE SENSITIVE TEETH NEED A DENTIST

See your dentist if:

❑ Teeth are sensitive to pressure, heat, or cold.
❑ You have pain that lasts longer than one hour.
❑ A single tooth is sensitive.
❑ Gums around the sensitive teeth have changed color.
❑ You have obvious decay.
❑ Sensitivity persists for two weeks despite self-care.

❑ ❑ ❑

❑ Rinse with over-the-counter fluoride rinses.
❑ Use less pressure when you brush, and brush in a small, circular pattern rather than back and forth.
❑ Never use chewing tobacco.

Whiter and Brighter Teeth

Lots of things can cause your teeth to look dingy—coffee, tea, colas, red wine, soy sauce, tobacco. Aging tends to turn teeth more yellowish as enamel thins and the dentin shows through. Even some medications, such as tetracycline, given to children or taken by their mothers during pregnancy can cause permanent staining.

Only your dentist can remove tough stains from your teeth, but you can use these strategies to keep your teeth whiter.

❑ Cut down on coffee, tea, and colas.
❑ Stop smoking.
❑ Don't use smokeless tobacco (chewing tobacco, spit, or snuff).
❑ Brush and floss at least twice each day.
❑ Brush with a baking soda paste.
❑ Use "stain-removing" toothpastes no more than two or three times a week. Because they can be harsh, you may brush away enamel.
❑ Avoid do-it-yourself bleaching kits.

There's Help for Sensitive Teeth

Coping with Sensitive Teeth

When you drink something hot or cold or bite down on a sweet food, does an electric tingling sensation send you out of your seat? You've got sensitive teeth.

Plenty of things can make your teeth react to hot, cold, sweet, sour, and even pressure. You may have chomped down too hard and injured one or more teeth. Often teeth feel sensitive after being cleaned or filled. Grinding your teeth or clamping the jaws tightly can make teeth sensitive, too. If your teeth are sensitive to sweet foods, it means they've been compromised in some way. In most cases, this sensitivity is caused from exposed dentin from dental decay, a defective restoration, or abrasion.

If your teeth feel sensitive, have a dentist check them out to ensure there is no decay or other problem that requires professional help. Then try these tips:

❑ Use a soft toothbrush.
❑ Try a desensitizing toothpaste.

Easing Toothache Pain

Pain in a tooth is a signal you need to see a dentist. However, these strategies can help until you can get to the dental office.

❏ Take an over-the-counter pain reliever.

❏ Apply oil of cloves. Be sure to follow label directions and apply only to the tooth, *not* the gums.

❏ Put an ice pack on your cheek.

❏ Rinse your mouth with warm water to clean out any food debris.

❏ Use dental floss to remove any food that might be trapped between teeth and causing the pain.

❏ Cover the affected tooth with gauze if it's sensitive to air.

Do You Grind Your Teeth?

Bruxism (from the Greek *brychein* meaning "to gnash the teeth") is dental lingo for tooth grinding. Plenty of people grind, clench (bite down with continual pressure), or tap (click) their teeth together. These habits can cause facial and jaw soreness and pain, headaches, and fractured and abraded teeth.

What causes bruxism? Most dental authorities believe it's an unconscious method of relieving stress. They say 98 percent of adults clench their teeth together in response to emotional distress at some time or other. For unexplained reasons, women are four times more likely than men to report symptoms typically attributable to bruxism.

Occasionally, bruxism may occur because teeth don't fit together (malocclusion) or are improperly positioned. The body tries to "grind" the teeth into proper position. However, tooth grinding can also *cause* malocclusion. When we bite or chew food, we exert 25 to 50 pounds of force. When some persons grind or clench, they exert as much as 500 pounds of force. It's easy to see why grinding, clenching, and tooth tapping can harm your oral health.

You may grind your teeth and not even know it. In fact, experts estimate as many as 20 percent of us grind our teeth when we sleep, but we're seldom aware of it. Since bruxism is largely an unconscious habit, one solution is to become aware of the condition. Right now, is your jaw clenched? If so, consciously relax it and try to keep your teeth slightly apart. To identify your habit, ask yourself these questions:

● Do I wake in the morning with my neck and jaw muscles sore or tight?

● Do I clench my jaw when I feel stressed?

● Do I often feel the need to massage my face and jaw joint muscles because they are tight or sore?

● Do my teeth ever feel loose?

● Are my teeth sensitive to hot or cold?

● Does my jaw ever ache?

As Many as 20 Percent of Us Grind Our Teeth when We Sleep

A "Clicking" Jaw May Be a Sign of TMD

If you answered "Yes," you might be a tooth grinder. You can help "retrain" yourself out of a daytime clenching habit. Try these strategies:

❏ **Consciously relax your face and jaw.** If you feel yourself becoming tense, focus on stretching and loosening your facial muscles.

❏ **Try stress-relieving techniques.** Instead of clenching or tooth grinding, take a walk or breathe deeply.

❏ **Avoid stimulants.** Caffeine and over-the-counter decongestants, for example, can make you tense your muscles.

❏ **Manage your stress load.** Ask yourself, "What's bothering me? What's causing me to feel anxiety? What are some of the things I can do about it?" Consider taking a class in stress-reduction techniques such as meditation or biofeedback.

❏ **Relax before you retire.** Take a hot bath, listen to soothing music, drink a glass of warm milk.

❏ **Before sleeping, repeat this phrase to yourself:** "Lips closed, teeth apart, jaw relaxed."

❏ **See the chapter *Coping with Stress*, page 127.**

Self-care may not relieve bruxism, especially if you're a nighttime grinder. If it doesn't, get help pronto. Psychotherapy, counseling, and relaxation therapy can often help deal with the anxiety, emotional upset, and work stress that may contribute to your bruxism. Your dentist can also make you a custom-fit plastic appliance called a splint or a night guard, which protects the surfaces of your teeth from the effects of grinding.

Dealing with TMD

Do you have headaches, clicking and popping in the jaw, or pain in your face or neck? You may have temporomandibular joint disorder (TMD) or a misalignment of the jaw joint.

TMD can have many causes:

• Bad posture (including cradling a phone on your shoulder)

• Tooth grinding

• An injury to the jaw or chin, or whiplash

• Poor fitting teeth

• Disorders affecting bones and joints, such as arthritis

• Gum chewing

Treatment of TMD has involved everything from massage to jaw joint replacement. Most experts recommend starting with conservative treatments such as gentle exercise, chewing modifications, and posture correction. Surgical procedures to treat TMD are very serious interventions with many possible complications. Always seek a second opinion before undergoing any surgical intervention.

You may be able to ease your discomfort with these tips:

❏ Use over-the-counter pain relievers.

❏ Don't chew gum.

❏ Consciously avoid clenching your jaws.

❏ Alternate hot and cold packs on the jaw joint.

❏ Massage your jaw, neck, and shoulders.

Coping with Dry Mouth

Dentists call it "xerostomia." You experience it as a pasty feeling in your mouth. It's dry mouth caused when salivary glands do not produce enough saliva.

Saliva isn't something you really think much about. That is, until you don't have enough of it. Lots of things can cause your salivary glands to become less productive—diabetes and other diseases, anxiety, depression, or drugs such as antihistamines, decongestants, tranquilizers, antihypertensives, antidepressants, diuretics, nicotine, alcohol, and marijuana.

Dry mouth contributes to the development of dental cavities, so if you have dry mouth you should floss regularly, brush with fluoride toothpastes or gels, and have your teeth professionally cleaned at least once a year. If your dry mouth condition is severe, you may need to see your dentist every three to six months. People who have xerostomia and wear dentures are at higher risk for developing a yeast overgrowth in the mouth and may need to use an antifungal product such as Mycelex. Some people combat oral fungal infections by lining their dentures with a thin film of this cream before inserting them. (Do so only after consulting with your dentist.)

Here are some tips for coping if you have dry mouth:

❑ **Have a medical checkup.** Your doctor should rule out underlying health problems.

❑ **Change medications.** If your dry mouth is a side effect of a medication, talk with your physician or pharmacist about finding one with a less drying effect.

❑ **Use an oral lubricant.** Products such as Oralbalance are long-lasting lubricants that coat the mouth and help prevent moisture loss.

❑ **Chew carrots or sugarless gum.** Chewing gum or hard vegetables, such as carrots or celery, temporarily stimulates increased saliva production.

❑ **Try artificial saliva.** Saliva substitutes sold over-the-counter, such as Moi-stir and Salivart, can help replace saliva.

❑ **Give up saliva robbers.** These include tobacco products, alcohol, caffeine, and mouthwashes that contain alcohol.

Dealing with Denture Troubles

If you've ever had denture troubles, you know the signs and symptoms well—pain, pressure, slippage, and sore spots. Dentures often cause trouble during the initial "adjustment phase" when they are new, and after several years of wearing, when gums have shrunk and the appliance no longer fits properly. These hints can help you stop denture discomfort:

❑ **Keep your dentures clean.** This is especially important during the break-in period

Xerostomia Is the Medical Term for Dry Mouth

121

Care of Replacement Teeth Is Vitally Important

when your gums are still healing. Clean your dentures with toothpaste, a special denture cleanser, or plain soap and water.

❑ **Brush your gums regularly.** Gum brushing stimulates the gums and helps them stay healthy.

❑ **Give your mouth time to adjust to new dentures.** Eat soft foods at first and avoid hard foods such as corn on the cob. Even after you've adjusted, stay away from foods like apples that are hard to eat with dentures.

❑ **Take your dentures out for 24 hours if you develop sore spots.** Pain means you've probably developed a soft tissue injury. Give your mouth time to heal.

❑ **Rinse your mouth with warm salt water.** Use one-half teaspoon salt to four ounces warm water every three or four hours. Salt "toughens" the tissue and helps eliminate bacteria.

❑ **Take over-the-counter pain relievers.**

❑ **Wear your dentures only half the time.** Never sleep with your dentures in.

❑ **Schedule annual dental exams.** While denture wearers obviously do not have teeth that require a dentist's care, they are subject to many types of oral tissue problems, resulting from either trauma or infection. In addition, the age of most denture wearers puts them in a high-risk group for other oral diseases (including oral cancer). Many of these conditions, as well as side effects from medications, can be detected during a regular dental examination.

Caring for Crowns, Bridges, and Implants

Your dentist has given you new teeth! Well, sort of. Tooth decay, gum disease, or injury has left you with a few gaps in your smile. But your dentist has filled these in with crowns, bridges, and implants.

A crown, or cap, is a restoration applied by the dentist that covers the entire tooth. A bridge is a tooth replacement attached to your natural teeth. An implant is an artificial tooth secured by a metal post surgically set in your jaw. Having these tooth replacements really makes you feel like you have a whole new mouth. Even though these artificial teeth can't decay like your natural ones, the natural tooth holding a crown can, and the areas around the replacements are great places for food to catch and plaque to build up, contributing to infections of the gum tissue.

Care of replacement teeth is, therefore, even more important. Follow these tips to take good care of your new teeth:

❑ **Brush and floss regularly.** Try an interdental brush—a tiny brush designed for hard-to-reach areas such as between artificial teeth. When you can't brush, at least rinse your mouth with water.

❑ **Brush the gumline.** With a soft brush, gently brush the gums. For an extra ounce of prevention, rinse with an antiplaque mouthwash after you brush.

- **Use a stimulator.** Have you wondered what that rubber tip is that comes on some toothbrushes? Use it to clean the gum area around crowns and artificial teeth.
- **Ask your dentist about flossing fixed bridges.** You may need a special floss or a floss threader to floss between the bridge and your gums.
- **Try an irrigation device.** Tools such as a Water Pik can help remove trapped food. Look for a model bearing the American Dental Association's seal of acceptance.

Caring for Kids' Teeth

Taking care of your children's teeth begins *before* they're born. Pregnant women should eat a well-balanced diet full of the nutrients needed for the formation of teeth—calcium, phosphorus, protein, iron, and vitamins A, C, and D. They should also avoid taking tetracycline, which can stain baby's teeth.

Even before a baby's teeth have erupted, it's important to keep baby's gums clean. Wipe the gums with gauze or a clean cloth after feeding. Also, avoid "baby bottle tooth decay"—severe tooth decay in infants and young children caused by putting them to bed with a bottle of juice, sugar water, milk, or formula. If they need a bottle at bedtime or naptime, give them plain water only.

Once teeth emerge, use a damp piece of gauze to clean. As soon as your child has molars (the largest teeth in the back of the mouth), switch to a soft toothbrush with a small head. Scrub every surface of each tooth, gently and quickly. Use a fluoridated toothpaste, but use only a small, pea-sized dab, and teach the child to spit out—not swallow—the toothpaste. Follow the tooth brushing with gentle flossing.

When Children Can Take Over

It's important not to let your children care for their teeth before they have the fine motor skills to do it well. A good guideline is if children don't have the motor coordination to write, they won't be able to brush or floss thoroughly. You can teach your children the basics of cleaning their own teeth by the time they're aged two or three years, but you must carefully supervise tooth brushing until they can do a good job (about the age of eight). You can gently floss children's teeth, and they can usually learn to do it themselves by the age of six or seven.

Your Child's First Trip to the Dentist

It's important to start professional dental care early. Your child's first trip to the dentist should take place by the time the child is two years of age. The American Dental Association recommends your child see a dentist as early as 6 to 12 months of age.

Don't wait until dental decay develops for your child's first dental visit. Early dental care, includ-

Don't Wait Until Decay Develops for Your Child's First Dental Visit

123

THE COMINGS AND GOINGS OF KIDS' TEETH

Kids lose 20 "primary" teeth and acquire 28 to 32 "permanent" teeth as they grow from toddlers into teens. While not all children's teeth come in or fall out at the same time, this is about the timetable you can expect:

Aged 6–12 months: The central incisors, the teeth right in the middle of the jaw, appear on the top and bottom.

Aged 9–13 months: Lateral incisors appear.

Aged 16–22 months: The "canines" (cuspids) come in.

Aged 13–19 months: The first or "baby" molars appear.

Aged 25–33 months: The child's second baby molars emerge.

Aged 6 years: The first permanent teeth, much larger and usually less white than baby teeth, start to emerge. Four molars come in behind existing baby teeth.

Aged 7 years: Call the tooth fairy because by the age of seven, your child will likely lose those first four front incisors, leaving enchanting gaps in your child's smile. Usually these gaps won't be fully filled in until about aged 10.

Aged 8–10 years: The primary molars, one by one, fall out and are replaced by permanent bicuspids.

Aged 10–13 years: This is the age when the canines loosen and fall out. They are replaced by permanent teeth. Also during this time the second permanent molars appear behind the first molars that appeared around aged 6.

Aged 15 years and up: By the time your child is 15, he or she has 28 permanent teeth. Third permanent molars, the wisdom teeth, may or may not appear.

❑ ❑ ❑

ing professional cleaning, can prevent serious dental problems later on. And remember, fluoride is important for developing teeth. If you do not live in an area with fluoridated water, talk to your dentist about fluoride supplements. (See *Bring on the Fluoride*, page 103.)

Here are a few tips to make your child's first visit to the dentist a pleasant one.

❑ **Take your child to the dentist's office before the day of the examination.** Your child can meet the dentist and see the clinic area.

❑ **Schedule your child's exam in the morning.** Your child will be well rested, and the examination will be less likely to interfere with meals or naps.

❑ **Treat the visit as a new adventure.** Explain that the dentist is a friend who wants to make sure the child stays healthy.

❑ **Use positive language to describe the dental examination.** If you are anxious about your own dental exams, you may unintentionally communicate your own anxiety to your child.

❑ **Never threaten a child with going to see the dentist for misbehaving.** And don't resort to bribes to overcome a child's resistance to a visit to the dentist.

❑ **Be aware that some dental clinics are more child-friendly than others.** Pediatric dentists, for example, are especially skilled at dealing with young children.

❑ **Set a good example. Brush and floss your own teeth daily and schedule regular visits to the dentist.** Have the child brush with you. This practice provides your child with positive reinforcement and allows you to monitor the child's toothbrushing technique, including use of the appropriate amount of toothpaste.

Easing Teething Discomfort

One definition of "cranky" is a child whose first teeth are erupting through the gums. Symptoms of teething include irritability, crying, fussiness, gum inflammation, difficulty sleeping, decreased appetite, and drooling more than usual. A few babies develop a mild rash from exposure to their saliva. Sometimes teething also causes a mild fever, congestion, and ear pulling like that with an ear infection. A fever or rash may also indicate another problem, so notify your doctor if these symptoms occur.

The first signs of teething usually occur when a child is around six or seven months of age with a single lower central incisor. Most children have all of their primary or "baby" teeth by the age of three years, but all children are different. If your baby doesn't develop his or her teeth right on schedule, it's usually nothing to worry about. Some children don't develop their first teeth until they're one year old; others have a first tooth at two months of age. (See *The Coming and Going of Kids' Teeth,* page 124.)

The process of teething can be painful. These strategies can ease baby's (and your) discomfort.

- ❏ **Massage baby's gums.** Gently massage the gums with a clean finger. The pressure can often relieve pain.

IS IT REALLY TEETHING?

Discomfort is common and normal for teething babies, but sometimes the crankiness and fever signal something else is wrong. At about the age of six months, when babies begin teething, they lose their maternal protection against the herpes simplex virus (HSV 1), the culprit that causes cold sores and mouth blisters. If the baby has herpes mouth sores, some of the commercial teething products can be irritating and painful.

Fussy and feverish babies who are especially miserable should be checked out by a pediatrician or a pediatric dentist to rule out the presence of HSV 1 before using over-the-counter products. If the baby does, in fact, have HSV 1, the doctor can prescribe medication for the pain and fever. Make sure the baby gets plenty of fluids to prevent dehydration. An HSV 1 outbreak usually lasts ten days to two weeks.

Ear infections can also mimic teething symptoms. Ask your doctor to check carefully for any signs of infection.

❏   ❏   ❏

- ❏ **Offer a cold washcloth, chilled pacifier, or frozen banana.** Cold not only soothes inflamed gums, it also distracts your cranky baby. Frozen bananas are especially good because babies like the sweet taste.

- ❏ **Give children's pain relievers (not aspirin).** Try over-the-counter pain relievers such as Children's Liquid Tylenol. They can provide relief for up to four hours. Never give more than three times in a 24-hour period.

- ❏ **Apply oral anesthetic teething gels.** You can give baby temporary (30 to 40 minutes) relief with over-the-counter anesthetic gels such as Oragel.

- ❏ **Use herbal "teething tablets."** Ask your pharmacist about these quickly dissolving tablets.

If You're Not Sure Teething Is Causing Your Baby's Fussiness, Call Your Doctor

TEST YOUR WISDOM TEETH IQ

Wisdom teeth, or third molars, are the four permanent teeth that come in behind the upper and lower second molars in adults of about 17 to 21 years of age. (But it's not unusual for an individual not to have all four wisdom teeth.) Often, wisdom teeth need to be removed if they exert too much pressure on the second molars or if they erupt only partially, leaving an opening for harmful bacteria to enter. Some wisdom teeth do not come in at all but are "impacted," meaning they are unable to move into their proper position. This can occur if the jaw is too small to accommodate the extra teeth. Your dentist can evaluate your wisdom teeth to determine if they require removal.

❑ ❑ ❑

❑ **Let them chew.** Chewing helps the baby work the tooth through the gum. For very young babies, you can wrap an apple wedge in a soft wash cloth and hold it for them to chew. Let older babies nosh on apple wedges themselves (watch for choking).

❑ **Play with them.** Distraction is a powerful tool with teething babies. Play peek-a-boo, engage them with their favorite toy, or rock or swing them to take their mind off discomfort.

Mouth Injuries

Mouth injuries can occur as a result of a bike or auto accident; a sports, recreation, or work-related incident; a fight; or even just during play. Proper action could save a tooth. Follow this advice for handling dental emergencies:

❑ **When the jaw may be broken:** Tie a cloth (handkerchief, necktie, towel) around the jaw and over the top of the head to keep the jaw from moving. Seek medical treatment immediately.

❑ **When a tooth is knocked out:** Do not remove any tissue fragments. Rinse the tooth in water and wrap it in a cloth soaked with water or milk. Go to the dentist immediately!

❑ **When a tooth chips or breaks:** If a tooth chips or breaks, your dentist will need to check the extent of any damage. The loss of part of a tooth may seem minor, but it can be painful and make your tooth or gum vulnerable to infection. You should phone your dentist immediately. He or she will instruct you whether you require immediate treatment.

❑ **When an injury bleeds:** To control bleeding of the lips or tongue, apply pressure to both sides of the wound with a moist cloth or gauze. To control bleeding of the gums or roof of the mouth, apply direct pressure with a moist cloth or gauze. To control bleeding of the teeth, apply pressure to tooth or socket, or bite down on cloth or dressing placed on the tooth or socket.

❑ **When an object is caught between teeth:** First, try using dental floss or a soft interdental stimulator (such as Stim-U-Dent) to remove the object. (Be careful not to push the object into the gums.) If floss does not work, go to the dentist. Do not risk injury to your mouth by trying to remove the object with sharp or pointed instruments.

CHAPTER 5

COPING

WITH

STRESS

*E*motional stress can come from a variety of sources—from an overflow of work at the office to the death of a loved one. Sometimes stress is self-imposed. Other times, it is the result of an external circumstance an individual has no control over. Regardless of its origins, however, stress can take a serious toll on body, mind, and soul.

You can't avoid stress—it's everywhere. However, you can learn how to control your responses to stress, thereby preventing it from detracting from your quality of life. This chapter helps you identify the causes of stress in your life and gives you simple, concrete strategies for coping. So cancel all your appointments, take the phone off the hook, and cozy up with a nice cup of tea. It's time to relax!

❑ ❑ ❑

Stress May Contribute to the Development of Heart Disease

Stress and Disease

At one time, the idea that emotional stress could cause physical symptoms seemed far-out, ludicrous. In fact, the only people who would admit to such a fringe belief were New-Age hipsters and aging transcendentalists.

These days, however, medical science is linking psychological stress to a variety of diseases. Although the research is still in the early stages, here are some recent findings:

- It has been estimated that up to 75% of all physician visits are made by people with stress-related complaints.

- In a survey of people infected with genital herpes, most participants reported that stress caused a recurrence in their symptoms.

- Evidence shows stress can depress the immune system, predisposing individuals to illness. Preliminary studies employing strategies such as relaxation, hypnosis, and exercise have shown some reversal of this effect. (It is not yet known whether these strategies can actually help prevent disease.)

- Dermatologists have found many skin conditions, such as hives and eczema, are related to stress.

- Stress may contribute to the development of heart disease. Some doctors, such as Dean Ornish, M.D., a cardiologist in Sausalito, California, believe stress reduction should play a prominent role in the treatment of heart disease. In his work with people with severe coronary heart disease, Dr. Ornish found that atherosclerotic disease was actually *reversed* among participants who underwent a program that included stress reduction.

- Stress is thought to be a common cause of everyday aches and pains, such as headaches, backaches, and indigestion.

Is All Stress Unhealthy?

Have you ever known someone who seemed impervious to pressure? Someone who seemed to experience life as a stroll through the proverbial park? Did you ever wonder how they got that way?

These people were not born with any special type of antistress gene. They have simply learned how to relax under pressure. They have developed effective mechanisms for coping with stress.

But chances are you're not the serene type. (Otherwise, why would you have turned to this chapter?) It's more likely you go through life stymied by an invisible obstacle that prevents relaxed, purposeful action during periods of stress. Without your conscious consent, something inside you makes a decision to see external pressures as stumbling blocks, rather than as opportunities to flex your emotional and mental muscles.

Fortunately, there is hope. You, too, can learn healthy ways to cope with stress. You can recognize and conquer your personal mountains.

Knowing your opponent is the first step in conquering it. To this end, experts divide stress into the following categories:

Healthy stress: Stressors that push you to perform better and achieve more than usual (such as a deadline at work or school, for example).

Unhealthy stress: Stressors that overtax you, wearing down your coping mechanisms, inhibiting your immune system, and predisposing you to illness.

It doesn't take a Ph.D. to figure out that what represents healthy stress for some people is a source of unhealthy stress for others. Some people thrive under pressure. Others wilt. The difference lies in how the individual interprets and reacts to the specific stressor. In simpler terms, by learning to change your reactions to stressful situations, you may be able to cope more effectively (and, perhaps, avoid some forms of stress-related disease). You can't control the world around you. But you can control the effects it has on you.

The rest of this chapter is dedicated to helping you minimize the damage caused by the unhealthy stressors in your life. It describes common stressors, helps you recognize the conditions that trigger your stress response, and offers techniques to help you cope. It is designed to help you reorganize, reprioritize, and relax. You may never learn to laugh in the face of stress. However, with a little practice, you'll soon be able to view difficult situations as challenging routes to personal growth.

Getting Help to Cope

If you don't feel better after trying the techniques presented here, or you feel stress severely detracts from your quality of life, seek professional help. This is nothing to be ashamed of. *If you don't think you can cope any longer, or if you have suicidal thoughts, get help.* You are not alone. People do want to help.

A therapist or counselor may be able to help you manage your time, help you deal with stress on the job, or help you improve your family relationships. And if you're in dire financial straits, you may be able to find a sliding-scale clinic that treats you at rates you can afford. See *Choosing the Right Therapist*, in Chapter 6, page 162, for advice on finding a therapist.

Identifying Your Stress Triggers

We all experience stress for different reasons. Situations that make one person want to run for the hills may be nothing more than a minor inconvenience or a challenge for another. The first step in conquering your own personal demons is to find out where they lurk.

Stressors usually fall into one or more categories:

Experts Divide Stress into Healthy Stress and Unhealthy Stress

A Variety of Factors Can Trigger Stress

Emotional stressors include fears and anxieties, such as worries about whether you'll be fired, or whether you'll make a good impression on a blind date. These stressors are very individual. For example, the pressure to pay your bills on time may overwhelm you, while your spouse may not give it a second thought until the final notices appear in the mailbox.

Family stressors can include changes in your relationship with your spouse, a divorce, or an extramarital affair. Other types of family stressors can be coping with an unruly adolescent or having a grown-up child leave home.

Social stressors arise in our interactions within our personal community. They can include dating, parties, public speaking, or the dynamics that occur within a group situation. As with emotional stressors, social stressors are very individualized (you may love speaking in public, while your colleague quakes in his boots at the mere suggestion).

Change stressors are feelings of stress related to any important changes in our lives. This may include moving, getting a new job, moving in with a significant other, or having a baby.

Chemical stressors are any drugs a person abuses, such as alcohol, nicotine, caffeine, or tranquilizers.

Work stressors are caused by the pressures of performing in the workplace (or in the home, if you are a homemaker). They may include tight deadlines, seemingly endless loads of laundry, a capricious boss, or long hours.

Decision stressors involve the stress caused by having to make important decisions, such as about the choice of a career or a mate.

Commuting stressors revolve around the pressures of getting to and from work. If you must drive long distances in heavy traffic, or if you spend every morning and evening packed tightly between other subway passengers, you may be experiencing commuting stress.

Phobic stressors are those caused by situations you are extremely afraid of, such as public speaking, airplanes, or heights.

Physical stressors are situations that overtax your body, such as working long hours without sleep, depriving yourself of healthy food, or standing on your feet all day. They may also include pregnancy, premenstrual syndrome, or excessive exercise.

Disease stressors are the products of long- or short-term health problems. These may cause stress (say, by keeping you in bed), be triggered by stress (such as herpes flare-ups), or may be aggravated by stress (such as migraine headaches).

Pain stressors can include acute pain (meaning it starts suddenly, is very painful, and usually does not last for a very long time) or chronic pain (meaning it continues over a long period of time). Like disease stressors, pain stressors can cause stress or be aggravated by stress.

Environmental stressors include forces in the world around us, such as noise, pollution, a lack of space, too much heat, or too much cold.

Using the above list as a reference, write down and categorize the main stressors in your life. You may even find some stressors fall into more than one category. Then read the next section for advice on how to start to eliminate, reduce, and cope with stress.

Taking Control of Stressors

After reading the previous section, and creating a (big?) list of things, people, and situations that cause you stress, you're ready to get down to business. In general, stress reduction is a three-part plan: You need to eliminate some stressors, reduce the potency of others, and learn to cope with the rest.

Eliminating stressors, at the outset, sounds like an attractive proposition. However, reality probably steps in and prohibits you from quitting your high-pressure job, divorcing your out-of-control teenagers, and selling your house the minute it gets dirty. The trick is to figure out which stressors you can realistically eliminate without resorting to extremes.

There are probably items on your list of stressors you can let go of, however. If having to clean the entire house on your day off every week is preventing you from having any leisure time, perhaps you can fit a cleaning lady into your budget. If ironing your husband's work shirts is keeping you up late at night, send them to the cleaners instead. If these seem like luxuries you can't afford, try to reorganize your budget a bit. Remember, your time is valuable, too.

Reducing the potency of your stressors is usually a more viable option than eliminating them entirely. For example, if you are having trouble concentrating on your work because of loud noise in the office, consider investing in a pair of earplugs. If your morning commute forces you to drive two hours in heavy traffic every day,

try another option, such as mass transit or a car pool, and bring along the morning paper or a good book.

Coping is undoubtedly your only option for the majority of the items on your list of stressors. However, this doesn't have to be as hopeless as it sounds. This chapter offers several techniques for learning to stay calm and clear-headed under pressure. As you master these techniques, even your biggest stressors will pose less and less of a threat.

Go back through your list of stressors and mark an E, an R, or a C for each item you can eliminate, reduce the potency of, or must learn to cope with. For the items marked with an E or an R, jot down any ideas you have on how to accomplish these goals (for example, sending shirts to the cleaners or buying ear plugs).

ELIMINATING STRESSORS

Once you've categorized your list of stressors into Es, Rs, and Cs, you're ready to get busy. Start by separating out your E-list—the list of stressors you've decided you can eliminate from your life.

Take a good gander at this new list. As you do, inhale deeply through your nose and exhale slowly through your mouth. If you're like most people, you should already be feeling just a tiny bit better. That's because your E-list is like a stress-busting SCUD missile. It is designed to hit and vaporize lots of little targets that make up your overall stress base.

If you've got a short E-list, consider the following ways to add items:

❑ **Is your schedule overloaded?** Do you feel as though you have little or no time for yourself? If so, go back through

Eliminate Some Stressors, Reduce the Potency of Others, and Learn to Cope with the Rest

To Reduce Stress, You Must Reorganize and Reprioritize

your list of stressors and see if there aren't more tasks you could hire out or delegate to others.

❑ **Do you have a physical ailment you haven't seen to?** Resolve to seek medical treatment.

❑ **Is your working environment (or your boss) beyond coping with?** If possible, make a note to start preparing your résumé and looking for a new job.

❑ **Is caffeine making you jittery?** Make a commitment to gradually reduce, then eliminate, your intake of tea, coffee, and soda.

❑ **Are you losing sleep because you're awakened every morning by the raised voices or pounding feet of your neighbor's children?** If you've tried every diplomatic approach you know, consider finding a new place to live.

The goal of this exercise is to be as creative as possible without being extreme. There's no harm in taking a strong stand on issues that have an appreciable effect on your sanity. The trick is to measure the impact of your stressors and weigh the costs of eliminating them against the toll they take on your health and well-being.

REDUCING STRESSORS

Like the E-list, the R-list is about controlling the external forces that repeatedly get the better of you. Although the E-list offers instant gratification by literally erasing your worries, the R-list requires a bit more creative fiddling. It is about reorganizing and reprioritizing. It is about finding ways to make some unavoidable stressors seem less threatening.

Here are some tried-and-true R-list techniques:

❑ **Invest in an appointment diary or electronic organizer.** The 1990s seems to be the era of the overloaded schedule. Between jobs that require ever-longer hours, extra-long commute times, and families that require as much attention and care as they ever did, most people spend many hours a day feeling as though they are being pulled in five directions at once. Does all this running cause stress? You bet. Factor in an appropriate fear of forgetting small details, and you've got quite a bit to worry about.

An appointment diary or a simple calendar like those banks, auto shops, and card stores give their customers free of charge (or if you want to get really fancy, an electronic organizer such as the Sharp Wizard or Apple's Newton) can't clear your schedule, but it can help ease the mental burden of having to remember what you're supposed to be doing within the next 15 minutes. And for some people, being able to quickly glance at the day's priorities can offer reassurance and a sense of direction.

❑ **Discover the underrated art of making lists.** Along with keeping a daily, weekly, and monthly schedule, list-making can also help clear an overly cluttered mind. While some people find lists (and yellow sticky notes on the bathroom mirror) a bit compulsive, others find them a therapeutic mental dumping ground.

The idea is to take your worries off of your mind and put them down on a list. There's no need to fret about forgetting something when you know it's safely noted on a piece of paper (or in the brain of a computer).

If you do begin to derive some relief from your lists, consider trying what the master list-makers do: Maintain two lists—one for short-term tasks you need to accomplish today, and a long-term list of goals you need to accomplish within the month or the year. Call the latter your "worry" list. It can include house- or car-maintenance needs, purchases you need to make, or tasks you need to accomplish (such as cleaning out the garage). It doesn't matter what you put down, only that you let yourself believe if it's on the list, you'll eventually take care of it.

❏ **Seek gentle compromise.** Many stressful situations—even those that can't be entirely eliminated—can be mitigated through negotiation. For example, if you are suffering because your boss keeps you at work until all hours of the night, try to make a deal with her: Suggest that you are happy to work late one or two nights a week, as long as you can go home on time the rest of the days. If a neighbor's stereo wakes you up at six o'clock every morning, negotiate a time for quiet and a time for noise. (For example, maybe it doesn't bother you to be woken up during the week, as long as you can sleep in on weekends.) You're not eliminating these stressors, but you are reducing their potency.

❏ **Reorganize your life.** Once you've started making a schedule and keeping lists, consult them each morning before you set off to face the day. Try to figure out where you can consolidate tasks to reduce the amount of energy it takes to accomplish them. See if you can put some items off until the weekend, when you'll have more time. Coordinate tasks, so you can accomplish more at once (such as running the washing machine while you fix dinner and paying the bills while the casserole is in the oven).

Think of every hour you organize away as an hour you'll be able to spend relaxing and de-stressing. If you organize well enough, you may stop feeling as though you're drowning under the weight of your myriad responsibilities.

❏ **Change your priorities.** Whenever you find yourself becoming truly overwhelmed, take five minutes and rank the items on your to-do list in order of importance. Then, put one foot in front of the other and proceed from top to bottom. Even if you can't accomplish everything, at least you can be secure in the fact that you've dealt with the highest imperatives.

If your list of daily tasks starts to spill over onto the next page and beyond, perform the ranking exercise described above, then draw a cutoff line. Move everything below the line to the next day. And don't panic: The world will survive without you until tomorrow.

The rest of this chapter is designed to help you deal with your C-list—the list of stressors you know you cannot eliminate or minimize. These strategies are aimed at helping you cope—and relax.

Learn the Art of Negotiation and Compromise

Let Go of the Reigns

Perfectionism and Stress Often Go Hand in Hand

Perfectionism is a character trait that can make a significant contribution to your stress level. If you feel a compulsive need to accomplish everything and accomplish it perfectly—you're doomed to feel a lot of pressure. Many people find perfectionism grows out of a need to control the world around them. As a result, perfectionists have a hard time delegating tasks and end up with even more on their overburdened to-do lists.

Here are some tips to help you temper your perfectionism:

❏ **Try the "how-important-is-it?" technique.** When you find yourself stressed-out because your house is a bit untidy or you're running late for an appointment, ask yourself what the consequences would be if you put off the cleaning or show up ten minutes late. Play out the worst-case scenario in your head (your mother-in-law dropping by and thinking you a bad housekeeper, your lunch date leaving the restaurant before you arrive).

Sometimes, it really may be important that you perform perfectly. Many times, however, you should be able to convince yourself the world will understand if you are human. The latter, more forgiving, attitude can help turn down the volume on your stress level. But *you* need to adopt this for-

giving attitude, too, and cut yourself some slack. Don't berate yourself over some dust bunnies and a missed luncheon appointment. Learn to *accurately* assess the relative importance of each stressful situation.

❏ **Delegate tasks.** Many people live by the motto "If you want it done right, you have to do it yourself." This kind of attitude can keep you overwhelmed by leaving you with an overly large volume of work to accomplish.

Employing the how-important-is-it technique described above, ask yourself what the worst-case scenario would be if you delegated a task to someone who performed it incompetently or, worse, didn't perform it at all. Then try playing out a more realistic scenario where, perhaps, the person accomplishes the task, albeit less perfectly than you would have done.

When you do delegate a task, take steps to reduce the margin of error, such as explicitly spelling out your expectations. And cultivate sources of help you trust to competently carry out your instructions.

❏ **Practice imperfection.** This is not to suggest you purposely flub important projects, simply that you give yourself a break once in a while. For example, when you're dog-tired, save the dishes for tomorrow and go to bed. When you're really overwhelmed, reschedule an appointment or renegotiate a deadline. The reduction in your stress level will make you even more productive when you do get a chance to take care of what you've put off.

Setting Aside "Me" Time

Feeling stressed is a strong signal from your subconscious mind that something is amiss. Somehow, you're not getting your needs met. More than likely, you're devoting more time to work, meeting other people's needs, or dealing with a distressing situation (such as job loss or divorce) than you are to taking good care of yourself. Even if you must continue to overextend yourself for a certain length of time, it's important to make space for yourself in your busy schedule.

Here are some tips for getting an adequate amount of "me" time:

❏ **Take a lunch break.** Even if you have a very demanding job, make an effort to schedule a midday break, even if just for 20 minutes or so. If necessary, tell your boss you've got to pick up a prescription, drop off a letter at the post office, or make a bank deposit. Use the time to walk around the block, collect yourself, breathe deeply, and relax. You'll be amazed at how much good a short break can do.

If you're a busy parent whose kids don't take naps, set them up with a coloring book or deposit them in the playpen for a few minutes, and take a time-out. Go into your bedroom, shut the door, and spend a few minutes rejuvenating. If your kids do take naps, resist the urge to rush through all your usual nap-time chores. Split the time in two, and reserve half for relaxation.

❏ **Leave one hour of time unscheduled every weekday and two (or more) hours a day on weekends.** Make it a rule and live by it. Even superhumans need a little time off.

During your hour, don't pay bills, clean dishes, or sort mail. Take the phone off the hook. Use this time to do relaxing activities: Take a bath, lie down, meditate, read a book, or watch television.

❏ **Go to bed early.** If you can't seem to convince the world to carry on without you for an hour or two, beg off and pretend to turn in early. Once alone, grab a good book or listen to relaxing music with headphones. And don't feel guilty: This is perfectly acceptable behavior.

Venting Feelings on Paper

Keeping a diary of your feelings can be a healthy way to blow off steam. It can also serve as an effective stress "barometer," allowing you to gauge the pressure you're under and its effect on you. Here are tips for keeping a stress journal:

❏ **Choose blank pages.** Don't buy one of those books that posts the date on top of every page. Instead, invest in a free-form notebook of some sort. This way, if you miss writing for many days, you won't feel guilty (this isn't school!).

Make Space for Yourself in Your Busy Schedule

Writing Can Help You Discover What You Think and Feel

❑ **Take a breath before you plunge in.** Before you start to write, spend a few minutes with your eyes closed, trying to get in touch with all the feelings you have at this moment. Are you angry? Overwhelmed? Tired? Relaxed? Sad? Happy? Open your eyes and write down all the feelings that come to mind.

❑ **Describe the day's events.** Write about what led you to have the feelings you have now. This might clue you in to some of the reasons you feel stressed.

❑ **List any worries lurking in the back of your mind.** Sometimes, we are not consciously aware of what is really bothering us. Getting it down on paper may give you some insight.

❑ **Try writing a note of encouragement to yourself.** Writing to yourself as though you were writing to a dear friend who needed cheering up can be an effective way to give yourself the support and caring you may be lacking.

❑ **Draw pictures.** Sometimes, words may not be adequate to express what you feel inside. At these times, illustrating your feelings may be easier and more therapeutic.

❑ **Free-associate.** When you feel blocked, try an exercise used in psychology as well as in writing classes: Simply write whatever comes to mind, even if it seems to start from nowhere or makes little sense. Omit punctuation entirely, if it improves your flow of thought. Certainly, don't stop to correct yourself. Just allow your thoughts to flow freely. When you run out of steam, go back and read what you've written. You may be surprised to discover previously hidden clues to your emotional state.

❑ **Rewrite reality.** If a situation left you feeling frustrated or angry during the day, write it down the way it happened. Then try rewriting it with a new ending, the way you would have liked it to happen.

❑ **Don't allow your journal writing to become yet another chore.** If you feel as though writing in your journal is just one more task you've got to slog through before you can go to bed, try another approach. Remember, this exercise is designed to help you release your pent-up anxieties, not provide you with additional ones. Try to see your journal-writing time as a way to let go of the day's stress.

❑ **If you're angry, use every expletive you can think of.** This book is for your eyes only. Go wild. You can always rip up the pages later. Write down elaborate fantasies about escaping your life and moving to a deserted island with nothing to occupy you but walking on the beach. Write down what you would say to your boss in a perfect world where no one ever got fired.

Meditation for Skeptics

The word "meditation" may conjure up visions of gurus with shaved heads, flowing robes, and prayer beads, but it needn't. Meditation can be a very practical, nonreligious technique for relaxing, reducing stress, and clearing your head. Consistent practice helps you become better and better at stilling your busy mind. At that point, you can tap into that stillness whenever you feel your stress level start to rise.

There are hundreds, perhaps thousands, of ways to meditate. To describe just a few:

- Sitting silently with your eyes closed, focusing on your breathing

- Movement, such as the martial art *t'ai chi chu'an*

- Sitting facing a blank wall (to empty the mind)

- Sitting with the eyes closed and repeating a single word or phrase, called a *mantra*

- Sitting silently and staring at a candle or other object

- Silent prayer

With so many options, how can you tell what method is right for you? First, you should consider your natural inclinations. If you have a hard time sitting still, you may wish to start with a form of dynamic (movement-oriented) meditation, such as t'ai chi chu'an (see *Martial Arts*, page 144). Otherwise, try one of the sitting meditations. Make sure you give your selection a fair trial of at least two weeks. After that, if you feel it's not right for you, try something else.

Meditation is not easy, especially for people who are prone to high stress levels. Stilling the mind requires a great amount of discipline, self-control, and practice. It may take awhile before you see any fruits of your labor. However,

the benefits are very real (just ask the millions of people around the world who swear by it). With practice, you will gain a peace of mind you may never have thought possible.

The following are two sample meditations you can try. You are also free to design your own. There is no right way to meditate. It all depends on what works for you. Pick a time of the day when you can be alone and undisturbed for at least 15 minutes. Take the phone off the hook, tell your family to leave you alone, and close yourself in a quiet room. At first, you may not be able to sit for more than a few minutes. If necessary, set a timer for five minutes and slowly increase your time with each session. And remember, it's not the length of time that counts, but the quality of the time spent. Enjoy!

Sample Meditation #1: Breathing

Find a comfortable sitting position, either on the floor with your legs crossed ("Indian style"), or on a comfortable chair or sofa. Sit with your back straight, abdomen lifted, your arms resting comfortably on your knees or beside you.

Close your eyes and take a deep breath in through your nose. Notice how the breath feels as it enters your nostrils, and follow its path as it flows deep into your diaphragm. Allow your abdomen to expand as you fill your lungs with air. Hold the breath for a moment, noticing how it feels. Then, exhale through your mouth, following the breath's path with your mind and allowing your chest and abdomen to deflate as your lungs empty. Repeat throughout the duration of your session.

This exercise sounds much easier than it is. You may find you can concentrate on your breath

Stilling the Mind Requires a Great Amount of Discipline, Self-Control, and Practice

Mastering Progressive Relaxation Is Like Discovering the Volume-Control Knob for Your Stress

only for a very short time before your mind begins to wander. Do not criticize yourself for this. This type of concentration takes years to develop! When you notice your mind wandering, simply lead it back to your breath, again and again. The more you practice, the more you will notice an improvement in your concentration.

Sample Meditation #2: Repeating a Mantra

Mantra meditation is based on ancient Hindu practices but was popularized in the United States by the transcendental meditation (TM) movement. It consists of repeating a single word or phrase throughout the entire session.

Mantras are usually of a spiritual nature. Many are in the ancient Indian language Sanskrit, or in Hindi, the modern Indian language. Some examples are "Om," which means peace, love, and God in Sanskrit, and "Ram," which is another Sanskrit name for God. Some Christians chant the name of Jesus or repeat a short prayer. But you can choose any mantra you like, as long as it conjures peaceful images for you.

Choose a mantra and continue as follows:

Find a comfortable sitting position, either on the floor with your legs crossed ("Indian style") or on a comfortable chair or sofa. Sit with your back straight, abdomen lifted, arms resting comfortably on your knees or beside you. Allow your breath to settle in a slow, natural rhythm. Begin to repeat your mantra, saying it or chanting it rhythmically. If you do not wish to say your mantra aloud, you can repeat it silently to yourself.

Try to keep your thoughts focused on your mantra. If they wander, gently lead your attention back to the word or phrase you are repeating.

Progressive Relaxation

Progressive relaxation is similar to meditation in the sense it usually requires sitting or lying down with the eyes closed. But it is a bit more physical in that it involves tightening and relaxing all of the muscles in the body. It is based on the principle that people hold residual tension in their muscles, even when they try to relax. Tightening the muscles increases the awareness of where the tension is stored. It also emphasizes the contrast to the relaxation you feel when you release the tension.

Mastering progressive relaxation helps you become more in tune with your stress level. You will notice muscle tension when it develops and will learn how to release it without much conscious effort. The effect is like discovering the volume-control knob for your stress level.

The following is a standard progressive-relaxation technique. Ideally, you should practice it once or twice a day for a period of 20 to 30 minutes. Try to wait a full hour after eating before performing this exercise, or you may fall asleep. Make sure you will be undisturbed for the duration of the exercise. You should lie down or sit in a comfortable chair (such as a recliner). Loosen any restrictive clothing and remove any jewelry that is uncomfortable.

For each muscle group listed below, perform this sequence:

138

1. Isolate the muscle and tense it up as tightly as you can. Hold this tension for about five seconds.

2. Release the tension. Imagine a wave of relaxation washing through the muscle.

3. Inhale deeply, then exhale, allowing the muscle to relax even further.

The following is the sequence of muscle areas to tighten and relax during progressive relaxation:

- Forehead
- Eyes
- Mouth (open widely)
- Tongue (press it against the roof of the mouth)
- Jaw
- Neck
- Shoulders
- Arms (flex your biceps muscles)
- Hands (make a fist)
- Chest
- Back
- Stomach
- Buttocks
- Thighs
- Calves
- Feet (curl your toes under)
- Feet (bend your toes back, up toward your knees)

After you have gone through the whole sequence, tense up your whole body and hold the tension for five seconds. Then release. Feel a sense of calm washing over you, bathing every muscle group.

Take a few more minutes to experience the relaxation. Breathe deeply in and out. When you are ready to end your session, slowly begin to wiggle your fingers and toes, then open your eyes.

If, during the course of your day, you start to feel tension, try to recall the feeling you had at the end of the progressive-relaxation exercise. Take a deep breath, then exhale while silently telling your muscles to relax.

Visualization and Affirmation

Remember the story of *The Little Engine Who Could?* Its main character was a determined little locomotive who puffed up a hill, repeating to himself "I think I can. I think I can." This mental reinforcement was more than just Pollyanna-ish positive thinking. The engine's belief in himself actually gave him the strength to achieve his goal.

The story described above is more than just a children's fable. As adults, we can interpret it as a reminder of the power of belief.

How does this relate to coping with stress? Simple: If you believe you can face stressful situations head on, remaining calm and relaxed throughout, you can. Visualization and affirmation are two techniques for cultivating the kind of belief that can help you scale your own personal mountains.

VISUALIZATION
A Positive Outcome

Visualization is akin to a mental rehearsal conducted in advance of the actual event (say, for example, a speech you have to give). The idea is to repeatedly conjure an imaginary picture of a situation

Visualization and Affirmation Help You Face Stressful Situations Head-On

The More Often You Practice Your Visualization, the More Powerful It Will Become

turning out the way you want it to (you see yourself confidently delivering your flawless speech to the sound of deafening applause). In this manner, you attempt to "train" the subconscious into leading you toward success.

The technique is as easy as using your imagination. Here's an example of how you would use visualization to help you cope with the stress of asking your boss for a raise:

❑ Close your eyes and take a few deep breaths. If you like, you can perform the progressive-relaxation exercise described in the previous section.

❑ Form a mental picture of yourself getting ready to go to work. You put on your most professional-looking outfit. You are confident and relaxed, ready to face your 9 A.M. appointment with your boss.

❑ See yourself calmly entering your boss' office. You flash her your most self-assured smile and extend your hand for a strong handshake.

❑ Without a single hint of self-doubt in your voice, you diplomatically state your purpose: You feel your performance has been strong throughout the last months. You met or beat every deadline your boss set for you. You were on time or early for work, even during the most adverse weather conditions. You haven't taken a sick day in six months. You enjoy your job and are anticipating a bright and productive future with the company. And you feel it's time the company reviewed your performance and gave you a ten percent raise.

❑ Throughout this imagined tête-a-tête, picture your palms warm and dry; your heartbeat

slow and even. Since you believe in what you are saying and feel sure the boss appreciates your performance, you do not fear you will be turned down. You smile again and await the boss' reply.

❑ Picture your superior nodding thoughtfully and returning your smile. Then imagine that she assures you your good work has not gone unnoticed. She says she will consult with her boss and recommend you get a ten percent increase. She'll get back to you by the end of the week.

❑ You stand up, thank your boss for her time, and shake her hand. With an unassuming air of confidence, you leave the office.

You can design a similar visualization for any situation that causes you stress, such as coming home and facing a sink full of dishes or completing a project on a high-pressure deadline. The more often you practice your visualization, the more powerful it will become. Try to run through it a few times a day for several days. You may find it makes a real dent in your stress level.

A Negative Outcome

Visualization can also be useful for improving your reactions to failure and disappointment. Say, in the above scenario, that your boss responds angrily to your request for a raise by listing all of your shortcomings, then threatening to fire you. If you're like most people, your stress response would probably go into overdrive.

❑ Try the visualization again—this time with the most nightmarish outcome you can realistically imagine.

❏ Instead of feeling your blood pressure rise and your heart beating in your throat, conjure an image of yourself listening calmly and objectively to what your boss has to say. See yourself nodding sincerely and saying that you'll give her opinions some thought.

❏ Practice separating your feelings of self-worth from the consequences of the situation.

Remember that regardless of what anybody says or does to you, it remains your responsibility to be your own best friend. It's up to you to consistently reaffirm your dignity and worth as a person, even in the face of adversity. Visualization is one way to accomplish this.

AFFIRMATION

Affirmation—which involves repeating a positive message to yourself (like the little engine did)—is an effective adjunct to visualization. It serves to counter the negative, doubting messages we often give ourselves when we face stressful situations. Here's how to employ affirmation, again with the example of asking your boss for a raise:

❏ Sit down with a piece of paper and a pen and draft a positive message to yourself in strong, decisive language, using the present tense. The message should be concise—no more than a sentence or two; for example: "I am a diligent, conscientious worker. I deserve a generous raise," or "My boss sees me as a strong performer. I feel calm and relaxed about asking her for a raise."

❏ Copy your affirmation 25 times, twice a day. Also, repeat it to yourself ten or more times, twice a day.

❏ Post copies of your affirmation on your bathroom mirror, on your refrigerator, and on the dashboard of your car. The more you read it, the more it will sink in.

Biofeedback

Many of the stress-management techniques described in this chapter—meditation, progressive relaxation, visualization, and affirmation—are all about training yourself to relax and controlling your responses to stress.

How can you tell whether you are really releasing your tension and controlling your stress level? You can look to your body for answers.

At the most physical level, stress is what is known as the fight-or-flight response: It is the nervous system's way of preparing itself to deal with adversity (flee a predator, take on an enemy, and so on). It can manifest in the following ways:

● A raised blood pressure level

● A surge of adrenaline

● A quickening heartbeat

● Rapid, shallow breathing

● Constricted blood vessels that cause the hands and feet to feel cold

Biofeedback is a system developed to monitor the physical stress responses and to report (or "feed back") information on those responses to the person being monitored. As the individual tries to relax, he can get an immediate idea of how effective his efforts are. With practice, the person

Biofeedback Is One Way to Control Your Body's Response to Stress

learns to control his physiological stress responses.

If you think you would benefit from biofeedback, ask your family physician or internist to refer you to a qualified professional who has a biofeedback machine and can instruct you.

You can also do a limited form of biofeedback on your own using a heartbeat meter (available at some sporting good stores). While this is an expensive item (most cost over $100; some are closer to $150), it allows you to witness the continuous changes in your heartbeat. With the use of the relaxation techniques described in this chapter, you can practice slowing your heartbeat. As you progress, you'll find you can draw on this training to calm yourself when you encounter stressful situations and feel your pulse quicken.

Massage

A Massage Can Rub Away Tension and Troubles

Many people find massage a luxurious and pleasant way to relax and relieve muscle tension. Not only does it give you an opportunity to lie down with your eyes closed and have someone pamper you, but it can also help relieve the pain caused by muscles that have worked themselves into knots.

If you've got a willing partner, try this relaxation ritual:

❑ Soak yourself in a soothing tub of warm water for about 20 minutes (use scented bath salts, if you wish). While you soak, have your partner set up a room with candles, a potpourri burner, and soothing music.

❑ After you get out and dry yourself, lie down in the massage room and cover yourself with a sheet or light blanket.

❑ Have your partner rub you down all over, making sure to adjust the pressure of the strokes to your taste (a scented oil is a nice touch). Your partner should uncover one body part at a time, then cover it again when it's time to move on to the next part (so you don't get a chill).

❑ As long as you're not modest, ask for a full-body massage, starting with the scalp and face and proceeding down through the neck, shoulders, back, buttocks, legs, and feet. If you feel self-conscious about being so exposed, simply have your partner rub your neck, shoulders, and back. Either way, you're sure to feel the tensions of the day floating away!

If you don't have a partner to trade massages with, you can opt to pay for a professional massage therapist. Some masseuses will come to your home (although you should probably meet him or her elsewhere first), and others will have you come to their office. Choosing a massage therapist out of the Yellow Pages may not be the best idea (you want to make sure you can really trust a person you will remove your clothes for). Instead, try getting a referral from a friend, a local chiropractor, or a health club.

When you speak to a potential candidate over the phone, ask the practitioner whether he or she has had any formal training. Ask about rates (which usually range from $35 to $60 or more for an hour-long massage) and what forms of payment are acceptable. Tell the masseuse about any special health conditions you may have (including pregnancy) and ask whether he or she has any experience in dealing with your condition. Lastly, ask what style of massage the therapist is trained in.

The following is a quick lexicon of the most common massage therapies.

Reflexology: A massage therapy that focuses solely on the feet. It is based on an ancient Egyptian theory that points on the feet correspond to specific body parts.

Sports, or deep-tissue, massage: Therapeutic, deep-tissue massage specifically aimed at treating and restoring flexibility to injured areas of the body.

Swedish: Gentle stroking and kneading aimed at improving circulation of blood to constricted muscles. This is what most people picture when they hear the word "massage."

Shiatsu (acupressure): Similar to acupuncture but without the needles. The practitioner puts pressure on points on the body believed to correspond to the major organs. This system is based on Chinese medical theory.

If you cannot find a reputable massage therapist in your area, contact the American Massage Therapy Association at 708-864-0123. This organization can refer you to a trained, certified practitioner in your area.

Yoga

Like meditation, yoga has been somewhat tarnished by a fringe, hippie-ish image. But something that's been going strong for 4,000 years must have something to it, right? The truth is, the goal of yoga need not be to contort your body into complicated, pretzel-like positions while reciting ancient Hindu scriptures. It can be a great way to manage stress, improve flexibility, release muscle tension, and relax.

Medical studies have turned up many health benefits to practicing yoga, including relieving chronic pain, inhibiting secretion of stomach acid, calming asthma, lowering blood pressure, and improving the range of motion in arthritic joints. The Lamaze breathing techniques so many women use during childbirth originated from yoga. Even the renowned cardiologist, Dean Ornish, M.D., uses yoga in his Sausalito, California-based heart-disease program. Students need not become yoga masters to reap its benefits: The positive side effects of slow, relaxed breathing and gentle stretching show up almost immediately.

There are many types of yoga, but most center around a series of poses (positions) held for several minutes. While holding the poses, students breathe slowly and deeply, which produces, some say, feelings of tranquility and well-being. Many classes teach stretching routines and visualization techniques. Some classes may also have a period of meditation at the end, where students sit silently with their eyes closed and focus on deep abdominal breathing.

If you're interested in trying yoga, you can rent or purchase one of the handful of instructional video tapes on the market, or join a class. Look in the Yellow Pages under "Yoga" for a program near you. Some hospitals and clinics offer yoga classes as well.

Yoga Is a Time-Honored Way to Manage Stress

Most of the Martial Arts Are a Form of Active Meditation

Martial Arts

Most types of exercise tout stress reduction as a pleasant side effect. But many forms of martial arts (primarily the non-competitive types) go one step further, emphasizing the connection between mind and body and making relaxation and spiritual development primary points of focus.

When you think about martial arts, chances are you think about violence and combat (after all, the word "martial" means war). And it is true most of these disciplines took root in the traditions of the ancient Asian warriors. However, most of the martial arts focus first on self-control and mental and physical awareness and second on martial skills. Students develop a respect and empathy for their opponents, instead of anger or hostility. They seek to defuse, not engender, conflict. Inner peace and awareness—not brute force or excessive physical strength—are primary keys to mastery of these arts. They are, in fact, a form of active meditation.

In Japanese, "do" (pronounced "doe") means "the way to enlightenment." Therefore, the Japanese martial arts whose names end in "do" focus more on spiritual development than on combat. These disciplines—in addition to the Chinese martial art t'ai chi chu'an—are probably the most effective for those seeking an active, physical route to stress reduction.

Here is a brief introduction to the martial arts that can be most effective for stress reduction:

T'ai chi chu'an (tye-chee'-chwahn): A noncompetitive Chinese system of exercise characterized by very slow, formalized sequences of movement. Among all the martial arts, this is probably the most meditative.

Aikido (eye-kee'-doe): A modern Japanese martial art that focuses on spiritual development and blending with or defusing an attack (so as not to harm the attacker). Its founder, Morihei Ueshiba, called aikido "the loving protection of all beings." His goal in creating it was to find a technique for harmonious resolution of conflict.

Judo: An unarmed martial art that focuses primarily on throwing and rolling, as opposed to the kicking and punching so prevalent in karate.

Tae kwan do (tye-kwahn'-doe): A Korean military martial art that integrates more kicking and punching than judo.

Kendo: "The way of the sword" involves practicing combat with bamboo swords.

If you are interested in trying any of these martial arts, look in the Yellow Pages under "Martial Arts" to find a program near you. Most centers have classes for men, women, and children of all ages, sizes, and strengths.

Dealing with Stress in the Moment

So far, the techniques for coping with stress described in this chapter have dealt with ways to reduce your overall stress level through time-and-task management, relaxation practices, visualization, and affirmation. While spending half an hour meditating or repeating affirmations every morning may help you start your day feeling calm and peaceful, how can it help you when you run into a stressful situation at 3:00 in the afternoon?

Well, the theory goes that when you become skilled at achieving a state of relaxation, you can easily return to it within seconds, whenever you need to. For example, when a client moves up a deadline at the exact moment the staff member responsible for the job quits in a huff, you may feel your pulse begin to race and your anxiety level start to rise. However, instead of panicking, you can remember the abdominal breathing you learned in yoga class and start to use it. Ideally, your heartbeat slows down and you begin to relax.

However, there is more to coping with acute stress than physiological relaxation. Experts find there are usually one of two emotional states involved in stressful situations: anxiety or anger. Finding effective ways to cope with these emotions can turn a potentially stressful situation into a pleasant challenge.

One technique for coping with anxiety and anger is changing the way you view adversity. You can do this by reprogramming what you tell yourself when you encounter difficult situations. The sidebar *Lighten Up* illustrates positive substitutions for the destructive messages we often tell ourselves when we are anxious or angry.

LIGHTEN UP

ANXIETY

Destructive message	Positive self-talk
I can't handle this.	I need to make a plan to accomplish this.
Why does this always happen to me?	I can handle whatever comes my way.
I'm getting nervous.	A bit of nervousness might give me the edge I need to come out ahead in this situation.
I'm going to make a fool of myself.	I plan to do my best and maintain my dignity, no matter the outcome.
This person hates me. I just know it.	I am a likable, competent person. Other people's opinions of me are inconsequential.

ANGER

Destructive message	Positive self-talk
This person is really getting my dander up.	I'm feeling a bit angry, but I can handle it.
This situation is going to escalate into a fight.	We can deal with this peacefully.
This person had better watch his step.	I'm going to keep my cool and be as diplomatic as possible.
I'll look like an idiot if I back down.	I'm going to stay focused on what I want out of this situation and figure out how to get it—regardless of how I appear to anyone else.

Practice Positive Self-Talk

Review the messages and practice some positive self-talk. If you simply can't shake your negative feelings, or if you have any self-destructive thoughts, seek help from a professional. Chapter 6 contains a checklist (page 153) that can help you determine if what you're feeling is more than stress. (Also see the section, *There's Help for Depression*, page 160.) Counseling can help you determine the source of your stress, help you cope with your stress, and help put you back on the road to self-confidence.

Of course, long-term bad habits are impossible to change overnight, but you can practice substituting more positive messages for your old standbys. Here's how:

❑ Read the sections on progressive relaxation (page 138) and visualization (page 139) in this chapter.

❑ Perform the progressive-relaxation exercise, going through all the muscle groups until you have reached a state of deep relaxation.

❑ Choose a situation you fear will be a stressful experience. Begin to visualize the scene.

❑ Next, instead of viewing the scene from outside of your body, try to listen to the self-talk going on inside your head. Are you getting angry or anxious? What are you telling yourself?

❑ Practice substituting positive self-talk for any destructive messages you give yourself.

You can use this exercise once or twice a day for a week or two before a stressful event you are anticipating. The more you rehearse the positive self-talk, the easier and more automatic it becomes.

Consider a Stress-Busting "Vacation"

If you've been riding yourself hard and are starting to feel as though you've reached the breaking point, maybe you should pack it in and take a few days off. A vacation might be just what you need to reduce stress and lift your spirits.

If stress-relief is your goal, you want to make sure the vacation you take is one that helps you wind down—not gear you up even more (heavy traffic, crowds, and long lines aren't exactly relaxing). Where can you go to really take the edge off? Here are some ideas:

❑ **Check into a spiritual retreat.** Believe it or not, there are still places in this country where you can go to completely escape the hustle and bustle of the modern world and experience peace and quiet. Many of these places are monasteries, abbeys, and spiritual retreats that provide lodgings for visitors of all faiths.

What can you expect when you take this kind of meditative vacation? It depends on where you choose to go:

• Accommodations may range from large rooms with private baths to modest monk's cells with shared bathrooms. Most places welcome men, women, and children.

• Some places require guests to participate in their religious rituals or pitch in and help with chores, but many do not.

You are usually expected to change the sheets on the bed when you leave.

- Prices usually run from $12 to $50 per night, including meals.

- Visitors are expected to be unintrusive and respectful. Most of these spiritual oases are quiet and contemplative. Guests are expected to behave as the members of the community do.

- You will need to make a reservation, since many spiritual centers book retreat groups weeks or months ahead.

Find out about spiritual sanctuaries in your area by talking with local clergypeople. There are also directories available, such as *Sanctuaries: A Guide to Lodgings in Monasteries, Abbeys, and Retreats of the United States,* by Jack and Marcia Kelly. Check your local library or bookstore.

❑ **Get pampered at a spa.** At wit's end? Treat your frazzled nerves to a luxurious spa vacation. Indulge in languorous massages, soothing jacuzzi soaks, invigorating workouts, and healthful gourmet cuisine. In no time, you'll be back on your feet, stress-free, and ready to face your life's toughest challenges.

What does a spa have to offer that other vacations don't?

- One-stop shopping. At a spa, you usually pay one price for the whole kit-and-caboodle: meals, workouts, classes, facilities, and instruction are all included. Certain services (such as massage, facials, body wraps, and so on) are included at some spas, extra at others. However, you don't have to wander around a resort town looking for a good gym; everything you need is easily accessible.

- A stress-free atmosphere. A spa vacation won't have you frantically running around, waiting in lines, or purchasing earplugs to block out the noise of party-happy fellow travelers. Spas are geared toward stress relief. The staff does everything it can to make sure your visit is as pleasant and relaxed as possible.

- Healthful food. For many health-conscious travelers, a vacation may turn into a never-ending search for meals that won't add unwanted pounds or send their cholesterol levels soaring. At spas, however, low-fat cuisine is a given. However, don't imagine for a second you'll go hungry. Most spas tout top-of-the line gourmet chefs who make eating healthfully a true pleasure.

There are spas all over the world, each with its own distinctive flavor and range of facilities and services. Many boast beautiful, exotic locales and scenic landscapes. You can contact your travel agent for more information, or call Spa-Finders, an agency that refers you to a spa that meets your needs, and makes all the necessary reservations and arrangements. Spa-Finders can be reached at 800-255-7727 (exclusive of New York state), or at 212-924-6800.

If a week-long vacation doesn't fit into your schedule (or your budget), consider a quick refresher at a local day spa. Day spas don't usually focus on fitness as other spas do, but they offer a range of stress-dissolving services, such as massage, facials, manicures, and pedicures. To locate a day spa in your area, try the Yellow Pages under "Beauty Salons," "Massage," and "Skin Care."

Consider a "Meditative Vacation"

Turn Your Home into a Weekend Mini-Retreat

You Can Bring a Stress-Bashing Vacation into Your Home

If your brimming schedule or your financial situation makes it impossible for you to get away, consider bringing a relaxing, stress-bashing vacation home. You can integrate almost all of the elements of a spa vacation—at a much less expensive price—and end up relaxed and serene on Monday morning, ready to face yet another hectic week.

The following is a guide to designing a weekender you won't soon forget.

Two weeks ahead:

❏ **Start to think about what you want out of your weekend.** Would you simply like some peace and quiet, some time alone? Would you like your spouse or a friend to join you? How would you like to spend the time? How about a challenging workout, 18 holes of golf, a pick-up game of basketball, or a long walk and a picnic? Maybe you'd like a massage or just an afternoon nap in a sunny spot. Make a list of the elements you'd like to integrate.

❏ **Clear your schedule.** Cancel or reschedule all your appointments, and make time to do all your weekend chores ahead of time. This means no lawn mowing, no cleaning, no laundry. It won't be a vacation if you have a plethora of obligations to attend to.

❏ **Inform your family of your plans.** Maybe your spouse could use this weekend to visit his parents. Maybe he'd even like to bring the kids along (starting to get the idea?). Or maybe Grandma and Grandpa or Uncle Jeff and Aunt Susan would like to have the kids for a weekend if you and your spouse want to relax together. Even if you can't entirely rid your home of distractions, perhaps you can reserve some space that's off-limits to everyone but you. If all else fails, plan to use nap time and bedtime to its fullest and include your family in some of your plans.

❏ **Make a list of needed supplies.** Using the list of activities you want to do as a guide, jot down the ingredients you'll need to make it happen. Massage oil, workout or stretching videos, and your favorite music (keep it low key, though) can all be part of the package. Go ahead, be self-indulgent!

❏ **Make appointments.** If you'd like to treat yourself to any professional services (massage, facials, manicures, and so forth), make your appointments now. If you need to book a tee time at the golf course or a racquetball court at the health club, do that, too. You won't want to miss out just because you waited too long.

One week ahead:

❏ **Make a schedule.** Map out a general plan for your weekend. This way, you know exactly what you can look forward to. You'll also know exactly what you'll need to make it happen the way you intend it to. (See the sample schedule.) But the plan is just a guide; don't let it turn you into a clock watcher on your weekend "off."

❑ **Append your list of supplies.** Go through your schedule and add any supplies you didn't write down the first time around. Don't forget a grocery list of healthful, easy-to-prepare foods.

❑ **Plan your meals.** Perhaps you don't want to prepare any meals during your weekend. Consider cooking ahead and freezing foods, or decide on cold dishes you can make a day ahead.

❑ **Go shopping.** Mine health-food stores, herb shops, and department stores for all they're worth. Consider a new workout outfit, new balls for your tennis match, new tees for your golf game. Preparation is half the fun.

One day ahead:

❑ **Buy perishable items.** Go to the grocery store and get everything you'll need for the whole weekend (stay out of the stores on your "vacation"). On the way home, pick up a big bouquet of fresh flowers to greet you on the first morning.

❑ **Go to the video store.** Video stores hold a treasure trove of workout, relaxation, and yoga videos. Also consider a travel video: If you can't get away, you can always visit far away places on video. You can also pick up a movie or two if it contributes to your stress-relief efforts. You're the boss.

❑ **Plan shorter activities as well as longer ones.** If you need ideas for what to do during your vacation at home, see the sidebar *Simple Stress Busters*.

SAMPLE DAY'S SCHEDULE

8:00 Wake, dress.

8:15 Have a quick glass of freshly squeezed orange juice, then head outside for a brisk walk. As you walk, concentrate on taking deep cleansing breaths. Stretch your muscles, observe the world around you.

9:15 Breakfast on whole-grain waffles; fresh, sliced strawberries; and nonfat vanilla yogurt (or whatever strikes your fancy). Linger over a cup of tea and the morning paper.

10:30 Perform a low-impact aerobic workout along with a video, or do a stretch routine for the workout activity that follows.

11:30 Participate in your activity of choice. (Don't forget a good lunch!)

5:00 Come home, pour yourself your favorite beverage, turn on some soft music, and sit down in your comfiest chair. Pull out some paper and a pen and spend time writing about what you would do if you won the lottery. Let your imagination roam.

6:00 Prepare yourself a dinner of flour tortillas filled with steamed shrimp and vegetables, low-fat cheddar cheese, salsa, and nonfat sour cream. Add a side of corn on the cob and pears poached in zinfandel for dessert.

8:00 Perform yoga or, if you're sharing your "spa" experience, share a massage.

9:00 Read a captivating novel or watch a movie.

11:00 Turn in.

❑　　❑　　❑

Experiment with Stress Busters

If reading a book on a Saturday afternoon just makes you feel guilty, then it's not the right stress buster for you. If sending the kids to your parents for the weekend so you and your wife can be alone just causes you to worry about whether Grandma and Grandpa can cope, you won't be able to relax. The point is, you have to do what works for you.

Some people relieve stress through physical activity—strenuous exercise, sports, gardening, cleaning. Others do it through watching old movies or comedies or putting on headphones and "vegging" out to their favorite music. Video games may work for some people; for those who are particularly competitive, they may be more stressful and frustrating. Experiment till you find what soothes your savage beast.

Here are some everyday stress-reduction tips:

❏ **If you're feeling stressed at work, take 10.** If possible, find a spot where you can be alone for a few minutes—a conference room, an empty office, the bathroom. Focus on your breathing and on relaxing your tense muscles. Or walk to the farthest point away from your work area, then return.

❏ **At home, before you do anything else, shed the work day—literally.** Remove the clothing you wore to work and get into something comfortable, even if you wear casual clothes to work.

❏ **Change your environment.** One of the most effective stress reduction techniques is a change of scenery—for a week, an hour, or even for a few minutes. Go for a walk or a drive. Sit in a park, or find a quiet spot, perhaps in your local library. Some people find people-watching at a shopping mall or train station a good way to take their mind off their troubles.

❏ **Have friends for dinner, but ask everyone to bring a dish.** That way you can spend time with friends but not worry about all the preparation. You can relax a bit—and sample a variety of dishes!

SIMPLE STRESS BUSTERS

❏ Play a game.

❏ Walk on the beach.

❏ Do something that made you happy when you were a kid—buy ice cream from the street vendor, build a sand castle, run through a sprinkler, make S'mores.

❏ Drive under the speed limit.

❏ Listen to your old phonograph records.

❏ Take off your watch.

❏ Fly a kite.

❏ Take a bubble bath.

❏ Watch the sun rise.

❏ Watch the sun set.

❏ Read the Sunday newspaper from first page to last at one sitting.

❏ Stop for coffee or lemonade at a cafe that has seating outdoors.

❏ Remain at the supper table after your meal and talk with your family.

❏ Turn off the TV.

❏ Return to the days of yore: Share an electricity–free evening with your family.

❏ Write a letter to an old friend.

❏ Write a poem.

❏ Draw or paint a picture.

❏ Light some candles to create a relaxing atmosphere.

❏   ❏   ❏

CHAPTER 6

EMOTIONAL

AND

MENTAL HEALTH

Our emotional and mental health are as important to our complete wellness as our physical health. In fact, doctors are discovering just how closely the two are related. Research has shown, for example, that emotional stress can lower the immune system's response, making the body more vulnerable to illnesses. Likewise, physical ailments can induce mental health problems such as depression.

All of us have to cope with day-to-day stresses—work, relationships, money. At times, we may also face trials such as the death of a loved one or a serious illness. This chapter can teach you about common mental health problems—how to recognize them, what you can do to help yourself, and when you need to seek professional help.

❑ ❑ ❑

Is It the Blues or Depression?

Mental Health Experts Define Three Basic Types of Depression

Life has its stresses, and everyone, at some time or another, feels emotionally down or luxuriates in a bit of self-pity. But clinical depression—depression serious enough to require treatment—is different. When you're clinically depressed, you have no energy. You feel listless, hopeless. You may withdraw from friends and family. Eventually, if the depression goes untreated, you're unable to function normally in your life. You may think about or even attempt suicide.

Mental health experts define three basic types of depression:

Major depression: If you're severely depressed, the sad, frustrated, pessimistic feelings are very intense and last for two weeks or longer. You may think these feelings will last forever.

Chronic depression (dysthymia): If you're chronically depressed, the joyless feelings may come and go, but they usually persist for more than half the time. Some people with this less intense, longer-lasting form of depression feel constantly depressed, never realizing their permanently gray view of the world isn't normal.

Bipolar depression: Also called *manic-depressive disorder*, bipolar depression causes the person to swing widely from emotional highs to emotional lows. If you have bipolar depression, you probably experience periods where you feel incredibly excited, energetic, and even euphoric. However, these periods are followed by periods of low energy and depression.

Causes of Depression

Mental health experts say depression is either *reactive* (also called situational) or *endogenous*.

Reactive depression: Nearly everyone experiences reactive, or situational, depression in response to a specific event or series of events such as the death of a loved one, a divorce, or a physical illness. A person with reactive depression may feel anxious, have difficulty sleeping, and avoid friends and family. The good news is that situational depression usually lasts days, weeks, or months as opposed to years. As the situation that has prompted the depression resolves or the grief from it is dulled by time, the person usually begins to feel better.

Endogenous depression: Unlike reactive depression, endogenous depression originates inside the person rather than from external events. If you're suffering from endogenous depression, you may have little or no appetite, have heart palpitations, and have difficulty remembering, concentrating, and making decisions. You may feel guilt, shame, despair, and hopelessness.

Left untreated for a long period, reactive depression can become endogenous depression and remain long after the situation that originally caused the depression.

The following factors may place you at greater risk for experiencing clinical depression:

- **Family history of depression.** Some types of depression run in families.

- **Personal history of depression.** It's not uncommon for depression to recur.

- **Chronic medical conditions.** The pain and frustration of illness can cause depression. In addition, some conditions, such as cancer and thyroid disease, cause changes in the body's chemistry, which may result in the symptoms of depression.

- **Recent personal loss.** Death, divorce, job loss, relocation, a child going to college or moving away, and other such major life losses can precipitate depression.

- **Depressive personality.** Some researchers now argue that persons with certain personality traits, especially the tendency to brood, criticize, and be pessimistic, are more prone to depression.

- **Drugs and alcohol.** Some drugs, particularly sedatives and tranquilizers, can induce depression. In addition, studies have long linked heavy alcohol use with depression. (See sidebar, *Common Medications that May Cause Depression,* page 158)

- **Winter weather.** In some people, the dark, gloomy days of winter can bring on a form of depression called *seasonal affective disorder,* or SAD. This type of depression lifts with the spring sunshine and returns with the winter darkness. (See *You Don't Need to Be SAD,* next.)

Are You Depressed?

If you feel down, how do you know whether you're experiencing one of life's normal dips or a more serious depression? Read through the following list of symptoms of depression, and check off those items you've experienced nearly every day, all day, for at least two weeks. If you have five or more of these symptoms, you need to see a professional for diagnosis and treatment. More signs and symptoms appear on page 154.

DEPRESSION CHECKLIST

___ 1. I feel sad or down in the dumps.

___ 2. I feel worthless and guilty.

___ 3. I have trouble concentrating, remembering, or making decisions.

___ 4. I'm experiencing changes in my appetite or changes in my weight.

___ 5. I feel tired and lack energy all the time.

___ 6. I don't care much about things I used to enjoy.

___ 7. I'm not particularly interested in sex.

___ 8. I have trouble sleeping or I've been oversleeping.

___ 9. I think about death or suicide or I've attempted suicide.*

___ 10. I have frequent headaches.

___ 11. I have frequent aches and pains.

___ 12. I have digestive troubles.

___ 13. I feel pessimistic or hopeless.

___ 14. I'm anxious and worried.

___ 15. I feel slow and lethargic, or I feel restless and can't seem to sit still.

* This symptom alone warrants diagnosis and treatment from a professional.

❏   ❏   ❏

It's Not Uncommon for Depression to Recur

You Don't Need to Be SAD

Many of us may regard the onset of winter as an annual inconvenience with its accompanying snow, ice, and frigid temperatures. But for some people, gray winter days mean severe depression, lethargy, and irritability. These people experience seasonal affective disorder, or SAD.

Lack of sunlight is thought to trigger this form of depression by altering the brain chemistry. Researchers at the National Institute of Mental Health estimate as many as 20 percent of Americans suffer some form of SAD: 25 million of us experience mild to moderate winter depression, and as many as 10 million develop SAD symptoms extreme enough to jeopardize careers, disrupt personal lives, and even drive some people to suicide.

As would be expected, SAD affects more people where winter nights are longer and days are shorter. At the latitude of Maine or Minnesota, more than 30 percent of residents experience some SAD symptoms. In Florida, the rates are less than 10 percent.

Doctors discovered the link between the darker winter months and seasonal depression about ten years ago. Scientists know that daylight, acting on the eye, triggers chemicals that regulate the body's normal rhythms. When people are deprived of light for long periods of time (in underground caves, for instance), their sleep, temperature, and hormone cycles change dramatically. The same types of changes happen in the winter to people who suffer from SAD.

Researchers aren't sure exactly why seasonal light changes plunge some people into deep depression. Some theorize that SAD sufferers have an unexplained defect in the retina at the back of the eye that makes it unable to absorb the weaker winter light and send the appropriate signals to the brain. Others believe the problem may

SIGNS AND SYMPTOMS OF DEPRESSION

- Difficulty falling asleep
- Waking early and inability to fall back asleep
- Sleeping too long
- Vivid, disturbing dreams
- Change in appetite
- Weight loss or gain
- Overeating or binge eating
- Nausea, vomiting, indigestion, heartburn
- Diarrhea or constipation
- Self-criticism
- Feelings of guilt
- Pessimism and hopelessness
- Loss of self-esteem
- Feelings of sadness
- Memory problems
- Fatigue unrelated to exertion
- Mood swings
- Headaches
- Shortness of breath
- Chest pain
- Vague aches and pains not related to illness
- Loss of interest in sex
- Feelings of resentment and anger
- Loss of motivation
- Thoughts of suicide or suicide attempts

❏   ❏   ❏

be abnormally low levels of serotonin, a chemical that helps carry messages from the eye to the brain and influences appetite, sleep, and body temperature. Still others think SAD symptoms may be caused by increased amounts of the hormone melatonin released by the pineal gland during the darker days of winter.

Whatever the cause, there is help for SAD sufferers. Doctors have discovered that light therapy, in which patients are exposed to specially designed bright lights from 15 minutes to 2 hours per day, may chase away SAD symptoms within a few days. But too much light can be overly stimulating, leaving patients feeling anxious and irritable, so having the right type of light in the right dose is important.

If you experience SAD symptoms, here are some self-help strategies:

❏ **Try lightening up your home.** Remove the drapes, trim back shrubs, paint walls and ceilings in lighter colors, install skylights and brighter bulbs.

❏ **Make time for winter vacations in sunny locations.**

❏ **Get outside.** Most of us stay indoors most of the time in the winter. But scientists have found that native peoples who live in areas that have darkness six months of the year stay physically active outdoors year round and do not experience SAD. Some SAD sufferers find as much relief from a morning walk as they do from light therapy. Morning light between 6:00 and 8:00 A.M. appears to be particularly effective.

❏ **Eaten sensibly, carbohydrates can lighten your moods.** An intense craving for carbohydrates is one of the symptoms of SAD. Try eating one or two ounces of carbohydrate such as cereal or pasta.

❏ **Synchronize your body clock to a regular schedule.** Get up and go to bed at the same time, even on weekends.

❏ **Avoid self-medicating.** Some people try to deal with the lethargy of SAD with caffeine. But too much caffeine can cause anxiety, muscle tension, and gastrointestinal problems. Others may use alcohol to cope with the depression of SAD. But alcohol is a depressant, so it can exacerbate depression.

❏ **Get professional help.** If these self-help strategies don't completely alleviate your SAD symptoms, consult your doctor. What you believe to be SAD might, in fact, be some other health problem such as a thyroid disorder.

If your doctor does diagnose SAD, light therapy may help. Many light devices are small enough to be easily portable. Researchers have also achieved good results with other light-type devices such as "dawn simulators."

Children and Adolescents Experience Depression, Too

Bummed Out Kids

Depression serious enough to require treatment doesn't just affect adults. Children and adolescents experience depression, too. Researchers suggest about 5 percent of all teenagers and 2 percent of children younger than 12 years of age may have the condition.

EMOTIONAL AND MENTAL HEALTH

Suicide Is the Third Leading Cause of Death Among Adolescents 15 to 24 Years of Age

Depression in teenagers can be especially difficult to distinguish from normal adolescent behavior. Unhappiness is an inevitable part of adolescence as the myriad of physical and hormonal changes of puberty cause emotional turmoil. Changes in body image can lead to a loss of self-esteem. Fears and anxieties about peer acceptance, sexuality, and the future are bound to occur.

But there are differences between "normal" teenage bouts of the blues and more serious depression. Depression in children and adolescents that is chronic and caused by seemingly inconsequential circumstances should be taken seriously. Kids with family histories of depression are two to three times more likely than others to have the condition. Children who are under constant stress, such as those who are chronically ill, are more vulnerable to depression.

Young people experience many of the same symptoms as depressed adults, including sleep disturbances, sadness, and fatigue. Consider depression a possibility if your youngster or adolescent displays any of the following behaviors:

- Aggressive behavior
- Inability to concentrate
- School difficulties
- Promiscuity
- Reckless "daredevil" behavior
- Alcohol or drug abuse

Unfortunately, depression in children or adolescents may be overlooked, especially when it's mixed with other behaviors such as hyperactivity or delinquency. However, depressed kids shouldn't be ignored, particularly if they threaten suicide. The third leading cause of death among adolescents 15 to 24 years of age, suicide is often an outcome of depression (see the sidebar, *Take it Seriously*).

If you think your child is depressed, seek professional help. Most depressed children and adolescents can be helped with psychotherapy or a combination of medication and psychotherapy.

TAKE IT SERIOUSLY

Eight out of ten children who threaten suicide attempt it. Watch for these signs. Then seek professional help.

- Increased sadness, tearfulness, moodiness, or irritability
- Withdrawal from favorite people or activities
- Evidence of drug or alcohol use
- Change in sleeping or eating habits
- Change in grooming habits
- Problems in school
- Preoccupation with death
- Giving away material goods
- Recent personal loss (such as a friend moving away or the death of a family member, friend, or pet)

❏   ❏   ❏

Coping with the Baby Blues

You've just given birth to a beautiful baby. You should be deliriously happy—and you are grateful the baby is healthy. But you feel irritable, fearful, and anxious, and you can't sleep.

You've got the "baby blues," or what doctors call postpartum depression. The condition is so common that most experts consider postpartum depression a normal part of pregnancy and childbirth. They estimate about 80 percent of women experience some "let-down" a few days after childbirth. Ten to twenty percent of those others move from the baby blues to clinical depression serious enough to require treatment.

Doctors suspect the causes of postpartum depression are many. One factor is the sudden change in body hormones which can dramatically alter mood. Another is the anticlimax many new mothers experience after so many months of awaiting the baby's birth. Still another cause may be the fatigue and uncertainty most new mothers feel, as well as the changes in lifestyle that motherhood demands.

Remember, it's normal to feel a little depressed the first few weeks after delivering your baby. Here's what you can do:

❑ **Get some rest.** Obviously, this isn't going to be easy with a newborn in the house. But you must snatch all the shuteye you possibly can to avoid becoming overly tired. For example, nap when the baby does—don't use this time as a chance to catch up on house-cleaning.

❑ **Arrange a shift system with your partner.** Share the responsibility of caring for the baby when he or she cries. If you're breast-feeding, consider pumping out some milk or supplementing with formula so your partner can feed the baby. This not only gives you a break, but it allows your partner important time to bond with the baby.

❑ **Ask for help.** Don't reject offers from friends and family to run errands, shop, and spell

you from the baby. And don't hesitate to ask for this help either.

❑ **Talk with your doctor.** If your baby blues get worse or persist for several weeks, let your doctor know. Most women can be helped with psychotherapy with or without medication. In a very few cases, new mothers need to be hospitalized.

Help for Depressed Older People

Depression is one of the most common mental health problems older people face. It's not hard to see why. As we get older, we must cope with physical, financial, and personal changes. We may end up feeling sad, empty, alone, and rejected.

There are plenty of causes for depression in an older person. One of the biggest is accumulated lifetime losses, which often include reduced income, changes in housing, loss of meaningful activities, changes in relationships, loss of pets or important possessions, dissatisfaction with personal image or accomplishments, loss of support as friends and family die or move away, and changes in physical and mental health.

Another common cause of depression in the elderly is medication. Often, older people take a large number of drugs. Many drugs, such as sedatives, tranquilizers, anti-inflammatories, and high blood pressure medications, can cause depression. Dangerous drug interactions can also cause

Depression Is One of the Most Common Mental Health Problems Older People Face

COMMON MEDICATIONS THAT MAY CAUSE DEPRESSION

One side effect of many prescription drugs is depression. If you take any of these drugs for the conditions listed below and feel depressed, talk with your physician about the possibility of taking a different drug or treatment.

Anxiety or sleeping problems
Dalmane, Halcion, Librium, Restoril, Valium, Xanax

Arthritis
Indocin

Heart problems and high blood pressure
Corgard, Inderal, Lopressor, Reserpine, Tenoretic, Tenormin

Seizures
Dilantin, Mysoline, Zarontin

❑   ❑   ❑

depression, mental confusion, and a host of physical problems.

There are special concerns when an older person is depressed. Depressed people are more vulnerable to infection and other illnesses and don't recover as quickly from illness as those who are not depressed. In addition, depressed elders are at increased risk for suicide.

Sometimes it's difficult to tell if an older person's symptoms are due to depression, normal age-related changes, or other health problems. *It's important to get a professional assessment and not self-diagnose depression.* See a professional if the symptoms listed below last two weeks or longer in an older individual, *and get professional help immediately if the person talks about or makes suicide attempts.*

- Sleeping difficulties
- Changes in eating and elimination habits

- Changes in behavior, mood, or thinking
- Physical complaints

If a loved one in your life exhibits any of these signs of depression, you can do much to help. Try these strategies:

❑ **Show your affection.** Touching is a particularly effective way to show caring and affection. Give hugs or offer back rubs and hair combing. Simple gestures such as these can mean a great deal.

❑ **Be sure your language communicates respect and dignity.** How you talk to older persons can make a tremendous difference in how they feel about themselves. Also consider any physical barriers to communication. For example, if the person has difficulty hearing, be sure to face him or her when speaking, and use short sentences.

❑ **Respect life-long patterns and routines.** Like all of us, older people need a sense of continuity. Respect their personal preferences, and value items the person likes and finds familiar.

❑ **Help the person feel in control.** It's natural to want to "take over" for an older person. But no one likes to have his or her control and dignity stripped away. Avoid overprotecting older persons. Encourage them to make their own decisions, and respect their privacy.

❑ **Provide meaningful activities.** It's important for all of us—and perhaps especially for older people—to stay involved in life. Help them become engaged in volunteer activities, hobbies, or other interests.

Red Flag: Recognize Suicide Warning Signs

Suicide is the most serious outcome of depression. Some experts estimate depression is a factor in 80 percent of all suicide attempts. For some people, talking about or attempting suicide is a cry for help. They don't really want to die, but they desperately need help. For others, suicide is the only option they see to end their pain. They are serious about dying and don't want anyone to interfere with their efforts.

Thinking about suicide does not necessarily mean a person will actively plan or attempt to end his or her life. It does, however, reflect the feeling life isn't worth living and is a measure of the person's level of distress.

Some people are at greater risk for suicide than others. People living in cities are more apt to commit suicide than those living in rural areas. Older people and teenagers are at higher risk. More men successfully commit suicide than women, although women make more attempts. And suicide rates among psychiatrists, musicians, lawyers, and police officers are higher than among persons in other occupations. The following factors indicate an increased risk of suicide:

- History of previous suicide attempts
- Family history of suicide
- A plan for committing suicide
- Widowed, separated, divorced, or never married
- Job loss or job failure
- Physical health problems, including recent major surgery, physical pain, or chronic or terminal illness
- Drug or alcohol use
- Withdrawal from friends and family
- A sense of hopelessness and inevitable doom
- Recent loss of a spouse, child or, particularly for a child, recent loss of a pet
- Lack of a social support system

One of the biggest mistakes people, including some mental health professionals, make in dealing with people who may be suicidal is not talking honestly with the person about it. They fear that bringing up suicide will "put the idea in the person's head." It will not. However, talking honestly and openly with someone who is thinking about suicide may help prevent suicide.

Always take threats of suicide seriously and urge the person to get professional help. If you know someone who is suicidal, try these suggestions:

- ❏ **Acknowledge the person's pain.** Help him talk about how he feels.
- ❏ **Tell the individual about the specific behaviors that concern you.** "I'm worried that you're drinking a lot more recently."
- ❏ **Urge the person to find medical help and counseling.** Recent research indicates many suicidal people have low levels of the brain chemical serotonin. Their depression can likely be treated with counsel-

Always Take Threats of Suicide Seriously

EMOTIONAL AND MENTAL HEALTH

ing and/or drug therapy. Offer to take the person to a mental health professional, and be sure he knows how to contact a suicide prevention hotline.

❑ **Offer a message of hope and support.** Tell the person how much you care about his well-being. Stress that he does not have to go through this alone.

There's Help for Depression

Most People Can Be Helped with Therapy, Medications, or a Combination of the Two

The good news about depression is most people can be helped with therapy, medications, or a combination of the two. Without treatment, major depression can last 6 to 12 months and may become chronic. Early treatment can help you feel better faster, reduce your risk of suicide, and help prevent recurrence of depression.

Short-term psychotherapies such as behavioral, cognitive, and interpersonal therapies have proven quite successful in treating depression. Unlike traditional psychotherapy, which focuses on unresolved childhood conflicts and can take years to produce results, these therapies concentrate on the present and are often effective within a few weeks or months.

Behavioral Therapy

Behavioral therapy stresses current behaviors that may be causing or contributing to depression and substituting these "negative" behaviors with more positive and productive ones. The idea is that emotions follow behavior. Change the behavior and you change the depressive emotions. For example, maybe you typically respond to depression by eating a gallon of ice cream which, in turn, causes you to gain weight and feel even more depressed. A behavioral therapist might ask you to substitute binge eating with a more positive behavior, such as taking a walk or getting a massage.

Cognitive Therapy

Cognitive therapy helps the person identify negative thoughts and beliefs that contribute to depression. Here are a few common negative thought patterns:

Overgeneralization. People who overgeneralize believe if one aspect of their life goes wrong, everything is bad.

All or nothing thinking. People believe if they're not perfect at everything, they must be worthless.

Jumping to conclusions. People believe the worst without evidence.

In cognitive therapy, clients are encouraged to examine false thoughts and beliefs and substitute them with more realistic views. (See *Change Your Negative Thinking*, page 166.)

ELECTROCONVULSIVE THERAPY

Electroconvulsive therapy is a form of treatment used for people who are so depressed they cannot function at all, for severely suicidal patients, or for those who are delusional or unresponsive to drugs or psychotherapy. Doctors aren't certain exactly how it works, but sending a controlled jolt of electric current to the brain, producing a mild brain seizure, can lift depression.

❑   ❑   ❑

EMOTIONAL AND MENTAL HEALTH

Interpersonal Therapy

Interpersonal therapy helps people resolve conflicts with spouses and other family members, friends, bosses, and coworkers. The focus may be on past or current relationships and their dynamics. For example, if you and your spouse yell at one another all the time, an interpersonal therapist might help you examine expectations each of you have, the roles you play, and how you communicate. The therapist might give you exercises or "scripts" to improve how you relate to one another.

Sometimes depression results from the loss of intimate relationships with significant people in our lives. An interpersonal therapist might focus on unresolved feelings following the loss of a parent or on family crises.

Medications

Medications, usually prescribed in combination with psychotherapy, can play an important role in treating depression. Researchers are only fairly recently beginning to understand the link between brain chemistry and depression. People with major depression are often given antidepressants. These medications can help increase appetite, ease sleep difficulties, increase energy, and correct the brain chemical imbalance that causes the depression.

Three types of antidepressants commonly used are: tricyclic antidepressants, monoamine oxidase inhibitors (MAOs), and lithium. Tricyclics, such as Elavil and Tofranil, and MAOs, such as Nardil and Parnate, ease depression by modifying brain chemistry. However, they aren't without side effects, such as weight gain and sedation. Tricyclics can also cause dry mouth, constipation, and irregular heart beat. MAOs can be fatal in combination with certain foods, including aged cheeses, beer, wine, yogurt, and sour cream. Lithium, a mood-altering drug used in treating manic depression, can cause weight gain, increased thirst, vomiting, and hand tremors.

A new class of antidepressants with fewer side effects has become available in the last few years. The most well known of these is fluoxetine, sold under the brand name Prozac. Unlike tricyclics and MAOs, these new antidepressants rarely trigger constipation, dry mouth, or sluggishness. These drugs are quite expensive, however.

Tips on Finding a Therapist

If you feel your mental and emotional issues are beyond self-help, you may opt for professional therapy. Clinical studies have shown the majority of those who seek therapy benefit from it. However, therapy is costly, both emotionally and financially, so it pays to shop around.

Here are some tips on finding a therapist:

❏ **Ask your physician for a referral.** You can also call the American Psychological Association at 202-336-5700 for help finding a qualified therapist in your area.

❏ **Talk to trusted friends who are or have been in therapy.** Ask them if they liked their therapists and why. Get phone numbers of therapists who come highly recommended.

People with Major Depression Are Often Given Antidepressants

❑ **Talk to a few therapists on the phone or in person before making a selection.** Explain what you need help with and ask candidates if they've had any experience in this area. Try to determine which therapists you feel a "chemistry" with. Also ask about the therapists' training and qualifications.

Choosing the Right Therapist

Your Rapport with Your Therapist Is Crucial to the Success of Therapy

You've done your homework, you've spoken on the phone with a few therapists, and you've made an appointment with one you liked. How do you know this is the right therapist for you?

Keep in mind you are investing *your* money, time, and effort, and no therapist, no matter how skilled, works equally well with all clients. The goal is to find the right fit between your personality and problems and the therapist's personality and expertise. Here are some qualities to look for:

• **Genuineness.** Does the therapist appear to be authentic and genuinely interested in what you're saying? Or do you feel like the person is playing a role? Did the person respond to your questions and concerns?

• **Empathy.** A therapist must be able to walk temporarily in his or her client's shoes. Does this therapist seem to understand what you're saying? Is he or she a good listener? If you feel you and your therapist are frequently miscommunicating, look for a new therapist.

• **Warmth.** Do you feel your therapist is interested in you and concerned for your well-being? Remember, however, a therapist must maintain a balance between caring and concern and professional distance and objectivity.

• **Acceptance.** A therapist should accept you "just as you are," yet be able to challenge and confront some of your specific behaviors. If you don't feel accepted and safe, you won't be willing to explore your "darker" sides.

• **Point of view.** Seek a therapist who is sensitive to your sex, race, religion, sexual orientation, or other personal issues.

• **Experience.** Look for a therapist who has successfully dealt with clients with your type of problem. Your therapist should have enough experience to have refined his or her therapeutic skills.

• **Training.** There are as many schools of psychological training as there are approaches to therapy. Ask your therapist about his or her training and theoretical approach. Mental health professionals must be state-licensed or certified to practice. This license assures you the therapist has the minimum qualifications.

Note: It's important that you feel the counselor is right for you. In a counseling situation, you should feel safe—physically and emotionally. If for any reason you feel uncomfortable during your counseling sessions about anything your counselor says or does, express your feelings. If the counselor rejects or minimizes your concerns or seems otherwise closed to criticism, seek counseling elsewhere.

Therapists—What Do All the Letters Mean?

When choosing a mental health therapist, you may be confused by the seemingly endless list of letters such as M.S.W., L.C.S.W., or Psy.D., among others. Here's a lexicon for deciphering what they mean.

Psychiatrists (M.D.): These are medical doctors who complete medical school and then spend four or more years in a psychiatric residency. These are the only mental health professionals who can prescribe medications. Treatment from this group tends to be the most expensive mental health therapy.

Psychologists (Ph.D. or Psy.D.): These are individuals who have received a doctorate in Philosophy (Ph.D.) or Psychology (Psy.D.). They cannot prescribe medications, but they often have more training than psychiatrists in behavioral and psychological research and psychological testing and diagnosis.

Social Workers (M.S.W. or L.C.S.W.): Social workers have a master's degree in social work. While they have fewer years of formal training than either psychiatrists or psychologists, the training is often very practical, and they receive more continuing supervision of their therapy. A social worker who is licensed (L.C.S.W.) has completed a specified number of supervised clinical hours in addition to those required by the master's program.

Marriage and Family Therapists (M.F.T. or M.F.C.C.): These are master's level mental health professionals. Marriage and Family Therapists are especially trained to deal with issues such as marriage conflicts and intergenerational problems. They are usually less expensive than psychiatrists or psychologists, but their counseling may not be covered by some insurance companies.

Counselors: In addition to the professionals listed above, there are mental health counselors who have a wide range of training. Some deal with specific issues such as grief or substance abuse. Others work only in educational or pastoral settings. Some may have only bachelor's level training, while others may have a master's or doctorate degree. Insurance companies may or may not cover therapy with these individuals.

Getting the Most Out of Therapy

If you decide to seek professional help, here are some strategies to ensure the treatment has the best chance of lifting the depression.

❑ **Keep all of your appointments.** Psychotherapy works gradually, and it can only work if you keep your appointments. Also, if you're taking antidepressant medication, your doctor will want to check the dosage and inquire about any side effects.

❑ **Take your medication as directed.** Don't stop taking your medication or change the dose, even if you begin to feel better, without first talking

Do Not Seek Treatment from an Unlicensed Therapist

BE SURE TO ASK

If a doctor prescribes antidepressants, be sure he or she answers the following questions:

1. When and how often should I take the medicine?
2. What side effects can I expect?
3. Are there any foods I should not eat while taking the medication? Can I have beer, wine, or other alcoholic beverages?
4. Can I take other medications while I'm taking these drugs?
5. What should I do if I forget to take the medication?
6. How long will I have to continue the medication?
7. How will I know if it's working?
8. How much does it cost? Is a generic brand available?

❏   ❏   ❏

Self-Help for Mild Depression

Not all bouts of depression require professional care. Bad moods catch up with all of us at one time or another. Here are some ways to shortcut them.

❏ **Get some rest.** Often depression and the blues have physical roots such as lack of sleep. When there's a disparity between your energy level and what you need to accomplish, it's sure to deflate your mood. One way to head off a serious depression is to take some time off. A day spent in retreat is not an indulgence if it helps you deal with the blues and return to your daily life feeling renewed.

❏ **Limit sugar.** Many people rely on sugary foods to give them a lift. But a few hours after eating sugar, you're likely to experience a big let down (the "sugar blues"). Cut the sugar, eat a balanced diet, and see if your moods don't improve.

❏ **Stay away from alcohol.** Some people try to "drown their sorrows" in alcoholic beverages. Don't. Alcohol is a depressant, and it can only contribute to your down moods.

❏ **Exercise.** Exercise lifts the spirits, increases energy, and can make personal problems seem less overwhelming. Exercise releases endorphins, the body's own "feel good" chemicals. Even a brisk 10- to 15-minute walk can improve your mood for hours.

Part of Therapy Is Trying New Behaviors and New Ways of Thinking

with your health-care provider. Also be sure to ask your doctor for information about your medication. See the sidebar, *Be Sure to Ask.*

❏ **Report any side effects.** Talk with your doctor or mental health professional about any side effects you experience. If the side effects are too bothersome, you may be able to switch to another medication.

❏ **Be honest and open.** Your mental health professional can help you only if you're honest and open about your thoughts and feelings.

❏ **Try to do the tasks your mental health professional assigns to you.** Part of psychotherapy is trying new behaviors and new ways of thinking.

❏ **Let your therapist know how the therapy is working.** Your feedback can help you both determine how long your therapy should continue.

❏ **Rely on friends and family for support.** Talking with another person about how you feel helps. Give yourself permission to unburden yourself. Ask a close friend or family member to listen to how you feel without judging or giving advice.

You need friends and family, but they're especially important during difficult times. *Before* you find yourself down in the dumps, take a look at your social support system. Do you have close friends and family members you can talk with and rely on? If not, start building those relationships now.

❏ **Be kind to yourself.** An emotional slump is an indication some personal resource has been depleted; you need a little more attention. Don't try to deny or ignore your feelings. Start taking better care of yourself.

❏ **Learn relaxation techniques.** Research shows soothing music helps patients facing surgery feel calmer and more in control. It can make you feel better, too. Deep breathing is also a great way to release tension.

Sit in a quiet place, place one hand on your chest and one on your stomach. Take a deep breath through your nose. Concentrate on making the hand on your stomach rise but leaving your chest hand still. Now breathe out through your mouth. You can use five to ten minutes of deep breathing as a form of daily relaxation or you can take a few deep breaths anytime you feel tense. (See Chapter 5, *Coping with Stress*, for additional relaxation techniques.)

❏ **Try to distract yourself.** When you feel down, get together with friends or participate in fun activities. Distraction can help you take a breather from your problems and return with a better perspective.

❏ **Use humor.** Give yourself permission to laugh. Go see a funny movie or a comedy act. Read a humorous book. While things often don't seem funny when you're depressed, even a chuckle can do a world of good.

❏ **Get organized.** Sometimes the sheer volume of what we have to accomplish can make us feel down. Make a list, prioritize it, and get going on those tasks you can accomplish quickly.

❏ **Establish a routine and stick to it.** You may wake up and feel like doing nothing. But routines can serve as a ladder for climbing out of the pits. Formless, empty spans of time can emphasize the feeling that "nothing will ever change." If you work or go to school, keep going. If you work at home, try to structure your days by making lists of brief, manageable tasks whose completion will give you a sense of accomplishment.

❏ **Examine your thinking.** When the blues and depression are a regular part of your life, you need to examine ingrained thought patterns that contribute to your moods. Writing down your thoughts and feelings can help you get some perspective on your problems. Do you always look at the darker side of a situation? Do you jump to negative conclusions or always expect the worst? These kinds of negative thoughts are habits you can consciously change.

Don't Try to Deny or Ignore Your Feelings

Change Your Negative Thinking

Could the Way You Talk to Yourself Be Making You Unhappy?

Sometimes our thoughts are our worst enemy. Mental health experts say how we think, especially the *self-talk* messages we constantly give ourselves, affects how we see the world and how we feel. If those messages are negative and destructive, we'll find ourselves caught in a cycle of feeling anxious, depressed, and unfulfilled in our relationships with others. By learning to identify your negative thought processes, then applying relatively simple intervention techniques, you can change your outlook and start to feel better.

Aaron Beck, M.D., the father of a behavior-changing technique called cognitive therapy, has identified several types of distorted, negative thinking. Look over this list and see if you can find your destructive thinking patterns that distort your reality.

All or nothing thinking. This is black or white thinking. If your performance isn't perfect, you see yourself as a failure. "The boss made some changes on my report. Obviously, I can't handle this job."

Overgeneralization. A single negative event leads you to conclude nothing can be right: "My car wouldn't start this morning, and I was late for work. Nothing ever goes right for me."

Disqualifying the positive. You ignore or discount positive experiences. They don't count: "He was just being nice. He didn't really mean what he said."

Jumping to conclusions. Without supporting evidence, you negatively interpret events: "The way my boss looked at me today, I know he's going to fire me."

Mind reading. You decide people are reacting negatively without really checking it out: "Alice didn't even look up when I said 'Good morning.' I'm sure she hates me."

Fortune telling. You anticipate negative outcomes and then act as if they've already happened: "I go in for surgery Thursday. I've arranged for my funeral."

Magnification or minimization. You exaggerate your errors and belittle your successes: "I stumbled all over my words during my speech. I sounded like an idiot." Or "It's only a small award. The company gives them to everyone."

Emotional reasoning. You base reality on the negative emotions you feel: "I feel it, therefore, it must be true."

Shoulds. You try to motivate yourself because you think you "should," "must," or "ought to": "I have a million things to do, but I have to go to that fund-raiser tomorrow."

Labeling. You attach negative labels to yourself instead of simply describing errors in behavior: "I left the water running. I'm such a scatter-brained idiot."

Personalization. You see yourself as the cause of negative events you were not responsible for: "It's my fault John lost his job."

Here are some tips to change your negative thinking.

❑ **Tune in and listen.** Begin to pay attention to your self-talk, the constant stream of messages you give yourself.

❑ **Write down the negative messages.** Don't let the negative thoughts buzz around in your head. Write them down. Then underline the negative elements in your messages such as, "If I only had ...," "I'm such a ...," "I can't ever ...."

❑ **Identify your negative thinking.** Compare your self-talk with the negative thinking list. Which types of distorted thinking apply to your thoughts?

❑ **Stop.** As you become more aware of your distorted thinking, you'll be able to "hear" those messages as you think them. Stop negative thoughts as soon as you become aware of them. For emphasis, tell yourself out loud to stop.

❑ **Revise the message.** Change negative messages into positive, objective ones.

❑ **Use affirmations.** Years of negative self-talk and distorted thinking can be difficult habits to overcome. They can also take a toll on your self-esteem. Begin to use affirmations, positive statements about yourself, such as "I can easily handle my job responsibilities," or "I'm a caring and trusting person."

Why Do I Feel So Anxious?

You know the feeling. You can't relax. You feel tense, always on guard, but you can't say just why. When life becomes stressful, your hands sweat, your heart races, and your muscles tense. With your boyfriend, you often feel jealous and fear he'll leave you. At work, you're defensive and quarrelsome. You're sure your coworkers are trying to make you look bad. You know something is wrong with your life, but you don't know what. You're experiencing anxiety.

Everyone experiences some anxiety. Perhaps you feel tense about giving a presentation at work. Or you're restless and ill-at-ease about going out with a new person. These are normal anxieties. A certain amount of anxiety is even helpful. Anxiety helps us stay alert and adapt to the ever-changing demands of a complicated world. Mental health experts say some types of extreme anxiety, such as fear of falling, are normal. These common anxieties may be the body's "early warning system" against harm.

Your Natural Alarm System

You can best understand anxiety if you think of it as your body's alarm system. When we feel danger, the alarm goes off to warn us and prevent injury. The body responds immediately to the alarm emotionally, physically, and behaviorally. Emotionally, we may feel fear, doom, or anger. Physically, our hearts race, muscles tense, breath becomes rapid, and palms and feet sweat. And we respond behaviorally by getting ready to fight or flee from danger.

The anxiety warning system works fine when there's clear and present danger. But anxiety can become a problem for people when they perceive harmless situations or people as dangerous. For

Anxiety Is a Problem when You Fear Harmless Situations

Caffeine Is a Common Anxiety-Producer

example, you might think your boss' feedback and suggestions are intended to prevent your promotion when, in fact, he or she is trying to help. Some people become anxious and fearful about everyday activities such as driving a car or going to the grocery store. This anxiety can become so intense it develops into a phobia that prevents them from carrying out those activities. (See *When Fear Is a Phobia*, page 172.)

Causes of Anxiety

There is no single reason why some people experience episodes of anxiety. Here are a few potential causes:

- Mental health experts say heredity plays a major role in certain types of anxiety, especially severe panic attacks in which the person experiences overwhelming physical and emotional anxiety (see *Help! I'm Having a Panic Attack!*).

- Histories of childhood trauma or loss, recent loss, or extreme stress may precede the onset of anxiety attacks.

- Any physical change, such as illness, can also cause anxiety. Anemia, diabetes, premenstrual syndrome, menopause, thyroid disorders, hypoglycemia (low blood sugar), pulmonary disease, endocrine tumors, and other conditions can cause anxiety symptoms.

- Drugs can be a factor in anxiety, too. Caffeine is a common anxiety-producer. In some people, one cup of caffeinated coffee is enough to produce an anxiety reaction. In high doses, caffeine can cause panic attacks. Over-the-counter diet pills, amphetamines, and cocaine can all cause anxiety symptoms.

Help! I'm Having a Panic Attack!

Panic attacks are severe, spontaneous episodes of anxiety. They often occur without warning and are accompanied by multiple physical symptoms, including shortness of breath or the sensation of smothering or choking, dizziness or faintness, a racing heart, trembling, nausea, numbness or tingling sensations, hot flashes or chills, chest pain, fear of dying, feelings of impending doom, and an overwhelming feeling of terror.

Usually no obvious danger or threat causes the attack, but people who experience them often mistakenly relate the symptoms to whatever they are doing when the attack occurs. They assume the subway, elevator, or crowded store caused the attack. Then they go out of their way to avoid situations or objects they associate with the attacks. Many people who experience panic attacks limit their lives so much, they eventually become agoraphobic, afraid to leave their homes.

If you suffer from panic attacks, help is available. Panic attacks respond well to both cognitive and drug therapy. Cognitive therapy teaches participants to identify thoughts and behaviors that contribute to their anxiety. They also learn relaxation techniques to calm the physical symptoms that can provoke panic attacks. Drug therapies include the use of tricyclic antidepressants and

EMOTIONAL AND MENTAL HEALTH

monoamine oxidase inhibitors. These drugs increase the levels of two neurotransmitters in the brain, norepinephrine and serotonin, and reduce anxiety.

Ways to Cope with Hyperventilation

You feel dizzy and short of breath, your heart is pounding, and your chest hurts. Are you having a heart attack? You may just be overbreathing, or hyperventilating, a common component of anxiety. When we feel frightened or anxious, we tend to breathe shallowly, blowing off too much carbon dioxide and causing the blood vessels in the brain and elsewhere in the body to constrict. As blood flow to the brain slows, the frightening hyperventilation symptoms appear.

You can help yourself before you hyperventilate to the point of fainting. Here's how:

❑ **Breathe into a paper bag.** Carbon dioxide levels in the bag build up; breathing this air can restore normal CO_2 blood levels.

❑ **Take slow, deep breaths.** Try to breathe in through your nose to a slow count of ten. Slowly exhale through your mouth, again to the count of ten. Repeat until you feel more relaxed.

❑ **Use your mind.** Picture a soothing scene—a walk on a beach, a quiet mountain meadow, a forest path.

DON'T IGNORE CHEST PAINS

Symptoms of hyperventilation may actually be the signs of other more serious health problems such as diabetes, heart disease, or thyroid disease. If you experience chest pains, numbness, shortness of breath, or dizziness, a trip to the doctor or emergency department is in order. Keep in mind, *a heart attack is a potentially life-threatening medical emergency.*

❑   ❑   ❑

There are also steps you can take to prevent episodes of hyperventilation:

❑ **Learn to relax.** Practice relaxation techniques, such as biofeedback, to learn how your body responds to stress and how you can learn to relieve that stress response. (See Chapter 5, *Coping with Stress.*)

❑ **Avoid caffeine, diet pills, and other stimulants.** All of these can cause or heighten anxiety.

❑ **Exercise regularly.** Regular exercise that is vigorous enough to make you breathe deeply helps defeat stress and stimulates the body's release of calming chemicals called endorphins.

Anxiety's Link to Sexual Dysfunction

Anxiety can negatively impact many areas of life, including your sex life. Anxiety may interfere with arousal any time during lovemaking. For example, some men and women are unable to become aroused in a normally stimulating situation. Others may experience anxiety

Hyperventilation May Be a Sign of Anxiety or a More Serious Health Problem

Anxiety Can Lead to Loss of Sexual Desire

later in the midst of arousal. Sometimes sexual anxiety occurs no matter what the sexual situations. Other times, it occurs only in certain situations such as when a partner becomes involved in an extra-marital affair. Anxieties can become so strong couples lose sexual desire and avoid sex altogether.

Anxiety in Men

Many men have "performance anxieties" regarding their sexual prowess. Worries and anxieties about performing sexually can cause a man to experience premature ejaculation, in which he ejaculates before full arousal; retarded ejaculation, in which the penis stays erect for a long period of time with delayed or no ejaculation; or erectile dysfunction, in which the man is unable to achieve or maintain an erection.

Men with sexual difficulties often are worried about the size of their penis. They tend to be overly sensitive to their partner's comments about their anatomy and their lovemaking ability.

Anxiety in Women

In women, sexual anxiety can cause vaginismus, in which the muscles of the lower third of the vagina suddenly contract during lovemaking. This contraction makes sexual penetration nearly impossible. If penetration is forced, the woman usually experiences pain and further muscle contractions. Sometimes the anxiety is caused by fears associated with earlier painful intercourse, rape or rape-like situations, or penetration associated with injury or impregnation.

Anxiety can also make it difficult for a woman to achieve orgasm. Instead of enjoying the pleasurable feelings of a sexual encounter, she focuses on the "goal" of having an orgasm. Unfortunately, the more she worries about having orgasms, the less likely she is to achieve them.

Causes of Anxiety

The causes of sexual anxiety are numerous. Perhaps the messages you got about sex as a child were inaccurate: "Sex is dirty." "A lady doesn't enjoy sex." "A man should always take the lead in sex." "A man can have an erection any time he wants." "Sex without intercourse isn't really sex." Maybe the sexual anxiety had its origins when the male partner had his first difficulty achieving or maintaining an erection. Or perhaps past sexual experiences have made sex an emotionally charged issue for you.

Whatever the cause, the cure is to find the psychological or physiological cause and then alleviate the anxiety.

❑ **See your doctor.** If you or your partner are having sexual difficulties, first have a thorough physical examination to rule out any health problems or medications that may be contributing to the problem.

❑ **Seek professional counseling.** If no physical problem is found, try short-term counseling with a mental health professional trained in sex therapy. A skilled therapist can help you improve your communication and, in most cases, a few sessions of therapy can eliminate feelings of anxiety, guilt, and inadequacy and help you introduce fun and spontaneity into your sex life.

Anxiety: A Common Problem for Older People

Perhaps you've noticed that an older relative or friend seems increasingly anxious and worried. The person is afraid of things that wouldn't have bothered him or her in the past. Little troubles become large worries. The person may feel alone and unneeded.

Generalized anxiety is common among older people. Aging often causes physical limitations and personal stresses that can increase an older person's feelings of vulnerability. Older people often fear becoming ill and, as a result, physically helpless and dependent on others. They may be afraid they'll be impoverished. They often fear they'll become victims of violent crime.

Your older loved one may manifest his or her anxiety in rigid thinking, mistrust of others, or physical illness. Some older people may be able to talk about their fears and anxieties. Others may not. If you sense that an older person you care about is experiencing generalized anxiety, here's what you can do to help:

- **Encourage them to discuss their fears and anxieties.** Show empathy and concern for their situation.

- **Check their medications.** These may contribute to anxiety. Talk with the person about the drugs he or she is taking, and check with the doctor or pharmacist about what effect the medication may be having and whether other options are available. (See sidebar, *Common Medications that May Cause Depression*, page 158.)

- **Eliminate health concerns.** Suggest the older person have a thorough checkup to rule out physical causes of anxiety. A confirmation of good health by a doctor can also help allay fears about a debilitating illness.

- **Help them feel safe.** If personal safety is a concern, help the person install safety devices in the home and car. Perhaps a pet or in-home companion would help.

- **Get them involved.** You can't force an older person to get involved in meaningful activities, but you can make specific suggestions about volunteer opportunities, classes, or groups to get them more involved with others.

- **Include them in your life.** Loneliness is a major cause of anxiety in older people. The anxiety is understandable when you consider they may have been left alone because loved ones and peers have died. Try to include the older person on a regular basis. Perhaps he or she can join you for dinners, Sunday drives, or shopping trips. Sometimes just talking to older people about your daily activities and your family makes them feel valued as a listener.

- **Suggest professional help.** If anxiety is interfering with the ability to enjoy life, suggest the older person talk with a mental health professional. Often anxieties stem from issues such as unresolved grief from the death of a spouse. Talking with a professional can help.

Anxiety is Common Among Older People

Phobias Trigger a Level of Terror that Far Outweighs the Actual Threat

When Fear Is a Phobia

All of us are afraid sometimes. A reasonable level of fear is a normal response to danger; it acts to keep us safe. For instance, fear of being run over by a car or truck can make us wait for a green light to cross a busy street. But when an object or situation that isn't dangerous causes us persistent, excessive fear, or when fear is out of proportion, it becomes a phobia. Phobias trigger a level of terror that far outweighs the actual threat. For 23 million people in the United States, phobias are so intense they interfere with normal, everyday living.

People with phobias go to almost any length to avoid the object or situation that causes the fear. Someone who is afraid of flying might be able to white-knuckle it and feel relieved when the plane lands. But people with a phobia of flying would rather drive cross country or miss an important event than face their fear of flying. Some people with phobias quit their jobs, drop out of school, or refuse to leave their homes for years because of their fears.

You can develop a phobia to nearly anything. Common phobias include fear of flying, heights, public speaking, crossing bridges, and closed or open spaces. Experts classify phobias into three categories:

- Simple phobias, the most common, include fear of specific objects or situations, such as fear of spiders or fear of heights
- Social phobia, which is fear of ridicule and embarrassment from others
- Agoraphobia, or fear of open places

Mental health experts aren't sure exactly what causes phobias. Some speculate they may be a manifestation of an underlying anxiety or depression. Others believe phobias have their roots in unpleasant childhood experiences which have usually been long forgotten. Still others suggest a predisposition to phobias may be inherited.

Are You Sure You're "Just Shy"?

You've been invited to a gathering in your new neighborhood. Most of your neighbors are strangers to you. As you approach the door where the party is being held, your stomach feels jittery, your breath is shallow, and you feel like bolting for your car. Do you have a case of shyness or are you a social phobic?

Nearly everyone is uneasy in situations where making a good impression is important—among new friends, at work or school, in front of an audience. If you've ever spoken to a group of people, you know how uncomfortable it can be to have everyone's attention focused on you. This kind of social anxiety is normal and even healthy. For example, the fear you'll embarrass yourself ensures you'll thoroughly prepare your speech. Once you start talking, your fears generally ease, and the next time you give a talk, you're not quite so frightened.

But for an estimated two to three percent of us, the fears are not so easily overcome. In fact, for those with social phobias the fear of what others think of them is so paralyzing they often go to extreme lengths to avoid putting themselves in situations with others. They are sure other people will scrutinize, reject, and embarrass them. A person with a social phobia is disabled by fear, not advancing at work because he or she is unable to express ideas, and unable to make friends, fearing the reactions of others.

Some people with social phobias experience fears only in certain settings. For instance, some are afraid of eating in public. As long as they stay away from these situations, they are fine. At the extreme end of the social phobic spectrum, however, are what mental health experts call "avoidant personality disorders." To avoid feeling unsafe and insecure, these individuals do not form any close relationships.

•Some mental health experts suggest the jittery stomach, fluttering heart, sweaty palms, and shortness of breath related to social phobias may, in fact, be an inherited trait. Individuals with these reactions, according to the theory, have an especially sensitive nervous system that makes them over-respond to social situations with intense fear.

In addition to professional help, if you have a social phobia or are just socially a little shy, try these strategies to help yourself:

❏ **Know you're not alone.** People with social phobias often believe they're the only ones feeling socially awkward. One-third to one-half of all people in any given social setting feel just as uncomfortable as you do.

❏ **Don't expect perfection.** You're human, not perfect. You don't have to be witty and wonderful. Just try to be yourself. You—with all your flaws— are unique.

❏ **Go easy on the alcohol.** Some people who feel socially awkward try to grease the social machinery with alcohol or drugs. Chemical courage is an illusion and can make you look foolish. It also puts you at increased risk for drug and alcohol dependence.

❏ **Stay focused.** Concentrate on conversations you're having instead of thinking about what others might be thinking of you. Focusing on others helps you stop thinking about yourself.

A Person with a Social Phobia Is Disabled by Fear

Conquer Your Fear of Flying

Fear of flying afflicts millions of Americans. For many of us, avoiding airplanes means limiting ourselves—missing career opportunities, vacations, and visits with far-away family and friends.

For some people, fear of flying stems from a simple lack of knowledge about the aviation industry. When combined with headlines

THE PHYSICAL RESPONSE TO ANXIETY

Under stress, the adrenal glands secrete a hormone that causes your heart to beat faster, your breathing rate to increase, and your muscles to tense. As the stress builds without physical release, your breathing becomes more shallow, which increases the production of carbon dioxide. As you breathe faster and less deeply (hyperventilation), the blood's carbon dioxide levels fall, and you may experience dizziness, shortness of breath, chest pains, shaking, nausea, and confusion.

To control the physical response, take slow, deep breaths in through your nose and out through your mouth as soon as you begin to feel anxious. As you continue to breathe in this fashion, concentrate on relaxing your muscles.

❏ ❏ ❏

Fear of Flying Afflicts Millions of People

about airplane crashes, hijacking, and safety scandals, the result is fearful flying. For others, the problem is panic attacks—severe episodes of terror and anxiety-producing physical symptoms, such as a pounding heart and shortness of breath. Since people who experience panic attacks often avoid situations where a panic attack occurred, those who experienced a panic attack on an airplane avoid flying.

Most airlines and many mental health clinics now offer programs that combine education, relaxation exercises, cognitive therapy, and a process called "desensitization" to help people overcome their fear of flying. These programs boast an 85 to 90 percent success rate. Here are some of the components of the program:

- Participants learn the facts about air travel. For example, most people with a fear of flying don't know the average age of an airline pilot is 43, and he or she has an average of 14 years' experience.

- Participants learn to relax with deep breathing and other relaxation exercises.

- They use cognitive therapy to identify irrational and erroneous beliefs and thoughts and replace them with more realistic ones. A catastrophic thought might be: "The pilot might have a heart attack." Participants learn to replace such thoughts with more realistic ones: "A pilot's health is frequently tested and if anything goes wrong, there's a co-pilot to take over."

- Participants experience desensitization, progressively exposing themselves to flying-type experiences and then actually flying. Desensitization might include visualizing oneself sitting on the plane, then actually boarding a plane, and eventually taking a flight.

If there isn't a fearful flyer program in your community, you can still help yourself overcome your fear of flying:

❏ **Learn about flying.** Much of your fear may stem from misinformation. The aviation industry is one of the safest. (According to experts, you're 30 times more likely to die in a car crash than in an airplane crash.) Airline pilots must have flown a minimum of 2,000 hours before being hired by an airline, and they take refresher courses and are tested every six months. It takes five to ten years to become an airline pilot. Airline maintenance is rigorous, too. Most planes are checked out thoroughly each day and given monthly in-depth inspections. Planes undergo major overhauls every four years.

❑ **Learn to relax.** The physical symptoms of anxiety are frightening and can produce even more anxiety and distress. (See the sidebar, *The Physical Response to Anxiety.*)

Learn to stop the physical reactions before they start. Sit in a relaxed position with one hand on your belly, one on your chest. Breathe deeply in through the nose, making the belly hand rise, but keeping the chest hand relatively still. Hold the inhalation for three seconds. Then slowly exhale through your mouth. As you exhale, relax your muscles and quiet your thoughts. Continue breathing like this for several minutes until you feel relaxed.

❑ **Use your mind.** Practice desensitizing yourself to flying by rehearsing the experience in your mind. Close your eyes and see yourself confidently getting on the plane, chatting comfortably with other passengers, enjoying the takeoff and landing.

❑ **Occupy yourself.** The takeoff and landing are the hardest parts of flying for many people with flying phobias. Give yourself something to do during these times. Progressively tense and relax your toes; shrug your shoulders; breathe deeply. Also, if you're involved in an engrossing book, talking with others, or another activity, you won't be thinking about your fears.

❑ **Move around.** Once the seat belt light has been turned off, get up, stretch, walk around. Go to the washroom and splash water on your face. Keeping your muscles loose helps keep your mind relaxed.

❑ **Reward yourself.** After a successful flight, do something especially nice for yourself. Take a long, hot bubble bath, have a massage, treat yourself to something you've been wanting.

Self-Help for Anxiety and Phobias

You can't eliminate genetics that may make you prone to anxiety and phobias, but you can do plenty to help yourself feel less anxious. Try these strategies:

❑ **Learn all you can.** Take the mystery out of phobias and panic attacks by learning about them. Send a postcard and request a free information packet from the Anxiety Disorders Association of America, 6000 Executive Blvd, Suite 513, Rockville, MD 20852-3801, or a free booklet, *Phobias and Panic*, from the National Institute of Mental Health, Rm 15C-05, 5600 Fishers Lane, Rockville, MD 20857.

❑ **Give up caffeine.** You may think you can't live without it, but if anxiety is a problem for you, try cutting the caffeine from your diet. Keep in mind caffeine occurs not only in coffee and tea, but also in cocoa, cola soft drinks, chocolate, and many over-the-counter drugs.

❑ **Exercise regularly.** Aerobic exercise vigorous enough to get your pulse up to 60 to 85 percent of the maximum recommended for your age group can

Learn to Stop the Physical Reactions Before They Start

You Can Overcome Anxiety and Phobias with Professional Help

do wonders for your anxiety (see Chapter 3, *Determining Your Aerobic Target Heart Rate*, page 76). Exercise releases anxiety-relieving chemicals called endorphins. It also helps make you feel more capable, powerful, and in control of your life.

❏ **Get some sleep.** Being overly tired can make you anxious.

❏ **Relax.** People who are anxious can relieve tension with relaxation techniques, such as meditation, biofeedback, music therapy, and progressive relaxation. Many community colleges offer classes in relaxation techniques. (Also see Chapter 5, *Coping with Stress*.)

❏ **Keep a journal.** Write down your thoughts and feelings. Ask yourself, "What's making me feel so anxious?" "What can I reasonably do about this situation?" "Who can help me with this problem?"

❏ **Try self-help groups.** Plenty of peer- and professionally lead groups exist for people with specific anxiety problems. Your local mental health agency or community hospital can provide referrals.

Professional Help for Anxiety and Phobias

Self-help strategies can go a long way toward easing anxieties and phobias and giving you new feelings of self-confidence. But sometimes you can't do it alone. Sometimes, you need the help of a professional.

When anxiety and phobias require professional help, treatment usually includes psychotherapy, medication, or a combination of the two.

Psychotherapy
This form of mental therapy involves identifying and facing the fears that underlie anxiety. Often these fears stem from traumatic events in childhood. The client uncovers and addresses these fears by retelling the anxiety-producing experiences to a skilled therapist. Two common types of psychotherapy are behavioral therapy and cognitive therapy.

Behavioral therapy deals with the present anxiety-producing situation as opposed to identifying historical, underlying causes. This treatment is especially effective for phobias. A behavioral approach often involves desensitization in which the person progressively addresses his or her fears.

Cognitive therapy also ignores past events and focuses on current destructive thinking and beliefs that contribute to anxieties and fears. This form of therapy helps the person identify types of distorted thinking, such as overgeneralization, all or nothing thinking, and jumping to conclusions, and replace these thought patterns with more realistic ones.

Drug Therapy
Severe anxiety and phobias often require medications such as anti-anxiety benzodiazepines, MAO inhibitors, and beta blockers. These drugs can be quite effective in easing anxieties, but they do have side effects. (See *Medications*, page 161.) Usually, medications are most effective when used in combination with behavioral or cognitive therapies.

Understanding Your Grief

We experience many losses in life, but the death of a loved one may be the most profound and painful. All of us have faced or will face grief, a process of overwhelming feelings of sadness and loss often accompanied by physical aches, pains, and even serious illness.

We are never really prepared to lose someone we love, even when the death follows a long illness. Mental health experts say there is no way to prepare for the full impact of the death of a loved one and the ensuing emotional roller coaster that can last for months or even years. Our culture does little to prepare us for death and grief. We often behave as if everyone will live happily ever after. In the past—before hospitals and major medical advances—when death usually occurred at home, everyone learned about death naturally. Death and grief were accepted as part of life.

Today, however, we often deny death and our grief. Grief rituals such as wearing black for a period of time are less commonly practiced. We protect our children from rituals of mourning, believing these events are morbid. The result is most of us are totally unprepared to deal with the intense emotions that come with the death of someone we care about.

Often grief emotions are so strong and foreign to us, we fear we are losing control or going crazy. Childhood fears of abandonment may resurface. Death also forces us to look at our own mortality. But understanding the grief process can help you successfully cope with it and grow from the experience.

Death and dying experts say when we lose someone close to us, we go through somewhat predictable stages of grief:

- An initial phase of shock, numbness, and denial

- A middle period that can include anger, helplessness, depression, guilt, and fear

- A final stage of acceptance and adjustment

We do not necessarily pass from one stage to the next; rather, we move back and forth among stages. The feelings from each stage overlap during the grieving process.

Stage One: Shock, Numbness, and Denial

The first reaction to a major loss is shock. During this phase, it seems the death can't be real. We resist the finality of death because it's so difficult to let go of someone we love. People in this phase often behave as if they were in a trance. Filled with disbelief, they are unable to imagine life without the person who has died.

During this stage, the person is likely to be in a physical state of alarm with icy fingers, sweaty palms, and trembling. As blood moves away from the intestinal tract, the person loses his appetite and may feel nauseated. He may feel restless, causing him to pace, fidget, and move aimlessly about.

The trauma or level of shock an individual feels during this first stage of grief is often related to how the death occurred and when and where it happened. If, for instance, the death was totally unexpected, as in an auto accident or homicide, the shock to friends

There Is No
Way to
Prepare for
the Full
Impact of
the Death of
a Loved One

When We Lose Someone Close to Us, We Go Through Stages of Grief

and family is likely to be more severe than the death of an older person following a long illness.

Stage Two: Anger, Helplessness, Depression, Guilt, and Fear

This is the middle stage of grief when pain is felt most acutely. A person in this grief stage becomes aware of her loss and often see-saws through the day with strong emotions and uncontrollable weeping. During this period, the person may yearn strongly for the dead person and feel frustration that the yearning is unfulfilled. She may feel angry at the person who died, at herself, at friends and family, at a higher power. Feelings of guilt and fear may also come up. Could she have done something to prevent the death? Could she have been kinder during the person's lifetime? What happens now that she is left alone?

Stage Three: Acceptance and Adjustment

The final stage of the grieving process often comes as a gentle turning point. While there are no defined marks of change, the person begins to feel more energy and less sadness and is willing to participate a little more in life.

Sometimes an external event such as a vacation, a new job, or a move to a new residence initiates this final healing phase of grief. During this period, the person assumes control of his life and accepts a new role that does not include the person who has died.

This final stage of acceptance and adjustment may be a long time in coming. For some people, it takes months. For others, years. In the end, people who successfully move through the grieving process come to some degree of acceptance of their loss and begin to rebuild a life for themselves.

Self-Help for Your Grief

Grieving is difficult. But you can take steps to help yourself and make the process a little easier. Try these strategies:

- **Grieve fully.** You can't escape the pain of your loss. Give yourself permission to grieve. Let yourself feel the full impact and intensity of your emotions. Expressing how you feel is not a sign of weakness. Cry, be angry, or yell if it helps.

- **Take time out from decision-making.** Now is not the time to make major decisions about your future. Most people cannot evaluate all aspects of a situation immediately after the shock of a death.

- **Let others nurture you.** Let others—friends, family, coworkers—carry some of the load, and allow yourself to lean on them. Not only will it give you comfort, it will make them feel useful and needed. If you're not getting the support you need, ask for it. Often people aren't sure how to respond to someone who is grieving. Let them know the kind of help you need.

- **Give yourself time.** Grieving takes time and lots of it. In our fast-paced culture, we expect everything to move quickly. But the process of grieving can take several months or even years.

- **Give yourself time off from grief.** This item may seem to contradict the previous item, but it is equally important to allow yourself to enjoy the moments you can. Sometimes people who are grieving feel guilty if they aren't feeling sad or lonely every minute. It's okay to spend time with friends and family laughing and enjoying your time together. You aren't disloyal if you have a good time. These breaks are important sources of renewal to enable you to get through the hard work of grieving.

❏ **Take an active part in planning the funeral or memorial service.** Death makes us feel out of control. Having a say in the ritual arrangements can give you a sense of control during a time when you really need it.

❏ **Use ritual to heal.** You don't have to be religious to benefit from the closure that rituals around death can provide. You might share your thoughts and feelings with a group of friends, perhaps through flowers, songs, or poetry.

❏ **Exercise.** You probably won't feel like exercising, but your body needs a way to process all the extra adrenalin it's putting out. A physical workout can help relieve the tension of pent-up emotions. Don't push too hard, however. You need to conserve your energy.

❏ **Try to eat a balanced diet.** You won't feel like eating, especially at first. But your grieving body is using up vast amounts of energy and needs good food to keep going. If fixing food is too much to deal with, ask friends for help or eat out.

❏ **Talk it out.** People who are grieving need to repeatedly talk about the death and about their feelings. Find people who are willing to listen without judgment or advice-giving. But recognize that unless they've experienced the grief surrounding death, most people can't understand the intensity of it. Don't expect friends and others who have no experience with the grief of death to fully understand what you're going through. You'll likely find support from others who have been through a similar experience.

❏ **Attend a grief support group.** Because our culture is so fearful of death, it's often hard to find people who have experienced grief and are willing to talk about it. It may help to join a grief support group where you can talk with like-minded people about how you feel and learn some important coping strategies.

❏ **Get professional help.** If you can't find others to talk with and share your grief, talking with a counselor trained in grief counseling can help.

❏ **Say goodbye.** One of the most healing activities you can do after losing someone you love is to say goodbye. Write the person a long letter, telling them everything you wish you had been able to say.

❏ **Meet new people.** Part of the healing process is learning new ways to interact, especially after the death of a spouse. Find new people to enjoy.

❏ **Take up new hobbies.** Find an activity or skill you always wanted to try. Take courses or seminars.

❏ **Go inside.** Use meditation, prayer, or any other method that helps you go inside yourself and get in touch with the depth of your feelings.

Allow Yourself to Grieve Fully

Every Moment Is Precious

What Grief Can Teach Us

Losing someone we love is never easy. It can, however, teach us some valuable life lessons. These lessons usually only become evident during the later stages of grief, when some of the initial pain has subsided.

❑ **Live in the present.** Losing someone dear teaches us that this moment is all we can really count on having. Every moment is precious.

❑ **Be spontaneously joyful.** Grief makes us aware of the gifts of joy, laughter, and play.

❑ **Value time.** It isn't something we can save or hold on to. We all waste time with daily distractions.

❑ **Simplify.** It's only after we lose someone or something valuable to us that we recognize its worth. Give less energy to the daily transactions of life and let go of the need for perfec-

tion. Learn to enjoy time spent with one another.

❑ **Embrace change.** Everything changes. We can either fight it or embrace and enjoy it. We can either grow and change or wither.

❑ **Be patient.** Grief teaches us that life can't be hurried. Everything has its own time and place. Try to understand and be patient with yourself and with others.

❑ **Enjoy laughter.** A belly laugh recharges and renews us—both physically and emotionally. Let the silly side of yourself emerge.

❑ **Get involved and belong to the human race.** The truth of the saying "No man is an island" becomes evident during the grieving process. We do need others. We need to lean on others and belong to one another. Give others a chance, and connect with your heart.

❑ **Share yourself.** Too often after a death of someone we care about, we regret the things we didn't say. Be open with others. Trust and share your thoughts and feelings.

CHAPTER 7

EVERYDAY HEALTH PROBLEMS

*A*t every stage of our lives, even the hardiest among us face minor health problems: sore throats and sniffles, heartburn and headaches. The question is not whether we'll endure aches and pains, but how we'll take care of them when they occur.

The steps we take to prevent and treat everyday health problems shape not only our physical but also our emotional health. You probably know someone who treats every little discomfort as a major crisis, and also someone who ignores even serious symptoms and avoids the doctor for years on end. Fortunately, most of us fall somewhere in between these two extremes. This chapter is designed to help you prevent many everyday health problems in yourself and in your family, tell you how to treat them when they do occur, and point out symptoms that might indicate the need for a professional opinion.

❏ ❏ ❏

Does Acne Have ESP?

There Is No Medical Evidence that What You Eat Affects Acne

It never fails—the day of the big date, the school photo sitting, the crucial job interview—a huge pimple suddenly appears on your face, as if it knew you needed to look good. Pimples are the bane of adolescence and sometimes surprising and unwelcome visitors well into adulthood. Genetics, stress, hormones, and other factors play roles in producing pimples, but you can take steps to minimize the problem.

What Causes Breakouts?

Acne is the result of blocked skin pores. Normally, your pores constantly shed dead skin cells and release oil. When the pores and follicles—canals that contain hair shafts—become blocked by dead cells, oil builds up and bacteria feeds on the oil and multiplies. The bacteria produces chemicals that break down the follicle walls, allowing the trapped material—oil, bacteria, and shed skin cells—to escape and produce bumps. The bumps are whiteheads and pimples. Blackheads occur when the oil is exposed to the air. Contrary to myth, they are not caused by trapped dirt.

Why We Get Pimples

When children reach puberty, their levels of male hormones rise, (in both boys and girls), and their skin's sebaceous (oil) glands get bigger, especially in the face, upper back, and chest areas. Oil output increases, causing dead skin cells to stick together and sometimes plug pores or follicles. Adults, especially women, also get acne, although it tends to appear more on the chin, jawline, or neck in women, and on the upper back and chest in men. Women may also experience breakouts at certain points in their menstrual cycle and due to the use of oral contraceptives. Sometimes an overabundance of androgen, a male hormone, causes acne breakouts in women.

Acne Triggers

You may be convinced the bag of potato chips you just ate will result in at least one pimple by morning. But there is, in fact, no medical evidence to suggest that what you eat affects acne. That doesn't mean the act of eating the chips is unrelated to a breakout. Perhaps you ate the whole bag when you saw your Visa bill or while you were preparing a major presentation for work. The stress may have triggered the emotional eating and at the same time affected your hormone level enough to worsen a minor blemish. (See sidebar, *Mythical Acne Causes*.) The following factors, however, may provoke or worsen breakouts:

- **Physical contact.** When you squeeze a pimple, you risk

MYTHICAL ACNE CAUSES

For such a widespread problem, acne is the subject of a lot of myths and misinformation. Contrary to popular belief, these do not cause acne:

- Chocolate, fried foods, or anything else you eat

- Sexual activity, or lack of it

- Dirt

❏   ❏   ❏

spreading the bacteria and worsening inflammation. It may also result in scarring.

- **Stress.** Although a link is not medically proved, many people notice flare-ups when they're experiencing tension.
- **Cosmetics.** Greasy makeup and moisturizers may clog your pores.
- **Drugs.** Some medications, such as lithium, may worsen acne.

Caring for Acne-Prone Skin

Follow this advice to pamper your precious skin.

- ❑ **Be gentle.** Vigorous scrubbing can irritate the skin and worsen blocked pores. Besides, while washing gets rid of oil on the skin's surface, it's the oil trapped beneath the surface—which no amount of scrubbing can reach—that causes breakouts.

- ❑ **Try gentle washing with warm water and soap or skin cleanser once or twice a day.** Again, the important word here is *gentle*. Because pimples often appear on the forehead, regular shampooing is also a good idea.

- ❑ **Don't "pop" pimples.** In fact, try to keep your hands away from your face as much as possible.

- ❑ **Try skipping the moisturizer.** If you're pimple prone, use only cosmetics labelled *noncomedogenic*, which means they won't block pores. And always remove your makeup each night with soap and water.

- ❑ **Check your medications.** Consult your doctor or pharmacist about the possible effects on your skin of any drugs you're taking.

- ❑ **Try over-the-counter products containing salicylic acid or benzoyl peroxide.** These are helpful products to treat mild acne. Start with the weakest formulas, and work your way up as necessary.

- ❑ **See your family physician or dermatologist.** If your acne doesn't get better after a few weeks of home treatments, seek professional help.

How Doctors Treat Acne

Too many teens and adults resign themselves to pimples because they believe not much can be done about acne. But studies show up to 80 percent of all people who seek treatment for the problem can be helped. If you seek a doctor's help in ridding yourself of pimples, explain to him or her what you've been doing to combat the problem, and what, if any, oral medications you take regularly.

Once your physician determines your problem is acne (instead of, say, an allergic reaction to makeup, lotions, or drugs or another skin disease), you might be given a prescription topical or oral medication to curb the problem. In severe cases, a physician might prescribe hormone therapy, or a drug called *isotretinoin,* a strong, last-resort drug.

Be sure to ask about side effects and precautions you need to take when using the drugs. Some topical creams, for example, increase your sensitivity to sunlight; antibiotics can upset your stomach or increase your risk of yeast infections; and isotretinoin has been linked to birth defects when used during pregnancy.

Avoid Vigorous Scrubbing— Treat Your Skin Gently

Living with Allergies

One Out of Every 11 Office Visits to a Doctor Is for an Allergic Condition

Allergies are extremely common—about one out of five Americans suffers from them, according to the National Institutes of Health, and estimates are that one out of every 11 office visits to a doctor is for an allergic condition.

Yet the causes of allergic diseases are still being debated by researchers, and many health problems—such as a food intolerance—are sometimes wrongly blamed on allergies. If some substances, such as pollen, household dust, or cat dander, cause your eyes to water and make you sneeze, you probably have a sensitivity to them, which can not only make you uncomfortable, but make you less productive at work, home, or school.

What Are Allergies?
Allergies occur when the body's immune system—designed to combat infection and disease—reacts inappropriately to a substance, called an *allergen*. Heredity is believed to play the largest role in determining who gets allergies, but the influences of other factors, including hormones, viral infections, and smoking, are still being studied. It's possible for someone to "outgrow" allergies—or suddenly develop them as an adult.

An allergic reaction occurs when an infection-fighting protein, known as the IgE antibody, encounters an allergen in the body and triggers the release of histamine and other chemicals from mast cells, which are most heavily concentrated in the skin, the linings of the nose and lungs, the gastrointestinal tract, and the reproductive system. The chemicals released from the mast cells then react with the tissues of the body, and produce problems: sneezing, watery eyes, asthmatic wheezing and coughing, skin conditions such as hives or eczema, or shock-like symptoms.

Diagnosing The Problem
If you consult a physician because you suspect you have allergies, you may have to undergo a skin test to determine if you've got the condition—and precisely which substances trigger a reaction. A physician uses a needle to put a drop of allergen just under the skin's surface. The test, which is essentially painless, takes about five minutes to administer; it takes about 15 minutes to get the results. A doctor might also check for elevated levels of IgE antibodies in a patient's immune system by drawing blood.

SELF-HELP FOR SNEEZERS
Your doctor can help treat many allergies, but the best first line of defense is to avoid or limit exposure to whatever it is that makes you miserable. If you have a problem with allergies, here are a few ways to decrease your exposure to common allergens, including dust, dust mites, and pollen. (Also see the sidebar, *Darn Those Dust Mites*, page 185.)

❏ **Try to stay inside when pollen counts are highest, early in the morning.** Bright, sunny, breezy days in the spring and fall are generally the worst for allergy sufferers.

❏ **Keep your house or car windows closed.** If you have it, use air-conditioning, switched to the "recycle" mode, when indoors or in a car—it can filter out 99 percent of all the pollen- and allergen-producing material in the air outside.

❑ **Keep your face covered.** If you must work outdoors, wear a scarf, bandanna, or "surgical mask" around your nose and mouth.

❑ **If your home uses forced air heat, cover each room's heat outlet with a dust filter made of cheesecloth or nylon.** Change the filter frequently, and change or clean furnace or air-conditioning filters every two to four weeks.

❑ **Don't forget to dust the ducts.** Heating and air conditioner ducts are ideal places for bacteria, dust mites, and mold to multiply—and enter your living space when the ducts are operating.

❑ **Try not to use carpets, except for washable throw rugs.** All carpets, especially the shag variety, trap dust and house dust mites.

❑ **Use "dustable" furniture and furnishings, such as wooden chairs and lightweight curtains.** Venetian blinds and upholstered furniture attract dust, and dust mites can breed in the upholstery. Wash curtains once a week.

❑ **Use air cleaners.** The most effective room air cleaners are fitted with high-efficiency particle-activating (HEPA) filters.

❑ **Don't keep furry or feathered household pets.** Cats are an especially bad idea for an allergy sufferer because their saliva—which they use to wash their fur—triggers allergic reactions.

DARN THOSE DUST MITES

Dust what? Perhaps you didn't realize you are sharing your home with thousands of microscopic creatures. In fact, allergists believe the real culprit in most dust allergies is the dust mite. These tiny insects live—and multiply—in dusty, humid areas as well as furniture, bedding, curtains, and other common household items made of fibrous materials.

Look around your home. If you have overstuffed furniture, carpets, or even lots of stuffed animals, dust mite corpses and droppings may be the reason you can't shake your allergy symptoms. See *Self-Help for Sneezers* for advice on how to limit your exposure to these varmints.

❑ ❑ ❑

Hints for an "Anti-Allergy" Bedroom

Most of us spend a good deal of time in our bedrooms. But this most-restful room can be a veritable minefield of allergens. Here's how to make the bedroom more hospitable to the allergy sufferer.

❑ **In bedroom closets, encase clothing in zippered plastic bags, and keep shoes in boxes rather than on the floor.** These storage methods keep dust buildup to a minimum.

❑ **Encase your bed's box spring, mattress, and pillows in zippered plastic covers.** Dust mites love to take up residence in the fibrous material of these items. As unpleasant as it sounds, covering these items keeps the mites already inside

True Food Allergies Are Very Rare

from getting out, and keeps others from getting in and sharing your bed.

❑ **Use synthetic-filled mattress pads, pillows, and comforters.** Many allergy sufferers are sensitive to feathers. Also avoid wool blankets since many people have a sensitivity to wool. Launder sheets and blankets frequently.

❑ **If the allergy sufferer is a child, keep nonwashable toys out of their bedroom.** Avoid stuffed animals. Keep all toys in a closed toy box or chest when the child isn't playing with them.

❑ **Clean the bedroom daily with damp cloths or oil mops.** After each cleaning, close the doors and windows until the dust-sensitive person is ready to reenter the room.

❑ **Make the bedroom off limits to pets.** Keep any household pets with fur or feathers out of the bedroom at all times.

Ask Your Doctor for (Achoo!) Help

Other than avoiding the sources of potential "allergy attacks"—which isn't always possible, you have a number of options when you seek relief from allergy symptoms.

- Nasal steroids (prescribed by your physician) and antihistamines (available over the counter) may help stop allergy symptoms.

- Your doctor may prescribe an ophthalmic (eye) steroid to help relieve the eye symptoms

of allergies, including itchy, watery eyes.

- Some drugs, including cromolyn sodium nasal spray, may prevent allergic reactions from taking place.

- Allergy shots, administered by a doctor, can reduce your body's production of the IgE antibody and encourage production of another antibody, IgG. Eighty-five percent of people with allergic rhinitis (hay fever) who receive the shots get some measure of relief, according to the National Institute of Allergy and Infectious Diseases, although it generally takes one to two years of routine treatment for them to notice results.

Allergic to Food?

Despite what you may think, true food allergies are very rare. Although one out of three people in the United States says they or someone in their family has a food allergy, the National Institutes of Health reports only about three percent of children and one percent of adults have an allergy to any type of food.

Many of these alleged "allergies" are, in fact, an intolerance to certain foods. Many people, for example, are lactose intolerant, which means they're deficient in an enzyme that breaks down milk protein.

If your doctor diagnoses a food allergy, you should avoid eating the food (which means you'll need to read ingredient labels carefully). If you have a severe allergy to shellfish, peanuts, or eggs, you may need to protect yourself in the event you inadvertently consume the food by carrying a kit to ward off potentially fatal anaphylactic reactions. The kit, available by prescription, includes a syringe of adrenaline, which should be administered immediately. You should then seek *immediate* medical care. (People who have severe allergies to insect stings may also need to carry such a kit.)

Take a Stand Against Athlete's Foot

An itching, burning feeling on the soles of your feet, between your toes, or on the palms of your hands, usually accompanied by a red rash, may indicate a fungal infection commonly called athlete's foot.

The fungus that causes this mildly contagious problem thrives in warm, moist areas, such as public showers and locker rooms—hence the name. But you don't have to spend time in a locker room to acquire this infection. Even couch potatoes can get athlete's foot. It is also spread by sharing towels, or by stepping on a contaminated bath mat; therefore, it's important to take preventive steps if you share a bathroom with anyone who has athlete's foot.

COMBATTING ATHLETE'S FOOT

Here are a few tips to prevent and treat athlete's foot fungus.

❑ **Keep your feet as dry as possible.** Towel them dry carefully after bathing or showering or when you step out of a pool. And don't share your towels. Incidentally, although you may *feel* safer wearing rubber sandals into a communal shower or locker room, there's no evidence they prevent athlete's foot.

❑ **Change into clean, dry socks or hose frequently.** Health professionals disagree over the best material for keeping skin dry: some say synthetic materials, others choose cotton. Try a pair of socks made with each material and see which keeps your feet drier.

❑ **Wear comfortable shoes.** Choose shoes that don't pinch your feet or cause them to sweat excessively. Leather is a more "breathable" material than rubber or vinyl.

❑ **Use antifungal powders.** Available over-the-counter in most pharmacies, these products may help prevent athlete's foot or control the problem if it occurs.

❑ **See your doctor.** If these tips don't help and the problem persists, schedule a visit with your physician.

Answers for Aching Backs

If you've ever had a backache, you're not alone. About six million Americans suffer back pain each year. Most backaches get better after a few days of rest. But about one out of six people has experienced a severe episode of back pain that lasts for at least two weeks.

The Fungus that Causes Athlete's Foot Thrives in Warm, Moist Areas

Most Lower Back Problems Are Caused by Improper Lifting and Moving of Heavy Objects

Back pain can hurt your wallet, too—after the common cold, episodes of lower back pain are the most frequent cause of lost work time in adults younger than 45 years of age. Fortunately, relatively few back problems require surgery.

Why Your Back Hurts

Lower back pain has many causes, including muscle strain or problems with the bones in the spine (vertebrae) and the disks of shock-absorbing material that separate them. The lower back is the most vulnerable part of the spine, probably because it isn't supported by the rib cage. Lower back injuries often occur because you've used muscles that aren't usually exercised. If you're not physically fit, your back and abdominal muscles are probably weaker than they should be, and, as a result, unable to handle strain. A "slipped disk" can also result when twisting causes a disk to bulge and put pressure on nerves. Some types of arthritis can also cause stiffness and pain in the back, neck, or hips.

Risk Factors

You're more likely to suffer back pain if your back and abdominal muscle tone are weak and:

- your job requires lots of bending and lifting.
- you take care of a bedridden or wheelchair-bound person who needs to be lifted and moved frequently.
- you bend your back rather than your knees when lifting objects.
- you lift and move heavy objects when in a hurry or off balance.
- you are overweight for your age, height, and sex.
- you're pregnant.

- you slouch when sitting or standing.
- you do not engage in regular exercise that specifically strengthens back and abdominal muscles.

PREVENTING BACK PROBLEMS

Because most lower back problems are caused by improper lifting and moving of heavy objects, learning the correct way to manage those tasks, as well as maintaining good back and abdominal muscle tone, can help prevent most problems. Follow these steps when lifting or moving a heavy object or a person:

- ❏ Plan ahead and take your time.
- ❏ Stand with your feet shoulder-width apart. This gives you a solid base of support.
- ❏ Bend at the knees.
- ❏ Tighten your abdominal muscles.
- ❏ Position the person or object close to your body.
- ❏ Lift with your legs *and don't bend at the waist!*
- ❏ Try not to twist your body. To move, point your toes in the direction you want to move and pivot in that direction.
- ❏ If you need to move an object on wheels, push rather than pull it.
- ❏ Wear flat shoes, or heels no higher than one inch.
- ❏ Seek assistance if you need to lift an object that's too heavy for you or too awkward for you to carry alone. Showing off will only damage your back.

TREATING BACK PAIN

Back pain requires some pampering. Follow these treatment tips.

❑ **Rest in bed.** In most cases, bed rest can help you recover from an episode of back pain. For best results, place pillows under your knees, or lie with your knees up and your feet flat, to take pressure and weight off your back.

❑ **Take over-the-counter anti-inflammatory medicine.** Aspirin or ibuprofen can help relieve pain.

❑ **Try ice packs and massages.** Some people also like heating pads, but use a heating pad for no more than 30 minutes at a time to avoid irritating the skin.

❑ **After a few days, get a little exercise.** Light activity keeps your muscles from getting weak. Walk around for a few minutes every few hours at least, even if it hurts. Build up slowly, gradually increasing the length and frequency of your activity.

When to Call a Doctor

Seek professional medical care if you experience the following symptoms.

● Pain that radiates from your lower back to the buttocks or down your leg

● Numbness in the leg, foot, groin, or rectal area

● Back pain accompanied by fever, nausea or vomiting, stomachache, weakness, or excessive sweating

● Loss of control of your bowels or bladder

● Intense pain

● Pain caused by an injury (If the injury is work related, you may need a doctor's report to file a disability claim with your employer.)

FOR MORE INFORMATION

To learn more about safe lifting techniques and back pain prevention, call the American Academy of Orthopaedic Surgeons at 1-800-824-BONES, or send a stamped, self-addressed business-sized envelope to:

Lift It Safe
American Academy of Orthopaedic Surgeons
P.O. Box 1998
Des Plaines, IL 60017

❑ ❑ ❑

Build a Better Back

Performed every other day, these exercises can help you strengthen your back, hip, leg, and abdominal muscles in order to prevent back injury. Do not perform these or any other exercises to the point of discomfort. Skip the exercise if you feel any pain. In fact, it's wise to consult your doctor before beginning any exercise program, especially if you haven't been physically active recently.

Wall Slides (*strengthens back, hip, and leg muscles*). Stand with your back against a wall and your feet shoulder-width apart, keeping your back against the wall as if you were sitting in a chair. Slide down into a crouch, until your legs form a 90-degree angle. Count to 5 and slide back up the wall. Repeat 5 times.

Arm and Leg Raises (*strengthens the upper and lower back*). Lie

Bed Rest Can Help You Recover from Back Pain

189

Exercise Regularly to Strengthen Back and Abdominal Muscles

on your stomach with your forehead resting on the floor, your arms extended on the floor in front of your head. Extend your legs, and rest your feet on the inner side of the big toes.

Slowly and gently lift the right arm and the left leg on 2 counts and lower on 2 counts. Then lift and lower the left arm and the right leg. Do 8 repetitions of this set, and progress to 3 sets of 8.

Easy Back Extension (*conditions the lower back*). Lie on your stomach with your forehead resting on the floor. Bend your elbows and place them alongside your chest, with your forearms resting flat on the floor. Extend your legs, and rest your feet on the inner side of the big toes.

Exhale as you slowly and gently lift the upper body, keeping your elbows and forearms on the floor. Keep your hip bones on the floor and lift only as high as you can go without pulling your elbows off the floor. Return to the starting position. Do 8 repetitions.

Abdominal Crunch (*strengthens stomach muscles*). Lie on your back with your knees bent and your feet flat on the floor. Slowly raise your head and shoulder blades off the floor and reach your hands toward your knees. To flex the abdominal muscles without risking back injury, do not raise your upper body beyond the shoulder blades. Count to 10, then lower yourself back to the floor. Repeat 5 times.

Back Leg Swing (*strengthens hip and back muscles*). Stand behind a chair. Using the chair for support, lift one leg back and up while keeping the knees straight. Return it slowly to the original position. Repeat with the other leg. Repeat the exercise 5 times with each leg.

Excuse Your Belching

In some ancient cultures, a cook's ability in the kitchen was judged by the loudness of the dinner guests' belches. (It's now customary to praise the chef by merely asking for recipes.) While most of us frown upon burping in public, it's still a natural, and at times necessary, function of the digestive system. Burping results from the following conditions:

- Eating too much food or too much of certain kinds of foods
- Eating too fast
- Drinking certain beverages such as beer or soda
- Swallowing too much air

The feeling of having "gas" or fullness in the upper abdomen usually doesn't indicate a buildup of intestinal gas, but an irritation of the upper stomach area. Over-the-counter antacids, either in tablet or liquid form, can cause you to belch and help relieve the pressure. Just remember to say "Excuse me."

Breast Care for Nursing Moms

Nursing is great for a baby, enabling him or her to bond with Mom and supplying nutrients needed for growth and good health. But breast-feeding can be tough for a new mother.

190

She may endure dry, cracked, sore nipples. Breast infections may occur. And the let-down reflex that helps milk flow can be triggered at the most inopportune times.

Here are hints to prevent sore nipples and make nursing a positive experience for both mother and child.

❑ **Make sure the baby is sucking properly.** If the sucking hurts, start over. Put your finger in the corner of the baby's mouth to stop baby's sucking action.

❑ **Let your nipples air dry between feedings.** A hair dryer set on low can help speed up the process.

❑ **At the start of a feeding, offer baby the nipple that is least sore first.** Sometimes the baby's sucking becomes less vigorous after feeding for a few minutes.

❑ **Change breasts often.** Switching breasts more often may alleviate some soreness.

❑ **Try rubbing lanolin or vitamin E oil on your nipples to soothe them.** Make sure you wash these products off before feeding the baby.

❑ **Wash your nipples daily with warm water.** This helps to prevent infection. Be sure to dry breasts thoroughly.

❑ **Don't wear plastic bra pads.** The plastic cannot wick moisture away from your breasts. Moisture increases your risk of breast infection.

❑ **Express milk until your let-down reflex occurs.** This helps make milk flow more readily (so your baby won't have to suck as hard).

❑ **Nurse the baby often.** This prevents your breasts from becoming engorged with milk.

❑ **Don't limit the time of feedings.** Stopping a feeding session before milk ducts empty can result in engorgement.

Is It a Breast Infection?

Sore, red spots on the breasts of a nursing mother—at times accompanied by fever—could indicate a breast infection, *mastitis,* a condition that's relatively rare in women who aren't nursing babies.

Call your doctor if you experience these symptoms; you may need an antibiotic. Your physician may also suggest an analgesic, such as aspirin, acetaminophen, or ibuprofen, for the pain and fever. The drugs shouldn't have any effect on the nursing baby, but you may want to switch to feeding the infant with the noninfected breast until the problem subsides. To prevent infections, keep your nipples clean and dry between feedings. (Be sure to read *Breast Care for Nursing Moms*, page 190.)

Breast Lumps: Are They Always Serious?

With all the recent media focus on breast cancer, you may be reassured to learn that not all breast conditions are cancer.

Nursing Moms Should Take Steps to Prevent Breast Infections

Perform Regular Breast Self-Exams

A number of other disorders can affect the female breast. These vary in degree of seriousness and discomfort. Some of the most painful conditions are treated quite simply, while some of the most serious conditions cause no pain or discomfort.

BREAST LUMPS

Few experiences are more frightening than finding a lump in your breast. But most breast lumps are benign (noncancerous) and caused by factors that have nothing to do with cancer (especially in women younger than aged 40). But only your health care practitioner can tell you whether you need to worry about a lump in your breast or unusual nipple discharge. See *The Breast Self-Examination,* Chapter 8, page 271, for details on how to examine your breasts for lumps.

Perhaps the most common source of breast lumps are fibrocystic changes, an umbrella term doctors give to the numerous kinds of thickening that occur in the second half of a woman's monthly cycle as her body prepares for pregnancy and nursing. The condition, which most often affects women between the ages of 25 and 50, involves tenderness and lumps that may include cysts, small, fluid-filled cavities. (Another condition, a *fibroadenoma,* is caused by harder, benign growths.)

The cause of fibrocystic changes, which usually abate once the menstrual period begins, is unknown. Likewise, there is no proved treatment for the condition, but here are a few suggestions for symptom relief.

- ❏ **Reduce caffeine intake.** Many women claim cutting down on caffeine eases their symptoms.
- ❏ **Take a mild diuretic.** If your doctor approves, use of a diuretic may also help ease discomfort caused by swollen breasts.
- ❏ **Use a mild analgesic.** Aspirin or ibuprofen may also ease pain.

Recovering from Bronchitis

Bronchitis is a viral infection of the mucous membranes that line the bronchi, the tubes that lead into the lungs. Smokers are more likely to get bronchitis, although any adult or child can suffer from it.

Although often caused by the same virus that results in the common cold (in fact, bronchitis is often the result of a cold virus that has spread to the mucous membranes), these symptoms often signal that your body is fighting off more than a simple cold:

- Wheezing
- Tightness in the chest
- Severe, loud coughing
- Yellow or greenish phlegm

TREATING BRONCHITIS

Remember, bronchitis is more serious than a cold, so take care of yourself. Follow these tips:

- ❏ **Rest, drink fluids, and avoid exposure to irritants.** A bronchitis sufferer must be pampered because an untreated case of bronchitis could turn into a much more serious case of pneumonia. Rest, drinking extra fluids, and avoiding lung irritants such as tobacco smoke help recovery.

❑ **Relieve symptoms with over-the-counter medicine.** An analgesic such as aspirin or acetaminophen helps reduce fever, and an over-the-counter cough suppressant helps relieve violent hacking, which can irritate the bronchi. If you have chronic heart or lung problems (including asthma), consult your doctor before using a cough suppressant. (Note: If treating a child with bronchitis, see the section *Fever Facts,* page 211.)

Easing the Ache of Bursitis

It used to go by the rather old-fashioned name "housemaid's knee," but there's nothing quaint about painful bursitis. For one thing, bursitis doesn't only occur at the knee; it can affect any major joint—your shoulder, elbow, hip, ankle, heel, or the base of the big toe.

Bursitis occurs when a bursa—a small sac of fluid that prevents friction between tendons and bones—becomes swollen and irritated. Repeated stress on a joint or repeated use (such as kneeling to scrub a floor, or throwing a ball hundreds of times in an afternoon) can cause bursitis.

TREATING BURSITIS

If you can stand a little discomfort, most cases of bursitis clear up on their own in a week or two

IS IT MORE SERIOUS?

If you experience the following symptoms, contact your physician; they may indicate pneumonia.

● Fever and chills
● Productive cough (cough that brings forth mucus or sputum)
● Sputum that is rusty or greenish
● Shortness of breath
● Chest pain

❑   ❑   ❑

(although you should be warned they tend to recur in the same place). To cope, try the following hints:

❑ Rest the joint.
❑ Keep pressure off the tender area.
❑ Take mild anti-inflammatory drugs such as aspirin or ibuprofen to relieve pain.
❑ Consult your physician if you experience prolonged or severe pain.

If your doctor determines your problem is indeed bursitis, he or she might be able to aspirate the bursa (inject a needle into it to draw off excess fluid); inject corticosteroids into the bursa; or prescribe or administer additional anti-inflammatory drugs.

Care for Carpal Tunnel Syndrome

The median nerve performs important work all day long, yet few people have heard of it. The nerve, which travels down the forearm and into the hand

Most Cases of Bursitis Clear Up on Their Own

If You Must Perform Repetitive Tasks Daily, Protect Your Wrists

through a "tunnel" in the wrist formed by bones and ligaments, helps regulate the nine tendons that help your muscles and bones bend your fingers and thumb. Usually, the median nerve quietly goes about its business, but when synovial membranes in the carpal tunnel of the wrist become swollen or irritated, putting pressure on the nerve, a painful condition called carpal tunnel syndrome can result.

Symptoms of Carpal Tunnel Syndrome
If you experience any of these symptoms, you might have carpal tunnel syndrome:

- Numbness or tingling in your hand that's worse at night or after using your hands to do a task (such as typing)
- Decreased feeling in your thumb, index finger, or middle finger
- Clumsiness when handling objects
- Occasional pain radiating from the hand up the shoulder

Causes of Carpal Tunnel Syndrome
These are common causes of this painful condition:

- Repeated and forceful grasping with the hands
- Repeated bending of the wrist (such as while typing, playing an instrument, or working a cash register)
- A broken or dislocated wrist
- Arthritis

- Thyroid dysfunction
- Diabetes
- Hormonal changes, such as those that accompany menopause or pregnancy

Protecting Your Wrists

If you must preform repetitive tasks on a daily basis, be sure to take these precautions:

- **Don't rest your wrists on hard edges.** This pressure can contribute to stress and swelling.
- **Adjust your chair height properly.** When seated at your workstation, your forearms should be parallel to the floor, and your wrists should not have to bend to reach the keyboard or work surface.
- **Take breaks.** A rest from the repetitive task now and then can prevent fatigue, which is a signal you are overstressing your wrists.
- **Exercise your hands.** When you take that break, stretch and rotate your hands to get the blood flowing properly.

TREATING CARPAL TUNNEL SYNDROME
If your physician diagnoses carpal tunnel syndrome, he or she may recommend the following:

- Many cases can be treated with rest and over-the-counter pain relievers, such as aspirin or ibuprofen.
- Splints can help keep your hand immobile so it can heal while still allowing you the use of your fingers. Splints may be

especially helpful in quelling nighttime symptoms.

- If you have a severe case, your doctor might recommend an injection of a medication such as cortisone into the carpal tunnel to help shrink the swollen membranes in the wrist and soothe your pain.

- If the above treatments fail, surgery—which is often performed on an outpatient basis—may be necessary to cut the ligament that forms the roof of the "tunnel" to relieve pressure on the median nerve.

Chafing: There's the Rub

If your skin has been rubbed painfully raw by tight-fitting clothing or by some other source of friction, you need to take two steps to help it recover: Protect it and lubricate it.

- ❑ **Determine why your skin is chafing.** Are you wearing clothes that are too snug or a size too small for you? Take steps to alleviate the problem.

- ❑ **Apply moisturizer to your skin.** Moisturizers lubricate the skin and make it less vulnerable to the wear and tear caused by friction. (See the sidebar, *The Best Moisturizers*.)

Signs of Other Skin Conditions

Chafing is a wearing away of the top layer of skin in one area of your body. If you suffer from frequent patches of red, blistering, scaly, oozing, itchy skin—and notice the problem usually gets worse at night—you might instead

THE BEST MOISTURIZERS

When choosing a moisturizer, keep this hint in mind: The "gunkier" (thicker and oilier) it is, the more effective it will be. Doctors tout plain old petroleum jelly as a highly effective means to keep your skin soft. It penetrates the top layer of skin to replenish the fats beneath the surface. Although it may feel uncomfortable to slather on such a thick gel, experiment with the product. Generally, the skin quickly absorbs a thin layer of petroleum jelly. For best results, apply any moisturizer immediately after washing, bathing, or showering while the skin is still damp to lock in water.

❑ ❑ ❑

have some type of eczema, an umbrella term given to a number of skin conditions, some of them caused by allergies. If you suspect you have eczema, see your physician. (Also see *When the Diagnosis Is Dermatitis and Eczema*, page 201.)

Kiss Chapped Lips Goodbye

As the weather becomes cold and dry, your lips may start to feel rough and cracked. They may even bleed. For most people, chapped lips can be prevented by locking in precious moisture.

- ❑ **Carry your favorite over-the-counter lip balm with you always.** Apply it often. Petroleum jelly also works well and may even help repair damaged skin.

- ❑ **Try not to chew or lick your lips.** These nervous habits can make chapped lips worse.

❑ **If nothing helps, see your doctor.** If chapped lips don't heal themselves with preventive care, your doctor might be able to prescribe a steroid cream to speed up recovery.

Nice Catch: You've Got a Cold

Healthy Adults Average Two or Three Colds Annually

It's one of those mysteries that continues to baffle modern scientists despite decades of research: how to cure the common cold. Children, whose immune systems are still developing (and who spend lots of time in the company of other children in school or day care), get an average of 8 to 12 colds a year. Healthy adults average two or three colds annually, although parents of young children may get more. Although there is no cure for cold misery, you can take steps to prevent colds and to seek relief from sniffles, coughing, and sore throats when they occur.

Cold Culprits?
Myths and folklore about colds abound. You may be surprised to learn what conditions don't lead to colds:

● **Cold, wet weather.** In fact, the virus thrives in cool, dry environments. Cold weather makes your nose run, however, even if you don't have a cold.

● **Going out in public.** In fact, you're more likely to catch a cold at home because of the close, intimate contact you have with your family members. (Colds are most contagious in the first three days of symptoms.)

● **Smoking.** It may make a cold you already have worse (and make you more vulnerable to bronchitis), but there's no evidence it gives you more colds.

Careful with that Cold!

To avoid catching the cold virus or passing it to others (especially during cold and flu season, which runs from late August until May in most of the United States), integrate these steps into your daily routine:

❑ **Keep your hands clean.** Wash them often with soap and water, especially after helping a child blow his or her nose. Cold viruses pass most rapidly when they get on your hands; they then enter your body when you touch your nose or rub your eyes.

❑ **Try not to rub your eyes or touch your nose.** If you must, wash your hands first.

❑ **Use disposable facial tissues when you blow your nose.** When disposed of properly they are more sanitary than cloth handkerchiefs.

❑ **Cover your mouth when you cough or sneeze.** Teach children to do the same. The airborne cold virus can make others sick.

TREATING COLD SYMPTOMS

Your mother was right: Rest and drinking lots of fluids help speed your recovery from a cold. Although not all doctors are convinced home remedies, such as vitamin C and chicken soup, have much effect on colds, they may make you feel you're at least putting up a fight.

When shopping for over-the counter cold relief, choose single-action products that target your symptoms (for example, a decongestant for a stuffy nose, a cough suppressant for a dry, nagging cough). Multisymptom cold remedies probably contain ingredients that combat symptoms you don't even have and may expose you to additional side effects. Always read the label of any medication to learn about possible side effects and cautions for people with certain medical conditions.

When to Call the Doctor

If your cold hangs on for more than a week, seek medical attention. You could have influenza (which isn't merely a "bad cold," but another illness entirely), bronchitis, strep throat, or an infection of the sinuses or the middle ear (which is common in children). Recurrent "colds" may in fact be allergies, especially if they're not accompanied by fever.

Cold Sore Care

Cold sores are not only an annoyance, but a sign of an incurable virus called herpes simplex type I. Type I herpes is contagious and spread through casual contact, but do not con-

STEAMING YOUR SINUSES

Some cold sufferers swear hot or cold steam produced by vaporizers or humidifiers helps clear their nasal passages and ease their breathing. But if not cleaned often, these devices can grow all kinds of bacteria, which are then expelled into the air and can prolong your misery by giving you a sinus infection.

To guard against bacteria buildup, empty and clean the device often, and change or clean any filters as recommended in the manufacturer's manual.

❏ ❏ ❏

fuse it with herpes simplex type II (genital herpes). Type I virus announces its arrival with sores, usually on the lip, and sometimes swollen glands.

The following factors may precipitate a cold sore outbreak:

- Stress
- A cold or fever
- An injury (from dental work or biting your lip)
- Sun and wind exposure

After the first episode of the virus (which typically lasts seven to ten days), you may experience recurrent outbreaks, which usually appear as single sores on the lip. The sores usually appear in the same place over and over again and may be preceded by a tingling feeling in that area.

COPING WITH COLD SORES

Although the sores disappear on their own after seven to ten days, your doctor can prescribe the antiviral medication acyclovir, which is available in either ointment or capsules.

Here are some tips to cope with cold sores while you're waiting for them to disappear.

Rest and Drinking Lots of Fluids Help Speed Your Recovery

❏ **Keep cold sores to yourself.** Cold sores are highly contagious. Avoid direct contact (yes, that means kissing) and sharing towels, makeup, and drinking and eating utensils.

❏ **Avoid salty, spicy, and acidic foods.** They can irritate cold sores.

❏ **Use aspirin or ibuprofen.** These over-the-counter medications can reduce inflammation and pain. Choose them over acetaminophen, which is not an anti-inflammatory.

Calming the Baby with Colic

Each Baby Responds Differently to Attempts to Soothe Crying

If you've got an infant younger than 12 weeks old who has suddenly started crying with a vengeance at night, there's probably no cause for alarm. Often babies who cry inconsolably are experiencing some abdominal pain and cramping.

A baby's temperament—and yours—may influence how he or she behaves at this stage: Fussy babies are often more "colicky," crying louder and longer than docile ones, and infants may pick up on parents' anxiety about the situation, making it worse.

The best advice: Stay calm, rock and cuddle the baby when the crying starts, and be patient.

Each baby responds differently to attempts to soothe the crying. Parents become very creative when it comes to discovering what works. Some of the favorites:

● **Singing.** It doesn't matter if you can sing on key; if you feel comfortable singing or humming, your baby will like the sound of your voice.

● **Running water.** Place a bowl in the sink and turn the faucet on. Hold your baby next the sink so he or she can hear the sound of the water running into the bowl.

● **A vacuum cleaner.** Sometimes a louder noise is what baby likes. But watch your child's reaction carefully—the noise may frighten some babies.

● **A ride in the car.** Nearly every parent swears by this one. You may also be able to simulate a car ride: Some parents say placing the baby in a car seat and placing the car seat on a running clothes dryer works, too. *Never leave baby unattended!*

● **Rocking.** Babies love to rock. You can rock them while you stand or sit, or place baby in a baby swing. *Again, never leave baby alone in a swing!*

Ruling Out Crying Causes

There may be simple reasons for your youngster's wailing. Your baby may need to be burped, or perhaps a stray hair wrapped around a baby's finger or toe is causing distress. A well-meaning parent's frantic attempts to entertain and distract a baby can result in overstimulation when all the child really needs to do is snooze.

Constipation: A "Regular" Problem?

Despite what you hear on TV commercials, there's no such thing as being "regular." Some people have bowel movements three times daily, while others may have them three times a week. If, however, you notice a sudden change in your bathroom habits, have to strain to move your bowels, or feel uncomfortable even after you've attempted to have a bowel movement, you may be constipated, which happens when stools pass too slowly through your intestines.

Causes of Constipation

Here are some common causes of constipation:

- Not enough fluids
- Not enough dietary fiber
- Not enough physical activity
- Not going to the bathroom when you feel the urge
- Certain drugs
- Laxative overuse
- Depression
- Hyperthyroidism
- Colon cancer

GETTING THROUGH A CASE OF CONSTIPATION

The advice to prevent and treat constipation is the same:

- ❏ Drink fluids (water is best).
- ❏ Eat fiber-rich foods.

Drinking plenty of fluids (the equivalent of six to eight glasses of water daily) and eating plenty of fiber should help prevent constipation, and should be tried first when you do feel blocked. Ideally, two to four servings of fruit and three to five servings of vegetables a day, plus any extra grains (such

FIBER-RICH FOODS

- Unprocessed wheat bran
- Unrefined breakfast cereals, such as shredded wheat
- Whole wheat, rye, or pumpernickel bread
- Fresh or dried fruit (except bananas)
- Vegetables (except for potatoes)
- Legumes (chickpeas, baked beans, lima beans, soybeans)

❏　❏　❏

as bran breakfast cereal) should be your daily goal. See the sidebar, *Fiber-Rich Foods*, for a list of some good choices. (Also see *Increasing Your Fiber Intake*, in Chapter 1, page 23.)

If the problem persists despite dietary changes, increased exercise, and the use of bulk-forming laxatives (the kind that contain psyllium), talk to your doctor.

Why Laxatives Don't Help Long-term

Occasional use of bulk-forming laxatives—which add water to your stools, softening them and making them pass more easily through the intestines—may help if you're constipated, but they shouldn't be your first line of defense. Overuse of other types of laxatives, which stimulate muscle contractions in the intestine, can actually make the problem worse. And enemas are not considered a recommended treatment for constipation. Here are the reasons daily or frequent use of laxatives is counterproductive:

- Your intestines can become dependent on laxatives, and may have trouble functioning on their own once you stop using them.

To Prevent Constipation, Drink Fluids and Eat Fiber-Rich Foods

Follow Your Contact Lens Cleaning Schedule Exactly

- Laxatives can interfere with your body's ability to metabolize drugs.
- Laxatives can move food through your digestive system so quickly that water and nutrients can't be completely absorbed.

Signs of Serious Problems

In rare cases, the inability to have a bowel movement isn't mere constipation, but the sign of an obstruction of the digestive tract. Such blockages, most common in people older than age 40, might be caused by a benign or even a malignant tumor. If you've never been constipated before and suddenly have great trouble moving your bowels, or if you experience any of the following symptoms, see your doctor:

- Bloody or black stools
- Constipation that lasts three weeks or more
- Abdominal pain or pain upon moving the bowels

Correcting Contact Lens Problems

Today, there are several different kinds of contact lenses, freeing people who need their vision corrected from eyeglasses. But contact lenses, whether hard, soft, daily wear, extended wear, or disposable, can present problems of their own (such as protein buildup and corneal infections) if you do not care for them properly.

If you wear contacts, ask your eye care professional about the proper way to clean and store your lenses. Follow the cleaning schedule exactly to prevent protein buildup and infections. In addition, here are some helpful hints:

- ❑ **Wash your hands thoroughly with soap before handling your lenses.** Choose a soap without additives, and one that doesn't leave a film on your hands.

- ❑ **Don't rub your eyes.** If your eyes feel irritated, remove your contacts.

- ❑ **Don't use tap water or saliva to lubricate your contact lenses.** Keep a travel-size bottle of saline solution in your car, desk, and work area.

- ❑ **Use any aerosol products (deodorant, cologne, hair spray)** *before* **inserting your lenses.** If you must use one of these products when wearing contact lenses, shut your eyes tightly, then quickly leave the area while the cloud of spray disperses.

- ❑ **Don't wear contacts when applying chemical products to your hair.** These include hair dyes, permanent wave lotions, or medicated shampoos.

- ❑ **Apply any cosmetics before inserting your lenses.** And remove contacts before removing your makeup.

- ❑ **Use only water-soluble cosmetics and "water-resistant" mascara.** Do not use "lash-building" or "waterproof" mascara. Choose pressed powder makeup rather than loose powder. And don't wear false eyelashes.

- ❑ **If you must apply eyeliner, use a soft pencil.** Liquid or cake-type eyeliners can flake. Never apply eyeliner to the inner edge of the lid or above the lash line on the lower lid.

❑ **Never apply eye makeup when you're in motion.** In other words, don't put your makeup on in a moving vehicle.

Coughs: Halting the Hack

Coughing is more than an annoyance—it's a reflex that protects your breathing passages, including your lungs, from secretions that can clog them and hinder your intake of oxygen. But coughing can also serve as an important signal of serious health problems, including upper respiratory infections, pneumonia, asthma, and illnesses caused by cigarette smoking.

TREATING COUGHS

To prevent coughs, follow the advice for preventing colds and flu (see pages 196 and 214). Also, avoid cigarette smoke, and kick the habit if you smoke. Follow these directions for treating different kinds of coughs.

❑ **Dry cough accompanied by ticklish or sore throat:** Try sucking on hard candies or medicated throat lozenges.

❑ **Cough with thick phlegm:** Expectorants, over-the-counter syrups that increase the lubricants in your throat, can help you cough or spit up the material. Drinking plenty of fluids also helps and is ultimately more crucial than medicine from the pharmacy.

❑ **Dry, irritating cough:** A cough suppressant that contains codeine and prescribed by your physician or an over-the-counter substitute may help you rest.

When to Seek Help

Notify your physician for the following cough conditions:

● If you have a persistent cough that doesn't improve after ten days of treatment, especially an unexplained cough, or one that's dry and hacking

● If you have a cough that produces thick, foul-smelling, rusty or greenish phlegm (a sign of pneumonia)

● If you experience chest pain when you breathe

● If you ever cough up blood

When the Diagnosis Is Dermatitis and Eczema

If you suffer from frequent patches of red, blistering, scaly, oozing, itchy skin, you might have some type of dermatitis, also called eczema. Both are umbrella terms given to a number of skin conditions that result in inflammation. With medication and, in some cases, lifestyle changes, most dermatitis outbreaks can be controlled.

Here are some common types of eczema:

Atopic dermatitis, which most often affects people with a

Coughing Is a Reflex that Protects Your Breathing Passages

Stress Can Provoke a Case of Eczema

family history of hay fever or asthma, usually appears as red, blistering, oozing, crusting skin patches that become itchier at night. (As the patient ages, the lesions become drier and darker, sometimes appearing brownish-gray rather than red.) About ten percent of infants and three percent of all children and adults in the United States have this condition, according to the American Academy of Dermatology. Although the problem is most common in people younger than 25 years of age, about 60 percent of people suffer from eczema throughout life.

Infantile eczema is a type of atopic dermatitis that appears in infancy. Lesions most often show up on the child's face and scalp. A telltale sign of the problem is a youngster who constantly rubs his or her head and cheeks to relieve itching. The problem usually improves before the child reaches two years of age.

Allergic contact eczema, or **contact dermatitis**, describes itchy, blistering patches of skin that have come into contact with a substance that causes an allergic reaction, such as poison ivy, sumac or oak; cosmetics; chemicals; dyes; or detergents.

Seborrheic dermatitis appears as yellow-pinkish-brownish, thickened, greasy, scaly patches of skin, usually on the scalp and center of the face. Dandruff is a mild form of seborrheic dermatitis. The cause is generally unknown and, while treatment can control this form of dermatitis, it may not eradicate the problem.

Nummular eczema shows up as round, red, oozing, crusting patches on the shoulders, backs of the forearms and lower legs, and buttocks. Like seborrheic dermati-

tis, the cause is often unknown, but a dry environment (indoors in the winter) or stress can lead to the condition.

BALANCING THE SCALES

Here's what you can do to cope with your itchy skin:

❑ **Try not to scratch!** Scratching only makes the problem worse.

❑ **Note what you wear or put on your skin.** Rough, tight, scratchy clothing, such as woolens, or strong soaps, lotions, or cosmetics might be aggravating the problem.

❑ **Reduce stress.** Emotional stress might also make eczema worse. See Chapter 5, *Coping with Stress*, for stress reduction techniques.

❑ **Call your doctor.** Your physician can prescribe topical creams, such as corticosteroids, and oral antihistamines, to control itching and speed healing. In some cases, your doctor might prescribe antibiotics to combat a secondary infection. In severe instances, ultraviolet light therapy (administered at a medical facility) might be tried. If you have a severe or stubborn case of eczema, your doctor might prescribe systemic steroids.

Diaper Rash: Pamper Baby's Bottom

A baby's skin is sensitive, and sometimes even the most pampered infants can suffer an irritated, red, burn-like rash caused by exposure to a soiled diaper.

To prevent your child from enduring this painful annoyance, follow this advice:

❑ **Check and change diapers often.** Keep baby's bottom clean and dry by washing the area with a clean wet cloth and then wiping carefully each time you change the diaper.

❑ **Apply petroleum jelly.** Diaper rash usually goes away on its own, but you might want to rub a little petroleum jelly onto the affected area to soothe a baby's discomfort.

❑ **If a rash is accompanied by red, pimple-like dots on the edges, notify your doctor.** He or she might prescribe antifungal cream to soothe the area.

Fending Off Diarrhea

Whatever its cause—a virus, bacteria, parasites, the use of antibiotics, rich foods, spoiled foods—few experiences are more unpleasant than diarrhea. Although watery, uncontrollable bowel movements are actually your body's attempt to make itself healthy—to rid itself of an infection or irritant—diarrhea can lead to dehydration, a problem that may require medical attention.

You may not have realized it, but most cases of diarrhea are preventable.

❑ **Wash your hands before cooking or serving food.** A simple rinse isn't good enough to eliminate diarrhea-causing bacteria. Be sure to use soap and warm water.

❑ **Wash your hands carefully after changing a diaper or using the bathroom.** Again, use warm water and soap.

❑ **Dispose of diapers properly.** Always put used diapers in a closed trash can or diaper pail.

❑ **Ask your doctor about the possible side effects of any prescriptions you receive.** Antibiotics, vitamin C supplements, magnesium-based antacids, some heart disease and cancer medications, and laxatives (when used excessively) can all cause diarrhea. If you think your medication may be causing your diarrhea, consult your doctor. Do not, however, change the dosage or stop taking any medication without first talking with your physician.

❑ **Check your diet.** If you're lactose intolerant (sensitive to milk sugars), dairy products may be at the root of your diarrhea. Try soy-based milk substitutes, or take lactase supplements instead. (See *Coping with Lactose Intolerance*, in Chapter 1, page 34.)

❑ **Avoid products that contain sorbitol, the artificial sweetener.** Some people are unable to digest this product.

❑ **Learn to manage stress.** Stress can aggravate irritable bowel syndrome and other digestive problems associated with diarrhea. (See Chapter 5, *Coping with Stress*, for stress-reduction techniques.)

❑ **Store food properly.** Follow the advice found in the section *Ensuring Food Safety,* in Chapter 1, page 31, to avoid eating spoiled food.

Most Cases of Diarrhea Are Preventable

When Diarrhea's Got You Down

Diarrhea is a natural and necessary process. The body needs to eliminate what is making it sick, and diarrhea is one way to do that.

But if you feel you need relief, try the following advice:

❑ **Try over-the-counter medications.** Products such as Pepto-Bismol can help curb symptoms. In cases where diarrhea is caused by bacteria, your doctor may prescribe antibiotics to speed your recovery.

❑ **Drink fluids to keep from dehydrating.** If a child with diarrhea is also vomiting, try giving small, frequent amounts of liquid. You should wait at least 30 minutes after the last bout of vomiting to ensure the solution stays down. Read *Signs of Serious Illness,* and notify your doctor if diarrhea persists or is accompanied by any of the conditions listed. Dehydration is a serious condition, and delay in obtaining medical treatment can be dangerous.

SIGNS OF SERIOUS ILLNESS

Babies and small children can lose too much body fluid very quickly. If a child displays any of these signs after or during a bout of diarrhea or vomiting, seek immediate medical help. These symptoms may indicate a life-threatening condition. (An older child or adult who experiences feelings of faintness after an episode of diarrhea or vomiting may need extra fluids or even medical attention.)

● Irritability
● Loss of appetite
● Weight loss
● Light-headedness when getting out of bed or standing up
● Less frequent urination
● Darker-than-usual urine
● Fast pulse
● Dry mouth
● Extreme thirst
● Sunken eyes
● No tears when crying
● Sunken soft spot on the head of babies younger than 18 months
● Skin that feels doughy instead of springy to the touch

Other Warning Signs

Also call your doctor if a child with diarrhea or vomiting displays any of the following symptoms.

FOOD AND DRINK TIPS

❑ Diarrhea patients older than two years of age can drink broth, sports drinks (such as Gatorade), ginger ale, or noncaffeinated tea.

❑ Avoid soft drinks or other beverages containing caffeine, which is a diuretic—the last thing a diarrhea sufferer needs!

❑ Stay away from milk and dairy products (including ice cream and pudding) for three to seven days after diarrhea begins because milk protein (lactose) can aggravate the problem.

❑ Also avoid foods with lots of sugar or fat, such as gelatin or fried foods.

❑ Eat bland foods. In the first 24 hours of a diarrhea bout, the BRAT diet—**b**ananas, **r**ice, **a**pplesauce, and **t**oast—as well as unsweetened cereals can provide nutrition without upsetting the stomach of a child or adult.

❑　❑　❑

These symptoms are sometimes present in serious or life-threatening conditions.

- A fever greater than 102 degrees Fahrenheit
- Vomiting longer than eight hours, or severe vomiting
- Bloody or slimy stools
- Bloody or green vomit
- Bloated appearance
- Inability to urinate in eight hours
- A stiff neck
- Listlessness or excessive sleepiness
- Abdominal pain for more than two hours

Dry Skin: Searching for Softness

Some people suffer dry, itchy, chapped skin year round, but especially in winter. If your skin lacks the moisture it needs to keep it soft and supple, you need to put some moisture in—and keep what's already there from being drawn out.

- ❏ Wash and bathe when necessary, no more than once or twice a day, in warm (not hot) water. (Hot water removes oil.)
- ❏ Wear protective cotton, plastic, or rubber gloves when doing household chores, such as washing dishes.
- ❏ Use a moisturizer after washing or bathing to lock in water.
- ❏ Apply lotion to your hands frequently, especially after hand-

washing or dishwashing, to keep them from drying out.

- ❏ See the sidebar, *The Best Moisturizers*, page 195.

Take Care of Your Ears

There are a number of reasons you may experience ear discomfort. But whatever the cause, the effect is the same—it makes you feel uncomfortable and may make it difficult for you to hear. Infants and small children in particular are prone to ear infections. A common cold can block up your eustachian tubes, which lead from the middle ear to the throat. A dip in a pool can leave you with an annoying case of "swimmer's ear."

For advice on coping with ear infections and ringing in the ears, see those sections (page 206 and 207). And follow these tips to take better care of your ears.

CLEANING YOUR EARS

Next time someone suggests you "Get the wax out of your ears," tell them that earwax removal is neither recommended nor necessary.

First, some earwax is good for our ears: It protects the eardrum from foreign particles, such as dust and bacteria that could cause infection, and its lubricating effects prevent dryness.

Second, for the most part, ears are self-cleaning. The movement of your jaw when you eat and talk eventually pushes most of the wax to the outer ear where you can easily remove it.

Infants and Small Children Are Prone to Ear Infections

Earwax Removal Is Generally Not Necessary

Third, the ear contains plenty of delicate tissue that can be easily—and irreparably—damaged. So use of cotton swabs to remove earwax is a definite no-no. Besides the risk of perforating the eardrum, use of cotton swabs or other instruments may push the wax deeper into the canal, making it more difficult to remove, or against the eardrum, affecting hearing and perhaps even damaging the eardrum.

Still, some people's ears do produce a great deal of wax—more than can be removed naturally. Too much earwax can cause ringing in the ears, pressure or fullness, itchiness, and hearing loss. If you have a great deal of wax built up inside your ear (but have no fever, illness, dizziness, or ear pain), you might want to try the following flushing technique for earwax removal. Incidentally, over-the-counter earwax removal systems are safe, but are no more effective than the following technique. *Note: Never put liquid in your ear if you have a perforated eardrum.*

1. With an eyedropper, place a few drops of mineral oil (vegetable and baby oil work, too) in your ear twice a day for two or three days to loosen earwax.

2. After a few days of this oil treatment, flush your ears with a bulb syringe filled with warm water. Tilt your head down and pull your outer ear up and back (to straighten the ear canal), and gently squirt the water into the ear canal. Repeat until the wax falls out.

3. Fill an eyedropper with rubbing alcohol and use it to rinse your ear. The alcohol will absorb the water remaining in your ear canal. Let the alcohol drain from your ear.

If you are unable to remove the wax, or you feel continued pressure inside the ear, ask your physician to flush out your ears.

Is It an Ear Infection?

Middle ear infections are very common, especially in infants and young children. A physician can prescribe medication to treat infections. The symptoms of an ear infection can include the following:

- Feelings of fullness in the ear
- Earache
- Hearing loss or hearing difficulty
- Fever
- Dizziness
- Ringing in the ears
- Any drainage from the ear

Infants and small children might also exhibit the following signs:

- Crying
- Irritability
- Constant rubbing or tugging the ear

If your physician diagnoses an infection, prescription antibiotics might be required to combat the problem. Analgesics, such as aspirin, ibuprofen, or acetaminophen, might also ease your discomfort. Remember: Never give aspirin to a child because of the risk of Reye syndrome, a rare but potentially fatal disease. In some cases, surgery may be required to relieve pressure on the eardrum.

Ward Off Ringing in the Ears

You go to hear live music played one night, and for hours afterward, everything sounds as if you're underwater. But what if outside sounds stay muffled, and the ringing, buzzing noise in your ears doesn't go away? It could be a sign you've damaged your hearing. Ringing in the ears, or *tinnitus,* is a condition of the inner ear that can be triggered by exposure to loud noise, as well as by a host of other factors, including earwax buildup, allergies, ear infections, diabetes, anemia, heart disease, stroke, and trauma.

Your inner ear contains thousands of tiny hair cells that send electrical impulses to the brain in response to sound vibrations. The brain translates these impulses into sound. When the hair cells are damaged, they may send continuous impulses, even when no sounds are present and no vibrations are actually entering the ear. This constant sound is enough to drive anyone to distraction.

STOP THE RING BEFORE IT STARTS

To prevent tinnitus or at least attempt to make it more bearable, follow this advice:

❑ **Avoid situations that present dangers to your ears.** Use common sense. In other words, if you must go hear a rock band, don't stand in front of the amplifiers. If you must play your car stereo, don't turn up the volume until the windows rattle. If you must listen to music through headphones, keep the sound at a reasonable level—if other people can hear it, the music is too loud.

❑ **Wear protective gear.** If you work near loud machinery, wear the appropriate ear protection equipment (usually provided by your employer). Wear earplugs (available in most pharmacies) when attending a loud concert. If you own a gun and practice shooting at a rifle or gun range, wear protective ear covering.

❑ **Drink responsibly.** Too much alcohol can cause you to expose yourself to louder noise than you could tolerate when sober—and it can aggravate tinnitus.

❑ **Control your blood pressure.** Low or high blood pressure can cause inner ear problems that result in tinnitus. Have your blood pressure checked by your doctor, and follow his or her advice for getting your pressure to normal levels.

❑ **Cut down on sodium and stimulants.** Eliminating sodium has proved helpful in reducing tinnitus in some people with inner ear disorders. Stimulants such as caffeine found in coffee, tea, colas, or chocolate; smoking; and drugs can affect the hair cells and trigger tinnitus.

❑ **Limit aspirin.** Talk to your doctor if you take aspirin regularly and you experience ringing in the ears. Its use in large doses or over extended periods has been associated with hair cell damage.

Avoid Situations that Present Dangers to Your Ears

207

Excessive Perspiration Could Signal a Medical Problem

❏ **Maintain your overall health.** You'll reduce your risk of some of the conditions that impact tinnitus, such as heart disease and diabetes. Even reducing stress, getting enough rest, and exercising regularly can affect your ears!

COPING WITH TINNITUS

If you experience persistent ringing in the ears, see your doctor. He or she might give you a hearing test to gauge any reduction in your ability to detect sound. (Other symptoms of hearing loss might include difficulty understanding women's or children's voices, or difficulty sorting out sound when more than one person is speaking.)

Although most people with tinnitus simply have to learn to live with it, some manage by covering up the ringing with a more pleasant sound (such as a radio at night), or with the use of artificial hearing aids.

Coping with Excessive Perspiration

Sweaty palms, damp underarms—we all get them sometimes. If you feel perspiration is a problem, more frequent showering and use of a strong antiperspirant (as opposed to a deodorant, which helps curb odor but not sweating) may help. But if you find yourself soaking through your clothes on a daily basis, you should try to determine the cause.

Here are some possible causes and some advice for coping with profuse sweating.

❏ If you perspire a great deal whenever you physically exert yourself even mildly (such as climbing one set of stairs), see your doctor for a stress test. In this case, perspiration could indicate you're at risk for heart disease. At the very least, it probably discourages you from getting enough exercise, which you need for overall health.

❏ If you only sweat when faced with a situation that makes you nervous, such as going on a date or speaking in a business meeting, emotional stress and anxiety could be the culprits. You may need to seek help in dealing with your fears.

❏ If you suddenly develop a problem with profuse sweating for no apparent reason, in other words the perspiration is not associated with physical activity or an anxiety-producing event, see your doctor. In addition to a heart problem, perspiration could signal a medical condition such as a thyroid problem or infection among others. Also let your doctor know if you wake up during the night perspiring profusely—a condition called night sweats.

What Are Your Red Eyes Telling You?

If your eyes are the mirror of your soul, what message is your soul sending out when your eyes are red? Red eyes can signal a variety of troubles from not enough sleep, to a minor medical condition, to a major, vision-threatening illness.

If you've been getting enough sleep lately and you know fatigue isn't the problem, your eye redness could indicate the following:

- A small problem that will heal itself: a rupture, possibly caused by hard coughing or sneezing, of the tiny blood vessels of the conjunctiva, the film-like membrane that lines the eyelid and covers much of the eyeball

- An allergic reaction

- A bacterial or viral infection of the conjunctiva. (See *Conjunctivitis: The Perils of "Pinkeye."*)

- The onset of a sty (See *When a Sty Has You Stymied*, page 210.)

- Iritis, an inflammation of the uvea, the layer of the eye that includes the iris (Iritis may require drug treatment.)

- A trauma, such as a foreign object in the eye, which may require first aid, and possibly professional attention (For advice on removing a foreign body or substance from your eye, see *First Aid for Your Eyes*, Chapter 10, page 340.)

BRING BACK THE WHITE

Decongestant eye drops, which contain an agent that constricts blood vessels, are available over the counter in any pharmacy. But you should check with your family physician or ophthalmologist before using these products. The doctor may want to make sure the cause of your eye redness is not a serious medical condition. If you do use these products to relieve discomfort, be sure to follow the product directions carefully.

If red eyes are accompanied by other symptoms, such as pain, significant eye discharge, blurred vision, or severe sensitivity to light, consult a physician. These could indicate an inflammation on the inside of the eye, an ulcer of the eye, or even glaucoma.

Conjunctivitis: The Perils of "Pinkeye"

When the white of your eye turns pink or red, and you experience a gritty, itchy sensation when you blink, you may have an inflammation of the conjunctiva, the thin membrane that lines the eyelids and covers much of the eyeball.

Although allergies or environmental irritants can enlarge the tiny blood vessels of the conjunctiva (causing redness, an increased sensitivity to light, and watery or pus-like discharge), the problem is also often caused by bacteria or viral infections—a condition commonly known as "pinkeye." Although the problem is usually harmless, it should be treated early because conjunctivitis is extremely contagious.

AVOIDING CONJUNCTIVITIS

These hints should help you avoid getting a conjunctivitis infection from another person or from passing it on if you do get it.

- Wash your hands after contact with someone who has conjunctivitis.

- Don't use anyone else's handkerchiefs, washcloths, or

Conjunctivitis Is Extremely Contagious

A Sty Is Usually the Result of an Inflamed Eyelash Follicle

towels, and don't let anyone else use yours.

❑ Do not share eye cosmetics or makeup applicators.

❑ Don't smoke, and avoid exposure to secondhand smoke; smoke may cause or aggravate conjunctivitis.

COPING WITH CONJUNCTIVITIS

Follow this advice:

❑ Apply cool compresses to the inflamed eye to help soothe the discomfort.

❑ Notify your family physician or ophthalmologist. If your conjunctivitis is caused by bacteria, your doctor might prescribe antibiotic eye drops to help clear up the problem. Viral conjunctivitis, which might be accompanied by other symptoms such as a sore throat or runny nose, usually clears up on its own within two weeks.

Caution: Any conjunctivitis in a newborn baby should be treated without delay; it could threaten the child's vision.

When a Sty Has You Stymied

A sty is one of life's little unpleasant surprises. It appears suddenly as a painful, red swelling—resembling a pimple—at the base of an eyelash. Most often, a sty is the result of an infected follicle (the canals from which hairs sprout). If you notice a painful red area on the

eyelid itself, you might have a *chalazion,* which is the result of a blocked gland in the eyelid.

TREATING A STY

Both sties and chalazions go away on their own, although you may have to put up with up to a week of discomfort (or a month, in the case of a chalazion) and a less-than-ideal appearance.

In the meantime, follow this advice:

❑ Apply hot compresses to the affected area several times a day or soak your face in warm water to help draw the pus to a head, after which the sty bursts and begins to heal.

❑ Do not try to squeeze the sty to make it burst.

❑ Contact your ophthalmologist or family doctor if the sty or chalazion doesn't improve. Your doctor might suggest an antibiotic ointment to speed healing of a stubborn chalazion. If you have a sty that refuses to disappear, you might need to have it surgically removed.

Although nearly all sties and chalazions can be taken care of at home, you should consult your family doctor or ophthalmologist if the following conditions are present:

● The white of your eye gets red (which could indicate a more serious infection)

● There's a great deal of pus in the sty

● There is significant pain or swelling around the eye

● You experience double vision

Eyestrain: Help for Tired Eyes

Despite what your parents might have told you when you were a child, you won't go blind if you read in dim light or if you sit too close to the television set. But you could experience the temporary discomfort of eyestrain or, more accurately, eye fatigue.

"Tired eyes" can result from long periods of close work or reading. Although there's no evidence eye fatigue itself is damaging to your sight, it can cause red, watery, or dry eyes, fatigue, and difficulty focusing, and it can be accompanied by headaches.

PAMPER YOUR PEEPERS

Here's how:

❏ **Read in good light.** Dim light won't damage your eyes, but it does make it more difficult for you to see.

❏ **If it bothers your eyes, don't watch TV in a completely dark room.** Some people like to watch television in the dark—simulating the movie-going experience. But keeping a light on in the room, preferably beside the set or behind you, may reduce eye strain.

❏ **If you need corrective eyewear—either glasses or contact lenses—wear them.** Reading small print without your reading glasses won't hurt your vision, but you will have to strain to see what's written.

Computer monitors are a major source of eyestrain. If you use one, follow this advice:

❏ **Use a glare-cutting filter on your computer monitor.** Make sure the room's lighting does not add glare or reflections. And dust off the screen frequently to maximize visibility.

❏ **Get comfortable.** The monitor should be at or just below eye level and probably a bit farther away than you would hold a book you're reading. Make sure your chair is at such a position that your back, neck, or arms don't feel stressed after hours of work.

❏ **Take frequent breaks.** If possible, get up occasionally to stretch and walk around. Just looking at something else in the room for a minute other than the screen of your monitor can help you ward off fatigue.

SOOTHE TIRED EYES

Usually, your discomfort will cease once you stop doing the activity—reading, working on a computer—that caused your eyes to become fatigued. Over-the-counter eye drops, such as artificial tears or decongestant drops, may help soothe some of the symptoms. If the problem persists no matter what prevention steps you take, or you habitually have trouble focusing your vision, see your eye care specialist for an examination.

Fever Facts

A rise in body temperature when we're sick is a reflection of our bodies' attempt at fighting the infection that's got us down. Fevers of 104 degrees Fahrenheit are generally not considered dangerous by them-

Eyestrain Can Result from Long Periods of Close Work or Reading

Notify the Doctor if Your Infant Has a Fever

selves, but you should call the doctor if the fever is accompanied by other symptoms, such as abdominal pain, productive cough, seizures, severe headache, a stiff neck, swollen glands, or mental confusion. Although a rise in body temperature can occur along with a condition as minor as a cold, a fever may signal something more serious, such as meningitis, appendicitis, or gallbladder problems.

FEVERS IN CHILDREN

If you have an infant younger than three months of age who develops a fever—*any* fever—call the child's doctor immediately. Fevers over 101.4 degrees Fahrenheit in a child between three months and two years of age should be reported to a doctor as well, according to the American Academy of Family Physicians. *Never give aspirin to treat fever in a child—aspirin has been linked to Reye syndrome, a rare but potentially fatal disease.* Instead, use acetaminophen. (Since studies to determine if ibuprofen is safe for children with fevers are not completed, do not give ibuprofen.)

WHEN TO CALL THE DOCTOR

Mild analgesics, such as aspirin, acetaminophen, or ibuprofen, can help relieve low-grade fevers, but a high fever or a long-lasting one requires a doctor's opinion. A cool bath and rest under light sheets or blankets may also make a fever sufferer more comfortable.

If your child has a fever and any of these warning signs, consult his or her physician:

- Abrupt changes in behavior
- Constant vomiting or diarrhea
- Dry mouth
- Earache or pulling at ears
- Fever that comes and goes over a period of days
- High-pitched crying
- Irritability
- Loss of appetite
- Pale appearance
- Seizures
- Severe headache, especially one that wakes the child
- Skin rash
- Sore or swollen joints
- Sore throat
- Stiff neck
- Stomach pain
- Swelling of the soft spot of the head (in a child younger than 18 months)
- Lack of responsiveness
- Wheezing or other problems breathing
- Whimpering

Fingernails: Clues to Your Health

Your nails, produced by layers of protein called *keratin*, serve not only to protect the tender tissue underneath but also as an early indicator of changes in your physical health. Many problems, including poor nutrition and a variety of infections, reveal themselves through changes in the color or texture of the fingernails. For this reason, it's important to report any discoloration not related to an injury or any pitting of the nails to your doctor.

Injury to the area around the nail—especially the cuticle—can provide an entry point for bacteria and infection. The way we treat our nails can range from abusive (nail biting) to doting (professional manicures), but everyone should spend a little bit of time each week grooming nails to ensure their strength and health.

NAIL GROOMING

These nail care tips can help you prevent fingernail problems.

❑ Trim your fingernails with sharp manicure scissors or nail clippers.

❑ Use the fine side of an emery board to hone the edges of the nail. (For best results, groom your nails after bathing or showering, when they're softer and easier to cut.)

❑ Do not trim your cuticles; they protect the underlying tissue from infection.

❑ If you have a hangnail, don't pull it off—you could cause bleeding. Instead, gently trim it, and leave a small angle hanging outward to prevent it from growing the same way.

❑ Use moisturizing hand lotion to prevent many nail problems.

❑ Wear rubber or other gloves when using harsh chemicals, including household cleaning products.

❑ If you must use nail polish remover, which can dry out nails, apply it sparingly and no more than once a week.

Reducing Flatulence

"Passing gas" may make you unpopular, but it says little about your physical health—except you're probably eating lots of fiber. As your body digests food, it produces methane and other gases in the bowel, which are expelled through the anus. Flatulence is the natural consequence of eating many grains, legumes, and vegetables, although you might find other foods also give you "gas."

The situation can be exacerbated if you take deep, gulping breaths to make yourself burp because you'll fill your intestinal tract with air. If you experience a bloated feeling in the upper stomach area (like you have a bowling ball in your midriff), you may have heartburn or an irritated bowel, rather than mere "gas." (See the sections *Put Out the Fire of Heartburn*, page 225, and *Controlling Irritable Bowel Syndrome*, page 235.)

Gas is a natural and necessary part of your digestive process, but there are a few steps you can take to reduce flatulence.

❑ **Avoid overindulging in foods that give you gas.** See the sidebar, *Gas-Producing Foods*, for a list of some of the worst offenders and *Soak Your Kidneys* for advice on preparing beans (page 214). Use of Beano, an over-the-counter food modifier, may reduce the gas-producing effects of these foods.

Gas Is a Natural And Necessary Part of Your Digestive Process

GAS-PRODUCING FOODS

Certain foods are more likely to cause gas. Here are some of the worst offenders:

Beans   Cabbage
Beer   Carbonated beverages
Bran   Cauliflower
Broccoli   Milk
Brussels sprouts   Onions

Some people also have trouble with these foods:

Apples   Melon
Apricots   Potatoes
Bananas   Pretzels
Carrots   Prunes
Celery   Radishes
Citrus fruits   Raisins
Coffee   Soybeans
Cucumbers   Spinach
Eggplant   Strawberries
Lettuce   Wheat products

❑ ❑ ❑

SOAK YOUR KIDNEYS

No, not *those* kidneys . . . kidney *beans*, and lentils, and dried peas, and other legumes. The way you prepare beans can impact their gas-producing effects. Here's the scoop on how to reduce these effects:

1. Soak the beans overnight.
2. Replace the water with fresh water and cook the beans for 30 minutes. Drain the water again.
3. Add fresh water and cook another 30 minutes. Drain the water one more time.
4. Add fresh water and finish cooking.

❑ ❑ ❑

❑ **Reduce intake of milk and milk products.** You may be one of the many people who is sensitive to milk sugars, or lactose. See if cutting dairy products out of your diet helps reduce gas. Even if it turns out you're lactose intolerant, you don't have to give up milk on your cereal or that bowl of frozen yogurt for dessert. You can try soy-based milk substitutes or take lactase supplements. (See *Coping with Lactose Intolerance*, page 34.)

❑ **Exercise.** Mild aerobic exercise often assists foods' movement through the digestive system.

❑ **Manage stress.** Stress causes stomach muscles to tighten, which could worsen a flatulence problem.

❑ **Try antacids containing simethicone.** Over-the-counter products, such as Phazyme, Mylanta, and Maalox, can help curb symptoms.

When You Can't Flee the Flu

"The flu" is commonly used as a catchall term for many illnesses. In fact, for such a common ailment, the flu is very misunderstood.

First of all, there's no such thing as a "flu bug"—influenza is caused by a virus, not a parasite. Also, although many people claim they've contracted a "stomach flu" when they feel queasy, influenza virtually never results in only gastrointestinal symptoms. If your only symptoms are nausea, diarrhea, or vomiting, you've got another problem (perhaps food poisoning), but not the flu.

Signs of the Flu

Influenza, which is most contagious in the first four days after symptoms appear, may include any or all of the following:

- Fever
- Chills
- Cough
- Muscular achiness
- Extreme fatigue
- Nasal congestion

FIGHTING THE FLU

There are two types of viruses which can cause the flu: influenza A and influenza B. The most serious type, influenza A, fortunately responds to two prescription antiviral drugs, amantadine and rhinmantadine; however influenza B does not.

Whichever type of virus you contract, you may want to seek relief from your individual symptoms with home remedies and over-the-counter medications. (See *Nice Catch: You've Got a Cold*, page 196, for details.) In all cases, get plenty of rest and drink extra fluids to speed your recuperation.

Is It Really Fluid Retention?

Some women experience bloating and weight gain each month as part of a premenstrual syndrome, others retain fluid because of prescription medication (such as birth control pills and steroids), and still others retain water because their sodi-

FLU SHOTS

If you're older than aged 65 years or have a chronic illness (such as diabetes or emphysema), a case of the flu is especially dangerous for you because it could lead to pneumonia. Ask your doctor if you should have a flu shot each fall as a preventive measure. The vaccine is not recommended to those who are allergic to eggs, which are used to manufacture the serum. Pregnant women should also seek their doctor's advice about the vaccine.

❏ ❏ ❏

um intake is too high. But the hard truth is that most people who claim to retain water are actually just overweight.

If you think you're retaining water, your weight is the first factor you should evaluate.

- ❏ Find out what the ideal weight range is for your height, age, and sex (see the *Metropolitan Height-Weight Table* in Chapter 2, page 50).

- ❏ If you find you need to trim down, start with a low-fat, high carbohydrate diet and a program of regular physical exercise.

- ❏ If you are not overweight, mild diuretics taken at certain times of the month, coupled with reducing your intake of salt, may help alleviate the problem. Discuss the use of diuretics with your physician.

You Can Foil Food Poisoning

You went to the company picnic and spent the day in the sun, cooking out, playing ball,

If You Think You're Retaining Water, First Evaluate Your Weight

Symptoms of Food Poisoning Can Occur One Hour to Three Days After Eating Contaminated Food

and having a wonderful time. Just before you left late in the day, you couldn't resist eating one more deviled egg. It was warm but it tasted fine. You popped it in your mouth and forgot about it—until a few hours later when you were on the phone to your doctor, asking if the diarrhea and stomach cramps you're experiencing could be food poisoning.

Chances are it is indeed a food-borne illness that's got you camping out in the bathroom. Food-borne illnesses occur when disease organisms are present on food or introduced by food handlers from dirty equipment, hands, and utensils. Symptoms of food poisoning—severe cramps, stomach pain, nausea and vomiting, and diarrhea—can occur from one hour to three days after eating contaminated food. Most cases are mild, and symptoms last only a day or two. Notify your physician if symptoms are severe or last longer than two days.

The following are some common types of food-borne illness, their causes, symptoms, and steps to prevent them. As you will see by the similarity of the prevention steps, prevention of food poisoning is simple: The best means of control is proper hygiene and thorough cooking of foods.

BOTULISM

The most serious of the food-borne illnesses, botulism is caused by a bacteria that produces an extremely dangerous poison. The bacteria are usually found in canned—particularly home-canned—food. Symptoms generally begin two to eight hours after

eating contaminated food and include dry mouth, blurred vision, muscular weakness, and difficulty speaking, swallowing, and breathing. *Botulism can be fatal. Seek medical treatment immediately.*

To prevent botulism:

❏ Thoroughly heat home-canned or commercially canned food before eating. Food contaminated with the botulism bacteria may smell, look, and taste normal.

❏ Dispose of cans that show signs of possible contamination, such as leaks or bulging lids, and food with signs of spoilage such as mold, unpleasant odors, or discoloration.

❏ Follow proper home-canning guidelines to avoid contamination.

CHOLERA

Cholera is an acute bacterial bowel infection, marked by severe watery diarrhea, vomiting, muscle cramps, and dehydration. Cholera is transmitted through food and water contaminated with human waste of infected persons. The prevention tips are the same as those for traveler's diarrhea.

To prevent cholera:

❏ Do not consume unboiled or untreated water and ice. Carbonated bottled water or other carbonated drinks are usually safe, provided no ice is added.

❏ Avoid food and beverages from street vendors.

❏ Do not eat raw or partially cooked fish and shellfish. All cooked foods should be hot when served.

❏ Do not eat uncooked vegetables.

❏ Avoid uncooked fruits unless you peel them yourself.

GIARDIASIS

Symptoms of giardiasis, a disease caused by a parasite, include diarrhea that lasts a week or more, stomach cramps, gas, and fatigue. Like cholera, giardiasis is transmitted through food and water contaminated with human waste of infected persons, or person-to-person as a result of poor handwashing habits. Although the parasite itself is not life threatening, the severe diarrhea it causes can lead to dehydration and shock.

To prevent giardiasis:

❏ Do not drink water directly from streams or lakes, even if the water appears clean. (Backpackers and campers are often the victims of giardiasis.)

❏ Wash hands thoroughly after using the toilet, handling soiled diapers, and before eating or preparing food.

NORWALK VIRUS

Like many food-borne illnesses, Norwalk virus (named for an outbreak in a Norwalk, Ohio, grammar school in 1968) enters the food chain when infected food handlers do not wash their hands properly after using the toilet. The illness is also often associated with eating raw oysters and clams. Symptoms are similar to salmonellosis: diarrhea, cramps, vomiting, fever, headaches, muscle aches, weakness.

To prevent Norwalk virus:

❏ Wash hands thoroughly after using the toilet, handling soiled diapers, and before eating or preparing food.

❏ Avoid uncooked clams and oysters.

SALMONELLOSIS

The more than 2,000 types of bacteria grouped under the name *Salmonella* bacteria cause most cases of food poisoning. These bacteria are often spread through contaminated (and uncooked) meat, poultry, fish, raw eggs, and unpasteurized dairy products. Person-to-person transmission occurs during food preparation when food is not thoroughly cooked, or when uncooked food comes into contact with the bacteria. (Thorough cooking destroys the bacteria.) Salmonellosis symptoms are diarrhea, fever, headache, stomach cramps, and vomiting.

To prevent salmonellosis:

❏ Avoid eating raw eggs and foods containing raw eggs, such as homemade eggnog, ice cream, meringue, custard, and Hollandaise sauce. Commercially produced forms of these products are safe to serve since they are made with eggs that have been pasteurized, a process that destroys *Salmonella* bacteria. You can also use pasteurized eggs or egg substitutes in recipes calling for raw or undercooked eggs.

❏ Thoroughly cook all foods of animal origin. Refrigerate all meats and leftovers.

❏ Wash hands, utensils, equipment, and work areas with hot, soapy water before and after they come in contact with uncooked meat or eggs.

❏ Wash hands thoroughly after using the toilet.

TREATING A FOOD-BORNE ILLNESS

If you do feel queasy as a result of something you ate, follow these treatment guidelines:

Prevent Food Poisoning with Proper Hygiene and Thorough Cooking of Foods

Soak Your Aching Feet in a Pan of Warm Water

- If you have no diarrhea symptoms, do nothing. The nausea should pass.
- If you have loose stools when you go to the bathroom, take Pepto-Bismol tablets or liquid.
- If you have diarrhea, fever, chills, or sweats, you may need to take antibiotics. Consult your physician. Also, see the sections on Diarrhea for hints on preventing dehydration and a list of the signs of dehydration, pages 203–205.

Getting Relief for Your Aching Feet

You've been on your feet all day, and those dogs are barking. If your feet occasionally ache, they could just be reacting normally to the stress you've put on them for hours. Soothe your feet by soaking them in warm water, then sitting with your feet at or above the level of your heart for a while to ease your discomfort.

Other problems can cause foot pain. A bunion, a painful enlargement at the joint of the big toe, can be either inherited or caused by poorly fitting shoes. (For shoe-buying tips, see the next section, *The Cinderella Formula: Shoes that Fit.*) Corns or calluses, usually caused by pressure on the feet, result in sore feet for many people. (See *Caring for Corns and Calluses,* page 219.) If your aching feet are caused by misaligned bones, you may need surgery. People with diabetes or a history of circulation problems should consult their physician if aches continue.

The Cinderella Formula: Shoes that Fit

If you have persistent problems with aching feet, you should look for a more comfortable pair of shoes to wear during the day. Follow this advice when shoe shopping.

- **Stand while your foot is being measured.** Your feet expand when you put weight on them.
- **When you try on shoes, walk around in them on both carpeted and tiled areas.**
- **Select shoes that fit in the store.** Contrary to what a salesperson tells you, there is no "breaking-in period." Shoes should fit comfortably when you buy them.
- **Buy a shoe with plenty of toe room.** The area where the toes fit, the toe box, should be large enough for you to wiggle your toes. Unfortunately, many women's fashion shoes have narrow toe boxes that pinch the toes. Look for shoes that have a more rounded toe box.
- **Find shoes without heel slippage.** When you walk in your shoes, your heel shouldn't slip or come up.
- **Purchase shoes that are wide enough.** Your shoes shouldn't constrict any part of your foot. If your foot bulges over the side of the shoe, the shoe is too narrow.
- **Consider shoes that allow for padding.** Dress shoes, especially women's dress shoes, often don't provide enough support

or cushioning. Buy shoes large enough to add padding or arch supports.

❑ **Buy a low, thick heel.** The body can tolerate a one-inch high heel without problems. Heels higher than that cause the body to pitch forward. If you must wear high heels, buy the lowest heel you can find; one with a thick heel provides more stability.

Some guidelines for athletes:

❑ **Replace worn athletic shoes.** One cause of overuse injuries, such as stress fractures, is shoes that are worn out and no longer able to provide the support or cushioning the foot needs. Despite their high price tag, athletic shoes aren't long-term investments. Plan to replace your running shoes every 400 to 600 miles, walking shoes every 600 miles. Aerobic shoes are good for about six months, depending on how often you attend class, and tennis shoes last about 50 hours.

❑ **Try out athletic shoes first.** If you're buying an athletic shoe such as a running shoe, shop where they allow you to actually try out the shoes before buying them. Most reputable running shoe stores encourage shoppers to run in their shoes first.

Caring for Corns and Calluses

When skin is subjected to repeated pressure, the result is thickened or hardened skin, or corns and calluses. On the feet,

corns and calluses are often the result of poorly fitting shoes or two toes pressing together.

Usually the best way to bring relief is to remove the source of the friction. Some hints:

❑ Wear comfortable shoes. Shoes should conform to the shape of your feet and have no "pressure points." See *The Cinderella Formula: Shoes that Fit*, page 218.

❑ Try tiny adhesive foam cushions, available in pharmacies, to help ease friction on the feet.

Once the source of pressure has been removed, the toughened skin should disappear in a matter of weeks. If it doesn't, your physician might have to surgically remove the hardened skin. *Due to the risk of infection or other complications, never attempt to remove a corn or callus yourself!* Diabetics with severe corns or calluses may be at risk for infections or other problems. See a physician any time a patch of hardened skin becomes ulcerated or painful. If corns are caused by misaligned bones, your feet may require surgery.

Properly Clip Your Ingrown Toenail Problem

Toenails are meant to be cut straight across, rather than on a curve like fingernails. (You may notice fingernail clippers are curved, while clippers meant for use on the toenails have a straight edge.) Because many people groom their toenails in a

One Cause of Stress Fractures Is Worn Out Shoes

To Prevent Ingrown Toenails, Trim Your Nails Straight Across

curve, tiny "spurs" tend to form on the sides of toenails, especially those on the big toe. When the edge of a nail begins to dig into the skin (a situation that might be exacerbated by tight-fitting shoes), an ingrown toenail results—a development that can cause redness and discomfort if left untreated.

It's easy to prevent ingrown toenails:

❑ Make sure your shoes have toe boxes that are wide enough for all of your toes to fit comfortably without crowding.

❑ Trim your toenails straight across, about once a month. For best results, cut your nails after bathing or showering—they'll be softer and easier to trim.

❑ If you have an ingrown toenail, you need to keep the nail from becoming embedded in the skin and encourage it to grow straight out. To do this, lift the ingrown nail edge up, and cut it off straight with a nail clipper.

If an ingrown nail causes pain and inflammation, notify your doctor. If you have continuing occurrences of ingrown nails, your physician might suggest surgery to remove the troublesome portion of the nail permanently, thus eliminating the problem's source.

Eliminating Foot Odor

If you're dismayed to discover that you can clear a room when you take off your shoes, you'll be pleased to know you can prevent smelly feet.

Here are a few hints to get your nose and toes in sweet harmony:

❑ **Wash your feet daily in warm water and soap.** Antibacterial soaps may help prevent bacterial buildup.

❑ **Change into clean, dry socks or hose frequently.** Some health professionals recommend cotton socks to keep feet dry; others prefer synthetic materials. Experiment to determine which material works best for you.

❑ **Wear comfortable shoes that don't pinch your feet or cause them to sweat excessively.** Leather is a more "breathable" material than rubber or vinyl.

❑ **Ask your doctor about prescription powders.** If you have a severe problem with sweaty feet, these can help curb the situation.

Genital Herpes: What You Need to Know

Although rarely a serious health problem in nonpregnant persons, genital herpes—sores and blisters on the external sex organs caused by a virus that is usually transmitted through sexual contact—can be uncomfortable and emotionally upsetting to those who have it. The American College of Obstetricians and Gynecologists estimates about 30 million

American men and women have the condition, which can be treated with a prescription medication but currently has no cure.

Symptoms of Genital Herpes

Some people who carry the herpes virus experience no symptoms. If you do develop symptoms, about two to ten days after the virus enters your body you'll experience:

- Flu-like symptoms (swollen glands, fever, chills, muscle aches, fatigue, nausea)
- Clusters of small, fluid-filled blisters on the genitals, buttocks, or other areas
- Pain during urination, especially for women
- An itching or tingling feeling near the site where the virus first entered the body

Itching or tingling is a signal that persons with herpes are about to experience a recurrence of the condition. Pain running into the buttocks or knees could also signal another bout with herpes. About 90 percent of people with herpes experience recurrent infections, which are usually less severe than the first outbreak.

A Warning for Pregnant Women

If you are expecting a baby and have or have had an active herpes infection—or have had sex with someone who has the virus—tell your doctor. Herpes bouts are usually more severe during pregnancy, and they can pose a risk to your baby during birth. Your physician may want to schedule more frequent examinations and possibly test you for herpes if you've been exposed to the virus.

Reducing Your Risk

Follow this advice to reduce your risk not only of herpes, but of all sexually transmitted diseases:

- ❏ Limit your number of sexual partners and limit your contacts to those you know and trust.
- ❏ Tell your partner if you have the virus, and abstain from oral and genital sex when lesions reappear—in fact, until a few days after the scabs have disappeared. Condoms don't offer much protection against this infection because lesions uncovered by the latex still pose a danger to a partner. (Condoms are, however, effective in preventing transmission of other sexually transmitted diseases.)
- ❏ If you have herpes and share a bed, wear pajamas when the sores reappear to avoid infecting the other person.
- ❏ If you come in contact with herpes lesions, wash with soap and water to avoid reinfecting yourself or passing it on to others.

Caring For Genital Herpes

If you think you might have herpes, see a doctor. (If you're a woman, your physician can check for herpes and other STDs during an annual Pap test and pelvic examination.) Your physician may prescribe the drug acyclovir, which is available in oral, topical, or intravenous form. Although not a cure, it prevents the virus from multiplying, shortens the length of the first outbreak of sores—which usually lasts about three weeks—and reduces your discomfort. When taken in capsule form, it can also help prevent repeat outbreaks. Aspirin or acetaminophen might also relieve pain.

About 90 Percent of People with Herpes Experience Recurrent Infections

If you do have a recurrence of sores, help yourself heal faster:

❏ **Keep the lesions clean and dry.** Wash the sores gently with soap and warm water, and use a blow dryer on the low setting to dry hard-to-reach areas or sensitive blisters.

❏ **Wear loose-fitting cotton underclothes and avoid pantyhose.** Nylon and some other synthetics hold in heat and moisture and slow the healing process.

Halting Hangovers

The Only "Cure" for Hangovers Is Drinking in Moderation

Last night you wore a lamp shade on your head; this morning you're wearing an ice bag. Overindulging in alcohol gives you plenty of problems, but one of the most immediate is the headache and nausea known as a hangover.

When you have a hangover, blood vessels in your head are stretching and impinging on nearby nerves, causing the headache. A combination of alcohol's irritation of the stomach and its many effects on the nervous system cause the nausea and vomiting. You feel thirsty because alcohol causes dehydration. And that "all over awful" feeling comes from alcohol's depressant effect and acidosis, a disturbance of the body's acid-base balance, which leads to a build up of acids in the blood.

There's no such thing as a hangover "cure," other than teetotalism or drinking only in moderation. However, there are other ways to prevent intoxication and speed up your recovery from a night on the town.

Morning-After Remedies
Try these hangover remedies:

❏ **Drink plenty of water to replace lost fluids, relieve the acidosis, and soothe the stomach.** Broth is another good choice to replace lost minerals and fluids.

❏ **Drink coffee or tea.** That is, if you're stomach isn't too queasy. Caffeine constricts blood vessels, which can help relieve headaches.

❏ **Rest.**

❏ **Take acetaminophen or ibuprofen for the headache.** Avoid aspirin, which may further irritate your stomach.

❏ **Eat foods such as toast and soup that are easy on the stomach.** If you can't stomach solid food, try bouillon.

❏ **Vow to use *Tips for Safer Drinking* next time.**

TIPS FOR SAFER DRINKING

This advice is for *everyone* who drinks—even if you've never had a hangover:

❏ **Nurse your drinks, don't gulp them.** A good rule of thumb: Consume no more than one drink per hour (the time it takes most adults' bodies to process an alcoholic beverage) and preferably less than that.

❏ **Eat.** Eat food before, during, and between drinks.

❏ **When drinking hard liquor, choose fruit or vegetable juice mixers.** They contain fructose, a sugar that helps burn up alcohol.

❏ **Before retiring, eat a piece of toast spread with honey.** The fructose in the honey helps use up more alcohol.

Headaches: Types and Triggers

It's raining, you're stuck in traffic, your children are squabbling in the back seat, and just when life can't get any worse, your head starts throbbing in pain. Nearly everyone has a headache at one time or another, but an estimated 45 million Americans get chronic, recurring headaches, and as many as 18 million of those suffer from painful, debilitating migraines, according to the National Headache Foundation. Learning what triggers your headaches—and how to cope when they strike—will help you feel better and may also prevent you from missing work or missing out on life's pleasures.

A TRIO OF TYPES

Although there are nearly two dozen types of common headaches, they fall into three basic categories: tension, vascular, and organic headaches.

Tension Headaches

Characteristics: Dull, nonthrobbing pain, usually accompanied by tightness in the scalp or neck. About 90 percent of all headaches fall into this category.
Common triggers: Depression, stress.

Vascular Headaches

Characteristics: Intense, severe, piercing, throbbing pain. Cluster and migraine headaches fall into this category. Cluster headaches are so named because they occur in a cluster of time, for example daily for weeks or months. Vascular headache sufferers often can't sit still because of the intense pain.
Common triggers: Migraines are caused by heredity, diet, stress, menstruation, and environmental changes (such as exposure to cigarette smoke). The causes of cluster headaches are unknown, although excessive smoking or alcohol consumption can set them off.

Organic Headaches

Characteristics: Pain that gets increasingly worse and is accompanied by other symptoms, such as vomiting, visual disturbances, speech or personality changes, or problems with coordination. Indicates need for professional medical attention.
Common triggers: Tumors, infection, or diseases of the brain, eyes, ears, or nose.

THE MISERY OF MIGRAINE

Migraine headaches come in two varieties—"common" and "classic." Both types involve intense, piercing pain, usually on one side of the head, and may be accompanied by other symptoms, including nausea, vomiting, icy hands, shaking, or increased sensitivity to light and sound. A classic migraine, however, may announce its arrival up to 30 minutes before onset with an aura—warning symptoms that may include visual disturbances, numbness in the arm or leg, the smelling of strange odors, and even hallucinations.

More women than men experience migraines; in fact, about 70 percent of all migraine patients are female. Many women experience

The Three Categories of Headache Are Tension, Vascular, and Organic

migraines as part of their menstrual cycle; pregnant women usually experience fewer or milder attacks.

Migraine Triggers

Although heredity may be the biggest factor in determining whether you'll have migraines, other factors could lead to the intense pain of a migraine. Other triggers include the following:

- Certain foods, including ripened cheese, citrus fruits, chocolate, red wine, or excessive amounts of caffeine
- Missing or delaying a meal
- Emotional stress
- Hormones (Oral contraceptives and estrogen replacement therapy may trigger migraines in some women.)

- Erratic sleep habits (such as oversleeping on the weekend)
- Bright lights (either natural or artificial) and excessive TV or movie viewing
- Computer use
- Excessive noise
- Cigarette smoke
- Chemicals (such as those in some insecticides)
- Perfume
- Altitude
- Drugs (Cold and sinus medicines containing amines and some prescription medicines, such as lithium, may trigger headaches.)

CHILDREN AND HEADACHES

Like adults, children experience headaches, but for parents of young kids, finding out exactly where it hurts (and how much) can be a challenge. Children usually lack the vocabulary for detailing their symptoms. Migraine tendencies can show up in young children but may appear as frequent car or motion sickness rather than headaches. Most childhood headaches are harmless, but parents should be on the alert for symptoms that could indicate their youngster also has a head injury or illness. These signs may include those that follow:

- Extreme restlessness or irritability, especially in very young children
- Fever
- Nausea or vomiting
- Lack of muscle coordination
- Weakness or lethargy
- Seizures
- Abrupt personality changes

Remember: Never give aspirin to a child; aspirin has been linked to Reye syndrome, a rare but deadly illness.

❏ ❏ ❏

Relieving Your Headache

Fortunately, most headaches are fleeting episodes you can treat at home. The best advice: *Relax.*

❏ Rest, quiet, and removing yourself from the source of any stress (when possible) should help.

❏ Ice packs can sometimes help relieve discomfort.

❏ Biofeedback, a method of relieving stress by relaxing the muscles, may help you not only recover from a headache, but prevent their onset during stressful times (see Chapter 5, *Coping with Stress.*)

❏ Over-the-counter analgesics, such as aspirin, ibuprofen, or acetaminophen, may help constrict blood vessels and relieve pain.

❏ If you have chronic tension headaches, your physician

might suggest you find relief by using prescription anti-depressants.

❑ If you have frequent cluster headaches, you might benefit from medication containing the ingredient methysergide.

❑ If you experience chronic migraines, you might benefit from a number of prescription drugs, such as ergotamine, naproxen sodium, isometheptene, sumatriptan, and dihydroergotamine.

WHEN TO SEEK HELP

Consult your physician if these symptoms accompany headaches:

- Daily headaches
- Headaches after intense coughing, sneezing, or running
- Pain in the ear or eye
- Confusion
- Nausea or vomiting
- Vision changes
- Hallucinations
- Sensitivity to light and sound
- Weakness
- Dizziness
- Loss of consciousness

You should also contact your physician if you have an especially severe headache without any of these other symptoms. A severe headache may indicate another medical problem.

Put Out the Fire of Heartburn

Heartburn—a gassy, burning sensation in your upper abdomen, sometimes accompa-

FOR MORE INFORMATION

If you have additional questions or need some advice about headaches, the National Headache Foundation offers literature about identifying and treating all types of headaches. Call 1-800-843-2256.

❑ ❑ ❑

nied by the regurgitation of sour, bitter material into your throat or mouth—actually has nothing at all to do with your heart. It indicates that the lower part of your esophagus (or "swallowing tube"), the upper part of your stomach, or the first section of your bowel has become irritated, and the contents of your stomach have started to back up into the esophagus. Any child or adult can suffer from heartburn, and pregnant women are particularly susceptible.

Most cases of heartburn aren't serious. Here are tips to avoid and relieve a case of heartburn.

❑ Eat smaller meals.
❑ Stay trim.
❑ Avoid cigarettes.
❑ Drink only in moderation.
❑ Take over-the-counter antacids to help quell your symptoms. (These are most effective when taken after you eat and at bedtime.)
❑ Ask your doctor or pharmacist if heartburn is a side effect of any medications you're taking.
❑ Keep the upper part of your body elevated when you're lying down to help stop regurgitation. Put the head of your

Anyone— Child or Adult— Can Get Heartburn

bed on blocks to keep your upper body elevated when you sleep.

❏ If you experience daily or severe heartburn, ask your doctor for advice.

WHEN HEARTBURN ISN'T HEARTBURN

Some heart attack patients have mistaken early warning signs for heartburn. Even if you think you only have a case of indigestion, seek medical help if you also experience one of these symptoms:

- Severe pressure, fullness, squeezing, or pain in the center of the chest that lasts more than a few minutes, or goes away and comes back
- Pain spreading to the shoulders, neck, or arms
- Light-headedness, fainting, sweating, nausea, or shortness of breath

Don't Mistake Heart Attack Symptoms for Heartburn

Easing the Discomfort of Hemorrhoids

Painful hemorrhoids—also known as "piles"—are almost always caused by constipation or physical strain while attempting a bowel movement.

WARNING

Although bleeding can be a symptom of hemorrhoids, any episode of rectal bleeding should be reported to a doctor; rectal bleeding is also a warning sign of colon and rectal cancer. Don't simply assume hemorrhoids are causing the problem. Get it checked out.

❏   ❏   ❏

Pregnant women and adults who aren't getting enough fiber in their diet—which results in stools that are hard and difficult to pass—are at risk for the problem.

What Are Hemorrhoids?
The anus is essentially a ring of muscle. In the center, veins and loose tissue keep the orifice from leaking. But when you strain this muscle, these fragile veins can become swollen and may even rupture, causing bleeding during a bowel movement. A cluster of swollen veins is called a hemorrhoid. Sometimes a blood clot forms in a vein, causing you to feel as though a small pebble is caught in the rectal area. This type of hemorrhoid usually occurs on the outside of the anal canal, can measure up to two centimeters in size, and, with its blue or purple appearance, resembles grapes.

WHAT YOU AND YOUR DOCTOR CAN DO

Many people with mild hemorrhoid discomfort treat the problem themselves with soothing warm baths and an increase in dietary fiber (see the sidebar *Fiber-Rich Foods* on page 199.) Over-the-counter hemorrhoid treatments may make bowel movements less painful by lubricating the area and decreasing irritation.

If you experience rectal bleeding, notice a protrusion from the rectal area, or experience severe pain when moving your bowels, see your physician. A visual and digital examination (which might be aided by the use of scopes) can give your doctor an idea of the severity of your hemorrhoids and help him or her tailor treatment to your needs.

- For a mild case of hemorrhoids, you might be given prescription hydrocortisone suppositories to decrease inflammation.
- If you have an external protrusion, the doctor might push it back into the anal canal to eliminate swelling and pain.
- In more serious cases, the doctor might need to surgically remove the clot, or tie off a hemorrhoid until it drops off due to lack of blood flow, leaving healthy tissue in its place.
- In severe cases, surgery may be required to remove a troublesome vein completely.

Harnessing Hiccups

Everyone has hiccups at one time or another. Sonograms reveal that babies even have hiccups inside their mothers' wombs—possibly as an exercise to strengthen their diaphragm for all the crying and gurgling they'll do after they're born. Hiccups in children and adults are spasms commonly caused by irritations of the diaphragm or of the nerve that serves it.

Most cases of the hiccups fade by themselves in a few minutes or hours. Family folklore is filled with miracle cures—standing on your head, drinking sugar water, being startled by a sudden noise. But even the most widely accepted "cure"—holding your breath—may not help right away. If your hiccups last for more than a day or so, consult your doctor.

Coping with Hives

The sudden appearance of red, itchy welts on your skin—commonly known as hives, is a condition suffered by about one of every five people at some time during their lives, according to the American Academy of Dermatology. Often, the cause isn't known, but here are a few common hive triggers:

- An allergic reaction to a food or medication
- An infection
- Humidity
- Cold air
- Stress

Often the problem disappears as fast as it occurred. To ease itching and discomfort in the meantime, try a cool bath or taking an antihistamine. If the problem doesn't go away in a matter of days, if hives keep coming back, or if other symptoms are also present, such as severe swelling of the lips, tongue or eyes, see a doctor.

Impotence: Understanding the Causes

When a man can't achieve or maintain an erection long enough to have sexual intercourse, he is considered impotent. Most men are impotent at one time or another. Even men in their teens or 20s can experi-

Babies Even Have Hiccups Inside Their Mothers' Wombs

Impotence Is Not an Inevitable Sign of Old Age

ence impotence, although the condition is much more common in elderly men.

Impotence occurs as a result of a disruption in the process that sends blood or nerve signals to the penis. Something as simple as having one too many drinks, being tired, or being with a new partner may cause a man of any age to have trouble getting or maintaining an erection. But if the problem happens frequently—as it does for up to 20 million American men, according to the American Academy of Family Physicians—it may require medical treatment.

Impotence and Aging
Contrary to myth, the end of sexual function is not an inevitable sign of old age for a healthy male. The levels of male hormones, however, do decline as a man ages; it may take longer to achieve an erection. However, impotence is often the result of treatable medical or emotional factors. In other words, providing you stay in good health (and have a willing partner), there's no reason you can't enjoy sexual intimacy for the rest of your life!

Physical Causes
Diseases that damage your blood vessels or nerves can hamper the ability to achieve or sustain an erection. Lowered levels of testosterone or other male hormones may also cause impotence. These physical factors may include:

- Alcoholism
- Atherosclerosis
- Diabetes
- Brain or spinal-cord injuries
- Hypogonadism
- Liver or kidney failure
- Multiple sclerosis

- Parkinson disease
- Radiation therapy administered to the testicles
- Stroke
- Drugs (Some antidepressants and hypertension medicines and most tranquilizers may cause impotence.)

Emotional Causes
There's an old saying that the most important sexual organ is the one between your ears. Your state of mind, or the state of your relationship, might have some effect on your ability to enjoy intercourse. These emotional factors could include:

- Nervousness about sex (because of a new partner, a bad experience, or a previous problem with impotence)
- Stress at work or home
- Relationship problems
- Depression
- Self-consciousness

GETTING HELP FOR IMPOTENCE
Many men feel uncomfortable discussing impotence, even with a physician. But if you habitually have problems getting or maintaining an erection during lovemaking, you should consult your doctor because, in many cases, the problem has underlying medical or emotional causes that can be treated. Blood and urine tests may help uncover any physical problems; tests that can be done at home can determine whether you have erections while asleep (most men have an average of five per night).

If a physical cause for your problem is found, your doctor can treat it in a number of ways. The remedy might be to simply substitute another prescription drug for one you're now taking. Or it might involve hormone shots. Some men use devices to help them maintain erections. In some cases, surgery is needed to implant the devices.

How Counseling Can Help

No matter what method of treatment your doctor prescribes, counseling may help you and your partner understand each other's feelings and cope with the disruption of your physical relationship. Your partner might feel somehow to blame for your impotence or even be angry with you. A counselor can help both of you work through your emotions and offer suggestions to help your physical relationship recover. He or she might suggest you "start over" your sexual relationship, building up gradually, over a period of several encounters, from nonsexual touching eventually to intercourse. The counselor might also suggest you and your partner search for other ways to please each other without intercourse to reduce your worries about achieving erection.

Coping with Incontinence

Incontinence—the inability to control urination—is often a temporary problem that can be easily treated. Still, it can be not only embarrassing for the children and adults who have it, but the fear of having an "accident" can severely limit an individual's lifestyle (a child who wets the bed, for example,

may turn down invitations to slumber parties), and diminish his or her enjoyment of life. Learning why incontinence occurs—and what you can do about it—can help you deal with the problem should it happen to you or your children.

TYPES OF INCONTINENCE

Urinary incontinence can occur in several forms, and a person may experience more than one type. The types of urinary incontinence follow:

- **Stress incontinence** occurs during activity such as exercise, sneezing, laughing, or coughing.

- **Urge incontinence** is the sudden urge to urinate without a preliminary feeling of bladder fullness. The urge is so sudden and intense, the person with this form of incontinence often does not make it to the bathroom in time.

- **Reflex incontinence** is urine leakage without the person's awareness of the need to urinate.

- **Overflow incontinence** is lack of control over leakage that occurs when the bladder is full.

Although incontinence is a side effect of several illnesses of old age (such as Alzheimer disease), women of childbearing age are the most likely people among healthy adults to experience urine leakage. A woman who has recently vaginally delivered a baby may find she has stress incontinence— her urethra leaks urine when she coughs, sneezes, or laughs. In both

Incontinence Is Often a Temporary Problem that Can Be Easily Treated

Women of Childbearing Age Often Experience Urine Leakage

men and women, the condition can also result from illness, urinary tract infections, aging, fatigue, overweight, and other factors. Any sudden problem with incontinence should be checked out by a health professional, who can help rule out and treat any physical causes.

DON'T LET INCONTINENCE HINDER YOUR ACTIVITY

A few commonsense strategies can help you stay active and more confident:

❑ **Plan ahead and take necessary precautions.** Before starting off for an extended period—a lengthy car trip, for example—be sure to completely empty your bladder even if you don't feel the urge to do so.

❑ **Limit those foods and beverages known to irritate your bladder.** Acidic fruit juices, alcoholic beverages, coffee, tomato-based foods, and hot and spicy dishes have all been known to stimulate leakage.

❑ **Talk to your physician or ask your pharmacist about products available to assist the problem.** Many varieties of protective undergarments and external urine collection devices are available that could make your life a lot less complicated.

Help for Incontinent Women

An incontinent woman may find exercises can strengthen the muscles that control urination and gradually stop uncontrolled leakage. If you have stress incontinence but no other physical ailment, try to strengthen your pelvic muscles with a set of daily exercises that can be done anywhere—while sitting in an office chair, watching television, or driving a car. These controlled muscle contractions, called Kegel exercises, not only help you regain control over urination, but may also help you become more sexually responsive.

❑ Tighten and relax the muscles of your anus, vagina, and urethra—where urine eliminates from your body. Repeat 20 to 30 times. Repeat this several times a day.

❑ When using the toilet, try to stop and restart the stream of urine.

If you notice no improvement in your condition after a month of daily exercises, talk to your doctor again. There are prescription drugs available that may help the problem. He or she might also suggest you consult a urologist or gynecologist to determine if surgery is needed to correct the problem.

BED-WETTING MYTHS

These are not causes of bed-wetting:

• Stubbornness

• Spite

• Too much water or other liquids before bed

❑   ❑   ❑

Kids and Bed-wetting

Your four year old has been potty trained for a year and a half. But one morning, you notice your youngster's sheets are damp. The next morning, despite reminding the child to use the bathroom, the bed is wet again. What's going on?

If no physical illness or condition is to blame, then the situation could be rooted in heredity or your child's sleep patterns. Most child bed wetters have a parent who also wet the bed as a youngster. And many bed wetters are deep, almost "zombie-like" sleepers who have trouble waking up in time to heed the urge to urinate. Some incontinent kids even tell doctors they dream they're using the toilet when still in their beds—and inadvertently act out their dreams. Most children stop wetting the bed by the time they're six to eight years old, although some kids have the problem into their teens.

Treating Bed-wetting

Assuming the child is truly potty trained (and most are by the age of three or four, although some temporarily regress while still learning to use the toilet), incontinence may have a physical cause. A physician can help rule out bladder infections or other problems with a simple urine test.

If no physical cause can be found, bed-wetting can be treated with the prescription antidepressant Tofranil, which alters a child's level of sleep. A prescription nasal spray is available that stops the kidneys from producing urine—

and thus, the possibility of an accident—for up to eight hours. This medication can be helpful for some occasions such as a slumber party.

A few adjustments may need to be made in a child's sleepwear until he or she outgrows the problem. The youngster may need to wear a disposable diaper or "pull-up pants" at night. (You might place a plastic or rubber covering over the mattress to protect it.)

Finally, remember to be supportive of your child—making a youngster feel guilty or ashamed of bed-wetting won't make the problem stop any faster but it may damage your relationship.

Heredity and Sleep Patterns Often Play a Role in Bed-wetting

Infertility: Understanding Your Options

Perhaps no medical problem is as misunderstood as infertility, defined as the inability of a couple to conceive after 12 months of having intercourse without using birth control. Many couples deal with their disappointment and heartbreak by blaming themselves or each other, which might actually worsen the situation. (Emotional stress is sometimes a factor in infertility, but never the chief reason why a couple can't conceive.) But infertility, which affects about 14 percent of all couples in the United States, often has a specific and treatable cause.

The Fertility of Any Couple Declines as They Age

Successful Conception

Conceiving a baby is always a gamble. Basically, three events need to occur for a couple to conceive:

- **Ovulation**, the release of an egg from a woman's ovaries;
- **Fertilization**, the uniting of the egg and a man's sperm; and
- **Implantation**, the attachment of the fertilized egg into the lining of the woman's uterus.

Even assuming that both partners' reproductive systems work perfectly, the odds of a woman at peak fertility conceiving during her menstrual cycle are only 20 percent. These odds hold despite the facts that eggs can be fertilized for up to 24 hours after being released, and sperm can live for up to three days after being ejaculated into a woman's reproductive tract. The fertility of any couple declines as they age. Most women are at their peak of fertility in their early to mid-20s, and their ability to conceive drops precipitously after they reach 35 years of age. Male fertility also declines with age but not as rapidly.

Some Causes of Male Infertility

Your doctor will first evaluate these possible causes:

- Sexually transmitted diseases
- Fevers and infections, such as a case of the mumps suffered after puberty
- Surgery of the reproductive tract
- Vasectomy or other alteration or damage to the vas deferens, the passage that delivers sperm from the testes
- Injury to the testes, such as exposure to radiation
- Varicose veins in the scrotum
- Prescription drugs, such as those given to treat depression or hypertension
- Exposure of the testes to high temperatures, resulting, for example, from tight, constrictive underwear, excessive use of hot tubs, or workplace conditions
- Smoking
- Alcohol or marijuana use
- Certain medical conditions, such as diabetes
- Genetic or hormonal problems

Some Causes of Female Infertility

In women, a doctor will check for the following:

- Hormone imbalances
- Obesity (Being 30 percent or more over the ideal weight for your age and height can cause ovulation problems.)
- Scarring, tumors, or defects in the uterus
- Too little or poor quality cervical mucus
- Endometriosis
- Scarring inside the abdomen
- Pelvic inflammatory disease
- Production of antibodies that fight partner's sperm

THE EMOTIONAL COST

If you suspect you and your partner are infertile, carefully consider whether you want to begin infertility testing. The process can be long and expensive, and the treatments are not guaranteed to succeed in all cases. Adoption or settling for a smaller family may be an option for some couples. Counseling may help infertile couples cope with their emotions, regardless of the path they choose.

❑ ❑ ❑

- Some medical conditions, including thyroid disease and diabetes
- Genetic conditions
- Smoking
- Use of alcohol or marijuana

WHAT YOUR DOCTOR CAN DO

If you and your partner want to become parents and have been having sexual intercourse without birth control for 12 months without conceiving, you should consult your physician. Infertility tests, which may require several office visits by both you and your partner, usually involve the following exams:

- A semen analysis, performed on a semen sample provided by the man
- Tests that prove ovulation has occurred (These may include a blood sample to measure the hormone progesterone.)
- A postcoital (after intercourse) test of the cervical mucus to determine how the sperm move
- Evaluation of the woman's fallopian tubes, which can be performed by means of X rays, ultrasound, or other tests in a doctor's office

Treatment for infertility depends on the reasons for the couple's inability to conceive. In some cases, hormone shots that stimulate the production of sperm may be administered to a man, or fertility drugs that bring on ovulation may be prescribed for a woman. (An ironic footnote: Some fertility drugs carry the risk of creating a multiple pregnancy and, therefore, must be taken under close medical supervision.)

If infertility is linked to lifestyle factors, such as smoking, substance abuse, or being overweight, the couple should take steps to correct the problems. In some cases of infertility due to physical problems, such as a blocked fallopian tube or vas deferens, surgery may be required.

Other Conception Options

For some infertile couples, several medically revolutionary—but expensive—methods of "artificial" fertilization may help them realize their hopes of having a child.

Artificial insemination involves the placing of sperm (provided by either the woman's partner or by a donor) into the woman's reproductive tract.

In vitro fertilization involves removing mature eggs from the ovary just before ovulation and fertilizing them with sperm outside the woman's reproductive tract, in a lab dish, then reinserting the fertilized egg into the woman's uterus. In this procedure, unused fertilized eggs can be frozen and stored for future use.

Insomnia: When the Sandman Won't Come

You've tried counting sheep, drinking warm milk, pacing the floor, watching TV infomercials, and nothing helps you get to sleep. You might have insomnia occasionally, such as when you're not feeling well or are under stress at home or work. Or you might persistently have

Treatment for Infertility Depends on the Reasons for the Couple's Inability to Conceive

233

Sleep Patterns Can Be as Individual as Fingerprints

trouble falling asleep when you first go to bed, or wake up during the night and have trouble falling back to sleep, or awaken—and stay awake—much too early in the morning. Insomnia can make you tired, depressed, cranky, anxious, and much less productive during the day. It can also be a warning sign of serious health problems, including clinical depression. If you or someone in your family has a troubled relationship with the sandman, read on for some practical advice.

What Causes Insomnia?

Sleep patterns can be nearly as individual as fingerprints; some people can't function on less than ten hours of sleep a night, while others get by on six or less. If you're getting older, a change in sleep patterns might be just a sign of age; older people tend to need less than the average seven to eight hours of sleep per night, taking more naps during the day instead. If you don't feel sleepy during the day, you probably don't have insomnia.

Insomnia might be triggered by a number of factors, including:

- Emotional stress
- Caffeine
- Depression
- Changes in work shifts or daily schedules ("Swing shift" workers are prone to the condition.)
- Pain caused by medical problems, such as arthritis
- Sleeping pills (Many people notice their insomnia comes back as soon as they stop using sleep aids.)

Tips to Capture 40 Winks

Don't just hope you'll have better luck sleeping tonight. Take steps to encourage a restful sleep.

During the day, follow this advice:

❑ **Avoid caffeine (coffee, tea, sodas, and chocolate), decongestants, alcohol, and tobacco as much as possible.** Moderate alcohol drinking may help you fall asleep, but it may also wake you up in the middle of the night.

❑ **Exercise.** Regular exercise gives you more energy during the day and helps you sleep at night. Don't, however, work out shortly before bedtime when you should be winding down to prepare for sleep.

❑ **Set aside time during the day to think about what's bothering you.** For example, sit down after dinner and write down any problems you're having along with possible solutions. This helps you avoid the temptation to torture yourself with worry when you climb into bed at night.

❑ **Try a light snack in the evening but not immediately before going to bed.** A glass of warm milk or a few slices of cheese with crackers might help.

❑ **Don't nap during the day if you can't sleep at night.**

When it's time for bed, follow this advice:

❑ **Go to bed and wake up at about the same time each**

234

day. Try to avoid the temptation to oversleep on weekends. Not only does this make it harder to get to sleep at night, but you could get a headache from a disruption in your sleep schedule.

❏ **Keep your bedroom quiet and dark.** The drone of an electric fan or earplugs may help mask outside noise.

❏ **Follow the same routine each night in preparing for bed.** If you wash your face and read for a few minutes each night before bed, you'll start to connect these activities with sleep, and you'll feel drowsy.

❏ **Use your bedroom only for sleep or sex.** Don't read, eat, or talk on the phone in bed.

❏ **Don't think about falling asleep—just do it!** Thinking about it can make you self-conscious.

❏ **If you can't sleep after about 30 minutes, get up and go to another room.** Sit quietly. Watch television or read (but nothing frightening or upsetting) for about 20 minutes. Then go back to bed. Repeat this routine as necessary.

ASK YOUR DOCTOR FOR HELP

If you follow the advice given above and still persistently have trouble falling asleep, consult your physician. Sometimes insomnia has a physical cause, such as clinical depression or arthritis pain, that can be treated with medication.

You will probably be asked about your sleep habits and any stress you've been under lately or any habits you might have that are making it harder for you to sleep (such as drinking or smoking). In some cases, you might be asked to keep a "sleep diary" for a while to help pinpoint troublesome patterns. The doctor might also ask your bed partner to report any problems he or she has noticed, such as snoring, involuntary jerking of the legs, or short interruptions in your breathing known as sleep apnea, a condition that most often occurs in overweight middle-aged males (see *Snoring: Can You Achieve the Sounds of Silence?*, page 247).

Usually, insomnia goes away when the source of the problem (such as too much caffeine) is treated. If not, you might be referred to a professional counselor to deal with emotional stress or, in cases where a solution to your problem can't easily be found, a local sleep disorder clinic.

Controlling Irritable Bowel Syndrome

In irritable bowel syndrome (IBS), food does not move through the stomach and intestines normally. IBS also goes by the names spastic bowel, spastic colon, irritable colon, and functional bowel syndrome. It can be caused by reactions to certain foods, a deficiency of dietary fiber, and an inability to handle emotional stress. When the correct cause is identified, IBS can often be controlled.

Symptoms of IBS
So how do you know if food is moving through your system

Follow the Same Routine Each Night

235

Your Doctor Is More Likely to Prescribe Lifestyle Changes

"normally?" If you have IBS, you probably already have a pretty good idea that what you're experiencing isn't normal. Your symptoms may include:

- Bloating and gas
- Constipation
- Diarrhea
- The urge to have a bowel movement after having just had one
- The constant urge to have a bowel movement
- Mucus-covered stools
- Lower abdominal pain and cramping

Symptoms of IBS follow a pattern; you may notice symptoms in the morning or right after meals. Women with IBS may have IBS "attacks" during their menstrual periods. IBS may get worse when you're under stress, such as when you travel or attend a social event.

LIFESTYLE CHANGES MAY BE THE KEY

If your doctor diagnoses IBS, he or she is more likely to first prescribe lifestyle changes than medication. Because IBS is often a lifelong condition, it's in your best interest to learn how to control it with your diet and behavior rather than to become psychologically or physically dependent on drugs. Your doctor may discuss with you the following ways to control IBS:

- Adding more water and fiber to your diet (see the list of fiber-rich foods, page 199)
- Avoiding foods that give you trouble
- Eating smaller, more frequent meals each day (rather than three hearty ones) to help ease symptoms

- Finding ways to handle the stress in your life
- Using bulk-forming laxatives containing psyllium (a natural vegetable fiber). (Be sure to read, *Why Laxatives Don't Help Long-term*, page 199.)

If you do require medication, your doctor will probably prescribe an antispasmodic, a drug that helps relieve muscle spasms that cause the stomach pain associated with IBS, such as dicycolimine hydrochloride (Bentyl), chlordiazepoxide/clidinium (Librax), and hyoscyamine sulfate (Levsin, Donnatal, and Cystospaz among others).

FOOD AND IBS

Fiber, which creates bigger, softer stools, can improve the overall health of your digestive tract and reduce IBS symptoms. But be wary—too much of a good thing at once can actually increase bloating and gas.

If you haven't eaten much fiber before, add it gradually to your diet. Other foods might worsen your symptoms, although none actually causes IBS. Take note of any patterns you notice when you eat certain foods.

- Food and drink high in fat or caffeine can cause your intestines to contract or spasm.
- Sorbitol, an artificial sweetener, and the magnesium found in antacid tablets, may provoke diarrhea.
- Some foods are notorious for producing intestinal gas. (See the list of *Gas-Producing Foods*, page 214.) Some IBS sufferers also report problems with apple and grape juice, bananas, nuts, and raisins.
- If you're lactose intolerant—unable to digest milk protein, a

condition made worse by IBS—you should either avoid milk and dairy products, purchase lactase-containing milk or dairy products, or try lactase pills or liquid when you do consume those foods.

STRESS AND IBS

Stress seems to aggravate IBS symptoms. So even if your doctor prescribes tranquilizers or sedatives for the short term, you need to find a better way to handle emotional stress. Regular physical exercise, meditation, and relaxation techniques may help ease your anxiety. Your doctor might suggest professional counseling. If you're experiencing severe IBS symptoms and are feeling depressed, your physician might prescribe antidepressants. See Chapter 5, *Coping with Stress*, for some stress reduction techniques.

Soothe Your Aching Knees

Our knees take a lot of stress, and sometimes they react to that stress by becoming sore. A weekend athlete who overdoes it on the tennis court, and a teenager who takes one too many laps around the roller rink may feel aching in their knees for a couple of days, a problem that's easily treated. But you should also know what signs may indicate a more serious injury or the start of a degenerative disease—and the need for professional medical attention.

TRY RICE

To ease mild to moderate knee pain, follow the RICE (Rest, Ice, Compression, Elevation) program of self-treatment for a couple of days. If you feel no improvement or your pain worsens, consult your physician.

❏ *Rest.* Time is the best healer for most mild injuries to muscles or joints.

❏ *Ice.* Apply ice packs (using crushed ice rather than ice cubes). You can also rub a large piece of ice on the injured area to numb it—but don't hold the ice on any part of the skin for more than 30 seconds to avoid frostbite. (Avoid heating pads for at least three days after an injury—heat tends to draw fluid into the area and can provoke muscle spasms.)

❏ *Compression.* Try wrapping your knee in a bandage for at least a couple of days to avoid swelling and bruising.

❏ *Elevation.* When you sit or lie down, keep your knee raised at or above the level of your heart to prevent swelling.

In addition to the RICE treatment, over-the-counter anti-inflammatory medication, such as aspirin or ibuprofen, may also help relieve pain. Choose these medications instead of acetaminophen, which does not reduce inflammation.

When to Seek Help

Consult your physician if you experience any of these symptoms:

● Knee pain that doesn't get better after two or three days of home care

● Extreme redness

Follow the RICE Program of Self-Treatment

- A "hot" feeling in the knee
- Swelling
- A clicking or popping sound, either when you were injured or since the injury
- A feeling of instability or wobbliness when attempting to walk on the knee
- A knee that "gives way" when you try to walk on it

Finding the Voice Lost to Laryngitis

When You Have Laryngitis, Don't Even Try to Whisper

You went to a basketball game last night and screamed your lungs out; this morning, you can't even whisper. Laryngitis, an infection or irritation of the larynx, or voice box, can be caused by "straining" your voice or, more commonly in adults, by a virus.

If you experience hoarseness, a ticklish sensation, and a constant urge to clear your throat—but no other symptoms—your laryngitis should heal itself in a day or two. (If you have other problems, you might have a cold, the flu, or an infection that requires medical attention, such as strep throat.) The following tips can help speed your recovery:

- ❑ Drink warm liquids.
- ❑ Avoid alcohol.
- ❑ Avoid cigarette smoke.
- ❑ Give your voice a rest.

And remember: Whispering still counts as talking.

Embracing Menopause

Does life begin at 40? At 50? For millions of women, menopause—the end of the child-bearing years—signals a new stage of life, one that can be as rich and rewarding as any phase. Some women go through years of menopause with few problems or none at all! Others experience hot flashes, mood swings, depression, brittle bones, pain during intercourse, and other symptoms. Medical advances such as hormone replacement therapy have lessened some of the physical discomforts and health risks that occur during menopause, and modern society's heightened understanding has helped more women embrace this change of life.

Signs of Menopause
The average age when women stop menstruating entirely is about 50, but some women's bodies begin the process in their late 30s, producing less of the hormone estrogen, which triggers a host of physical changes. Many factors determine when you'll go through the change, including genetics (if your mother had an early menopause, you might, too), smoking (which may speed up the process by as much as two years), or the surgical removal of one's ovaries.

Here are some signs of menopause to watch for:

- Irregular periods, including skipped periods
- Hot flashes (sudden bursts of warmth, especially at night)
- Vaginal dryness or itching
- Painful intercourse
- Headaches
- Mood swings, irritability

Menopause or Aging?

The loss of estrogen causes other changes in a woman's body, but some are part of the normal aging process rather than a direct result of menopause. They include:

- Wrinkled skin
- Thinning hair and change in hair texture
- Increase in facial hair
- Loss of firmness and fullness in breasts
- Redistribution of body fat

SEXUALITY AT MID-LIFE

After menopause, women no longer have to worry about becoming pregnant—although you can conceive during menopause, up until your last period. Some women continue using the contraceptive methods they always have, some women (or their partners) opt for sterilization. However, because periods are irregular during the menopause years, "natural" family planning—abstaining from sex during certain times in your menstrual cycle—is not considered reliable.

In past generations, the onset of menopause too often meant the end of a couple's sex life. But the "change of life" can actually launch a rich—and romantic—phase in your relationship with your partner. An older woman and

SIGNS OF TROUBLE

Although menopause is marked by irregular periods, some abnormal bleeding could signal problems with the uterus or its lining. Call your doctor if you experience the following:

- A drastic change in your monthly cycle
- Very heavy bleeding
- Bleeding that lasts longer than usual
- Bleeding more often than every three weeks
- Bleeding after intercourse

❏ ❏ ❏

FOR MORE INFORMATION

The North American Menopause Society can give you information on health professionals in your area who can answer your questions about menopause. For a list, write:

North American Menopause Society
c/o University Hospitals of Cleveland
2074 Abington Road
Cleveland, OH 44106

If you'd like to seek out a menopause support group in your area, ask your doctor, or check the Yellow Pages.

❏ ❏ ❏

her partner may know more than when they were younger about how to please each other. And not having young children to care for may create more privacy for a couple—and more opportunities for lovemaking. If you experience discomfort, hormone replacement therapy or lubricating jellies—and longer foreplay—can combat vaginal dryness that can result from a loss of estrogen. And regular intercourse helps the vagina keep its natural elasticity and lubrication.

Build and
Maintain
Strong
Bones by
Getting
Enough
Dietary
Calcium

Menopause Health Risks: Hearts and Bones

There are some health risks associated with menopause. There are also steps you can take to reduce your risks of health problems.

A woman's ovaries produce estrogen. This hormone helps protect her heart by reducing plaque, which can block the blood vessels. When a woman begins menopause, the loss of that protective hormone puts her at increased risk for cardiovascular disease—the number one killer of women older than 50 years of age—and stroke. Hormone replacement therapy (HRT) can cut her risk significantly—most studies say by about 50 percent—but not every woman is a candidate for that treatment. (See *Hormone Replacement Therapy* for details.)

Estrogen helps women maintain strong bones. Although our bones lose their density as we get older, menopause, with its accompanying loss of estrogen, speeds up deterioration. This can lead to osteoporosis, or porous bones, which can make the hip, wrist, ribs, or spinal bones vulnerable to fractures. HRT can help bones maintain their density.

You can also help build and maintain strong bones by getting enough dietary calcium—at least 1,500 milligrams daily. Calcium is present in dairy products and some green, leafy vegetables. Regular, weight-bearing exercise— such as walking or weight lifting— may also help slow down bone loss.

HORMONE REPLACEMENT THERAPY

If you're experiencing uncomfortable symptoms, or if you're at high risk for osteoporosis or heart disease, your doctor may recommend hormone replacement therapy (HRT). HRT delivers estrogen— sometimes by means of pills, sometimes through skin patches or vaginal creams—to replace decreasing levels of those hormones in your body. Some doctors may add progesterone to the mix for a woman who still has a uterus because estrogen use alone has been linked with an increase in the risk of uterine and breast cancer. (In fact, if you've had breast cancer, endometrial cancer, uterine fibroids, or liver disease, HRT is usually not recommended.)

Before agreeing to HRT, make sure you've carefully discussed the risks and benefits with your doctor. If you do opt for HRT, communicate with your physician so the two of you can eventually settle on a dosage that works best for you. (Also see sidebar, *Pros and Cons of HRT*, in Chapter 8, page 301.)

Managing Menstrual Cramps

Cramps, which are especially common in teenagers and younger women, can mean anything from an annoying monthly inconvenience to a sign of underlying gynecologic problems ranging from endometriosis to sexually transmitted disease.

The timing and severity of the cramps can indicate how serious they are. If you have mild cramps that end with menstruation or pain that lasts only the first couple of days of your period, chances are you have nothing to worry about. Try the following to relieve pain:

❏ **Take a mild analgesic.** Aspirin or ibuprofen should take the edge off your discomfort.

❏ **Experiment to find the best remedy for you.** Although no home remedies have been proved effective, some women swear that warm baths, exercise, heating pads, and abstention from caffeine ease their symptoms.

❏ **Consider contraceptive pills.** Many women on oral contraceptives also report a decrease in premenstrual and menstrual symptoms, including cramps.

If, however, you experience severe cramps that last throughout your period (a condition called *dysmenorrhea*), consult your doctor.

Easing Morning Sickness

If you're expecting a baby and experiencing nausea on a regular basis, talk about the miracle of birth must seem a bit ironic. But morning sickness—a misnomer, because it can occur anytime—is a natural part of pregnancy for many women.

To soothe your queasiness, try eating several smaller meals during the day, rather than three hearty ones. And consult your obstetrician if you experience severe vomiting for more than a couple of days—it could indicate you have

an illness; you may also need intravenous feeding to replace the fluids and nutrients you've lost.

Motion Sickness: The Bane of Travelers

Some people can ride cross country in the back seat of a car for days and never feel queasy; others get nauseated by a quick jaunt across town. Some unlucky travelers are prone to motion sickness—nausea or light-headedness when traveling by car, plane, or boat. The problem is believed to be caused by a disruption in the inner ear, which regulates balance.

So what can you do? Over-the-counter antihistamine remedies, such as Dramamine, offer some relief, although they do cause drowsiness and, therefore, aren't recommended for drivers. If you're making a long trip, prescription patches that deliver antinausea medication to the skin behind your ear can help quell symptoms. The slow-acting patches can be worn for three days. Some other tips: Eat sparingly before a trip, avoid alcohol, and, in a car, try to sit up front.

Minimizing Muscle Pain

Muscles can rebel when they're stretched to their limit, whether as a result of playing

Morning Sickness Can Occur Anytime

241

Improve Muscle Strength and Flexibility with Regular Exercise

sports or going about your daily routine at work or home. Although most muscle strains are mild and can be treated at home (usually by taking it easy for a few days), any pain that doesn't improve after two or three days of self care should prompt you to seek professional medical advice.

The pain in your muscles may be due to one of the following conditions:

- A **strain** can result when a muscle or tendon—which connects muscles to bones—is stretched too much, or even tears partially or completely as a result of exertion.

- A **sprain** (a term often used interchangeably—and inaccurately—with "strain" to describe injuries), is a stretch or tear in one of your ligaments, the bands of connective tissue that join one bone to another. Sprains are most likely to occur in the ankles, knees, or wrists.

- **Tendinitis** is inflammation of a tendon. (See the section *Tendinitis: Tips for Weekend Warriors*, page 249.)

- **Bursitis** is swelling and irritation of the bursa, a fluid-filled sac located in the major joint areas, such as the shoulders. (See *Easing the Ache of Bursitis* on page 193.)

PREVENTING MUSCLE INJURY

To prevent the kinds of injuries that result in muscle pain, learn how to perform work and activities in a safe way and improve muscle strength and flexibility with regular exercise.

- ❑ **Use proper form when moving heavy or unwieldy objects.** If you must lift or move heavy objects, for example, lift them with your legs rather than your back, and try not to twist your body. (For more detailed instruction on safe lifting, see *Answers for Aching Backs*, page 187.)

- ❑ **Warm up and cool down each time you exercise.** If you play sports or engage in regular exercise, find out what warm-up and cool-down exercises are recommended, and do them every time (See Chapter 3, *Fitness*, for a complete program of warm-ups, stretches, and exercises that improve muscle strength and flexibility.)

- ❑ **Listen to your body.** If you feel tired or you notice muscle pain while engaging in an activity, stop doing it! "No pain, no gain" is no longer considered a wise motto for the exerciser. Exercise should not hurt; pain is your body's way of telling you something is wrong.

- ❑ **Follow the RICE program of self-treatment.** To ease mild to moderate muscle pain, remember RICE—Rest, Ice, Compression, Elevation—for a couple of days. (See *Soothe Your Aching Knees*, page 237.)

- ❑ **Try over-the-counter anti-inflammatory medication.** In addition to the RICE treatment, aspirin or ibuprofen can help relieve pain. (Forgo acetaminophen, which is not an anti-inflammatory medication.)

- ❑ **If you feel no improvement after a couple of days, consult your physician.**

Coping with Nausea and Vomiting

Vomiting can be caused by a virus, bacteria, parasites, the use of antibiotics, motion sickness, stress, or certain rich foods. It may also be caused by serious medical disorders, such as ulcer and gallbladder disease.

If you're not sure of the cause, or if nausea and vomiting are accompanied by severe stomach pain, a call to the doctor is in order. If vomit or stools are black or bloody, seek medical attention immediately.

Like diarrhea, vomiting is an attempt by your body to make itself healthy—to rid itself of an infection or irritant. However, excessive vomiting can lead to dehydration, a problem that may require additional fluids or even medical attention. See *Signs of Serious Illness*, page 204.

Here are a few tips for coping with short-term nausea and vomiting:

❑ Suck on ice chips.
❑ Drink clear liquids (water, 7-Up) if you can keep them down.
❑ Avoid sweetened beverages, such as apple juice or fruit-flavored soft drinks, and caffeinated beverages.
❑ Avoid solid foods for a while.
❑ Gradually add solid foods as your condition improves: Start with bananas, rice, applesauce, and toast (the BRAT diet), as well as clear soups and unsweetened cereals.

Premenstrual Syndrome: Is It All in Your Head?

Food cravings, mood swings, water retention, swollen breasts—no, these are not all in your head. For years, the American College of Obstetricians and Gynecologists has recognized 180 symptoms as part of a little-understood condition known as premenstrual syndrome (PMS). Most of the millions of women between puberty and menopause who experience PMS have only moderate symptoms. About 10 percent of women in their child-bearing years experience severe symptoms that affect their physical or emotional well-being.

What Is PMS?

Premenstrual symptoms are those you experience within the two weeks before your period begins. The discomfort ends rapidly once you start menstruating. Any problem that last longer than two weeks is probably not PMS and may require a doctor's advice; it could be a more serious condition, such as depression, or even an ailment, such as diabetes. You might want to keep track of your symptoms, their severity, and their timing by jotting them down in a journal for at least a couple of months. Having a record of your experience can help your doctor diagnose your condition and suggest treatments.

A High-Carbohydrate, Low-Protein Diet May Ease PMS Symptoms

243

Exercise Also Helps Relieve PMS Symptoms

There are four types of PMS symptoms:

- Fluid retention, which includes weight gain and swollen breasts
- Emotional problems, including mood swings
- Pain, which includes backaches and cramps
- Food cravings, especially for carbohydrates

THE GOOD NEWS ABOUT PMS

A whopping 60 percent of PMS sufferers report benefits from self-treatment, such as exercising, taking a warm bath, even hiring a baby-sitter for a few hours, which may be evidence that occasional pampering is good for all of us. But what works for some women may not work for you, so don't be discouraged if a warm bath does nothing for your PMS symptoms.

Your doctor may suggest treatments for specific symptoms. Here's a list of common symptoms and remedies.

- ❑ **Cramps, muscle aches:** Use mild analgesics, such as ibuprofen or aspirin.

- ❑ **Anxiety, tension, mood swings:** Reduce caffeine intake; take antidepressants (by prescription only).

- ❑ **Water retention, bloating, swollen breasts:** Reduce salt intake before your period; take mild diuretics, or "water pills."

- ❑ **Food cravings and insomnia:** Exercise. Doctors have also found that eating complex carbohydrates (whole grains, breads, pasta, fruits and vegetables) and limiting protein, sugar, and fatty foods can reduce PMS symptoms.

Easing the Discomfort of Psoriasis

Many of the nearly 4 million people in the United States who have the chronic, noncontagious but incurable skin disorder psoriasis experience very mild cases and, in fact, may go through life without ever knowing they have it. But psoriasis can also be unsightly and uncomfortable and can cause great emotional distress for people with severe cases. Fortunately, doctors now have a variety of weapons to combat the condition.

What Causes Psoriasis?

Psoriasis, which is thought to be passed on in the genes, is caused by an overproduction of skin cells. If you have the condition, your skin cells mature and turn over in a brisk three or four days, instead of the usual 28 to 30 days. The skin thickens and turns into red bumps covered by silvery scales, often on the scalp, elbows, knees, nails, groin, and lower back.

Although the problem can appear at any age, it most often starts in the early teens. Many people experience their first outbreak of psoriasis soon after the skin is cut, scratched, rubbed, or severely sunburned, although the connection between skin trauma and psoriasis outbreaks is uncertain. It can also be triggered by cold winter weather and some infections and medications.

CURBING PSORIASIS SYMPTOMS

If you seek help in curbing psoriasis symptoms, you have two challenges: to ease your discomfort and slow down rapid turnover of skin cells.

- In mild cases, over-the-counter shampoos containing coal-tar—which has been used for more than 100 years to treat psoriasis—may bring some relief.

- Your doctor might prescribe topical corticosteroids, or anthralin creams and ointments.

- Your physician might also suggest light therapy, in which you expose your skin to natural or ultraviolet light (which is administered in a medical facility). If light therapy is recommended, follow your doctor's advice to avoid raising your risk of skin cancer.

- In severe cases that don't respond to other treatments, an oral anticancer drug called methotrexate may be given.

On Pins and Needles? It May Be Restless Legs Syndrome

Bedtime should be peaceful, right? But many sleepers find they can't lie still—literally. A sudden jolting, jerking sensation right before you fall asleep is a normal reflex for millions of people, but if you experience a near-constant "pins and nee-

PSORIASIS AND ARTHRITIS

An estimated 10 to 15 percent of all people with psoriasis also have arthritis. Although doctors don't yet know why the two conditions appear to be linked, they can prescribe medication to ease the problem. Arthritis symptoms usually improve as a patient's skin responds to treatment.

❑ ❑ ❑

dles" feeling in your legs at night and are unable to keep them still (and, as a result, have trouble sleeping), you could be experiencing restless legs syndrome. The problem is most common among elderly people.

If you experience this problem, here are a few tips to help you rest:

- ❑ Try taking mild over-the-counter analgesics, such as aspirin or ibuprofen.
- ❑ Reduce caffeine intake.
- ❑ Try the tips for treating insomnia listed on pages 234–235.
- ❑ Consult your doctor if the syndrome persists despite self-treatment. Your doctor might prescribe a small dose of codeine, or phenobarbital, a sedative, to help you get some rest.

Shingles: An Old Virus Resurfaces

You had chicken pox as a child and thought you didn't need to worry about it ever again. Then suddenly, many years later, the virus makes a surprise reappearance—as

To Help Still Restless Legs, Forgo Caffeine

painful clusters of red blisters on the trunk, buttocks, or face known as herpes zoster, or shingles.

Although doctors don't know why the virus can lie dormant for decades, or what makes it reappear (most often after aged 50), they do think it takes advantage of periods of vulnerability in the body's ability to fight off disease. Although anyone who's had chicken pox can get shingles (in fact, about 20 percent of the population has them at some time in their lives, according to the American Academy of Dermatology), it seems especially common in some cancer patients, in AIDS patients, and in organ transplant recipients who are taking drugs to ward off transplant rejection—in other words, people with weakened immune systems.

Signs of Shingles

Here are the typical stages of shingles:

- The virus first announces its reappearance with burning pain, tingling, or extreme sensitivity in one region of the skin.
- After one to three days, a red rash appears, accompanied often by fever or headache.
- The rash soon turns into clumps of red blisters, which

eventually fill with fluid; this stage lasts up to three weeks. (Blisters on the face may be accompanied by temporary facial paralysis.)

- Next, the blisters crust over and start to disappear, although the pain may last longer.

COPING WITH SHINGLES

The good news is shingles usually clears up on its own, although your doctor will probably prescribe pain killers to ease your discomfort. In most cases, the antiviral drug acyclovir may be prescribed; it works best when given in the first few days of an outbreak of shingles, so for maximum benefits, consult your physician early. Some ointments, such as corticosteroids, may also be given by a doctor.

Note: If you have blisters near your eyes, tell your physician immediately—you could run the risk of permanent eye damage if they are left untreated. Cool compresses may also help dry the blisters and speed recovery.

Sinusitis: Cease Your Sniffles

If you have a cold that includes sniffles and lasts longer than a week, you may actually have sinusitis, a secondary bacterial infection of the sinuses, the cavities in the bone around your nose.

If you can't shake your sniffles, try the following:

❏ **Use vaporizers or breathe in shower steam.** These home

Anyone Who's Had Chicken Pox Can Get Shingles

IS SHINGLES CONTAGIOUS?

The virus that causes herpes zoster is contagious, but if passed on, it most likely causes chicken pox, not shingles. People with weakened immune systems, such as newborn babies or cancer patients, are most vulnerable to the virus—along with people who have never had chicken pox.

❏ ❏ ❏

remedies can help you breathe and loosen nasal blockage.

❑ **Try over-the-counter decongestants.** These might also help clear your nasal passages. Be sure to follow label directions, and do not use for more than three days.

❑ **Consult your doctor.** If you do have a bacterial infection (the most common cause of sinusitis, although a fungus or virus might also be the culprit), your doctor may prescribe an antibiotic to treat the problem. In some cases, a physician might recommend surgery to relieve chronic sinusitis.

❑ **Stop smoking.** Smokers seem particularly prone to sinus infections—yet another reason to kick the habit!

Snoring: Can You Achieve the Sounds of Silence?

Snoring—the sound produced when you're asleep by the relaxed muscles of the throat as you breathe—can range from a mild, endearing snuffle to a buzz-saw-like clatter. But it's usually not a problem for the snorer. (For an unlucky bed partner, however, it can be an annoyance or grounds for divorce.) In cases of persistently loud snoring and excessive daytime sleepiness, sleep apnea, an interruption of normal breathing caused by physical problems, may be the cause.

WATCH FOR SLEEP APNEA

Although most cases of snoring are harmless, a small number of them may indicate sleep apnea. In sleep apnea (which is most common in middle-aged, obese men), the sleeper snores loudly, then is unable to breath for periods ranging from about ten seconds to one minute. This lull in breathing results when the back of the tongue and other soft tissues in the throat close the airway during sleep. The silent period usually ends with grunting, gasping, or snorting sounds; then snoring resumes.

Sleep apnea prevents a person from getting the quality of sleep needed for daytime functioning. The sleep deprivation can result in headaches, memory problems, depression, decreased libido, and even a higher likelihood of falling asleep while driving. (People with apnea have a rate of automobile accidents ten times that of people without the condition.) The problem can be alleviated by following the prevention advice for snorers that follows, but if you notice headaches and excessive daytime sleepiness after trying the steps outlined below, consult your physician.

DIM THE DIN

If you snore, take the following steps to keep it under control:

❑ **Stay trim.** Overweight people are more likely to snore. Regular physical activity and a diet low in fat helps you maintain a weight that's ideal for your height, age, and sex.

❑ **Avoid alcohol and sleep aids.** Drinking—and taking sedatives—can aggravate the problem. If you must imbibe, drink moderately.

Do You Keep Others Awake When You Sleep?

247

- **Try sleeping on your side or stomach.** Spouses since the beginning of time have known that flipping a snorer on his or her stomach quiets down the noise. If you snore loudly and have trouble staying on your side, try to train yourself by sewing a sock filled with a tennis ball into the back of your pajama top.

Soothing a Sore Throat

A red, irritated throat—usually accompanying a cold or flu, and most often caused by a virus—can usually be soothed with a simple home remedy.

- Dissolve a teaspoon of salt into a glass of warm water and gargle with the solution.
- Repeat every four hours until you start to feel better.
- In addition to the salt water gargle, suck on menthol throat lozenges or use medicated throat sprays to ease the discomfort.

If your sore throat persists despite a day or two of home care or if it's extremely painful, see a doctor for a strep bacteria test. If you have strep throat, you may need antibiotics to get relief.

Subdue Your Upset Stomach

Nearly everyone eats something that "doesn't agree" with them from time to time. Maybe you shouldn't have entered that pie eating contest. Maybe it was those last ten fried shrimp at the all-you-can-eat shrimp bar. Or perhaps your stomach is rebelling against too many turns on the ferris wheel after that giant pink stick of cotton candy at the carnival. In other words, most upset stomachs are the result of eating too much, too fast, or too much of the wrong foods, especially sweet or fatty ones.

SOOTHING THE UPSET

Whether it was too many jelly beans or too much of Aunt Dorothy's fried chicken, pamper your stomach with these tips.

- **Sip decaffeinated soda.** Drinking ginger ale or 7-Up may help settle your stomach. For best results (and to prevent additional gas from the carbonation), drink these beverages warm and flat. Bartenders have their own "cure" for stomach upset: a small glass of soda water with two dashes of bitters.
- **Try antacids.** Some people find liquid antacids provide quicker relief from excess acid.
- **Don't drink milk.** If your stomach aches after eating gas-producing foods, a glass of milk may actually make the gas and bloating worse if you are lactose intolerant.
- **Avoid alcohol and coffee.** Both irritate the stomach.
- **Go for a walk.** Gentle exercise may help cramping muscles relax, aid digestion, and take your mind off your discomfort.

Most Upset Stomachs Are the Result of Eating Too Much, Too Fast

Keep Your Digestive Tract on Track

Here's some advice for preventing cases of stomach upset in the future.

❑ Eat more slowly.

❑ Eat smaller, more frequent meals.

❑ Add fiber to your diet.

❑ Avoid high-fat foods.

❑ Know which foods cause you problems. (See *Gas-Producing Foods*, page 214, for a list of potential troublemakers.)

❑ Limit sugary foods.

❑ Go easy on very spicy, peppery foods.

❑ Don't smoke.

❑ Exercise.

❑ Limit alcohol use.

When To See a Doctor

Be aware that in some cases stomach pain may indicate a more serious problem than simply overeating. Even if you think you only have a case of indigestion, seek medical help if you also experience one of these symptoms:

- An upset stomach that occurs at the same time every day

- An upset stomach that gets progressively worse as days go by, despite self treatment or preventive steps you've taken

- Vomiting or spitting up blood

- Black or bloody stools

- Severe pressure, fullness, squeezing, or pain in the center of the chest that lasts more than a few minutes, or goes away and comes back

- Pain spreading to the shoulders, neck, or arms

- Chest discomfort accompanied by light-headedness, fainting, sweating, nausea, or shortness of breath

- Severe stomach pain following an injury

Tendinitis: Tips for Weekend Warriors

You don't have to be a weekend athlete to get tendinitis, but weekend warriors often experience the condition. Injuries to the tendons—which connect the muscles to the bones—that result in inflammation, swelling, redness, and pain are called tendinitis. (The problem also goes by the names "tennis elbow" and "golfer's elbow.") It commonly happens as the result of playing sports or engaging in physical exercise, especially if you overdo it or don't take time to warm up properly, but tendons can become injured in the course of your daily routine, as well.

Kinds of Tendinitis

Although many tendon injuries are temporary and respond to time, rest, and treatment, some may indicate a more serious problem. Tendon injuries may include the following types:

- **Acute tendinitis.** This is a temporary problem that occurs due to an overuse injury.

Tendinitis Can Occur As a Result of Your Daily Routine

Take the Time to Warm Up Properly

- **Chronic tendinitis.** Pain that doesn't go away, or that returns often, may indicate a degenerative disease (such as arthritis), or simply the wear and tear on your tendons as the result of advancing age.

- **Split or torn tendons.** This can result from either of the first two types of tendinitis. Rotator cuff injuries—damage to the shoulder—may fall into this category, and some cases require surgery to repair them.

ARE YOU PRONE TO PAIN?

Some athletes are prone to tendinitis in specific parts of their bodies:

- Baseball or softball players, swimmers, tennis players, and golfers are most likely to have tendon injuries in their shoulders or arms.

- Soccer and basketball players, runners, dancers, and people who do aerobic dance workouts may be more prone to leg and foot injuries.

Find out what warm-up and cool-down exercises are recommended for your favorite sports, and do them every time. Also, if you notice muscle pain while engaging in an activity, stop doing it! "Feel the burn" is not a wise motto. Exercise is not supposed to hurt; pain is your body's way of telling you something's wrong.

RELIEF FOR TENDINITIS

Most cases of tendinitis can be taken care of at home, although you should see a doctor if you have severe pain or if the injured area doesn't feel better after a few days of self care. Time is the best healer of an injured tendon, but rest may be hard to get. The biggest challenge in treating tendinitis is that the muscles and tendons are constantly in motion. You might need to use a sling, for example, to steady an injured arm.

To relieve pain, try over-the-counter analgesics, such as aspirin or ibuprofen. After a few days, gently exercise the injured area to prevent it from becoming stiff. Remember: start slow! Overdoing it again can cause the problem to get worse; too much stress on an inflamed tendon can cause it to rupture, a serious situation that might require a doctor to put you in a cast or even perform surgery to repair the damage.

Avoiding Traveler's Diarrhea

You're planning a trip to another country. You're excited at the prospect of experiencing another culture, but there's one culture in particular you fear encountering—the bacterial kind that can make you ill. Water systems and food service industries in other nations aren't always required to heed the same stringent health codes the United States enforces. To prevent problems, here are some hints to ensure a happy, healthy journey.

Don't let the excitement of travel lead you to forget this basic advice for travellers:

- **Don't drink the water.** The old advice to help travelers avoid "Montezuma's revenge" still holds true. Drink only sterilized, chlorinated, or carbonated water. (Factory-bottled water is usually safe.)

❑ **Don't have your drinks over ice.** Not even alcoholic drinks, so forgo the frozen margarita. Alcohol does not kill the bacteria that causes "Montezuma's revenge."

❑ **Don't eat food sold by a street vendor.** It's usually been sitting out for long periods. Many carts lack proper refrigeration facilities.

❑ **Eat in reputable restaurants and hotels.** They're more likely to conform to American-style health guidelines.

❑ **Don't drink raw milk.** The pasteurization process kills bacteria.

❑ **Eat no undercooked meat.** Undercooked ground beef is a major source of food-borne disease. Make sure any meat you consume is cooked until no longer pink, and the juices run clear. Send undercooked meat back to the chef until done.

❑ **Eat fruit only if it can be peeled just before eating.** Pineapples, bananas, oranges, melons, and other fruit with a rind are your best choices.

CALM THE QUEASINESS

If you do feel queasy as a result of something you ate while abroad, follow these treatment guidelines, courtesy of the Centers for Disease Control and Prevention:

❑ **If you have no diarrhea symptoms, do nothing.** The nausea should pass.

❑ **If you have loose stools, take Pepto-Bismol.** Available in tablets or liquid, it's easy to take along with you.

❑ **If you have diarrhea, fever, chills, or sweats, you may need to take antibiotics.** See a physician for a prescription. (You might try getting a prescription from your doctor before you leave on your trip, for use in an emergency.) Also, read *When Diarrhea's Got You Down*, page 204.

Understanding Urinary Tract Infections

Painful, annoying urinary tract infections, or UTIs, are common—most of us will have at least one in our lifetime. Although commonly called a "bladder infection," the problem may be caused by bacteria in any part of your urinary tract, including your kidneys, ureters (the tubes that carry urine to the bladder from the kidneys), urethra (the tube that empties the bladder when you urinate), or bladder (the sac that "holds" urine before it is released through the urethra).

Because bacteria can spread quickly through the urinary tract, it's important to notify your doctor as soon as you develop symptoms of a urinary tract infection. The bacteria that cause urinary tract infections most often enter the urethra and travel up through the urinary tract. Physicians describe infections according to the portion of the urinary tract infected:

Urinary Tract Infections Are Commonly Called Bladder Infections

Women Are More Likely to Get Urinary Tract Infections

- An infection of the urethra is called *urethritis*.
- An infection of the bladder is *cystitis*, the most common infection.
- An infection that reaches the kidneys is *pyelonephritis*, a serious condition.

UTI Symptoms

If you have these symptoms, see your doctor; they could signal a urinary tract infection:

- A burning sensation when you urinate
- A frequent urge to urinate
- Feeling the urge to urinate even when you can't
- Urine leakage
- Foul-smelling urine
- Cloudy, dark, or bloody urine
- A low fever

If you have a kidney infection, you might also have these symptoms:

- Fever, chills, and sweats
- Abdominal pain
- Feelings of pressure in the lower abdomen
- Low back pain
- Nausea
- Fatigue

WOMEN AND UTI

Although men can also suffer infections of the urinary tract, women are much more likely to get them, for a number of reasons:

- **Anatomy.** Because a woman's urethra is shorter than a man's, bacteria can more easily reach the bladder. Also, because the urethra is closer to the rectum on a woman's body, bacteria from the rectum can more easily travel to the urinary tract.

- **Pregnancy.** Expectant mothers may be at higher risk for infections of the kidneys because a fetus can put pressure on the ureters.

- **Sex.** The act of sexual intercourse can push bacteria into the urethra. Wearing a diaphragm can also push against the urethra and make it harder to completely empty the bladder, causing bacteria to collect in the uneliminated urine.

MEN AND UTI

Urinary tract infections are commonly thought of as a "women's problem," but men get them too, although generally less frequently and at an older age than women. The symptoms are the same for men and women: frequent, painful urination and some difficulty when urinating. You feel the urge to go, but are able to void only a small amount.

The same bacteria cause urinary tract infections in men. Common factors that promote infection in men include:

- **Prostate problems.** An enlarged prostate may affect your urethra and prevent you from emptying your bladder completely, allowing bacteria to breed in the unreleased urine.

- **Inadequate fluid intake.** Drinking water, especially in warm weather, prevents dehydration and flushes bacteria from your urinary tract.

- **Frequent medical procedures.** If you've had medical treatment that required use of a catheter frequently or for an extended period, you may experience urinary tract infections. The catheter can introduce bacteria, and frequent catheterization may scar the urethra, causing it to narrow, which may in turn increase your risk of developing urinary tract infections.

Banishing the Bacteria that Cause UTI

Some people never get urinary tract infections, while others seem prone to them. You can help prevent painful infections of the urinary tract by following this advice:

❑ **Drink plenty of water to flush out bacteria.** Shoot for at least six to eight glasses every day.

❑ **Try drinking cranberry juice when possible.** Cranberry juice has long been a folk remedy with a good reputation, and now recent medical evidence supports its effectiveness in reducing the number of urinary tract infections.

❑ **Always heed the urge to urinate.** Holding in urine risks a buildup of bacteria.

❑ **Wipe from front to back after a bowel movement.** This helps prevent exposing the urethra to bacteria from the rectum.

❑ **Urinate after having sex.** This helps wash away any bacteria.

❑ **Consider using another form of contraception rather than a diaphragm.** Especially if you're prone to urinary tract infections.

❑ **Follow your doctor's advice about taking any medication.** This advice applies to medica-

tions taken to prevent or treat infections.

TREATING A UTI

If you suspect you have a urinary tract infection, your physician can diagnose it by checking a sample of your urine for bacteria. You may receive antibiotics to fight the infection. Although the symptoms of most urinary tract infections clear up within a day or two after you start taking the medication, you should finish all of the drugs you've been prescribed to completely rid yourself of the bacteria causing the problem. (Your doctor may prescribe a bladder analgesic along with the antibiotic. One side effect of this pain medication is bright-orange urine; don't be alarmed, this effect is only temporary.) If you're prone to urinary tract infections, your doctor might keep you on antibiotics longer to ward off recurrences, or give you pills to take when you have sexual intercourse to prevent infections.

Living with Varicose Veins

Swollen, twisted, bluish veins of the legs are not only unsightly, but they can be quite painful. You might be prone to varicose veins as you get older if your parents had them, but they're caused by more than heredity.

Why Varicose Veins Develop
Because we walk, stand, or sit upright, the blood flowing from the tissues of the leg must travel uphill to return to the heart. The muscles of the legs must help push

Drink Plenty of Water to Flush Out Bacteria

Be On the Watch for Complications of Varicose Veins

the blood flow upward. When a muscle relaxes, veins near the skin's surface (called superficial and perforating veins) suck blood into themselves and carry it into the deep veins of the leg, which transport blood to the heart. The deep and perforating veins contain tiny valves that prevent blood from flowing downhill, and back. If these valves don't work properly, blood may flow back into the superficial veins, making them swollen and twisted. This condition is called varicose veins.

Symptoms of Varicose Veins

Varicose veins, which occur more often in women than men, announce themselves by their appearance: protruding bluish veins on the leg, often on the back of the calf or up the inside of the leg. They may also appear around the anus, or even in the vagina (especially in pregnant women). Also, they may cause your legs to ache, especially in the afternoons (when you've been active for hours) or after you've been standing or walking for a while. Your feet may swell, causing your shoes to feel too tight by day's end.

Possible Complications

Varicose veins by themselves are usually not harmful to your

health. In some cases, however, complications can occur.

- Ulcers can develop if blood flow to the tissues of the leg is hampered. If a patch of brownish skin or a sore develops on or near a varicose vein, see your doctor.

- The swollen veins can bleed profusely if bumped or cut—a situation that requires immediate medical attention.

- Thrombophlebitis, or simply phlebitis, occurs when a clot forms in a vein, causing inflammation and swelling. If such a problem develops, your physician may prescribe anti-clotting drugs and you may need to be hospitalized; you may even need surgery. Your doctor may suggest that you take daily medication—usually aspirin—to prevent clots from forming.

Advice for Varicose Veins

Although there's nothing you can do to prevent varicose veins, you can take steps to ease the discomfort they cause and even to remove them.

- ❏ **Don't stand or sit for long periods.** To relieve your discomfort, take a break and walk around.
- ❏ **When sitting, try to keep your legs raised above the level of your chest whenever possible.** At home, rest your feet on a foot stool or hassock or sit in a reclining chair. Use pillows to elevate your legs even more.

FIRST AID FOR BLEEDING

If you cut a varicose vein:

- ❏ Lie down.
- ❏ Raise the injury above the level of your heart (if possible).
- ❏ Apply pressure to the wound with a clean handkerchief, bandage, or cloth.
- ❏ Seek immediate medical help.

❏   ❏   ❏

❑ **Wear strong support hose to help relieve some discomfort.** These are available in most pharmacies. For best results, put them on before getting out of bed in the morning.

❑ **Consider medical treatment.** Some patients opt for surgical removal of varicose veins, a procedure that may require hospitalization. Others choose a less radical (but in many cases, less effective) solution, in which a doctor injects chemicals into varicose veins that cause them to mat together and stop carrying blood. Recovery for both procedures takes several weeks.

Ward Off Warts

In fairy tales and folklore, warts cover witches and evil characters, but in real life, their nature is much less sinister—and you shouldn't need a magic spell to get rid of one. Warts are essentially scabs left after a viral infection; their raised appearance is due to a pileup of dead skin. The virus can be spread by touch. Although they can be unsightly, they rarely signal a serious health problem. Warts in the genital area, however, should be seen by a physician.

REMOVING WARTS

Many warts disappear by themselves. But here are a few treatment options if you wish to help them along.

● Some folk remedies may work, such as putting adhesive tape over a wart for 23 hours out of each day for a month.

● Salicylic acid patches, available in drugstores in over-the-counter "wart removal" kits, may help dissolve some warts. They're especially effective for warts on the feet but should never be used on the face or genital area.

● Your doctor can "freeze" a wart with liquid nitrogen, which helps it drop off. This procedure leaves minimal scarring.

● A physician might inject a wart with novocaine and literally cut it out of the skin, cauterizing the wound. For deeper warts on the bottom of the foot (called plantar warts), two or three such treatments might be required.

Understanding Yeast Infections

A yeast infection, also called *vaginitis,* is a common, irritating infection of the vaginal area. The organisms that cause vaginitis are normally present, but the vagina's acidic pH keeps these organisms in check. A yeast infection, then, indicates your vaginal pH has been altered so that, temporarily, it cannot control the growth of the vaginitis organism.

Several conditions can trigger this alteration:

● Menstruation

● Pregnancy

Warts Are Scabs Left After a Viral Infection

- Antibiotics
- Diabetes
- Stress
- Heat and moisture

Symptoms of Yeast Infection

These are the common symptoms of vaginitis. Be aware, however, that a yeast infection may not exhibit any symptoms at all; therefore, you can transmit the infection to your partner unknowingly during sexual intercourse. If your partner is not treated for the condition, your partner can then transmit the infection to you again.

- Unusual discharge from the vagina (white, foul-smelling, cottage cheese-like matter may signal the most common type of vaginitis, a yeast infection caused by a fungus)
- Itching and irritation in the genital area
- Pain during intercourse
- Pain in the lower abdomen
- Vaginal bleeding not associated with menstruation

Condom Use Helps Prevent Yeast Infections

Eliminating Yeast Infections

If you experience any of the symptoms above, consult your doctor who can tell you whether you have vaginitis. Yeast infections usually respond to treatment with miconazole or clotrimazole suppositories or creams, which are now available over-the-counter for women who suffer recurrent infections.

Remember that yeast infections can be transmitted from one partner to another during sex. If you have an infection, tell your partner, and urge your partner to seek treatment so you don't keep passing the infection back and forth.

If you're prone to yeast infections, here's how to prevent recurrences:

❑ **Practice safe sex.** Condom use help prevents not only common infections but many sexually transmitted diseases.

❑ **Consult your doctor to rule out diabetes, especially if you have frequent recurrences.** The fungus that causes yeast infection grows best in an environment rich in sugars.

❑ **Wear loose-fitting cotton underclothes.** Nylon and other synthetic materials trap heat and moisture, which allows bacteria to grow.

❑ **Avoid antibiotic use when possible.** They increase your risk for yeast infections.

YEAST INFECTIONS AND HIV

If it seems you're constantly battling recurrent yeast infections, see your doctor. You might need to be tested for human immunodeficiency virus (HIV), the virus thought to cause acquired immunodeficiency syndrome (AIDS). The Centers for Disease Control and Prevention says that repeated serious yeast infections are one of the first warning signs of HIV infection in women.

❑   ❑   ❑

CHAPTER 8

MAJOR

MEDICAL

PROBLEMS

If you live with a major medical condition, you already know how fragile the human body is and how important it is to take care of yourself. The medical problems described in this chapter are serious, potentially debilitating—even life-threatening— conditions that require a physician's treatment. If your physician has diagnosed a major medical problem, be sure to consult with him or her about any changes in your condition. And do not alter your treatment regimen in any way without your doctor's OK.

If you've never had a major medical condition, this chapter can help you identify your risk for a number of serious illnesses, such as cancer or heart disease, and provide you with information that may help you prevent disease and detect problems early if they do occur. If you are experiencing symptoms similar to those in this chapter, be sure to report them to your doctor.

❑ ❑ ❑

If We Improve Our Lifestyle Choices, We May Improve Our Health

The Choice is Yours

If you read about more than one major medical condition in this chapter, you'll see some messages repeated. These messages have to do with lifestyle choices. You see, by the way we live, we have some say in our health. Many of the health topics covered in this chapter are directly related to lifestyle choices such as: diet, smoking, sedentary lifestyle, sexual practices, and others. If we improve our lifestyle choices, we may improve our health.

Simply put, we have some control over our own good health. So if you seem to hear an echo as you read through the prevention and treatment tips in this chapter, it's because these are messages worth repeating:

❑ Don't smoke.
❑ Eat a balanced diet low in fats and high in fiber.
❑ Exercise regularly.
❑ Maintain ideal body weight.
❑ Manage your stress level.
❑ Practice safe sex.
❑ Drink alcohol in moderation only.
❑ Don't abuse drugs.
❑ Control your high blood pressure.
❑ Control your diabetes.
❑ Lower your blood cholesterol level.
❑ Discuss with your doctor the need for checkups.

We live in an age of medical miracles—if we develop health problems, we can receive the benefits of science and technology as well as the services of a wide range of health professionals. But there is so much each of us can do to *prevent* illness. It just takes a little knowledge and the desire to make healthy lifestyle choices. This chapter is designed to help you make more informed decisions about your health.

AIDS and HIV: What You Need to Know

Perhaps no major disease in this century has been the source of as much widespread misinformation and public fear as acquired immunodeficiency syndrome, or AIDS.

Since the first cases of the disease were reported in 1981, nearly 400,000 people in the United States have developed AIDS, and more than 220,000 have died (or nearly four times the number who died in the Vietnam War). In addition, the Centers for Disease Control and Prevention (CDC) estimates 1 million Americans—one in every 250 men, women, and children—are infected with the virus believed to cause AIDS. The disease is one of the three main causes of death for American men and women between the ages of 25 and 44, many of whom were exposed to the virus as teens and young adults.

Learning how to protect yourself from exposure to the virus that causes AIDS is the best defense against this deadly disease.

What Is HIV?

HIV, short for human immunodeficiency virus, is thought to be the virus that causes AIDS. When the virus enters the body, it gradually weakens the immune system by depleting the levels of $CD4^+$ cells (or T-helper cells), which, when plentiful, fight serious infections and some types of cancer. The virus can incubate in the body for years before symptoms develop or the infection leads to full-blown AIDS (the complete breakdown of the immune system). This means infected individuals can pass HIV on to many others before they ever discover they are infected.

THE STAGES AND SYMPTOMS OF HIV INFECTION

Often the term AIDS is inappropriately applied to describe any sign of HIV infection or to refer to persons who are HIV infected but have no signs or symptoms of illness. AIDS is the final stage of a process that began with transmission of HIV—perhaps years earlier. But not everyone infected with HIV shows signs of illness.

A person with HIV infection falls into one of three groups:

- Those who feel completely healthy
- Those with mild illness
- Those with the life-threatening disease AIDS

An important fact to note: Persons in all three groups can infect others.

In those people who have symptoms of HIV infection, the symptoms are often mild. But even severe symptoms can exist without the infections or cancers that mark the onset of AIDS. The early symptoms of HIV infection are common to many other illnesses so they may not alert an individual to the possibility of HIV infection. Symptoms may include the following:

- Fever
- Persistent diarrhea
- Weight loss
- Fatigue
- Enlarged lymph glands
- Persistent infections of the mouth or throat
- White spots in the mouth (called *thrush*)
- Persistent vaginal yeast infections
- Infections caused by the herpes viruses
- Shingles
- Night sweats

AIDS is the final severe disease stage of HIV infection. People who develop AIDS have been infected for at least four months and possibly as long as ten years. At this stage, the immune system is almost totally crippled, leaving the body susceptible to opportunistic diseases. "Opportunistic" describes diseases that take advantage of the weakened immune system—diseases that healthy bodies could fight off. Persons with AIDS battle many such opportunistic diseases. Each bout leaves them weaker and more disabled. Most people with AIDS eventually succumb to one of these diseases.

If an HIV-positive person develops AIDS, the breakdown of his or her immune system may also result in these conditions:

- Pneumonia
- Purple lesions on the skin (caused by a type of cancer called *Kaposi's sarcoma*)
- Tuberculosis
- Memory loss

AIDS Is the Final Stage of a Process that Began with Transmission of HIV

259

Use Latex Condoms Every Time You Have Sex

HOW HIV SPREADS

HIV is present in semen, blood, and vaginal secretions. The virus is passed in three ways:

- Sexual contact, whether anal, vaginal, or oral
- Sharing needles or syringes
- Childbirth (In some cases, mothers who are HIV-positive have passed the virus on to their newborns. Evidence also suggests that HIV can be transmitted through breast milk.)

There have been *no* reported cases of HIV transmission from the following:

- Saliva
- Tears
- Insect or animal bites
- Eating food handled by someone with the virus
- Sharing toilets, telephones, or clothes
- Sharing silverware, plates, or drinking glasses
- Touching, hugging, or kissing someone with the virus
- Playing sports with HIV-infected people
- Attending school, church, or working with someone who has the virus

PREVENTION TIPS

Protect yourself from HIV transmission:

- ❑ **Practice safe sex.** Limit the number of your sexual partners, and use latex condoms *every time* you have sex. Condoms protect you from a variety of sexually transmitted diseases and also help prevent pregnancy. Still, because condoms have a failure rate of around 12 percent, abstinence and a monogamous sexual relationship with someone who is also monogamous are the only completely reliable methods of avoiding STDs.

- ❑ **Avoid using drugs or drinking excessively.** If you're under the influence, you may be more likely to engage in unsafe sexual behavior.

- ❑ **If you do inject drugs, never share or reuse needles or syringes.**

- ❑ **If you are a health care worker, take "universal precautions."** Wear gloves, masks, gowns, and eyewear when performing procedures that expose you to blood, semen, or vaginal secretions. Wash your hands between patients. Properly dispose of used needles and other sharp medical tools.

THE BLOOD SUPPLY

In the early years of the AIDS epidemic, blood transfusions were a means of transmission of HIV infection. But blood screening programs implemented in 1985 have nearly eliminated transfusions as a means of transmission. In addition, since 1983, all blood donors have been screened based on their risk for the virus.

Incidentally, there is absolutely no risk of getting HIV by *giving* blood—a new, sterile needle is used for every blood donation.

❑   ❑   ❑

Living with AIDS and HIV Infection

Right now, there is no cure for AIDS, although some treatments have helped lengthen the lives of HIV-infected people. Three prescriptions drugs—

zidovudine (AZT), ddI, and ddC—are used to combat and slow the progession of HIV. A physician might also give a patient antibiotics or other drugs to prevent or treat some of the common opportunistic illnesses HIV-infected individuals may develop. Experimental drugs may also be available in some cases.

Self-Care for HIV Infection

In addition to drug therapy, HIV-infected individuals can do much to control their health. Here are a few suggestions:

❏ **Don't give up.** Be aggressive in your fight for health. A positive mental attitude is your best weapon against the progress of infection.

❏ **See a doctor regularly.** Your doctor will perform blood tests to monitor any change in your HIV status. You should also have regular eye and dental examinations. Be sure to inform all of your doctors of your HIV status.

❏ **Establish a network of support.** Talk with your friends, family, and partner about what you're experiencing physically and emotionally. Many communities provide services and activities for HIV-infected people where you can talk with others who are HIV infected and share your experiences.

❏ **Watch your diet.** Good nutrition is vitally important to maintain your health. (See Chapter 1, *Nutrition,* for a description of the foods in a balanced diet.)

FOR MORE INFORMATION

The Centers for Disease Control and Prevention (CDC) offers publications on a variety of AIDS-related topics, including guidelines for HIV prevention and for caring for AIDS patients. You can also get answers to any confidential questions you have about HIV or AIDS. The CDC National AIDS Hotline can be reached seven days a week, 24 hours a day at 1-800-342-AIDS (2437). The Spanish-language service, which is open from 8 A.M. until 2 A.M., EST, is available at 1-800-344-7432.

To learn about some experimental AIDS treatments, call the AIDS Clinical Trials Information Service at 1-800-TRIALS-A (874-2572). Your state or local health department or the local American Red Cross chapter can also tell you about services in your area.

❏ ❏ ❏

Who Should Have an HIV Test?

Anyone can become infected with HIV, but some people may be at higher risk. You should undergo testing for HIV infection if you answer "yes" to any of the following questions:

1. Have you ever had unprotected sex—anal, vaginal, or oral—with a man or woman who:

● you know was HIV infected?

● injects or has injected drugs?

● shared needles with someone who was infected?

● had sex with someone who shared needles?

● had multiple sex partners?

● you normally wouldn't have sex with?

2. Have you used needles or syringes that were used by anyone before you?

A Positive Mental Attitude Is Your Best Weapon Against the Progress of Infection

Is Arthritis an Inevitable Part of Growing Older?

3. Have you ever given or received sex for drugs or money?

4. Did you or any of your sex partners:

- receive treatment for hemophilia between 1978 and 1985?

- have a blood transfusion or organ transplant between 1978 and 1985?

Call your physician, local or state health department, or local AIDS organization for information about testing. Some states offer anonymous testing—your local health department can tell you if this service is available in your area. A blood test can detect the presence of antibodies to HIV within 12 weeks, although it can take up to six months before the body produces antibodies. *If the results of your test are positive for HIV, tell anyone you may have infected immediately.* If you're not comfortable doing this, ask a health department counselor to help you.

Arthritis: Is It Inevitable?

Most people, as they age, experience stiff or "creaky" joints from time to time. But is arthritis—which afflicts about one out of every seven Americans, according to the Arthritis Foundation—an inevitable part of growing older?

Not necessarily. Although it's true that most of the nearly 37 million people in the United States who have the disease are senior citizens, not every older person has arthritis. In addition, arthritis is not a condition that just affects the older generation. Many younger adults develop arthritis due to wear and tear on their joints or in conjunction with other medical conditions, such as psoriasis. And even children can develop juvenile rheumatoid arthritis, an inflammatory joint disease whose symptoms usually fade as the individual reaches adulthood.

Doctors aren't sure why some people get arthritis and others don't, although heredity, defective joints, and injury are thought to play roles. There's no prevention for the disease, but staying physically active, following your doctor's advice, and taking steps to protect your joints from injury can help you stay limber and keep symptoms to a minimum.

Why Joints Are Vulnerable

A joint—the structure where two bones meet—allows bending and movement, usually without pain. The ends of each bone are covered with a smooth material called hyaline cartilage, which cushions and protects bones from pressure and prevents them from scraping against one another as they move. The entire joint is encased in a capsule lined with a smooth membrane, which produces a fluid that lubricates the area to further re-

ARE YOU AT RISK?

The following groups are at increased risk for osteoarthritis:

- Older people
- Athletes
- People in jobs that require them to perform daily, repetitive movements (such as on an assembly line)

❑   ❑   ❑

duce friction. Although cartilage does suffer wear and tear the older we get, arthritis can accelerate the process, making movement· painful.

What Is Arthritis?

"Arthritis" is really a blanket term for more than 100 diseases that inflame the joints, making movement painful. The most common type, *osteoarthritis,* is also called degenerative joint disease; it results in the gradual wearing away of the cushioning cartilage surface that covers the ends of bones.

Although most elderly people have some degree of osteoarthritis, it can occur in younger people due to joint injury or overuse. (Weight-bearing joints, such as the knees, hips, and spine, are most vulnerable.) Rheumatoid arthritis, a chronic disease that affects many parts of the body, occurs when the body's immune system attacks and damages the joint surface, causing swelling, pain, and stiffness, even when the affected joints aren't being used. (Small joints in the hands, wrists, feet, and ankles are most often involved in these cases.)

Arthritis Symptoms

If you have any of these symptoms for more than two weeks, you may have arthritis:

- Swelling in one or more joints
- Stiffness, especially early in the morning
- Recurring pain or tenderness in a joint
- Inability to move a joint normally
- Redness or warmth in a joint
- Unexplained weight loss, fever, or weakness accompanied by joint pain

HELP FOR PERSONS WITH ARTHRITIS

These gadgets and devices may help protect joints and help people with arthritis stay active and handle daily tasks with more ease.

- ❑ Canes (When used correctly, a cane can reduce the amount of pressure walking puts on your hip joint by up to 60 percent.)
- ❑ Walkers
- ❑ Splints
- ❑ Shoe inserts, wedges, or cushioned pads
- ❑ Rubber, nonslip shoe soles
- ❑ Velcro clothing fasteners, instead of buttons or snaps
- ❑ Large grips for tools and utensils (You can wrap foam rubber or fabric around items with narrow handles, such as pens, for a surer grip.)
- ❑ Lightweight cookware and serving dishes, rather than stainless steel, glass, or ceramic
- ❑ Wall-mounted jar openers
- ❑ Electric knives, can openers, and other appliances
- ❑ Easy-to-open drug bottle caps (Note: These are not recommended for homes with small children.)
- ❑ Mobile shower heads
- ❑ Bath seats
- ❑ Railings or grab bars in the tub or shower

❑   ❑   ❑

Treating Your Stiff Joints

If you have arthritis symptoms, you and your doctor should discuss the following options to ease the aches of arthritis:

- You may find some pain relief with over-the-counter analgesics, especially anti-inflammatory medication such as aspirin or ibuprofen.

Help Yourself Remain Active and Limber with Regular Exercise

- Depending on the type and severity of your arthritis, your doctor might also prescribe any number of other drugs, including corticosteroids, gold salts, penicillamine, antimalarial medication, and drugs that suppress the immune system.

- When arthritis pain is severe, your physician might suggest an injection of cortisone, a strong pain reliever, as a temporary treatment.

- If medication and self-treatment (see the tips listed below) fail to bring relief, surgery might be recommended to remove, replace, or realign joints.

Self-Treatment Tips

In addition to taking any medicine your doctor prescribes, you can help yourself remain active and limber by following this advice:

- **Stay trim.** Being overweight can put more stress on your joints and bones and exacerbate arthritis pain.

- **Exercise regularly.** Weak, underused muscles can become stiff, causing you to lose your range of motion—and worsening arthritis symptoms. Perform physical activity for brief periods (to avoid injury and pain) as often as possible. Talk with your doctor about which kinds of exercise are best for you. Walking and swimming are two exercises often recommended for people who have arthritis.

- **Try physical therapy.** Although not everyone can afford physical therapy sessions, they may help you stay limber.

- **Protect your joints.** Use devices (see *Help for Persons with Arthritis*) to help you perform daily tasks. Avoid lifting heavy objects, and use safe lifting guidelines when you must lift something heavy. (See the guidelines in Chapter 7, *Answers for Aching Backs,* page 187.) Push rather than pull objects that must be moved.

- **Use heat or cold to relieve joint pain and stiffness.** Some arthritis patients say it is best to apply heat (by taking a warm bath or using a heating pad) before engaging in physical activity and cold afterward (by using an ice pack).

Understanding Asthma

The inability to breathe is one of the scariest experiences any child or adult can have, but it's very common. Asthma, which afflicts about 15 million people in this country, is the number one cause of school absenteeism and the most reported reason for the hospitalization of children. Although treatment can help prevent attacks and ease symptoms, and some

FOR MORE INFORMATION

To learn more about living with arthritis and treatment options, contact your local chapter of the Arthritis Foundation, or contact the national organization:

Arthritis Foundation
P.O. Box 19000
Atlanta, GA 30326
or call 1-800-283-7800

❑   ❑   ❑

patients "outgrow" the condition, asthma is serious—the disease kills up to 4,000 people in the United States annually.

What Is Asthma?

During an asthma episode, the bronchial tubes, which circulate air to and from the lungs, constrict as a result of spasms (called *bronchospasms*) and swelling bronchial tissue. Mucus clogs the smaller bronchial tubes. As a result of these events, stale air is trapped, and breathing becomes exhausting and painful. Asthma attacks produce the following symptoms:

- Wheezing
- Tightness in the chest
- Dry coughing
- Increased pulse rate

Asthma Triggers

Allergies are the most common cause of asthma, although asthma that develops later in life is less often caused by them. Here are other common asthma triggers:

- **Colds and sinus infections.** These viral infections often precede the onset of asthma.

- **Emotional stress.** It doesn't cause the condition, but it can aggravate it.

- **Stomach acid.** When you're lying down at night, acid may leak out of your stomach and into your esophagus, irritating its lining and setting off a reflex reaction in the chest.

- **Drugs.** Some drugs (including aspirin) can also trigger asthma attacks.

- **Exercise.** Strenuous physical activity can set off an asthma attack, but some form of exercise is also an important means

ASTHMA AND FOOD

Sulfites, a type of chemical preservative added to many kinds of foods and beverages, may trigger asthma attacks in some people. Here are some common foods with high concentrations of sulfites:

- Wine
- Lemon juice
- Dried fruits (such as apples or raisins)
- Fresh shrimp
- Instant potatoes
- Canned vegetables
- Fruit topping
- Molasses
- Wine vinegar
- Corn syrup
- Pizza dough
- Grapes
- Beer
- Instant tea

of maintaining good health, even for asthma sufferers.

- **Smoking.** Exposure to cigarette smoke can trigger asthma attacks. Also, studies show that children whose parents smoke are at greatly increased risk of developing asthma.

- **Pregnancy.** One-third of all women with asthma experience more symptoms when they're pregnant, but one-third also get temporarily better.

- **Weather.** Very cold or humid conditions can trigger an episode of asthma.

- **Certain chemicals.** Exposure to irritating chemicals (such as in the workplace) can trigger asthma symptoms.

Diagnosing Asthma

Doctors check for asthma by administering a pulmonary function test that measures a patient's ability to breathe out. You'll be asked to take a deep breath, then blow into a device called a *spirometer,* which measures how much and how quickly air is exhaled.

Some chronic asthma patients use a spirometer at home before and after taking bronchodilators—inhaled, airway-relaxing medication—to monitor their progress and to give them warnings when a serious attack is imminent.

Breathe Easier

Avoid Situations that Cause Asthma Attacks

Your doctor will advise you to avoid situations that cause asthma attacks.

❏ **Avoid causes of allergic reactions.** Because most cases of asthma—especially in children—are caused by allergies, one of the best ways to treat the condition is to limit exposure to allergens. (See the sections on Allergies in Chapter 7, page 184–187.)

❏ **Limit exposure to irritants in the air.** This includes cigarette smoke and chemicals in the workplace.

❏ **Listen to weather reports.** Weather forecasts provide air advisory warnings for persons with respiratory problems (such as on very hot, humid days). Try to stay indoors on these days. On very cold days, keep your mouth covered to avoid asthma attacks caused by breathing in icy air.

❏ **Manage your stress level.** Follow the advice in Chapter 5, *Coping with Stress*, for relieving stress, or seek professional counseling for ways to handle stress and reduce anxiety-induced asthma attacks.

❏ **Exercise.** Improving your level of physical fitness may help you cope with asthma. See *Asthma and Exercise* below.

❏ **Follow your physician's advice.** Your physician may prescribe drugs, such as inhaled cromolyn or inhaled corticosteroids, that can stop allergic reactions and can help stop airway inflammation and distress. Other medications your doctor gives you may help unblock or relax your airways and temporarily relieve asthma symptoms.

Be sure to ask your physician about possible side effects for any prescribed drug. Some bronchodilators can cause nervousness if overused and, therefore, may be best taken as you need them, rather than daily. You may also be put on a regimen of allergy shots in hopes of improving your condition.

When to Seek Help

Asthma is not something to take lightly—severe attacks can be fatal, especially if provoked by a sensitivity to certain foods or insect stings. Seek *immediate* professional medical care if an asthma episode is accompanied by these symptoms:

● Dizziness
● Itching of the ears, palms, genitals, or soles of the feet
● Hives
● Feeling of impending doom

Asthma and Exercise

Stereotypically, the person with asthma always sat on the sidelines during gym class, clutching a written excuse from his or her doctor. But while exercise *can* provoke attacks, it's still important for those with asthma to be physically fit, and that requires exercise.

❑ Consult your doctor about getting started on a fitness plan.

❑ Ask what kinds of activities would be best for you, how long and how often to try them, and which warning signs might indicate a need to take a break from an activity. Swimming is widely considered the best sport for people with asthma because the warm and humid environment of a pool is less likely to trigger an asthmatic reaction.

If you need inspiration to get started, consider this: Eight percent of the athletes who represented the United States in the 1988 Olympics had exercise-induced asthma.

Cancer: What You Need to Know

Cancer. It's possibly the most frightening word in the English language. But thanks to generations of medical research, and increased public awareness of healthier lifestyles and early detection, it's no longer a death sentence for millions of people.

More than 8 million Americans living today have a history of some form of cancer—and in about 5 million of those people, the cancer was diagnosed more than five years ago. The improving survival rates are encouraging, because the American Cancer Society estimates

TYPES OF CANCER

The following are the areas most often affected by fatal forms of cancer:

● Lung (most common cause of cancer deaths in both sexes)
● Colon and rectum
● Breast (most common type of cancer in women)
● Prostate (most common type of cancer in men)
● Pancreas
● Uterus and cervix
● Blood (Leukemia)
● Lymph nodes (Lymphoma)
● Skin (Skin cancer is actually the most common cancer, but it is not the most deadly.)
● Ovary
● Bladder
● Mouth and throat

❑ ❑ ❑

that one in three Americans will have some form of the disease at some point in their lives. By following preventive advice and maintaining a regular schedule of exams, both at home and with your doctor, you can increase your chances of avoiding or outlasting cancer.

What Is Cancer?
A blanket term for many different diseases, cancer occurs when cells begin to grow and spread abnormally. If the spread goes unchecked, these renegade cells can cause death. A cancer patient is said to be "cured" if he or she has no recurrence of the disease at least five years after treatment.

CANCER RISK FACTORS
Health professionals have much to learn about cancer, but they have identified some risk factors.

THE ROLE OF SMOKING

Cancer ranks second as cause of death for adult men and women in the United States (right behind cardiovascular disease), and lung cancer is the leading killer among malignant diseases, according to the American Cancer Society. Cigarette smoking is estimated by the American Cancer Society to be responsible for the overwhelming majority of lung cancer cases (about 87 percent overall). If you smoke two or more packs a day, you're up to 25 percent more likely to die of lung cancer than a nonsmoker.

❏ ❏ ❏

Researchers Have Identified Several Risk Factors for Cancer

- **Age.** Your likelihood of developing cancer increases you as get older, especially as you reach your 40s.

- **Heredity.** Some types of cancer, such as breast cancer and malignancies of the female reproductive system, are strongly linked to family history. Find out if you have a family history of cancer, including what kinds, and report this information to your doctor.

- **Personal history.** If you've had cancer in the past, you're at greater risk for a recurrence.

- **Smoking.** Research has linked smoking with several types of cancer. For more information, see the sidebar, *The Role of Smoking*.

- **Obesity.** If you're 40 percent or more over the ideal weight for your height, age, and sex, you're at increased risk for cancer of the colon, breast, prostate, gallbladder, ovary, and uterus. (See the *Metropolitan Height-Weight Table* in Chapter 2, page 50, to determine your ideal weight.)

- **Heavy drinking.** Heavy drinking—especially when accompanied by cigarette smoking or chewing tobacco—increases your risk for developing cancer of the mouth, larynx, throat, esophagus, and liver.

- **Diet.** Foods high in fat or nitrates and low in fiber increase your risk.

- **Sun exposure.** Time spent outdoors without protection from the sun's rays increases your risk for skin cancer.

- **Exposure to radiation or other environmental hazards.** Asbestos, nickel, chromate, and vinyl chloride are some of the industrial agents that can make you more vulnerable to cancer.

REDUCE YOUR CANCER RISK

You have control over many risk factors, such as sun exposure, smoking, diet, and so on. Here are additional steps you can take to reduce your cancer risk.

- ❏ **Do regular self-exams.** See the guidelines for breast and skin evaluations you can do at home (pages 271–272, 272–273).

- ❏ **Discuss the need for regular medical examinations with your doctor.** See the guidelines for early detection of cancers.

- ❏ **Stay trim.** If you are overweight, ask your doctor about a weight loss regimen that includes physical exercise and a diet low in fat.

- ❏ **Eat balanced, nutritious, varied meals.** Foods low in saturated fat and high in fiber—such as fruits, vegetables, and grains—may help lower your risk of lung, prostate, bladder, esophagus, colorectal, and stomach cancers. A diet high in fat may be a factor in the development of breast, colon, and prostate cancers.

❑ **Avoid salt-cured, smoked, and nitrate-cured foods.** They may contribute to stomach and esophagus cancers.

❑ **Stay out of the sun.** Tanning can be hazardous to your health. To protect yourself, the Skin Cancer Foundation advises that you stay out of the sun between 10 A.M. and 3 P.M. when the sun is highest in the sky. When you do go outdoors, wear a hat, and apply a sunscreen with a sun protection factor (SPF) of at least 15. (For more information on tanning, see *Your Tan Isn't Healthy,* page 273.)

❑ **If you're receiving hormone therapy and still have your uterus, take progesterone.** Postmenopausal women who take estrogen without progesterone are at greater risk for endometrial cancer.

Cancer: Early Detection

Physical examinations your doctor performs are important to prevent illness and maintain good health. You and your doctor should discuss the frequency of examinations—probably every one to three years if you are in good health. Your physician will consider your age and health history in setting up an examination schedule. The two of you can also set up a cancer screening schedule based on your health history and your risks for certain types of cancer.

Screening helps your doctor detect problems early, when treatment is most effective.

Watch for These Symptoms
Always report the following symptoms to your physician:

• Change in bowel or bladder habits
• Sores that fail to heal
• Any unusual bleeding or discharge
• Any thickening or lump in the breast or elsewhere
• Chronic indigestion or difficulty swallowing
• Any obvious change in a wart or mole
• Nagging cough or hoarseness

RECOMMENDATIONS FOR WOMEN
Women are at risk for breast and female reproductive cancers. They have three particular weapons against those illnesses, in addition to regular checkups.

Mammography. Doctors agree that women aged 50 and older should undergo an annual mammogram (an X ray of the breast tissue). There is, however, some disagreement among doctors about screening recommendations for women younger than 50 years.
The American Cancer Society is one group that recommends all women undergo a mammogram by the time they reach age 40. Then, if no problems are found, every woman should have another screening every two years until she reaches age 50, or annually if she is considered at high risk for breast cancer. A woman at high risk has a history of breast cancer or a direct relative—mother, sister, daughter—with breast cancer.

Cancer Screening Helps Your Doctor Detect Problems Early When Treatment Is Most Effective

269

Other doctors specializing in preventive medicine agree that women aged 50 and older should undergo annual examinations, but they point out that, currently, study results do not demonstrate any benefit in mammography examination in women 40 to 49 years of age.

Talk with your doctor about your need for regular mammograms. In addition, examine your breasts monthly, and have a doctor examine your breasts each time you undergo a physical.

Pap tests. Any woman who is sexually active should undergo a pelvic exam and a Pap test to screen for cervical cancer. A Pap smear involves the removal of cells from a woman's cervix to be examined for abnormalities. While many health practitioners recommend annual Pap smears, others say after three negative results, women can skip a year or two between tests.

Breast exams. Women 20 years of age and older can examine their breasts for lumps, thickening, and other irregularities. (See *The Breast Self-Examination,* for instructions.) A doctor should also examine a woman's breasts during her physical examination.

RECOMMENDATIONS FOR MEN

Approximately one of every ten men in the United States develops cancer of the prostate, a gland that contributes fluids to semen, by the age of 85. Talk with your doctor about the need for routine exams for prostatic abnormalities. Tests used to check for abnormalities include a digital rectal examination, an ultrasound (transrectal ultrasound), and a blood test called a *prostate specific antigen* (PSA), which detects antigens that may indicate tumors.

Talk with Your Doctor About Your Need for Regular Screening Exams

Cancer: Treatment Options

If your doctor diagnoses some form of cancer (possibly following the results of a biopsy, in which suspect cells are sampled and evaluated in a lab), your treatment will depend on the type of cancer you have, the stage to which it has progressed, and a host of other factors.

Your doctor might be able to take charge of the disease quickly; for example, in about 90 percent of skin cancer cases, the affected patch of skin can usually be removed in a doctor's office. If your doctor suggests more involved treatment, you owe it to yourself to find out all you can about the recommended procedure, including its side effects. It's always wise to get a second doctor's opinion before embarking on an intensive treatment strategy; some health insurance policies require you to do so as well.

Generally, cancer patients can undergo one or more of the following four types of treatment.

Surgery. Many kinds of cancer may require surgical removal of malignant tissue. In breast cancer treatment, for example, surgical removal of a breast (a mastectomy) may be recommended, although in some cases doctors may recommend a less radical lumpectomy, in which only tumors and some surrounding tissue are removed.

Chemotherapy. Chemotherapy, in which a patient receives intravenous anticancer drugs, usually over the course of several sessions, may be used as a follow-up to surgery, by itself, or in combination with radiation or other treatments. Chemotherapy may result in serious side effects, such as nausea, vomiting, and hair loss, which usually subside once treatment ends.

Radiation. Aiming a dose of high-energy radiation at cancerous tumors and cells can help break them down and destroy them. Radiation therapy, often delivered in several sessions rather than all at once, is used as a follow-up to surgery, in combination with other therapies, or alone. It may also result in serious side effects, such as nausea, hair loss, and lethargy. These, however, go away once treatment stops.

Immunotherapy. Researchers are constantly looking for ways to enhance the body's natural defenses against foreign cells. Some doctors, for example, use interferon, a naturally occurring protein, to combat certain types of lymph cancer and also hairy cell leukemia, a rare blood disease that afflicts mostly elderly patients.

Treatment—The Human Side

Any doctor will tell you a patient's state of mind can play a role in the progress—both positive and negative—of a serious illness. It's important for a cancer patient to be able to express feelings, including any fear, anger, and anxiety, and to focus on getting better. It's equally crucial that family members and loved ones—who may be facing the stress of caring for the patient—be able to express their emotions.

If you have cancer and need more emotional support than your family or loved ones can provide, you may benefit from professional counseling or a local support

FOR MORE INFORMATION

To learn more about cancer prevention, treatment, or to locate support groups or other recovery services, contact the American Cancer Society.

American Cancer Society
1599 Clifton Road, N.E.
Atlanta, GA 30329-4251

or call 1-800-ACS-2345

You can also phone the National Cancer Institute's Cancer Information Service:

1-800-4- CANCER (422-6237)

❏ ❏ ❏

group. Support groups, which have become very popular in the last decade, enable cancer patients and their families to meet and talk about their feelings and common experiences.

The Breast Self-Examination

Although women can hardly turn on the television or open a magazine without hearing about the need to perform a monthly breast self-examination, most women don't do them. The American Cancer Society reports that only about 29 percent of women in the United States regularly perform a breast self-exam—many don't because they don't know how.

Here's how to detect changes in your breasts:

❏ Stand or sit in front of a mirror, with your arms at your sides. Look for dimpling, puck-

Only About 29 Percent of U.S. Women Regularly Perform a Breast Self-Exam

271

A Breast Self-Exam Is Quick, Easy, and Painless

ering, or redness of breast skin. Press your hands tightly on your hips, and look at the area again. Do the same with your arms raised over your head.

❑ Lie flat on your back, with a folded towel or a pillow under your left shoulder and your left hand under or over your head. Using your right hand, gently feel your left breast. Feel for lumps or hard areas. Use small, clockwise motions, creating smaller and smaller circles as you get closer to the nipple, until you've examined all of the breast tissue.

❑ Examine the nipple area; gently squeeze the nipple and check for discharge. Examine the area below the armpits.

❑ Follow the steps above to examine your right breast with your left hand.

❑ Perform the exam at the same time each month. If you're still menstruating, the best time to check for irregularities is soon after your period ends.

Breast Cancer Warning Signs

Nearly every woman has some irregularity in her breasts, but these signs, which can be detected in a monthly breast self-examination, indicate a doctor's opinion is needed:

- Unexplained lumps or thickening in the breast or armpit
- Puckering or dimpling of the skin of the breast
- Discharge or bleeding from the nipple
- A recent change in the nipple, such as one that has retracted, or pulled inward
- A change in the breast's skin
- Breast tenderness

The Cancer You Can See: Skin Cancer

One in six Americans develops skin cancer in his or her lifetime, according to the Skin Cancer Foundation. Although more than 80 percent of those cases are slow-growing basal cell or squamous cell carcinomas, the number of cases of malignant melanoma, a fast-growing, potentially fatal cancer, are increasing. A careful, five-minute self-examination at least every three months can help you detect problems early, when they can be easily treated.

Skin Cancer Warning Signs

Let your doctor know if you discover any of these symptoms during a skin self-examination:

- Change in color of mole, or moles that are multicolored
- Changes in size (Watch moles larger than six millimeters across for signs of growth.)
- Asymmetric shapes (one side of the mole doesn't match the other)
- Moles with jagged borders
- Raised moles
- Any bleeding or crusted sores that won't heal

SKIN CANCER: SELF-EXAMINATION

Here are some hints for a quick and easy self-exam. Perform the self-exam in front of a full-length mirror.

- ❑ Look at your front and back. Raise your arms and look down the length of your left and right sides.
- ❑ Check the front and back of your legs in the mirror. (Women are three times more likely than men to develop malignant melanoma on the legs.)
- ❑ Look between your buttocks and around your genital area.
- ❑ Bend your elbows, and carefully look at your palms, then your forearms, then your upper arms. Remember to check the underside of your arms.
- ❑ With the help of a hand-held mirror, look at your face, neck, and scalp. (A comb or blow drier may help move your hair out of the way.)
- ❑ Examine your feet, including the soles, and the spaces between your toes.

Your Tan Isn't Healthy

There's no doubt about it—there's something attractive about a golden brown tan. Certainly, most of us believe we look healthier with a tan. However, looks can be deceiving: Our tanned skin certainly isn't healthier. The same damaging process that causes a painful, red sunburn occurs when we tan. Unfortunately, because much of the damage caused by repeated tanning, including skin cancers, may not show up for years, most of us continue to regularly bake to a golden brown.

Exposure to the sun's dangerous ultraviolet rays is a chief factor in the more than 700,000 cases of basal and squamous cell skin cancers diagnosed each year in this country. Two types of ultraviolet light from the sun that impact the skin are ultraviolet A (UVA), or long wavelength ultraviolet, and ultraviolet B (UVB), a shorter and stronger form of ultraviolet. UVA rays are the "tanning rays." Because UVA rays don't cause sunburns, for many years doctors believed they weren't a cancer threat. However, they now know that even small amounts of UVA light can enhance the damaging—and cancer-causing—effects of UVB rays. UVA rays are also able to penetrate the skin more deeply than UVB rays and damage the skin's elastic structure.

UVB, the so-called "burning rays," cause tanning *and* sunburning. These rays easily penetrate the skin's outer layer, the epidermis, and cause damage. Even one bad roasting can damage the epidermal cell membranes and DNA enough to trigger the development of skin cancer.

THE TANNING PROCESS

When the sun's rays penetrate the skin's various layers, they strike living epidermal cells, pigment-producing cells (melanocytes), and the inner skin structures. The ultraviolet rays cause the melanocytes to produce the brown pigment melanin. The melanin spreading out through the skin causes the tanned look. The extra melanin production, the body's protective response to the sun's harmful rays, blocks further penetration of ultraviolet light.

Exposure to the Sun Is a Chief Factor in the Development of Skin Cancer

People Who Are Fair or Freckled Are Particularly Susceptible to Skin Damage from the Sun

If the skin's melanin production can't keep pace with sun exposure, a sunburn results. When you touch a hot stove and get a minor burn, it causes the cells of the skin's outer layer (epidermis) to die. The same thing happens when you get a sunburn. You can easily see the sunburn damage under the microscope. Formerly healthy skin cells are dead and shriveled. Thick, red bundles of connective tissue are ground into gray smudge. Tiny, thin-walled blood vessels are dilated and leak fluid. DNA strands that contain information about how to repair and replicate cells and other structures are damaged, causing the skin to produce abnormal, precancerous cells and, in some cases, cancerous cells.

If you freckle easily, it means your melanin doesn't disperse evenly. If you're fair and don't tan, it means your skin isn't able to produce the protective melanin. People who are fair or freckled are particularly susceptible to skin damage from the sun.

TIME IS A RISK FACTOR

The damage over time rather than the temporary discomfort of an occasional sunburn is the real cause for concern. Repeated tanning or sunburning over many years breaks down the elastic tissues in the skin, making it look prematurely old and wrinkled. It can also cause red, rough patches of skin called solar keratoses, particularly in those with fair skin.

Even more disturbing than dry, wrinkled, sagging, splotchy skin is the fact that repeated sun exposure can cause precancerous changes in the skin and dramatically increase your risk of skin cancer. In fact, the Skin Cancer Foundation says that one in three cancers diagnosed this year will be skin cancer, and one in six of us will develop skin cancer during our lifetime.

You might want to keep this information in mind next time you're contemplating a few hours bathing in the sun.

Put the Stop on Sunburns

Doctors now know sunburns and prolonged sun exposure of any kind can stimulate cancer-causing changes in the skin. How at risk are you? It depends on how much unprotected time you spend outdoors. And the fairer your complexion, the greater your risk.

If you're of Irish, Welsh, Scottish, or English descent, you probably have the whitest and most vulnerable type of skin. Other Europeans and Asians are at risk, too. Individuals with "olive" or brown skin carry a lower risk. Dark-skinned blacks are the least vulnerable to sunburning and sun-induced cancers, but they're not immune. Even the darkest skin can burn and, decades later, develop skin cancer.

Prevention is the best course. Use these tips to keep the sun's rays at bay.

❏ **Block out the sun.** The Skin Cancer Foundation says the best and easiest way to prevent a sunburn is to wear protective clothing—wide-brimmed hats, long sleeves, and long pants. Tightly woven material will block more sun than more loosely woven or mesh materials and thus provide better protection.

When choosing a hat, opt for a wide-brimmed one that

protects your ears and neck. According to the Skin Cancer Foundation, 80 percent of skin cancers occur on the head, neck, and hands. Look for a tightly woven fabric such as canvas rather than a straw hat.

❑ **Use sunblock.** If you're fair-skinned, you should never go out in the sun without a sunblock with a sun protection factor (SPF) of at least 15. Don't forget sensitive areas such as the tops of the ears, nose, hands, hairlines, and "V" of the chest. Apply a thick layer of sunscreen 15 to 30 minutes before going into the sun to allow it to absorb into the skin. Reapply every two hours or more often if you're sweating or getting wet.

❑ **Apply zinc oxide paste.** This is the funny looking white stuff you see on the noses of lifeguards. For maximum protection of horizontal surfaces such as the nose, apply a sunblock with an SPF of at least 15, then put some zinc oxide on top of it.

❑ **Stay in the shade.** If your complexion is fair, your best bet is to stay out of the sun, especially between 10 A.M. and 3 P.M., when the sun's rays are strongest.

Keep in mind, however, sunlight can be scattered and reflected off sand, cement, snow, chrome, and rock. You can get a sunburn even while in the shade of a tree or an umbrella! While you're in the shade, put on some sunblock.

❑ **Use lip protection.** Many skin cancers occur on the lips. Use a lip balm with an SPF of at least 8.

If you do get burned, see *Easing Sunburn Pain,* page 358.

Choosing the Right Sunscreen

Any pharmacy or supermarket skincare section carries an overwhelming array of sunscreen products. How do you know which one to choose?

The Food and Drug Administration designates five degrees of protection, according to a product's sun protection factor (SPF):

SPF 2–4 minimal protection

SPF 4–6 moderate protection

SPF 6–8 extra sun protection

SPF 8–15 maximal sun protection

SPF 15+ ultra sun protection

The type of sunscreen you need depends on your skin type.

Skin Type	Minimum SPF
Very fair, freckles	15+
Fair, freckles	10–15
Average	8–10
Olive or brown	4–6

How About Tan in a Bottle?

You're convinced suntanning isn't a good idea, but you still love the bronze look of a tan. Now there are other ways to get a tan.

Two types of "bottle" tanning products exist. The first type is a bronzing makeup or tinting moisturizer. These often contain a sunscreen and are easily washed off.

The second type of bottle tan is a skin stainer. These products con-

The Type of Sunscreen You Need Depends on Your Skin Type

DECIPHERING SUNBLOCK LANGUAGE

Read the label of any sunblock product and you may come away confused. Here's a dictionary of commonly used sunscreen terms and ingredients.

Alcohol: In some sunblocks, alcohol is used as a base. If you have dry or sensitive skin, avoid alcohol-based blocks.

Anthranilates (methyl anthranilate): These ingredients offer moderate protection against both UVA and UVB rays.

Benzophenones (oxybenzone, sulisobenzone, dioxybenzone): These are UVA blockers found in products with SPFs of 15 or greater.

Cinnamates (octyl methoxycinnamate): A commonly used UVB blocker.

Noncomedogenic: Products that have this characteristic don't clog pores.

PABA (para-aminobenzoic acid): This highly effective UVB blocker was once widely used in sunscreens. Unfortunately, it often causes skin irritations and has been replaced with other ingredients.

PABA derivatives (octyl dimethyl PABA): Second cousins to the original PABA, they offer the protection from UVB without the irritants.

Parsol 1789 (avobenzone): A UVA protectant. The Food and Drug Administration (FDA) has approved this product as an effective UVA blocker.

Sun protection factor (SPF): A number from 2 to 30+ that indicates the sun-screening ability a product has. For example, if you would normally burn after one hour, you would burn after five hours after applying a sunscreen with an SPF of 5. However, keep in mind SPFs are calculated under ideal laboratory conditions. Other factors such as sweat, water, and thickness of application affect effectiveness.

Waterproof: FDA guidelines state a waterproof sunblock must remain effective even after four 20-minute swims.

Water-resistant: The sunblock is effective after two 20-minute swims.

Zinc oxide: An opaque block that protects against both UVA and UVB rays. It has an SPF of about 8.

❏   ❏   ❏

tain the colorant dihydroxyacetone. It gives the skin a temporary bronzing stain. With skillful application, these products can produce good results on some types of skin. However, the skin coloring lasts only three or four days. As old skin cells slough off and are replaced by new ones, the "tan" fades. These stains provide no protection from the sun, and you'll still have to apply sunscreen.

Some people have tried to achieve the golden brown look with so-called tanning pills. They contain a food colorant called canthaxanthin, which when ingested can turn the skin an orangey color. Although tanning pills are widely available, they're illegal and can be harmful and even deadly. Canthaxanthin may cause aplastic anemia, which kills red and white blood cells.

Chronic Fatigue Syndrome: When You're Tired All the Time

Everyone occasionally feels exhausted or depressed, but some people suffer a debilitating malaise that won't go away. They constantly feel tired and find themselves unable to muster the energy or enthusiasm for work, school, or family life.

Although this may sound like clinical depression, people who develop chronic fatigue syndrome (CFS) also suffer flu-like symptoms, such as muscle aches and sore throats. CFS (not a disease, but a blanket term for a set of other unexplainable symptoms) has only recently been recognized by doctors, and much about the condition—including its cause—is still unknown. CFS is usually not thought to be medically dangerous, but it can wreak havoc with your daily routine. For many people, the condition improves or disappears with time.

Who Gets CFS?

Once thought of as a "yuppie plague," CFS affects not only young professionals, but people of both sexes and all ages and ethnic and economic backgrounds, although young white women most often seek medical treatment for the illness. Here's what we know about CFS.

- It usually begins after a patient has an acute infectious illness, such as the flu, bronchitis, hepatitis, or mononucleosis, the "kissing disease" most often seen in teenagers and young adults.

- People with allergies may be more susceptible: Researchers estimate that between 50 and 80 percent of CFS patients had some kind of allergies before the illness struck, even though only about 17 percent of the population at large has allergies.

- Stress may also be a factor: Often, CFS strikes during a period of emotional upheaval in a person's life.

- A large percentage of CFS patients also have (or have had) depression or anxiety disorders, although it's unclear whether CFS and psychiatric illnesses are linked.

What Causes CFS?

There are many theories about the causes of CFS, but no conclusive evidence. Viruses may cause some cases of CFS. One possible culprit may be the Epstein-Barr virus, which about 80 percent of all adults are exposed to by the time they reach age 30. The virus causes mononucleosis, which often precedes CFS. Another possible cause of CFS may be malfunctioning of the body's immune system; for example, some researchers suspect that in CFS patients, the immune system keeps fighting infection even after an infection has been subdued.

Symptoms of CFS

If you experience the following symptoms persistently or frequently for more than six months, you may have chronic fatigue syndrome. Discuss these symptoms with your doctor.

- Headaches
- Sore throat
- Low-grade fever or chills
- Fatigue or weakness
- Tender lymph glands (lymph glands are located in the neck and armpits)
- Muscle and joint aches
- Inability to concentrate
- Problems falling or staying asleep
- Depression or malaise

Much About Chronic Fatigue Syndrome— Including Its Cause—Is Unknown

FOR MORE INFORMATION

To get more information on CFS and related diseases and to seek support groups in your area, write:

Chronic Fatigue and
Immune Dysfunction Syndrome Association
P.O. Box 220398
Charlotte, NC 28222

or call 1-800-442-3437

❑   ❑   ❑

Chronic
Fatigue
Syndrome
Often
Improves or
Disappears
with Time

Combatting Chronic Fatigue Syndrome

First, the good news: CFS is generally not a progressive condition. It doesn't get worse. Usually, symptoms are most debilitating early in the illness then fade over time. Some people recover almost overnight.

This is fortunate, because there isn't a medically proved treatment for the ailment, although doctors may try to combat CFS with prescription drugs, including antiviral, antidepressant, and immune-system-boosting medications. If you have CFS, the following advice may help improve your condition.

❏ Eat a balanced diet.
❏ Get plenty of rest.
❏ Engage in as much physical exercise as you can without worsening fatigue.
❏ Learn better ways to handle stress.
❏ Seek counseling with a physician, therapist, clergyman, or other trusted professional to help cope with both everyday stress and the ups and downs of the condition.

Coronary Artery Disease: Know Your Risk

Coronary artery disease occurs when one or more of the coronary arteries, which supply the heart with blood and oxygen, becomes blocked.

When blood flow decreases, there is a greater risk of angina pectoris, or chest pain (see the section, *Is It a Heart Attack or Angina?*, page 282), and myocardial infarction, or heart attack. Heart attack, in which a region of the heart muscle dies due to a deficiency of blood and oxygen, is the number one killer of American men and women, taking about 500,000 lives each year, according to the American Heart Association. Another million survive myocardial infarctions, but they may find the road to recovery long and their lives changed.

HEART DISEASE RISK FACTORS

These are the risk factors you can't control:

● **Age.** The older you are, the higher your likelihood of having coronary artery disease. Men are at greatest risk after they reach the age of 45, and women after the age of 55.

● **Race.** Blacks have higher rates of high blood pressure—and of heart disease—than whites.

● **Heredity.** If your biological family members had heart attacks (especially men before age 55 and women before age 65), you're at increased risk.

● **Personal history.** People who have already suffered heart problems or a stroke are at greater risk for having them in the future.

● **Diabetes.** More than 80 percent of people with diabetes mellitus die of some form of heart or artery disease. Controlling the condition with diet, insulin, or other medications also helps control the blood vessel damage that occurs as diabetes progresses.

You can control these risk factors:

- **Smoking.** Smokers' risk of heart attack is more than double that of nonsmokers. In addition, being regularly exposed to others' secondhand cigarette smoke increases your risk of heart disease.

- **Weight.** Being obese—defined as 30 percent or more above the ideal body weight for your height, age, and sex—increases your risk for heart disease and stroke, even if you have no other risk factors.

- **High blood pressure.** See page 295.

- **High blood cholesterol level.** See page 293.

- **Hormones.** Postmenopausal women who are not receiving estrogen replacement therapy are at increased risk for heart disease. Women who use oral contraceptives and have other risk factors may be at greater risk of blood clots.

- **Exercise.** If you lead a sedentary lifestyle, you're at increased risk.

- **Stress.** People who have trouble handling emotional upsets are prone to develop a number of health problems, including heart disease.

Reducing Your Risk of Coronary Artery Disease

Here are steps you can take to reduce some risk factors:

- **Stay trim.** Find out what your ideal weight is, and try to reach it. (See the *Metropolitan Height-Weight Table* in Chapter 2, page 50, to determine your ideal weight.) If you need to lose pounds, consult your doctor for advice tailored to your age and physical condition.

- **Pay attention to your diet.** If your doctor gives you a diet, follow it closely. Eating balanced meals low in saturated fat helps you maintain your overall health.

- **Drink only in moderation.** Moderate drinking—no more than one beer or one six-ounce glass of wine, particularly red wine, per day—may actually help raise the level of high-density lipoprotein, or "good" cholesterol. But heavy drinking increases your blood pressure. And because alcoholic drinks are high in calories, they make it that much harder to lose weight.

- **Don't smoke.** And if you do smoke, quit.

- **Exercise.** Aerobic physical activity, in workout sessions lasting from 30 to 45 minutes at least three times a week, helps you not only stay trim but exercises your muscles, heart, and lungs. You should consult your doctor if you have hypertension or a history of heart problems, but most people who have been sedentary for a while have no trouble starting out with such activities as walking or bicycling.

- **Learn to cope with stress.** If you have problems relaxing, try exercise. It not only helps you blow off emotional steam, but it helps you sleep more soundly at night, helps you trim your weight, and benefits

Heart Attack Is the Number One Killer of American Men and Women

279

your overall health. Other relaxation techniques, or even professional counseling, may help you handle emotional upsets and lower your risk of stress-related health problems. (See Chapter 5, *Coping with Stress,* for some techniques to reduce your stress level.)

When to Seek Help

The American Heart Association reports that about half of all heart attack victims wait more than two hours after the onset of symptoms before seeking help. Perhaps that's one reason about 300,000 Americans each year die of heart attacks before reaching the hospital.

Seek emergency medical help if you experience the following symptoms for more than a few minutes:

- Uncomfortable pressure or fullness in the center of your chest
- Squeezing or pain in the center of your chest

- Chest pain that spreads to your shoulders, neck, or arms
- Light-headedness or fainting
- Profuse sweating
- Unexplainable nausea
- Shortness of breath

Coronary Artery Disease: Early Detection

Your best weapon in the fight against heart disease is early detection. Learning you are at risk for cardiovascular problems before they have a chance to progress can encourage you to take steps to maintain your health. Your doctor will likely evaluate the following factors to assess your risk of heart disease:

- **Blood pressure:** Have it checked once a year.
- **Blood cholesterol:** After the age of 20, have it checked at least once every five years, or more often if your doctor so recommends.
- **Overall health and conditioning:** Regular medical checkups can help your doctor detect problems with your heart or lungs. A stress test, in which a person walks on a treadmill while the heart and lung functions are electronically monitored, is recommended for patients at increased risk, based on family history and lifestyle factors, for cardiovascular disease.

BODY TYPES: APPLES AND PEARS

The way in which fat is distributed on your body seems to indicate your risk of heart disease. For the purposes of lowering your risk, it's better to be "pear-shaped" than "apple-shaped," according to the American Heart Association.

To find out if you're truly "pear-shaped," take a minute to measure your waist and around the fullest part of your buttocks and hips. Then divide your waist measurement by your hip measurement. For example, if your waist measures 32 inches and your hips measure 35 inches, divide 32 by 35, for a result of 0.91. The safe range for woman is 0.8 or below. For men, it is 1.0 or below. If your result is above those guidelines, you probably need to lose weight. Talk to your doctor about a safe weight-reduction plan that includes exercise and a diet low in saturated fat, and read Chapter 2, *Weight Control.*

Coronary Artery Disease: Treatment and Recovery

Today, a person who experiences a heart attack has a better chance than ever of survival and recovery—from 1980 to 1990, the death rate from myocardial infarctions declined more than 32 percent, according to the American Heart Association. But the person must seek immediate medical help. Treatment and recovery in the long term involves the full cooperation of the patient, often including changes in his or her lifestyle.

EMERGENCY TREATMENT

When a heart attack victim is brought to a cardiac care unit, the medical team's first goal is to stop further damage to the heart. Often this is achieved by injecting the patient with a thrombolytic, or clot-dissolving, agent to unblock the coronary artery. To restore adequate blood flow in the long term, surgery might be recommended.

In one type of procedure, percutaneous transluminal angioplasty, a balloon-tipped catheter is inserted into an artery; when the balloon is expanded, the artery widens. In another common type of procedure, known as coronary artery bypass graft surgery, doctors take a blood vessel from another part of the body and construct a "detour" for blood to flow around the blocked part of a coronary artery.

RECOVERY TIPS

If you experience a heart attack, follow your doctor's advice regarding medication. Aspirin may be recommended, which can help prevent clotting. In addition, the following guidelines can help prevent a second heart attack.

❑ **Don't smoke.** The best gift you can give your heart is to stop smoking. Nicotine increases your heart rate, making the heart work harder. It also constricts blood vessels, impeding blood circulation. This, in combination with the inhalation of carbon monoxide, reduces the

HEART DISEASE AND WOMEN

The stereotypical victim of a heart attack is a middle-aged man, with an impatient "type A" personality, involved in a stressful career. But that stereotype doesn't match reality. Forty-five percent of all heart attacks occur in people older than 65 years of age. And women are nearly as likely as men to develop cardiovascular disease. Menopause, which brings with it a loss of the female hormone estrogen, increases a woman's risk (although hormone replacement therapy can help protect the heart). After they reach age 65, in fact, women are twice as likely as men to die in the first few weeks after a heart attack. There's controversy over the explanation. Here are some of the reasons suggested:

● Heart disease is harder to diagnose in women than in men due to a difference in symptoms.

● Some women tend to ignore heart disease warning signs.

● Some doctors may be too quick to dismiss such symptoms in women.

● Women tend to be older than men at the time of their first heart attack.

One thing is certain, however: Both men and women need to lead healthy lifestyles, maintain a regular schedule of preventive medical examinations, and take note of their individual risk factors for heart disease.

❑   ❑   ❑

Extra Pounds Place Stress on Your Heart

amount of oxygen available to the heart.

❏ **Exercise regularly.** Talk with your doctor about how much you should do and what kinds of exercise are best. You might benefit from a rehabilitation program sponsored by a hospital, which can help you get started on a safe, supervised exercise routine.

❏ **Stay trim.** Extra pounds place stress on your heart.

❏ **Stick to your diet.** Your doctor will probably suggest you eat well-balanced meals low in saturated fat, cholesterol, and sodium.

❏ **Learn to handle stress.** Seek professional counseling if you are experiencing personal upheaval.

❏ **Control your blood pressure and blood cholesterol.** See *Controlling High Blood Pressure,* page 296, and *Keep Tabs On Your Blood Cholesterol Level,* page 293.

Recovery and Sex

Many heart attack victims fear the resumption of sexual activity because they're worried the exertion may trigger another heart attack. But most heart patients are able to start enjoying physical intimacy three to four weeks into their recovery. Although it's best to start gradually—as with any activity—and experiment to find the most comfortable position for you and your partner, intercourse shouldn't pose a risk to your health. (Contrary to myth and made-for-TV movies, it's actually extremely rare for someone to suffer a heart attack during sex.) If you have concerns, talk to your doctor and your partner.

Is It a Heart Attack or Angina?

Do you suffer from chest pains when you're emotionally upset or after running or otherwise physically exerting yourself? If so, you could be among the more than 3 million Americans who have angina pectoris.

Angina is a symptom of a condition called *myocardial ischemia,* which happens because the heart muscle isn't getting enough blood to perform a certain level of work. In addition, the American Heart Association estimates as many as 4 million Americans may have episodes of silent ischemia—a deficiency of blood flowing to the heart without the pain of angina. Angina happens because your heart suddenly needs to work harder (while you're exercising, for example), and it isn't getting enough oxygen-rich blood to do the job. Angina is one of the major warning signs that you're at risk for a future heart attack.

What Causes Angina?

Atherosclerosis, the buildup of fatty deposits in the arteries, is the root cause of both angina and heart attacks. As you age, the arteries narrow and become less flexible. Other factors, such as a high blood cholesterol level, can speed this process considerably.

TREATMENT OPTIONS

If your doctor diagnoses angina (usually by giving you a "stress test," in which you walk on a treadmill while your heart and lung functions are monitored), you may be given coronary vasodilators, drugs that relax blood vessels and improve blood flow. The most common type are safe, inexpensive nitroglycerin tablets. Follow your doctor's advice on using the drug. A few general tips:

❏ To treat angina pain as it arises, keep nitroglycerin tablets on hand wherever you go.

❏ Get refills at least every six months. The drug can lose its effectiveness over time and when exposed to heat, light, and air, so follow your pharmacist's directions for storing the tablets.

❏ If your angina isn't better within 15 minutes after taking three tablets, *seek professional medical care immediately*.

In severe cases of angina caused by badly blocked arteries, your physician might suggest surgery.

Preventing Angina

Take steps to prevent the onset or recurrence of angina.

❏ **Think about the activities that bring on your angina.** Discuss these with your doctor. You may need to avoid some activities entirely (such as shoveling snow), alter some activities (walking rather than running for exercise), or use medication (such as before sexual intercourse).

❏ **Exercise—under your doctor's supervision.** Moderate physical activity can help decrease symptoms, but ask your physician what kind of exercises you should attempt.

FOR MORE INFORMATION

To learn more about preventing heart disease, including advice about exercise, controlling risk factors (such as hypertension, high cholesterol, diabetes, and smoking), and nutrition, contact the American Heart Association.

American Heart Association
c/o The National Center
7272 Greenville Avenue
Dallas, TX 75231

or call 214-373-6300

❏   ❏   ❏

❏ **Learn how to handle stress.** It's not always possible to avoid emotionally upsetting situations or work-related pressures. Meditation and relaxation exercises can help—to start, try relaxing all your muscles twice a day for 20 minutes each session. (See Chapter 5, *Coping with Stress*, for additional stress-reduction techniques.)

If you're dealing with long-standing personal or work problems, it might help to talk them over with a professional counselor or clergymember, or check to see if your employer provides an Employee Assistance Program. Let your physician know about such problems, too. In some instances, your doctor might prescribe mild tranquilizers.

❏ **Don't smoke.** And if you do, quit. Cigarette smoking usually makes angina worse—and it increases your risk of heart attack and other kinds of cardiovascular disease.

❏ **Eat smaller meals.** Digestion, like exercise, makes the heart work harder. Try eating smaller meals and avoiding heavy or rich foods. Relax for a while

Angina Is One of the Warning Signs that You're at Risk for a Heart Attack immediately after eating. Overeating is also a factor in weight gain, which increases your risk of angina and other forms of heart disease.

❑ **Don't drink heavily.** In fact, some angina patients are advised not to drink at all; ask your doctor's advice.

Diabetes: A Disease to Monitor

Diabetes, a serious disease of the endocrine system, affects about 13 million people in this country, according to the American Diabetes Association. Millions more may have the ailment and not recognize it until their symptoms become severe or they experience a medical emergency such as a diabetic coma.

TIPS ON TESTING YOUR BLOOD SUGAR

Follow this advice for best results when monitoring your blood sugar at home:

❑ Wash and dry your hands well before performing the test.

❑ Note the expiration dates on your test strips; don't use one that's past its prime.

❑ Make sure you've drawn enough blood to get a good result.

❑ Make sure the meter is set correctly. Keep it clean, and check its batteries often.

❑ Follow test instructions carefully. Wait for the full suggested amount of time between steps.

❑ Write down the results so you can show them to your doctor.

❑　❑　❑

What Is Diabetes?

In a healthy person, the pancreas produces hormones that help the body break down the food consumed. If you have diabetes mellitus, however, your body has a problem metabolizing a simple form of sugar called *glucose*.

For reasons scientists are still trying to discover, diabetics either don't produce enough insulin, the hormone that breaks down glucose, or their bodies are unable to use insulin in the right way. Because of this, glucose builds up in the blood to dangerous levels. In the long term, excess blood sugar can damage the eyes, blood vessels, nerves, and kidneys.

In addition to an excess of blood sugar (hyperglycemia), emergency episodes can also be created as a result of an excess of insulin (hypoglycemia), and a life-threatening kind of insulin deficiency that causes the body to start breaking down fats for energy instead of breaking down blood glucose (ketoacidosis).

Symptoms of Diabetes

Consult your physician if you experience the following symptoms and they do not subside promptly, especially if you're overweight or have a family history of diabetes:

- Increased thirst
- Increased urination (frequency and volume of urine)
- Weight loss, even if your appetite increases
- Fatigue
- Nausea and vomiting
- Frequent vaginal, skin, or bladder infections
- Blurred vision
- Impotence

What You Can Do About Diabetes

Although diabetes is incurable, you have some control over your condition through a combination of changes in your lifestyle (including what you eat and drink), daily monitoring of blood sugar levels, achieving and maintaining appropriate weight, and strict adherence to an individually tailored treatment plan.

If your physician determines you have diabetes, the treatment strategy he or she maps out for you will depend upon the type and severity of your illness. About five percent of all diabetics have type I, or insulin-dependent diabetes (which is also called "juvenile diabetes," because it's most often diagnosed in persons younger than age 30). The remaining 95 percent have type II, or non–insulin-dependent diabetes.

If the disease can't be controlled with dietary changes only (see *Diabetes: Dietary Factors*, page 287), your doctor may prescribe insulin injections (which you can administer to yourself) or oral hypoglycemic drugs, which stimulate the production of insulin. You may also be asked to monitor your blood sugar levels—perhaps several times a day—by means of a monitoring device specially designed for that purpose.

When to Call a Doctor
Seek medical help if the following conditions exist.

- You check your blood sugar level and it is high
- You start feeling very thirsty and urinate more frequently
- You feel nauseated or vomit more than once
- Your breathing suddenly becomes deeper and faster
- Your breath smells sweet or "fruity"
- You experience trembling, weakness, or drowsiness, followed by dizziness, confusion, or double vision
- You feel uncoordinated

FIRST AID FOR DIABETIC EMERGENCIES
If you notice someone exhibiting the symptoms listed above, try to determine if he is diabetic; many people wear medical alert bracelets or medallions that indicate they have the disease. Even if you're not sure if the person is experiencing an episode of high blood sugar (hyperglycemia) or low blood sugar (hypoglycemia), try to offer him something sweet, such as a cup of orange juice, a soft drink containing sugar, or a few pieces of candy. *Seek immediate medical help if the person's condition does not improve within 10 to 15 minutes after he consumes the sugar or he is unconscious.*

Avoiding Complications from Diabetes

Because the disease damages nerves and blood vessels, complications of diabetes may include impotence, heart and

Although Diabetes Is Incurable, You Have Some Control over Your Condition

Carefully Monitor Your Diabetes to Avoid Complications

kidney disease, stroke, blindness, and blood flow problems that may lead to the need to amputate feet or legs.

DIABETES AND IMPOTENCE

Many men who have diabetes—perhaps as many as 60 percent—are impotent (unable to achieve or sustain an erection long enough to have sexual intercourse). In some cases, impotence may be caused by damage to nerves or blood vessels. Certain medications, especially those given to control high blood pressure, may cause impotence in some men. And emotional stress may also play a role.

Follow this advice to help avoid impotence:

❑ **Don't worry.** Stress makes the problem worse.

❑ **Control your diabetes.** Make any necessary lifestyle changes to take charge of your disease.

❑ **Don't drink excessively.** Heavy alcohol consumption causes impotence.

❑ **Don't smoke.** Nicotine causes blood vessels to narrow, which can contribute to blocked arteries that make it more difficult to achieve erection.

DIABETES AND PREGNANCY

If you're a woman with diabetes and you're thinking of having a baby, talk to your doctor. It's important to carefully control your blood sugar levels from the moment you decide to start a family, for your own health and that of your baby. With careful attention paid to diet and doctor's orders, the chances of a diabetic women having a healthy child are better than ever.

Some women who are not diabetic may also develop gestational diabetes, a temporary condition that usually goes away after the baby is born.

TAKE CARE OF YOUR FEET

As diabetes progresses, damage to the nerves and blood vessels can cause deterioration of the extremities, especially the feet, with often tragic consequences. Diabetics are more than 11 times more likely than other adults to be hospitalized for amputations, according to the American Diabetes Association. To prevent problems, carefully monitor and control your diabetes. Report any sores or unusual discoloring of your feet or legs to your doctor as soon as they become apparent.

DON'T OVERLOOK EYE EXAMS

Diabetes has such a significant effect on the eyes that your ophthalmologist (eye doctor) can tell how you are controlling your diabetes from an eye examination. The most common eye disorders involve the retina and lens: People with diabetes are at risk of developing cataracts, an area of the lens that cannot transmit light, and diabetic retinopathy, which is damage to the retina.

Because they are prone to vision changes, diabetics should schedule regular eye examinations. Your ophthalmologist can recommend an appropriate examination schedule for you: Some people with diabetes may require eye exams every two or three months, depending on the number of years they've had diabetes and the progress of any eye conditions. Others with well-controlled diabetes may need an examination annually.

Diabetes: Dietary Factors

Food and drink—how much you eat, when, and what—play a big role in controlling your diabetes. The American Diabetes Association has established new dietary guidelines for people with diabetes.

If you thought you'd never be able to eat a sugary treat again, the new guidelines may be a sweet surprise. But get help sorting through the new guidelines and adapting the Association's recommendations to your lifestyle. In fact, the guidelines themselves recommend that diabetics consult a registered dietician for help tailoring their dietary needs to the type of diabetes they have, their weight, activity level, and eating habits and tastes. Simply put, each person with diabetes needs an individual diet plan. Here are a few general tips:

❑ **Stay trim.** Being overweight or obese (30 percent or more over the ideal weight for your height, age, and gender) will worsen your condition. Losing even 5 to 15 pounds can help lower not only your blood sugar level, but your blood cholesterol level and your blood pressure as well.

❑ **Eat plenty of fiber.** Fiber—found in many foods, but especially fruits and green leafy vegetables—is good for you for many reasons. It helps control your blood sugar levels by slowing the release of sugar from the foods you eat. It also can help lower your cholesterol and ensure easier and more frequent bowel movements.

FOR MORE INFORMATION

To learn more about treating and living with diabetes, contact the American Diabetes Association:

1-800-232-3472

(In Virginia and the Washington, D.C. metropolitan area, call 703-549-1500.)

❑   ❑   ❑

❑ **Don't drink too much alcohol.** Although you should consult your physician about a recommendation for you, many diabetics can drink occasionally, although one or two drinks once or twice a week (with meals) is considered the maximum. Drinking on an empty stomach can cause your blood sugar to drop.

❑ **Limit your sugar intake.** Don't add sugar to coffee or iced tea. And watch for "hidden" sugars in fruit juices and nondiet sodas.

❑ **Drink lots of water.** Many health experts recommend drinking six to eight glasses of water per day to ensure overall good health. Drinking a glass or two with meals helps you feel less hungry and helps improve your sugar control.

❑ **Exercise.** Exercise helps your body make better use of the insulin it has and lowers your blood sugar level.

Emphysema: Are Your Lungs at Risk?

Afflicting about 2 million Americans, emphysema is a disease of the lungs that causes

Each Person with Diabetes Needs an Individual Diet Plan

chronic coughing and short-ness of breath after even mild exertion such as walking or speaking. More than 42 percent of all people in the United States with emphysema report that their daily routine has been severely limited by the disease, according to the American Lung Association.

But the news is not all bad. Although some forms of emphysema have less controllable causes (heredity, asthma, and exposure to air pollution), the most common cause of the disease—cigarette smoking—is easily preventable. A small number of people with emphysema have a rare form called *alpha₁-antitrypsin deficiency*—an inherited deficiency of a protein that protects the lungs. Merely having the deficiency—as an estimated 70,000 Americans do—doesn't mean you'll get emphysema, but it does increase your risk.

What Is Emphysema?

Emphysema—or chronic obstructive pulmonary disease (COPD)—begins when structures in the lungs called *alveoli* (or air sacs) overexpand when you breathe in. Eventually the walls of the alveoli, which are very thin, break down and lose their elasticity. In the alveoli, oxygen you breathe in is transferred to the blood in exchange for carbon dioxide. But lungs with damaged alveoli trans-

Smoking Is the Most Common Cause of Emphysema

fer less oxygen to the blood. This results in shortness of breath. If left untreated, the disease progresses, making it harder and harder for a person with emphysema to breathe and eventually causing damage to the heart.

Controlling Emphysema

Here are some steps you can take to control risk factors of emphysema.

- **Don't smoke.** Cigarettes are responsible for 82 percent of all kinds of chronic lung disease, including emphysema, according to the American Lung Association. If you smoke—stop!

- **Avoid polluted air.** Doctors suspect that exposure to air pollution and airborne toxins (such as fumes or dust in a workplace) may aggravate or cause some cases of emphysema. At work, wear any recommended protective gear, such as face masks, and pay attention to air quality evaluations in TV and newspaper weather reports. When smog levels are deemed unhealthy, stay indoors as much as possible.

- **Treat colds and other respiratory problems promptly.** Respiratory infections can make emphysema worse; consult your physician when such an infection begins. Also, ask about getting a vaccine to prevent influenza and pneumococcal pneumonia.

- **Take care of yourself.** Get plenty of rest, exercise regularly, and eat a balanced diet that's low in saturated fat.

FOR MORE INFORMATION

To learn more about emphysema and other chronic lung diseases, such as chronic bronchitis, contact your local American Lung Association.

❑　❑　❑

Maintaining your overall health will lessen your chances of getting countless ailments that could worsen emphysema.

TREATING EMPHYSEMA

Emphysema has no cure, but if it is diagnosed early, you and your doctor can slow or stop its progression. Depending on your condition, your physician might suggest any or all of these steps:

- **Quitting smoking.** See Chapter 9, *Kick the Nicotine Habit*, page 318 for advice.

- **Medication.** Bronchodilators, prescription medications taken orally or inhaled, help relax and open air passages, making breathing easier. Your doctor might recommend antibiotics if he or she finds you have a respiratory bacterial infection. If your emphysema is due to an inherited protein deficiency, you may receive a drug to combat the problem.

- **Exercise.** First, you should try to stay as active as your doctor thinks is safe. Second, your doctor may also suggest breathing exercises that are specially designed to help you control the emptying of your lungs.

- **Oxygen.** Your doctor might suggest keeping a supply of oxygen at home. If you use oxygen tanks, follow safe handling and storage directions carefully.

Could It Be Epilepsy?

Throughout history, epilepsy has been widely misunderstood. The men, women, and

---

WHEN TO CALL AN AMBULANCE

Most seizures end in about five minutes and can be handled with simple first-aid measures. The following are signs you need to call for emergency medical help:

- If the person has a seizure while in water (such as a swimming pool)
- If you don't know whether the seizure is due to epilepsy
- If the person is pregnant
- If the person has diabetes
- If the person is injured
- If the seizure continues for more than five minutes
- If a second seizure starts shortly after the first ends
- If the person doesn't regain consciousness after the convulsion stops

❑　❑　❑

---

children who have the condition (once considered synonymous with madness) have at times been persecuted or isolated from society.

Even today, some people with epilepsy experience job and social discrimination, and children whose epilepsy has been undiagnosed and untreated can experience learning disabilities. But there's nothing sinister about epilepsy, a chronic medical condition that affects more than 2 million people in the United States.

In people with epilepsy, sudden changes in the electrical function of the brain produce seizures, which can range from convulsions to periods of fixed staring to alteration of sensory perception. Today, with early detection and treatment (which might include prescribed drugs, a special diet, or even surgery), most persons with epilepsy—up to 85 percent of those who get treatment—can expect to get control of their seizures.

Epilepsy Can Develop at Any Age

Possible Causes of Epilepsy

In more than 70 percent of all people with epilepsy, no cause for the condition can be found. Identifiable causes may include:

- Head injuries
- Brain damage due to oxygen deficiency at birth
- Brain tumors
- Genetic conditions
- Lead poisoning
- Fetal brain development problems
- Serious infections, such as meningitis or encephalitis

Signs of Epilepsy

Epilepsy can develop at any age, but it usually first shows up in childhood or early adolescence. The following signs indicate the need to consult your physician:

- Periods of blackout or confused memory
- Experiencing unexplainable odd sounds, smells, tastes, distorted visual perception, or feelings of fear and apprehension (This is known as an "aura," an unusual sensation that often precedes epileptic seizures.)
- "Fainting spells" followed by incontinence or extreme fatigue
- Episodes of uncontrollable staring or unexplained periods of unresponsiveness in children
- Episodes of uncontrollable blinking or chewing
- Involuntary movement of the arms or legs
- Convulsions, with or without an accompanying fever

First Aid for Seizures

If you see someone having a seizure, the first action you should take is to prevent him from hurting himself. Other than that, it's best to just let the seizure run its course. Here are some guidelines for helping a person with epilepsy who experiences a seizure.

Do:

- ❑ Look for medical identification, such as a bracelet or necklace.
- ❑ Move nearby hazards out of the way.
- ❑ Loosen the person's tie or shirt collar.
- ❑ Turn the patient on his or her side, to keep the airway clear and to prevent the person from choking on saliva.
- ❑ Reassure the patient when he or she regains consciousness.
- ❑ Offer to help the person get home, if he is not at home.

FOR MORE INFORMATION

The Epilepsy Foundation of America offers literature on the condition as well as programs to help patients and their families. For assistance, call the foundation's local chapter (check your Yellow Pages for the number), or contact the national foundation.

Epilepsy Foundation of America
4351 Garden City Drive
Landover, MD 20785

or phone 1-800-332-1000

❑   ❑   ❑

Don't:

❑ Restrain the person.

❑ Put *anything* in the person's mouth.

❑ Try to hold the person's tongue or open the mouth.

❑ Give liquids during or just after a seizure.

❑ Use artificial respiration unless the person is not breathing after the muscle jerks subside or unless he has inhaled water (such as while swimming).

Stay Alert to Signs of Glaucoma

Glaucoma is one of the chief reasons adults in the United States, especially those middle-aged and older, lose their sight. An estimated two out of every 100 people in the United States older than age 35 are at risk for this eye disease.

In about 90 percent of cases, glaucoma starts very subtly, and no symptoms appear until relatively late in the ailment's progression. By the time many people learn they have glaucoma, they've already suffered some permanent loss of vision. For that reason, you should have your eyes examined regularly to protect your sight.

What Is Glaucoma?

Glaucoma is a blanket term for a number of eye diseases that involve a change in pressure inside the eye. It results in damage to the optic nerve, which carries the images we see from the retina, the structure at the back of the eye that senses light, to the brain for processing.

LOW VISION HELPERS

If you've been left visually impaired by glaucoma or another eye problem, a number of devices are available to help you see better. (Good lighting can also make a big difference; even the average 60 year old with no eye disorder requires twice as much illumination as she did at age 20 to read comfortably.) Low vision aids include:

❑ Magnifying spectacles (available over the counter at many pharmacies)

❑ Hand magnifiers (also available in stores)

❑ Telescopes (Some people use tiny telescopes mounted in spectacles for sighting objects at distances, such as street signs.)

❑ Closed-circuit televisions (These produce an enlarged image on a TV monitor.)

❑ Large-print books, magazines, and newspapers

❑ "Talking" appliances, such as timers, clocks, or computers

❑ Enlarged telephone dials

❑   ❑   ❑

In a person who has perfect vision, the optic nerve serves as a sort of electrical cable, transporting visual messages by means of nerve fibers. In a person with glaucoma, pressure builds within the eye because aqueous humor, a clear eye liquid, is blocked from draining properly. The nerve fibers become damaged, and blind spots develop in one's vision. (Peripheral vision is usually affected first.) If the entire nerve is destroyed (which eventually happens if the problem isn't treated), blindness results.

ARE YOU AT RISK?

The following are risk factors for glaucoma:

● **Age.** Although in rare cases children can develop glaucoma, chances of developing the ailment increase as you age. People older than 40 years of age are at greater risk.

- **Heredity.** A family history of glaucoma or diabetes may indicate you're susceptible.
- **Race.** Blacks have a greater risk of developing glaucoma.
- **Previous eye injuries.** Injuries, as well as cataracts, often precede glaucoma.
- **Use of topical steroid medication.** These include eye drops.

Glaucoma: Early Detection and Treatment

Although there's no way to prevent glaucoma (and no cure once it's found), detecting the problem early and seeking treatment can help slow damage to the eyes and prevent further vision loss. The following eye examination schedule is recommended to prevent problems.

Get an exam every three to five years if:
- Your vision is unchanged

Get an exam every one to two years if:
- A close family member—parents, siblings, or grandparents—have or had glaucoma or diabetes
- You're of African ancestry
- You've ever had a serious eye injury
- You are using topical steroid medication

About ten percent of glaucoma cases either develop rapidly (angle-closure and secondary glaucoma) or are present from birth (congenital glaucoma, which afflicts infants and children). These cases need immediate treatment to prevent further vision loss.

A child or adult who experiences these symptoms should undergo an eye examination:

- Blurred vision
- Severe eye pain
- Unexplained, persistent headaches
- Seeing rainbow-colored "halos" around lights
- Unexplained, persistent nausea and vomiting

An infant or child whose eyes exhibit these symptoms of glaucoma should also undergo examination:

- Enlarging
- Cloudiness
- Watering and closing when exposed to light

If your ophthalmologist or physician diagnoses glaucoma, the treatment he or she recommends may depend on the cause of your ailment and how far it's progressed. Your doctor may prescribe eye drops and pills that decrease eye pressure. These work by either slowing the production of aqueous fluid or by improving drainage. Medication side effects, which can include anything from stinging, reddened eyes to drowsiness, bowel irregularities and even kidney stones, should be reported to your doctor. Your doctor may also suggest laser or other surgery, which can improve fluid drainage in the eye.

Early Detection and Treatment of Glaucoma Can Prevent Further Vision Loss

Getting Relief from Gout

Doctors thought for generations that gout—sudden, severe pain in a single joint, usually at the base of the big toe—was due to overindulgence in food and drink. Because gout often occurred in overweight men, the theory seemed credible.

Although doctors know an alcohol or food binge can bring on an attack of gout, it doesn't cause it. The real culprit—an overabundance of uric acid in the body—has been identified, and treating that situation can help relieve the pain of this chronic problem.

What Is Gout?

Some people produce too much—or have trouble excreting—uric acid. (This metabolic tendency is inherited.) When uric acid builds up in the body, it can form crystals in the fluid around the joints and cause the pain, swelling, and redness of gout. Attacks of gout may follow an injury, or may be a side effect of some diuretics used to treat hypertension. The pain usually subsides after one or two weeks. People who suffer from untreated gout may be at risk for developing kidney stones or arthritis of the feet or knees.

TREATING GOUT

Doctors once put gout patients on diets and warned them away from alcohol. Although it's always a good idea to drink only in moderation and to keep your weight down with low-fat meals, diet is no longer considered the most efficient way to treat gout.

The best way to relieve the pain is to prevent your body from producing uric acid, which can be accomplished with such prescription medications as allopurinol. Avoiding foods rich in purines (compounds that contain uric acid), such as liver, kidneys, sardines, anchovies, and sweetbreads, may also help prevent attacks.

Keep Tabs on Your Blood Cholesterol Level

Cholesterol—a type of fat (lipids) made in your liver, and present in meat and dairy products—comes in two varieties: "good" and "bad."

Everyone needs a certain amount of cholesterol to build cell

WHAT CHOLESTEROL TEST RESULTS MEAN

A cholesterol test evaluates a small sample of blood to determine the levels of HDL and LDL. The test results report your total cholesterol level and also break the findings into totals of HDL and LDL. Here are the guidelines doctors use to determine your risk of heart disease (the numbers are in milligrams per deciliter, or mg/dL):

Total Cholesterol Levels
- Best: under 200
- Borderline risk: between 200 and 239
- At risk: 240 or more

LDL Levels
- Best: under 130
- Borderline risk: 130 to 159
- At risk: 160 or more

HDL Levels
- Best: 60 or more
- At risk: under 35

❑   ❑   ❑

Every Adult Should Have a Blood Cholesterol Test at Least Once Every Five Years

membranes and maintain health. But too much of these blood lipids—especially too much of the "bad" low-density lipoprotein (LDL), can raise your risk for heart disease and stroke. Too little "good" cholesterol (high-density lipoproteins, or HDL), which helps remove fats from the bloodstream, can also pose a problem.

Although doctors are still trying to determine why some people are prone to high blood cholesterol levels, nearly everyone can lower their cardiovascular disease risk by eating foods low in saturated fat and adapting an overall healthier lifestyle.

The Benefits of Early Detection

If you have a "high" blood cholesterol level, the fats in the blood cling to the inside of arteries like scale inside a pipe. As time passes, the arteries narrow and become less flexible—the so-called "hardening" of the arteries that can increase your risk for stroke and heart disease.

To detect problems early (when they can be treated most effectively), every adult older than 20 years of age should have a blood cholesterol test at least once every five years, and more often if their doctor recommends it, according to the National Heart, Lung, and Blood Institute.

Risk Factors for High Blood Cholesterol

Some risk factors of high blood cholesterol you can control; others you cannot. Risk factors include:

- **Age.** Men older than age 45 and women older than age 55, or women who entered menopause before age 48 without receiving estrogen replacement therapy, are susceptible to high blood cholesterol levels.

- **Family history.** If your father or brother suffered a heart attack before age 55, or your mother or sister suffered one before age 65, you could be at greater risk.

- **Smoking.** Smokers tend to have lower levels of protective HDL cholesterol.

- **Excess weight.** Weight gain is associated with a consumption of fat, which can raise the blood cholesterol level.

- **Lack of regular exercise.** Regular exercise can help reduce blood cholesterol levels.

How to Lower Blood Cholesterol

There is much you can do to control your blood cholesterol level.

Lifestyle Changes

Change your diet and acquire new lifestyle habits:

- **Stay trim.** Find out what your ideal weight is, and try to reach it. (See the *Metropolitan Height-Weight Table* in Chapter 2, page 50, to determine your ideal weight.) If you need to lose pounds, consult your doctor for advice tailored to your age and physical condition.

- **Follow a low-fat diet.** If your doctor gives you a diet, follow it closely. Eat plenty of fruits and vegetables and foods high in fiber (such as oats and dark breads), and avoid fried foods. See chapter 1, *Nutrition*, for more "low-fat advice."

- **Don't smoke.** Smoking greatly increases your risk of developing cardiovascular disease.

❑ **Exercise.** Aerobic physical activity, in workout sessions lasting from 30 to 45 minutes at least three times a week, will help you stay trim and exercise your muscles, heart, and lungs. If you have hypertension or a history of heart problems, consult your doctor before beginning an exercise program. Most people can participate in walking exercise.

Medication

Changing your diet and lifestyle habits might be all you'll need to lower your cholesterol (and your risk of cardiovascular disease). In some cases, however—especially if you're older and at great risk for heart disease—your physician might prescribe drugs to lower your LDL and raise your HDL levels. Certain medications can help raise HDLs and lower LDLs, but they may induce side effects and are usually only used when other self-treatment efforts fail.

In postmenopausal women, hormone replacement therapy, which delivers a dose of the female hormone estrogen (a "protector" of the heart and arteries), may be recommended.

High Blood Pressure: Beware the Silent Killer

Blood pressure—the force created by your heart as it pumps blood into the arteries and by your arterial blood vessels as they resist the flow from the heart—is one way to measure the health of your cardiovascular system.

If you have high blood pressure—which can be diagnosed with a simple, painless test—you need to control it with lifestyle changes and perhaps medication. Otherwise, your heart has to work progressively harder to pump blood through your arteries. Your heart may enlarge, and you'll be at increased risk for heart attacks, stroke, kidney failure, and atherosclerosis (buildup of plaque in the arteries). Because you may go for years without knowing you have high blood pressure, it's been called a "silent killer." Relatively few people die simply of hypertension, but hundreds of thousands die each year of heart attacks and strokes.

CHECKING YOUR BLOOD PRESSURE

Blood pressure can be detected easily, and should be checked at least once a year by a health professional. An instrument called a *sphygmomanometer*, a gauge attached to an inflatable rubber cuff, is slipped around your upper arm and inflated by squeezing an attached rubber bulb. When full, it compresses a large artery in the arm, stopping blood flow. A stethoscope is placed on the arm near the cuff, the cuff is slowly deflated, and the doctor, nurse, or other health care worker listens with the stethoscope while watching the gauge.

The pressure recorded on the gauge when the first sound is heard (called the systolic pressure) and when the last sound is heard (the diastolic pressure) become your blood pressure reading. The sphygmomanometer measures blood pressure in millimeters of mercury, which is abbreviated mm Hg. If, for example, your systolic pressure is 127 and your diastolic pressure is 78, your reading would be 127/78 mm Hg.

Have Your Blood Pressure Checked at Least Once a Year

You Can Control Many of the Risk Factors for High Blood Pressure

RISK FACTORS

Are you at risk for high blood pressure? Here are common risk factors for the condition.

- **Age.** The older you are, the higher your likelihood of having hypertension.
- **Race.** Blacks are more prone to high blood pressure than whites.
- **Weight.** Being obese—defined as 30 percent or more above the ideal body weight for your height, age, and gender—increases your risk. If you're merely overweight—above your ideal poundage, but not greater than 30 percent above it—you're still at increased risk for higher than normal or mildly high blood pressure.
- **Heredity.** The likelihood you will have high blood pressure increases if one or both of your parents has it.
- **Pregnancy.** Some expectant mothers experience elevated blood pressure.
- **Oral contraceptive use.** Some women who take birth control pills develop hypertension, especially if they have other risk factors for the disease.
- **Alcohol use.** Heavy drinking increases blood pressure.
- **Sodium consumption.** Blood pressure increases in some people when they consume too much sodium (found in table salt and other foods).
- **Lack of exercise.** If you lead a sedentary lifestyle, you're at increased risk for obesity and hypertension.

Controlling High Blood Pressure

Take these steps to help control your blood pressure:

- ❑ **Stay trim.** See the *Metropolitan Height-Weight Table* in Chapter 2, page 50, to find out what your ideal weight is; then try to reach it. If you need to lose pounds, consult your doctor for advice tailored to your age and physical condition.
- ❑ **Follow a balanced diet.** If your doctor gives you a diet, follow it closely. Eating balanced meals low in sodium and saturated fat helps you maintain your overall health.
- ❑ **Don't drink—or do so only in moderation.** Heavy drinking increases your blood pressure. And because alcoholic drinks are high in calories, they'll make it that much harder to lose weight.
- ❑ **Don't smoke.** Although there's no evidence smoking has a direct effect on blood pressure, it does greatly increase your risk of developing cardiovascular disease.
- ❑ **Avoid sodium.** Consuming salty foods can help jack up your blood pressure. Ask your doctor whether you should be on a sodium-restricted diet. Read package labels, and learn how to cut down on the amount of salt you use in

HOW HIGH IS HIGH BLOOD PRESSURE?

There is no "ideal" blood pressure, only ranges of "normal" readings for adults. A person has hypertension—high blood pressure—when the systolic pressure (the first number in the reading) is 140 or more, and the diastolic pressure (the second number) is 90 or more, for extended periods of time.

❑ ❑ ❑

cooking. The National Institutes of Health recommends no more than 2.5 grams (2,500 milligrams) of sodium daily for most adults. Use herbs and spices to add flavor to food in place of salt.

❑ **Exercise.** Aerobic physical activity, in workout sessions lasting from 30 to 45 minutes at least three times a week, helps you stay trim, and exercises your muscles, heart, and lungs. Although you should consult your doctor if you have hypertension or a history of heart problems, most people who have been sedentary for a while have no trouble starting out with walking.

❑ **Avoid some over-the-counter medicines.** Some common medications–cold tablets, for example—can elevate blood pressure.

WHAT YOUR DOCTOR CAN DO

Your doctor may prescribe the following medications to combat your hypertension:

- Diuretics, which rid the body of excess fluid and sodium

- Beta-blockers, which reduce the heart rate and the amount of blood flowing from the heart

- Sympathetic nerve inhibitors, which prevent blood vessels from constricting

- Vasodilators, which relax tiny blood vessels in the arteries and help dilate the arteries themselves

Always ask about the side effects of any drug, and report any problems that begin after you start taking the medication to your doctor. Some antihypertension medications have serious side effects, such as impotence.

Although it's crucial that you follow any drug regimen, that's only part of the treatment. To improve your blood pressure and lower your risk for a number of cardiovascular problems, you should also follow the prevention tips listed above and any other suggestions your doctor gives for a healthier lifestyle.

What to Do About Kidney Stones

If you've never had kidney stones, consider yourself lucky. Passing a kidney stone—crystallizations of calcium salts, uric acid, or other substances—ranks with childbirth as one of life's most painful experiences.

The tiny stones, which usually measure no more than 1 or 2 millimeters in diameter, are expelled from the kidneys and down the tube-like ureter into the bladder, and are "passed" when you urinate. (The pain comes when the stone is in the narrow ureter, on its way to the bladder.) Kidney stones tend to run in families due to an inherited tendency to excrete more calcium (about 80 percent of all kidney stones are calcium-derived). But other factors, such as physical inactivity and not drinking enough water, can also lead to the formation of kidney stones.

SYMPTOMS OF KIDNEY STONES

If you have a family or personal history of kidney stones and experience any of these symptoms, you

Kidney Stones Tend to Run in Families

Kidney Stones Tend to Recur

may be in the process of passing a kidney stone:

- Gradually developing pain in the waist or back that moves to the groin or testicle area and becomes extreme

- A constant urge to urinate

- Blood in the urine

TREATING KIDNEY STONES

The bad news about kidney stones is this: There's not much a doctor can do for you until you pass it. The good news: Once you've passed it, you'll immediately feel much better. Here are some of the treatment options:

- **If you're in a lot of pain:** Your doctor can give you a strong anesthetic to relieve some of your discomfort.

- **If you're having trouble passing the stone:** A special kidney X-ray test, called an IVP (intravenous pyelograph) can help physicians find any abnormalities or problems. In some cases, a doctor might elect to "flush out" a kidney stone that's difficult to pass or causing such side effects as severe bleeding or a bladder infection.

- **If you're passing a kidney stone by yourself:** Your doctor might ask you to urinate through a strainer, so the stone can be recovered and evaluated to determine its makeup and whether medication might prevent such stones from recurring.

PREVENTION TIPS

If you're prone to kidney stones (they tend to recur), or have a family history of the problem, take these steps:

- ❑ **Drink lots of water.** Down six to eight glasses a day—at least one of them at bedtime—to dilute urine and keep crystals from forming.

- ❑ **Exercise regularly.** Leading a sedentary lifestyle aggravates the problem.

- ❑ **Ask your doctor about medication.** If you have a lot of kidney stones, you may need prescription drugs to keep calcium salts, uric acid, or other substances from accumulating in your kidneys.

Understanding Multiple Sclerosis

Multiple sclerosis (MS), a chronic disease of the central nervous system, is shrouded in mystery. Although researchers believe the disease is caused by an immune-system dysfunction, hard facts remain elusive.

Doctors have identified four patterns of symptoms (listed under *Types of MS*), but the disease affects each patient in a unique way. One person might have very few symptoms and long periods without any symptoms at all; another might experience severe disabling attacks for months or years at a time. Although there is currently no cure for MS, new treatments may give relief to some patients.

What Is MS?
Multiple sclerosis "attacks"—characterized by weakness, incoordination, double vision, slurred speech, and sometimes loss of bladder control and paralysis—occur because of damage to tissue, or

myelin, that wraps around nerve fibers in the brain, spinal cord, and optic nerves like a sheath. The myelin sheath insulates nerve fibers so they can do their job without interference, much the way insulation protects phone or electrical cables. In a person with MS, the body's immune system attacks the myelin. White blood cells called *lymphocytes*, or *T cells*, invade the central nervous system, breaking down and unraveling the protective myelin sheath. After the myelin has been ravaged by the T cells, lesions called *plaques* appear where there was once protective sheathing.

Who Gets MS?

An estimated 350,000 people in the United States have MS, according to the National Multiple Sclerosis Society. Overwhelmingly, MS is a disease that affects young women; twice as many women as men have the ailment, and about two-thirds of all persons with MS first experience symptoms when they are between the ages of 20 and 40—the years when many are attending school, starting careers, and caring for young families.

Although researchers believe a genetic factor determines who gets MS, the condition is not directly inherited.

TYPES OF MS

The categories of MS are divided according to their characteristic symptoms:

- **Benign** (20 percent of all cases): A person with benign MS has mild attacks with long, symptom-free periods.
- **Relapsing-remitting** (25 percent of cases): A person who has MS symptoms but also periods of recovery or stability is said to have relapsing-remitting MS.
- **Relapsing-progressive** (40 percent of cases): A person who recovers only modestly from MS attacks, or whose ability to function is impaired, is described as having relapsing-progressive MS.
- **Chronic-progressive** (15 percent of cases): A person whose condition deteriorates continuously for months or years, and who suffers life-threatening complications, has chronic-progressive MS.

MS: WHAT CAN BE DONE?

Although no cure for MS yet exists, the medical community can assist the person with MS in several ways:

- Physicians and physical therapists can help a patient control symptoms and keep a positive mental attitude.
- Some prescription drugs can help suppress muscle spasms.
- Corticosteroids and hormones can help reduce inflammation.
- For those with relapse-remitting MS, the new antiviral prescription drug Betaseron may help lessen the frequency and severity of MS attacks.

MS Primarily Affects Women Between 20 and 40 Years of Age

FOR MORE INFORMATION

To learn more about multiple sclerosis contact:

National Multiple Sclerosis Society
733 Third Avenue
New York, NY 10017-3288

or call 212-986-3240

❑   ❑   ❑

All Adults Lose Bone Mass After the Age of 35

Who Is at Risk for Osteoporosis?

Many older adults find themselves becoming shorter as they get on in years. This "shrinkage" is actually a sign of osteoporosis, or porous bones, the loss of bone mass that begins to occur in all adults after the age of 35.

Although men can also experience thinner, more porous bones as they reach their 70s or 80s, osteoporosis is a far greater risk for women, who lose bone density rapidly as their levels of the female hormone estrogen (which protects bones) plummet after menopause. Women are also more vulnerable to osteoporosis because they have less bone mass than men to begin with, tend to live longer, and, on average, take in less dietary calcium, which helps build bone density and keep bones strong.

RISK FACTORS

The following uncontrollable factors increase your risk of developing osteoporosis as you age:

- Family history of osteoporosis
- Early menopause (before the age of 48)
- Having fair skin (whites and Asians are at greatest risk)
- Hyperthyroidism
- Having a small-boned frame

These controllable situations also increase your risk:

- Calcium deficiency
- Lack of exercise (Physical activity, especially weight-bearing exercises such as walking or swimming, helps keep bones strong.)
- Smoking (It can make osteoporosis worse, and may cancel out the benefits of hormone therapy.)
- Alcohol abuse
- Having ovaries removed through surgery before menopause
- Being slender or underweight
- Using steroids

Symptoms of Osteoporosis

You might not know you're in danger of osteoporosis until you experience serious warning signs, such as the following:

- Lower back pain
- Loss of height (This happens over time because osteoporosis can cause the bones in your spine to collapse, a condition called compression fractures.)
- A hunched back
- A broken wrist, hip, or rib

Osteoporosis Treatment Options

If you have risk factors for osteoporosis, or if you're experiencing any of its symptoms, your treatment strategy may depend upon your age.

- **If you're premenopausal:** Taking steps to improve your overall physical health (quitting smoking, cutting down on alcohol, exercising regularly) and increasing your daily intake of calcium help you build bone mass and ward off future problems.

- **If you're at or past menopause:** You may need to supplement those steps with hormone replacement therapy (HRT), which supplies you with estrogen (and, in some cases, progesterone) that your body stops making at menopause or if your ovaries have been surgically removed.

HORMONE REPLACEMENT THERAPY

Hormone replacement therapy, sometimes referred to as estrogen replacement therapy (ERT), is exactly what its name suggests. After menopause, the ovaries no longer produce the hormone estrogen; HRT restores your estrogen level by means of pills or a skin patch—thus alleviating those discomforts associated with falling estrogen levels.

Although the therapy was strictly estrogen at one time, now HRT includes another hormone—progesterone. Doctors added this extra hormone because researchers found that estrogen therapy alone increases the risk of endometrial cancer (cancer of the uterine lining). The addition of progesterone nearly eliminates that risk.

However, even with progesterone, HRT is not without risks. HRT is not recommended for women who have any history of breast cancer, endometrial cancer, uterine fibroids, or liver disease. These risk factors and possible side effects make the decision to start HRT a complicated one.

Even if you do decide that HRT is right for you, you and your doctor must still decide on the proper dosage and the delivery method (pills or patch) that suit you best. Be sure to explore all of the issues with your doctor. See the sidebar, *Pros and Cons of HRT,* for more information on the positive and negative aspects of this treatment.

PROS AND CONS OF HRT

Here is a list of some of the pros and cons of hormone replacement therapy. Discuss these with your doctor.

PROS
- Prevention of bone loss (osteoporosis)
- Possible decreased risk of heart attack
- Relief of hot flashes
- Maintenance of skin's elasticity (helping you look "younger") and vaginal moisture (making sexual intercourse more comfortable)
- Possible decreased mood swings and improved memory

CONS
- Possible increased risk of breast cancer
- Irregular, continued vaginal bleeding or spotting
- PMS-like symptoms in some women (fluid retention, cramps, mood changes)

❑ ❑ ❑

THE ROLE OF CALCIUM

Before you experience menopause, your intake of dietary calcium (found in dairy products, dried beans, sardines with bones, and broccoli, among other foods) helps you build bone mass; after menopause, it helps you preserve bone density.

If you're a premenopausal woman or a postmenopausal woman receiving HRT, you need at least 1,000 milligrams of calcium each day, and up to 1,500 a day if you're pregnant, nursing, or postmenopausal but do not receive HRT. Your doctor might recommend calcium supplements if you're not getting enough in the foods you eat, but these might not be as effective as dietary calcium. (For example, some ingredients in milk and dairy products, such as lactose and vitamin D, help your body absorb calcium.)

Strokes Are the Third Most Frequent Cause of Death in the U.S.

Protect Brittle Bones

Here are practical tips for avoiding falls and broken bones.

❑ Don't use throw rugs in your home.

❑ Wear flat, rubber-soled shoes for best traction.

❑ Use a cane or walker if you need one.

❑ Put hand grips and safety mats in your tub or shower to prevent slipping on wet surfaces.

❑ Provide good lighting on stairways.

❑ Don't stoop when you need to pick something up. If you must reach for something, bend your knees and keep your back straight.

Lower Your Risk of Stroke

A stroke is a very serious form of cardiovascular disease—it is the third biggest killer in the United States after heart disease and cancer. Strokes primarily affect elderly people, although the American Heart Association estimates 28 percent of the people who suffer strokes in a given year are younger than 65 years of age. The incidence of stroke is higher among men than women, but everyone's risk climbs with each decade they're alive.

Some patients are left completely debilitated and permanently handicapped by a stroke, while others experience only temporary symptoms and recover quickly. Advances in preventive care and in treatment for strokes has given new hope to patients: From 1980 to 1990, the rate of death from stroke declined 32.4 percent.

What Is Stroke?

A stroke occurs because part of the brain is deprived of the blood it needs to function. The loss of blood flow may be caused by a rupture or blockage (usually caused by a blood clot) in a vessel leading to the brain. When the brain is deprived of oxygen-rich blood, nerve cells in the affected areas of the brain die within minutes. The parts of the body and their functions that are controlled by those nerve cells are disabled—often including speech, memory, eyesight, and movement.

Up to 80 percent of all strokes are caused by blood clots and other blockages. These varieties of the disease—cerebral thrombosis and cerebral embolism—are much less often fatal than those caused by ruptures of the blood vessels (cerebral hemorrhages and subarachnoid hemorrhages).

ARE YOU AT RISK?

Most of the factors that increase your likelihood of having a stroke cannot be changed, but it's good to be aware of them. They include:

● **Age.** After age 65, your stroke risk edges up one percent a year. If you've had a transient ischemic attack, or TIA, commonly called a "mini-stroke," your risk increases as much as 8 percent each year.

● **Sex.** About 30 percent more men than women have

strokes—and the gender gap widens among people younger than age 65.

- **Race.** Blacks, who are at increased risk for high blood pressure, also have a much greater risk of dying or suffering severe disability from a stroke.

- **Heredity.** The risk is greater for people with a family history of stroke.

- **Diabetes mellitus.** People with diabetes have a high rate of heart disease, circulatory problems, high blood cholesterol levels, and hypertension.

- **Hypertension.** High blood pressure is a major risk factor for stroke.

- **Your personal history of stroke.** People who have had a stroke are a greater risk of having another. TIAs may predict a major stroke—about 36 percent of people who have a TIA later have a stroke.

- **Asymptomatic carotid bruit.** This abnormal sound, heard when a stethoscope is placed over the neck's carotid artery, usually indicates plaque buildup on the artery walls—and an increased risk for stroke.

PREVENTING STROKE

Control some of the risk factors of stroke with these tips:

- ❑ **Don't smoke.** Cigarettes increase the risk of stroke for several reasons: Nicotine increases blood pressure; the carbon monoxide in cigarette smoke reduces the amount of oxygen in your blood; and smoke causes blood platelets to stick together, increasing the risk of clotting.

- ❑ **Watch your blood pressure and your diet.** If you have hypertension, seek treatment from your physician. Eat a well-balanced, healthy diet, and keep your weight within guidelines for your height, age, and gender.

- ❑ **Seek treatment for heart disease risks.** If you have heart disease, you have more than twice the normal risk of stroke. Ask your doctor to monitor your blood cholesterol level. (Incidentally, anything that increases your risk of heart disease, including obesity, a lack of physical exercise, or excessive drinking, indirectly increases your risk of stroke.)

- ❑ **Seek treatment for blood clotting risks.** If you have a high count of red blood cells (which thicken the blood), or have had a TIA, seek your doctor's advice. You may need treatments or medications that inhibit clot formation.

When a Stroke Occurs

See a doctor *immediately* if you notice one of these symptoms:

- Sudden weakness or numbness of the face, arm, or leg on one side of the body

- Sudden dimness or loss of vision, especially when it occurs in only one eye

- Speech problems—trouble either talking or understanding when others talk

- Sudden, unexplained headaches

- Sudden, unexplained dizziness, unsteadiness, or falling.

High Blood Pressure Is a Major Risk Factor for Stroke

Is There Such a Thing as an "Ulcer Personality"?

There's no sugar-coating the truth: Strokes kill many people, and disable many more. About 38 percent of people who have a stroke die within 30 days, according to the American Heart Association, and the disease is the major cause of serious disability in the United States.

But there's good news as well: Most recovery of functional ability occurs in the first month after a stroke (called *spontaneous recovery*), and half of the people who survive their first month of recovery are still alive seven years later. Recovery generally involves a combination of the following:

- Surgery, to remove arterial blockage or repair damaged heart valves

- Drugs, to dissolve or prevent blood clots

- Hospital care

- Rehabilitation

Because stroke survivors are at increased risk for clinical depression, compassionate and knowledgeable family members can lift a patient's spirits and make a big difference in his or her treatment.

You Don't Have to Be a Hothead to Have an Ulcer

Is there such a thing as an "ulcer personality"? Some doctors would say yes—many patients who seek treatment for sores in their digestive tract are tightly wound people who have trouble handling emotional upsets. But contrary to the popular stereotype, not every person with a "type A" personality gets ulcers.

Other factors, including heredity, a tendency to produce too much stomach acid, and such behaviors as smoking and drinking alcohol can cause sores to develop in the "swallowing tube," or esophagus (esophageal ulcers), stomach lining (gastric ulcers), or, most commonly, in the first part of the small intestine, called the duodenum (duodenal ulcers). Although ulcers can't be "cured" in the usual sense (and may recur), they can be healed through medication, a change in your lifestyle, and sometimes surgery.

What Causes Ulcers?

Ulcers happen when stomach acid and other juices that help digest food burn and irritate the lining of the digestive tract. Some people produce too much stomach acid; others get ulcers when the lining of the digestive tract is damaged and becomes more vulnerable. Esophageal ulcers occur when stomach acid backs up into the esophagus. In addition to emotional stress, heredity, diet, and lifestyle factors such as smoking, some ulcers may be caused by a type of bacteria called *Helicobactor pylori*.

Ulcer Symptoms

These are the common symptoms of ulcer:

- Consistent burning or dull stomach pain

- Stomach pain when you eat or drink

- Stomach pain that improves when you eat or drink but then resumes an hour or two after eating

- Stomach pain that wakes you up from sleep
- Feeling "full" without eating or drinking much
- Feeling bloated
- Vomiting
- Weight loss

Diagnosing an Ulcer

If you complain to your doctor that you're experiencing ulcer-like symptoms, he or she may give you medicine right away as a means of ruling out other sources for your pain. Inflammation in the esophagus or stomach lining, which is a mild ulcer-like condition, usually gets better about a week after treatment starts.

If your symptoms don't improve, your doctor might do additional tests to determine the extent of the damage to your digestive system and plot a treatment strategy. These examinations might include an endoscopy (a thin tube that enables the physician to look at your digestive tract) or a barium X ray (in which you drink a barium liquid that highlights any ulcers on the X ray).

Ulcer Healing Hints

When your doctor diagnoses an ulcer, any treatment he or she prescribes has three goals:

- To decrease the amount of acid your stomach produces (by means of drugs called H2 blockers and the stronger medicine, omeprazole)
- To neutralize the digestive juices the stomach does make (with over-the-counter antacids)

- To protect sores so they can heal (with a drug called *sucralfate*, which coats the ulcer)

If your physician determines bacteria are causing your problems, you might be given antibiotics. Most ulcers heal within eight weeks of drug treatment. In addition, your doctor will probably advise you to make changes in your diet and habits (see *What You Can Do*, below) not only to heal your current ulcer, but to prevent recurrences in the future. Surgery, which is recommended usually in only rare and severe emergencies, often involves removing ulcerated tissue, but it is not considered a cure for those with chronic ulcers.

WHAT YOU CAN DO

If you're prone to ulcers, follow this advice to avoid irritating your stomach:

- ❏ **Don't smoke.** Heavy smokers are more likely to develop ulcers than nonsmokers, and ulcers in smokers take longer to heal.

- ❏ **Avoid aspirin or ibuprofen.** Some anti-inflammatory arthritis drugs may also aggravate ulcers. Acetaminophen, an over-the-counter pain reliever, can substitute for aspirin or ibuprofen in most instances.

- ❏ **Avoid caffeine, alcohol, milk, and peppermint.** If you must indulge in any of these, have only a small amount, and then only on a full stomach. Milk, once a suggested balm for ulcer-prone digestive tracts, has since been found to stimulate the production of stomach acid.

- ❏ **Don't eat spicy foods,** such as hot peppers or chili powder, if you have stomach pain.

You May Need to Change Your Diet and Your Habits

Anxiety Can Play a Role in the Development of Ulcers

❏ **Eat small, frequent meals.** Big meals can aggravate your stomach if you're already experiencing discomfort.

❏ **Learn to manage stress.** Anxiety—and how you handle it—can play a role in the development or recurrence of ulcers. If you're ulcer prone, avoid stressful situations, learn relaxation techniques, and seek the help of a professional counselor if needed.

When to Consult Your Doctor

If you have or have had an ulcer and experience any of the following symptoms, they could signal your condition is getting worse and requires further medical attention.

- Vomiting blood (a sign of a serious "bleeding" ulcer)
- Vomiting food eaten hours or even days previously
- Feeling cold or clammy with no other explanation
- Feeling weak or dizzy with no other explanation
- Black or bloody stools (another sign of a "bleeding" ulcer)
- Persistent nausea or vomiting
- Sudden, severe stomach pain
- Continuing weight loss
- Pain that radiates to your back
- Ulcer symptoms that fail to respond to medication

S U B S T A N C E

A B U S E

Most of us have used substances to make us feel better at one time or another. We may turn to a cup of coffee when we're sleepy or a bowl of ice cream when we're feeling down. Others reach for a cigarette to relieve tension. Still others may look to a quart of whiskey every night or a syringe full of street drugs.

Too much of almost anything can become a bad habit. Practice a bad habit long enough and it can become a compulsive addiction. Addiction means you no longer have a choice about practicing your habit. It controls you. This chapter discusses some of the more common substances that can become addictions, how to tell whether you or someone you care about has a problem with substance abuse, and how to find help.

❑ ❑ ❑

Do You Have a Problem with Drugs or Alcohol?

Drugs and Alcohol Can Fool Us into Believing We Still Have Control

One of the biggest problems with addictions to substances such as drugs is they can fool us into believing we still have control. Many drugs can make us—at least temporarily—feel smarter, more at ease, more in control of ourselves and the world. Eventually, however, they stop working and instead of alleviating our problems, they create more.

Think about the substances that you use to make yourself feel better—cigarettes, alcohol, prescription medications, or so-called "recreational drugs." Then use the questions on page 309 to help assess whether you have an addiction problem.

Myths about Alcohol and Drug Abuse

Many of us hold beliefs about drug and alcohol abuse that simply aren't true. These myths can keep us from recognizing when we or someone we care about has a problem with substance abuse.

Myth: "I only drink beer" or "I use only pot." Drugs are drugs. People can abuse and become addicted to almost any drug. True, many drugs don't cause physical withdrawal symptoms like heroin or alcohol do. But many drugs can cause a powerful psychological addiction.

Myth: Only men are alcoholics or drug addicts. Substance abuse experts recognize that many drug and alcohol abusers are women. Unfortunately, women tend to be more secretive and private than men about their habit, so their problem may go unnoticed.

Myth: I'm too young to be an addict or alcoholic. Drug and alcohol addiction don't discriminate on the basis of age. More younger people are seeking help from drug and alcohol addiction than ever before.

Myth: I can't be an addict or alcoholic. I hold down a responsible job. Not all alcoholics or drug addicts are derelicts on the street. Substance abuse experts estimate that 10 percent of all business executives are alcoholics. Every day, the tabloids are filled with stories of celebrities and athletes admitting to drug dependencies.

Myth: I'm too smart to become dependent on drugs or alcohol. Intelligence has nothing to do with alcohol or drug abuse. In fact, many substance abuse experts believe the predilection to addiction may be inherited.

Myth: Drugs make me perform better. There's no evidence any drug improves work or school performance. Some people believe drugs or alcohol enhance their creativity. However, any short-term gains are outweighed by impaired memory, judgment, and reaction time; an inability to do complex tasks; and many long-term negative health effects.

Myth: My drug or alcohol use is my business and no one else's. If you have friends, family, and cowork-

ASSESS YOUR USE OF DRUGS AND ALCOHOL

Use these questions to evaluate your drug and alcohol use. The more "yes" answers you have, the more likely it is you're chemically dependent.

	YES	NO
1. People have commented on my drug or alcohol use.	❏	❏
2. Sometimes I feel guilty or ashamed about my use.	❏	❏
3. I often use drugs or drink alone.	❏	❏
4. I get drunk or high even when I intended to stay sober.	❏	❏
5. I've had one or more DWI (driving while intoxicated) charges.	❏	❏
6. Sometimes I can't remember what happened after a bout of drinking alcohol or using drugs.	❏	❏
7. My doctor has said my drinking or drug use is affecting my health.	❏	❏
8. Before a social gathering, I usually have a few drinks or take some drugs just in case there won't be enough at the party.	❏	❏
9. I've tried unsuccessfully to cut down my drinking or drug use.	❏	❏
10. I can handle my liquor or drugs better than most people.	❏	❏
11. Most of my friends drink or use drugs.	❏	❏
12. I'm really not interested in socializing if alcohol or drugs aren't available.	❏	❏
13. I keep drinking or using drugs even when it's not pleasurable.	❏	❏
14. I'm afraid to quit.	❏	❏
15. I use drugs or alcohol to comfort myself when life gets me down or is going poorly.	❏	❏
16. I use alcohol or drugs as an "eye opener" in the morning.	❏	❏
17. I get irritated when others question me about my alcohol or drug use.	❏	❏
18. I have experienced symptoms of withdrawal (such as trembling and irritability) during periods I have not used drugs or alcohol.	❏	❏

ers, you can bet your substance abuse affects them, too. That's because it affects who you are when you drink or use drugs. People who abuse alcohol or drugs have more accidents, are absent from work more often, have difficulties with relationships, and are more likely to commit suicide.

Substance Abuse: The Effects on Families

Drug or Alcohol Abuse Doesn't Just Harm the Abuser

Most people who are dependent on drugs or alcohol believe their drug use doesn't really affect others. But drug and alcohol abuse harms not only the abuser, but the person's family, friends, and coworkers.

Being dependent on drugs or alcohol causes abusers to behave in irrational, hostile, and embarrassing ways that make everyone around them miserable. Their abuse creates an unhealthy climate that strains the very bonds that hold families together. Drug and alcohol abuse sends people close to the chemically dependent person on a continuous emotional roller coaster. These are some of the emotional effects of their abuse.

- **Fear:** Family and friends of someone who is addicted to drugs or alcohol constantly fear what may happen as a consequence of the substance use. Their world becomes unpredictable. Will the abuser become irritable, angry, or even violent after the alcohol or drug use? How will the

abuser's behavior impact family finances? Will the person be able to deliver that important assignment at work? Those who grew up in families with drug or alcohol abuse often relate that they weren't able to bring friends home because they never knew if their home environment would be chaotic or peaceful.

- **Guilt:** As strange as it may seem, family members and close friends often blame themselves for the chemically dependent person's drug or alcohol addiction: "If only I weren't so ..." or "If only I were more ...." Children and spouses of drug or alcohol abusers are particularly vulnerable to this type of guilty thinking.

- **Suspicion:** As drug and alcohol abuse worsens, family members and friends become increasingly suspicious of the addict's behaviors. This suspicion often leads to accusations and conflicts.

- **Insecurity:** People who abuse drugs or alcohol become less and less dependable as their abuse progresses. Those around the addict feel less secure that their emotional and domestic needs will be met. For children who grow up in families of alcoholics or drug users, these feelings of insecurity can last a lifetime.

- **Disappointment:** A substance abuser's life is full of good intentions and broken promises. People who abuse drugs and alcohol aren't able to live up to their commitments and obligations and continually disappoint family and friends.

- **Isolation:** As the drug or alcohol problem gets worse, families may isolate themselves more and more from others to avoid the embarrassment or pain of facing the issue. They withdraw from outside contacts and support and develop unhealthy ways of coping with the situation. Their isolation prevents them from going outside the family for the help they need.

- **Resentment:** Alcoholics and drug addicts become progressively less able to handle their lives. Friends, coworkers, and family members often step in to carry the load. But as more unfair demands are placed on these loved ones, they often become angry and resentful.

Alcohol Abuse: Health Risks

Most adults drink alcoholic beverages from time to time. An occasional drink for non-pregnant individuals appears to have no negative effect on health. But drinking can progress almost imperceptibly over time from light social indulging to alcohol abuse. Health experts know chronic drinking can have major health risks.

Alcohol abuse affects every system of the body. These are some of the ways alcohol abuse can harm your health.

- **Brain and nervous system.** Alcohol dulls the brain and the nervous system, slowing reactions and making drinkers feel relaxed and tranquilized. It can also lower inhibitions and make a person aggressive or hostile. In higher doses, it may block memory ("blackouts") and impair concentration, judgment, coordination, and emotional reactions.

- **Liver.** The liver is one of the primary targets of chronic alcohol abuse. In alcoholic hepatitis, liver cells are damaged or destroyed as a result of fairly recent heavy drinking. Prolonged excessive drinking can lead to alcoholic cirrhosis, a condition in which large areas of the liver are destroyed or scarred. Symptoms of liver disease include swelling of the abdomen (ascites) and ankles (edema) and yellowing of the skin and eyes (jaundice). Liver damage is extremely serious and may be life threatening.

- **Skin.** The skin of heavy drinkers often appears flushed. Alcohol is a vasodilator that widens the skin's surface blood vessels. Over time, the blood vessels are unable to shrink back, and the skin takes on a permanently reddish look.

- **Heart.** Alcohol abuse takes its toll on the heart by damaging and weakening the muscular tissue, a condition known as cardiomyopathy.

- **Stomach.** If you've ever had too much too drink, you know alcohol can cause an upset stomach (gastritis). Alcohol is an irritant to the stomach lining. Over time, heavy drinking can cause chronic stomach problems, including peptic ulcer disease.

- **Accidents.** Alcohol is a factor in at least half of all traffic fatalities in the United States.

Chronic Drinking Can Have Major Health Risks

Alcohol Consumed During Pregnancy Can Harm the Fetus

Alcohol impairs coordination and judgment, so people under its influence often believe they are capable of driving. Motor vehicle injuries are only one type of accident related to alcohol use: Injuries and deaths from fires, boating accidents, water sports, snowmobiling, and other activities are also more common among participants who are intoxicated.

- **Reproductive system.** Men who drink heavily often complain of impotence. Alcohol dulls the nerves that control erection and ejaculation. Women who are chronic drinkers report lack of sexual drive. In addition, alcohol consumed during pregnancy can harm the fetus, resulting in fetal alcohol syndrome. Fetal alcohol syndrome is a leading cause of mental retardation in children. Low birth weight, slow development, and learning problems are also associated with alcohol consumption during pregnancy. (See *Alcohol: A Health Hazard for Women* below.)

- **Blood.** Chronic alcohol abuse can result in such problems as anemia and bleeding disorders.

Alcohol: A Health Hazard for Women

Alcohol poses special health risks for women. When given the same amount of alcohol as men, women develop a higher blood alcohol content per pound of body weight. Men have a higher proportion of body water (55 to 65 percent) than women (45 to 55 percent), so alcohol becomes more diluted in a man's body. This "concentration" effect may explain why women develop liver and brain disease after consumption of about half the amount of alcohol consumed by men.

Some researchers have suggested alcohol may be linked to the development of breast cancer. While the jury is still out on the alcohol-breast cancer question, some experts contend as little as three drinks per week may double a woman's risk of breast cancer.

Women who drink heavily have less regular ovulation and menstruation flow. They also have a lower sex drive.

Women who are moderate to heavy drinkers may bear children with fetal alcohol syndrome (FAS), which can cause a variety of health problems. Some symptoms of FAS follow.

- **Low birth weight and slow development:** FAS children tend to be small and emaciated. At puberty, FAS girls are often short, stocky, and overweight.

- **Mental retardation and learning disabilities:** Alcohol use during pregnancy causes one-third of all cases of mental retardation.

- **Central nervous system dysfunction:** Such dysfunction can include tremors, irritability, overreaction to sounds, feeding difficulties, speech problems, and hyperactivity.

- **Facial malformations:** These may be a small head; long, flattened midface; sunken nasal bridge; short, receding chin; and cleft palate.

- **Major organ malformation:** This includes muscle problems, skeletal defects, genital defects, kidney and urinary abnormalities, and heart valve defects.

Because no safe level of consumption during pregnancy or breast-feeding has been established, health professionals recommend that women abstain from all alcohol use during these times.

Alcoholism Warning Signs

Some people cannot use alcohol safely. Community studies in the United States have shown that between 13 and 15 percent of the adult population will have an alcohol abuse or dependence problem at some time in their lives. Warning signs that may signal a potential problem include:

- **A family history of alcohol abuse or dependence.** The predisposition for problems with alcohol appears to run in families, even among children not raised by alcoholic parents, which suggests a genetic link to this disorder.
- **An inborn "tolerance" for alcohol.** People vary widely in the amount of alcohol they can tolerate. Some appear to be able to drink large amounts with hardly any bad effects. This can lead to a "need" to drink more to obtain a high.
- **A growing tolerance for alcohol.** Even if someone isn't born with a high alcohol tolerance, over days, months, and

years of alcohol use, tolerance can grow and the person gradually "needs" to drink more alcohol to achieve the same effects.

- **Drinking to take care of life's problems.** Drinking alcohol as a way to cope with problems and stresses of life is a significant warning sign of potential problems.
- **Drinking to get drunk.** Some people, including a growing number of children and teenagers, drink with the goal of becoming drunk. This is a serious warning for alcohol dependence.
- **Increasing frequency of alcohol use.** Drinking more—and more often—can be a sign of potential alcohol dependence, especially if the person tries to hide his or her increased use.

If you're concerned with your level of drinking, or the drinking habits of someone you love, don't hesitate to seek help. *Alcohol dependence is a progressive disease that can be fatal.*

Tips for Wise Alcohol Use

Despite the dangers associated with alcohol use, not all use equals abuse. Most people can learn to use alcohol safely and responsibly. Try these ideas:

- ❑ **Set limits for yourself.** Decide not to exceed a certain number of drinks and then stick with this plan. A reasonable limit for a social occasion lasting several hours might be two beers or two mixed drinks.

The Predisposition for Alcohol Problems Appears to Run in Families

313

Many Prescription Drugs Can Be Addictive

❏ **Say no.** Friends may encourage you to have "just one more." Learn to say, "No thanks. I've had plenty."

❏ **Slow down and pace yourself.** The body is able to handle (metabolize) about an ounce of alcohol an hour. Sip your drinks and savor their flavor.

❏ **Dilute your drinks.** Your drinks last longer if you drink them diluted with water or a mixer such as soda or tonic. You'll still enjoy the flavor without the stronger effects of undiluted alcoholic drinks.

❏ **Eat while you drink.** Food slows the absorption of alcohol into the bloodstream.

❏ **Go nonalcoholic.** If you enjoy beer or wine, opt for nonalcoholic varieties that provide the flavor without the alcoholic effects. Or you can enjoy straight mixer.

❏ **Never mix drugs and alcohol.** Some drugs, including many prescription and over-the-counter varieties, can react adversely with alcohol.

❏ **Designate a driver.** Have someone in your party stay sober and drive.

What's the Effect of this Drug?

The term "drug" can refer to medicine or substances taken (usually voluntarily) to produce a temporary, often pleasurable effect. Sometimes medicinal drugs become so-called recreational drugs. For example, morphine can be used as a painkiller and it can produce a high that gives a sense of well-being and pleasure.

Some people believe prescription drugs are safe from abuse—after all, doctors prescribe them. But many prescription drugs, especially amphetamines ("diet pills"), depressants (barbiturates, tranquilizers), and narcotics (codeine, morphine) can be addictive.

The table on page 315 lists some of the drugs commonly abused, their effects, signs of their use, and their potential health risks.

Marijuana: Harmless Weed?

In the 1960s and 1970s, marijuana became the drug-of-choice for a generation. Since that time, more than 20 million people have experimented with this mind-altering drug derived from the *Cannabis sativa* plant. Many people believe marijuana is harmless. However, the drug's potency has increased in recent years, and so has the controversy over its use.

The "high" marijuana users experience comes from the plant's ingredient, delta-9-tetrahydrocannabinol, or THC. The effects of marijuana use include a faster pulse rate, bloodshot eyes, and a dry mouth and throat. The user may feel relaxed and happy. But the THC also impairs short-term memory, alters one's sense of time, and reduces the ability to perform tasks that require concentration, quick reactions, and coordination.

ILLICIT DRUGS

Drug	Effects	Signs of Use	Potential Health Effects
Amphetamines (uppers, speed, pep pills, bennies, diet pills)	Speeds up action of central nervous system (CNS): user feels energetic, excited	Weight loss, dilated pupils, insomnia, diarrhea, trembling	Hallucinations, heart problems, malnutrition, dependency, paranoia and violent behavior, death (from overdose); affects fetus
Cocaine (coke, blow, snow, crack, rock, ice)	Stimulates CNS: produces heightened sensations, sometimes hallucinations	Runny nose, dilated pupils, agitation, intoxication, shaking	Confusion, depression, convulsions, damaged nasal membranes, lung damage, dependency, coma, paranoia, cardiac arrhythmia/arrest, seizures, death
Depressants (barbiturates, barbs, goof balls, downers, blues; tranquilizers, Valium, Librium; methaqualone, soapers, quads, ludes)	Relaxes the CNS: produces drowsiness and lethargy	Intoxication, slurred speech, poor coordination, lack of balance	Confusion, loss of coordination, tolerance, dependency, seizures, coma, respiratory depression, potentially fatal withdrawal; especially dangerous with alcohol; affects fetus
Narcotics (heroin, H, horse, scag, junk, smack; morphine, M, dreamer; codeine; opium; methadone)	Lowers pain perception; produces temporary euphoria	Weight loss, lethargy, mood swings, sweating, slurred speech, sore eyes	Anxiety, depression, lethargy, apathy, loss of judgment and self-control, tolerance, dependency, convulsions, malnutrition, decreased sex drive, death; use of needles to administer drugs increases risk of hepatitis, HIV infection
Hallucinogens (LSD, acid; psychedelics; mescaline; designer drugs, MDA, DMT, STP; psilocybin; phencyclidine, PCP, angel dust)	Distorts reality: can produce both pleasant and frightening hallucinations	Dilated pupils, sweating, trembling, hot and cold sensations	Hallucinations, panic, flashbacks, long-term psychosis, depression, confusion, irrational behavior, tolerance, convulsions, severe neurologic damage, persistent memory and speech dysfunction, heart and lung failure, coma, death
Deliriants or inhalants (volatile substances: glue, cleaning fluids, lighter fluid, paint thinner, aerosol products; Amyl nitrite, poppers)	Produces mental confusion, hallucinations, giddiness, temporary euphoria	Dilated pupils, flushed face, confusion	Confusion, loss of coordination, hallucinations, nausea, convulsions, dependency, damage to lungs, brain, liver, kidneys, bone marrow
Cannabis (marijuana, pot, weed, dope, ganja, grass, Mary Jane, MJ; herb; hashish, hash, hash oil)	Alters mood, heightens perception, relaxes the body	Red eyes, dilated pupils, poor coordination, lethargy, nausea	Confusion, loss of coordination, decreased motivation, dependency, paranoia, impaired short-term memory and learning ability, decreased sex drive; may damage brain, heart, lungs, and reproductive system; affects fetus

Most Surveys Show Diet Pills Aren't Effective in Keeping the Weight Off

The results of research on other possible adverse effects of marijuana use is controversial at best. There is some evidence that smoking the drug may cause cellular changes in the lungs that may be a precursor to cancer. Other studies have suggested that pot may temporarily impair fertility in both men and women. Some researchers suggest that while the drug isn't physically addictive, some users may become psychologically dependent on it. But research on the drug is far from conclusive, and there's much scientists don't know about its long-term effects.

Marijuana's reputation as a "street drug" has impaired acceptance of its therapeutic use for certain health problems. Evidence suggests that marijuana can reduce eye pressure for glaucoma sufferers, decrease nausea in cancer patients receiving chemotherapy and radiation, and increase appetite in persons with AIDS.

The Skinny on Diet Pills

Most of us want to lose a few pounds at some time or another. If you watch the ads on television, maybe you've been tempted to try the over-the-counter "diet" pills.

Most appetite suppressants—both over-the-counter and prescription varieties—contain phenylpropanolamine, or PPA, a mild stimulant chemically similar to amphetamines. Taken in recommended doses (75 milligrams), PPA appears to cause few problems. However, many people, especially teenagers, take more than the recommended dose.

Studies have shown PPA may cause headaches, dry mouth, alterations in bowel movements, insomnia, and, in rare cases, irregular heartbeat. Experts say even minor overdoses of PPA can cause side effects.

If PPA actually worked it would be easy to understand the popularity of diet pills. But it doesn't. Some studies have shown participants in diet programs that include diet pills, exercise, and calorie restriction lose more weight in the short-term than dieters who do not take the pills. But after the dieters stop taking the pills, they quickly regain the weight. They may depend on the pills to keep the pounds off.

Most surveys show diet pills aren't effective in keeping the weight off. Pill manufacturers suggest dieters start taking the pills again as soon as they've regained a few pounds. However, doctors don't know what the health effects of taking PPA over a long period of time might be.

If you need to lose weight, the best advice is to stay away from diet pills. A well-balanced diet and regular exercise are the keys to weight loss (see Chapter 2, *Weight Control*).

Sleeping Pills: R_x for Sleeplessness

All of us have suffered through a sleepless night. And some of us who have difficulty sleeping turn to sleeping pills for relief. Sleep experts say sleeping pills may provide short-term relief, but they can also cause long-term problems.

Over-the-counter sleeping aids, such as Sominex or Nytol, are antihistamines, primarily diphenhydramines, which do indeed cause drowsiness. But these products interfere with the sleeper's ability to reach the stage of deep sleep. The person doesn't sleep deeply enough to wake refreshed.

In addition, antihistamines can leave one feeling "hung over" with drowsiness and can cause confusion and difficulty urinating. After a few nights of use, these sleep remedies may lose their sleep-inducing effectiveness.

Prescription sleeping pills are the more powerful benzodiazepines—sedatives that depress the central nervous system, relax the brain and muscles, and reduce anxiety. These drugs can induce the more restful stage two sleep and help those with insomnia break the cycle of sleeplessness. But for some users, they only help in the short-run. After a few weeks, the body adapts and their effectiveness wears off.

While the risk of benzodiazepine use is relatively low when the pills are taken in low doses for short periods, they can be dangerous if misused or taken for longer periods. They can cause nausea, fainting, dizziness, blurred vision, anxiety, and hallucinations. Extended use may result in liver damage. They can become habit-forming and cause users to experience withdrawal symptoms and "rebound insomnia" when they stop taking the pills.

NONDRUG ALTERNATIVES

Instead of sleep-in-a-pill, try these nondrug alternatives:

❑ Have a physical exam to rule out health problems.

❑ Cut caffeine.

❑ Eliminate alcohol, especially within two hours of bedtime.

❑ Go to bed and get up at the same time every day.

❑ Don't nap during the day.

❑ Exercise regularly, but not immediately before bedtime.

❑ Relax before retiring. Take a bath. Do some gentle stretching exercises.

❑ Read *Insomnia: When the Sandman Won't Come*, page 233.

The Steroid Rage

Kids and adults in gyms across the nation are swallowing or injecting huge amounts of anabolic steroids, synthetic versions of the hormone testosterone, to pump up muscles, be stronger, and look better. But they're putting their health at grave risk.

Anabolic steroids, known among users as "'roids" or "juice," can make muscles bigger and stronger in just a few months. But one of the biggest problems with steroid use is users usually take doses far greater than those recommended by the Food and Drug Administration for medical use. Users often "stack" steroids, that is, they take several different types of steroids during one "cycle" of several weeks or months of use.

Not all of the health effects, particularly long-term effects, of steroid abuse are known. However, experts do know that because steroids mimic the actions of testosterone, they shut down men's natural testosterone production. These are a few of the other possible side effects of these popular muscle-bulkers:

Sleeping Pills Should Be Used Only in Low Doses for a Short Time

Set a Date to Quit Smoking and Stick to It!

- Increased risk of liver disorders, kidney disease, immune system disturbances, and reproductive system disruptions
- Lower high-density lipoproteins (HDLs or "good" cholesterol) and increased risk of heart disease
- Increased risk of hypertension, heart attack, and stroke
- Decreased sex drive
- Increased breast size (in men) and, in both men and women, male pattern baldness, acne, and an increase in facial and body hair
- Lower sperm counts
- Personality changes, including bouts of rage and aggression
- Menstrual irregularities
- Premature stopping of bone growth in teens
- Spontaneous tendon rupture

In addition, steroid users risk becoming dependent on steroids.

Kick the Nicotine Habit

You know smoking is bad for your health, but if you've ever tried to quit, you know what a powerfully addictive drug nicotine can be. Nicotine may be so addicting because it can act as a stimulant, a relaxant, or a memory- or performance-enhancer. If you're a smoker, you know smoking can become an integral part of how you cope with life.

Try these proven quit-smoking strategies:

- ❑ **Make a list of all the benefits of being smoke-free.** These include more energy, better sense of taste and smell, less risk of lung disease and other medical conditions, and more spending money.
- ❑ **Set a quit date and stick with it.** Mark it on your calendar. Make sure it isn't a holiday or other stressful time.
- ❑ **Get support.** Friends, family, or ex-smoker support groups can help.
- ❑ **Develop alternative strategies to deal with stressful situations where you'll be tempted to smoke.** Carry snacks or gum. Learn relaxation techniques such as deep belly breathing (see Chapter 5, *Coping with Stress*, for relaxation techniques).
- ❑ **Stay away from temptations to smoke.** Avoid bars or other places you're likely to smoke.
- ❑ **Use your mind.** "See" yourself as a nonsmoker.
- ❑ **Set up a reward system.** Mark reward dates on your calendar. Treat yourself at one week smoke-free, two weeks, one month, and so on.
- ❑ **Exercise.** Regular exercise helps you beat stress and makes you feel better. It also helps keep off the extra pounds some people put on after they quit smoking.

WHEN YOU NEED HELP TO QUIT

If self-help strategies don't work, medical science has come up with two tools to help you kick the habit: nicotine gum and nicotine patches.

Surveys have shown that 85 percent of smokers have tried at one time or another to quit. Virtually all returned to smoking because they were unable to deal with the intense cravings. Nicotine gum (Nicorette), available with a prescription, allows the smoker to obtain nicotine in a safer form, without the carbon monoxide and other chemicals that contribute to cancer and heart disease. It enables smokers to stop smoking without going through the traumatic symptoms of withdrawal. Smokers stop smoking and use the gum for 4 to 12 months. Then they gradually taper off the gum.

But some would-be ex-smokers find chewing as many as 12 sticks of nicotine gum per day to alleviate cravings difficult. They may also experience unpleasant side effects such as hiccups, indigestion, nausea, and mouth irritation. Another tool in the fight against nicotine addiction is the nicotine patch. The nicotine patch has none of the problems of nicotine gum, except it can occasionally irritate the skin. Nicotine patches are available with a prescription.

Keep in mind, though, that neither nicotine patches nor gum can help you quit smoking unless you want to quit smoking. You've got to make the commitment to kick the habit—the patches and gum are tools to help.

Kids and Substance Abuse

Anyone can abuse drugs and alcohol, but young people are especially at risk. They want to look and act sophisticated and grown up. They're pressured

SMOKELESS TOBACCO

Some people chew smokeless tobacco, believing it is less addictive and safer than cigarette smoking. It is not a safe choice! The nicotine content of smokeless tobacco is quite high, making it highly addictive. Also, use of chewing tobacco has been associated with cancers of the mouth. Efforts to educate the public about the risks of smokeless tobacco are targeting teenagers who, wishing to imitate their favorite sports heroes or country and western stars, may pick up the habit without realizing the possible consequences.

❏ ❏ ❏

by friends or other peers to "just try it." They desperately long to fit in, and plenty of other kids are experimenting with drugs and alcohol. With a cornucopia of drugs and alcohol widely and cheaply available to young people, it's no wonder drug and alcohol use among our youth is rising at an alarming rate.

What can you do about the problem?

❏ **Take time to talk.** Spend time with your child talking about how he or she thinks and feels about drugs and other issues. Ask for your child's opinion about family decisions and other concerns. Help your child open up by asking questions such as, "How do you feel about that?" "What do you think about this?" When discussing drugs and alcohol, don't lecture or talk down to your child. And develop your listening skills. Help your children to talk freely with you without fear of reprimand or judgment.

Drug and Alcohol Use Among Our Youth is Rising at an Alarming Rate

Learn All You Can About the Signs of Drug and Alcohol Use

❏ **Help build your child's self-esteem.** Make your children feel special and appreciated by spending time alone with each child. Go shopping, play your teen's favorite sport, go out for dinner or for ice cream, go for a walk or see a movie. It doesn't matter what the two of you do together, as long as it helps strengthen the bond between you.

❏ **Set limits.** Part of your responsibility as a parent is to set limits for your children—what is acceptable and what is not. You have to let them know what behaviors you will not tolerate.

❏ **Be informed.** Learn all you can about the signs of drug use and the health risks. Give your kid the facts, not horror stories.

❏ **Stay involved.** Most of us are busy—often, so busy we don't make time to be involved in the lives of our children. Take time to get involved. Get to know your child's friends. Learn what your child does for recreation. Become knowledgeable about his or her school involvement. Spend time participating in antidrug activities together.

❏ **Provide your child with tools to resist peer pressure to use drugs.** Kids can give friends or acquaintances an excuse: "No, my parents would kill me." They can simply say why they don't want to use: "No, I've seen how it affects some of the kids at school and I don't want to use." They can use a delay tactic: "Thanks, but right now I don't want any." Changing the subject can work, too: "No thanks, but I'd really like a soda. My throat is dry." Or you can advise them to simply avoid situations where they might be pressured or tempted to use drugs or alcohol.

❏ **Face up to your own substance use.** You're in a poor position to advocate abstinence if you drink, smoke, or use other drugs. If you use alcohol or drugs and then proceed to confront your teenagers about their use, they will have every reason to resent the double standard.

❏ **Get support.** Talk with other adults—your spouse, friends, a counselor—to get some perspective on the problem.

❏ **Find help.** If your child needs help with a drug or alcohol problem, don't delay seeking that help. Too often parents don't want to face the problem, so they enable their child to continue using. Instead, face the facts and get help for your child and your family.

DOES YOUR CHILD HAVE A DRUG PROBLEM?

Sometimes it's difficult to tell whether your child has a drug problem. Signs and symptoms of drug abuse are similar to a teen's "normal" behavior—secrecy, independence from family, new interests. How can you tell whether your child uses drugs? Look for these signs.

• Change in performance at school

• Tardiness or absences

• Behavior changes

• Less interest in the family

• Erratic mood swings

• A new or different group of friends

• Paraphernalia (pipes, papers, tin foil)

• Physical symptoms (dilated pupils, red eyes, changes in weight)

❏ ❏ ❏

Finding Help for an Addiction

If you or someone you care about has a problem with drugs or alcohol, the good news is help is available. Try the following resources.

- **Referral sources:** You can get referrals to programs and substance abuse professionals through your employer's Employee Assistance Program (EAP), school guidance counselors, or state or local mental health agencies. Don't overlook your family physician as an important resource. Your doctor can suggest sources of assistance as well as evaluate any medical complications that may occur as a result of drug or alcohol use.

- **Professional help:** Ask for assistance from substance abuse programs or psychiatrists, psychologists, or mental health therapists trained in chemical dependency. Both residential and outpatient treatment programs are available.

- **Self-help groups:** Even with treatment, most people find they need the continuing support of self-help groups such as Alcoholics Anonymous (AA), Narcotics Anonymous (NA), or Cocaine Anonymous, among others. These are listed in the white pages of your phone book.

- **Information sources:** If you wish to learn more about drugs and alcohol, groups such as the National Council on Alcoholism and the National Institute on Drug Abuse can help.

Intervention: A Family Affair

Drug or alcohol addiction is a cunning disease. It actually fools the addict into believing he doesn't have a problem. For a time, the addict convinces himself he can handle it—that the drugs or alcohol aren't really causing problems. Even when problems become more obvious, some addicts maintain, "It's no big deal." This response is denial, and denial can keep a person in the cycle of addiction for years.

If you have a close friend or family member caught in denial, an **intervention** may be needed. Led by a trained drug and alcohol counselor, friends and family members confront the abuser with several specific incidents when the person's drug or alcohol use caused them pain. They speak with honesty and with love. The intervention is not meant to be punitive. At the end of the confrontation, each person says he or she is willing to break off contact with the addict unless the addict is willing to go into immediate treatment.

Interventions are difficult for everyone involved. However, they can be highly effective. They require advance planning and preparation. For example, each person who speaks in the intervention must practice what he or she is going to say. Arrangements must be made ahead of time to place the person immediately into a treatment center.

Denial Can Keep a Person in the Cycle of Addiction for Years

321

Interventions can also backfire. A confrontation that is too dramatic or punitive can provoke rage and more denial on the part of the addict. Interventions should only be conducted by a trained and experienced drug and alcohol counselor. Call addiction treatment clinics or the mental health society in your area for referrals.

Helping a Loved One Stay Drug-Free

You Can Help an Addict Stay on the Road to Recovery

No one can make another person face his or her drug problem. However, once the person has recognized a problem exists, you can help the addict stay on the road to recovery. Try these strategies:

❏ **Be available.** One of the biggest problems people with drug or alcohol problems face in sobriety is giving up the lifestyle associated with their substance use. It's likely many of their friends and acquaintances drink or use drugs. Now that your friend or family member is clean and sober, he may feel alone and without friends. Call him. Suggest a date for coffee or a movie. Let the person know you're available for companionship.

❏ **Encourage exercise.** Many people who use drugs and alcohol adopt other unhealthy habits such as a sedentary lifestyle. Encourage the person to become physically active—take a walk, ride a bike, play tennis. The exercise not only helps take her mind off using drugs and alcohol, but the physical activity helps release endorphins, the body's own "feel good" chemicals.

❏ **Offer to attend meetings.** Twelve Step support groups such as Alcoholics Anonymous and Narcotics Anonymous have proved very effective in helping people stay off drugs and alcohol. However, attending those first few meetings can be intimidating. Offer to go along. In most communities, meetings are available at a variety of locations throughout the day and evening.

❏ **Practice drug-free confrontations.** Being free of drugs or alcohol means facing difficult situations without a familiar crutch. After the person has some sobriety and has had other small successes in recovery, help him face those difficult situations without drugs. Perhaps one situation is talking to the boss without being high. Or maybe it's being in a favorite country western bar and drinking only soda. Do some role-playing first so he feels more comfortable in the real situation.

❏ **Listen.** Getting sober after years of drinking or drug use can provoke a wide range of emotions for the addict. Often people use drugs and alcohol to mask painful feelings such as sadness and anger. Without the drugs, these old feelings emerge. The person may also feel guilty and remorseful over incidents that occurred during her years of drinking or using drugs. Allow the addict to talk about these feelings. Be a good listener. Don't argue with the person or judge her actions. Show your concern by being actively attentive.

FIRST AID

AND

SAFETY

*I*f you or a loved one were bitten by a snake or broke a bone
and medical help wasn't readily available, would you know what
to do? According to the National Safety Council, more than
150,000 Americans die each year as a result of accidents. Many
of these deaths could be prevented with prompt first aid. Even
more could be avoided with some commonsense safety
precautions.

This chapter describes how to handle common medical problems
ranging from bites to sunburns. You'll get tips on first aid and
self-care, injury prevention, and recognizing when you need to see
the doctor. In addition, there's advice on auto, bike, fire, and
street safety, among other topics, to make your life a little safer.

❑ ❑ ❑

Do You Know Which Bites Require Medical Treatment?

Bites and Stings: Should You Self-Treat?

Bites and stings come in all shapes, sizes, and degrees of seriousness. They can cause a small, bothersome itch or a life-threatening wound. Some, such as mosquito bites, can be easily treated at home. Others, such as human bites or scorpion stings, require immediate medical care in an emergency department. The question is, how can you tell if you should self-treat or if you need to see a doctor?

Use these guidelines. See a doctor for:

- **A human bite.** Doctors agree human bites are especially dangerous because the human mouth is full of bacteria. In fact, humans have more bacteria in the mouth than any wild animal. A person with any blood-borne infection may be able to transmit it to others through a bite. Any human bite that breaks the skin should be treated by a medical professional.

- **A poisonous snake bite.** Fortunately, the United States has only a few types of poisonous snakes. The most common is the rattlesnake, which gets its name from the interlocking joints at the end of its tail which make a rattling or buzzing sound when shaken. Other poisonous snakes in this country include the copperhead, the coral snake, and the cottonmouth or water moccasin, all found mainly in the southern part of the United States.

- **A poisonous spider bite or scorpion sting.** Two U.S. spiders, the black widow and the brown recluse, are poisonous. In addition, the variety of scorpion found in Arizona and southern California can deliver a lethal sting. (See the sidebar, *Poisonous Insects*.) If you're bitten by a spider you can't identify, get medical treatment.

- **A wild animal bite.** Most animals in the wild stay away from humans. Those who get close enough to inflict a bite may have rabies.

- **Broken skin or a deep puncture wound.** Animal and human bites can introduce a large number of microorganisms into the body. These microorganisms can cause an infection. And unlike a cut or scrape wound, a puncture wound can carry debris and bacteria deep inside.

- **A bite that causes severe bleeding.** Apply pressure with your hand, a towel, gauze, or other dressing (don't cut off circulation). Elevate the area and go straight to the emergency department.

- **A bite on the hand or face.** Infection that enters a wound in the hand can spread quickly, possibly destroying tissue. Facial wounds should be closed as closely as possible for cosmetic reasons. In addition, with any facial injury, there is a risk that infection can enter the brain.

- **A bite that causes a severe reaction.** Some people react to bites or stings with a severe allergic reaction called anaphylactic shock. *This is a potentially fatal medical emergency that requires immediate medical attention.* See the sidebar, *Signs of Anaphylactic Shock,* page 331.

- **A bite that becomes infected.** Even bites that don't require immediate medical attention can become infected. See your doctor if your bite wound becomes red, swollen, and painful, or you develop red streaks in the area or a yellowish-greenish discharge.

BITE SELF-CARE

Many common bites can be safely treated at home. However, if you have any doubts, see your doctor. Use these self-care tips:

- ❑ **Stop the bleeding.** Use your hand, a clean towel, or a tissue and apply firm pressure directly to the area.

- ❑ **Wash the wound thoroughly.** Use soap and water to remove any debris.

- ❑ **Apply an antiseptic ointment.** To help prevent infection, apply a thin layer of an ointment such as Bacitracin or Neosporin. Cover with an adhesive bandage.

The Trouble with Ticks

Ticks attach themselves to humans and other mammals by burrowing their heads into the skin. The bites of most ticks are generally not serious, but some ticks do transmit disease. Two of these diseases are Rocky Mountain spotted fever and Lyme disease. If you develop the symptoms described here, and you were recently in a wooded or grassy area where ticks may be present, get medical treatment. Report any tick bites or exposure to your physician.

ROCKY MOUNTAIN SPOTTED FEVER

You'd never guess it by the name, but Rocky Mountain spotted fever occurs most often in the eastern part of the United States, usually in late spring and early summer. This disease is transmitted by the dog tick in the eastern regions, by the wood tick in the western states, and other ticks in the southern part of the country.

Symptoms, which usually develop in 3 to 14 days, occur in two stages. The first set of symptoms include the following:

- Severe headache
- Muscle aches
- Nausea and vomiting
- Sore throat
- Fever and chills

Some people also develop a cough, stomach pain, restlessness, and insomnia. About three days after the first symptoms begin, a red rash appears on the hands and feet, eventually spreading to the arms, legs, and chest. Most people recover from Rocky Mountain spotted fever when treated promptly with antibiotics, but severe cases can be fatal.

LYME DISEASE

Some deer ticks carry Lyme disease, which gets its name from an outbreak of the disease in Lyme, Connecticut, in 1980. Most cases of Lyme disease occur on the east coast from Massachusetts to

Many Common Bites Can Be Safely Treated at Home

POISONOUS INSECTS

Black widow spiders range in size from ¾ inch to 1½ inches long and have black, round bodies with a bright, red "hourglass" on the abdomen.

Symptoms of a black widow spider bite can include:

- A sharp, stinging pain
- Muscle cramps within 15 minutes to 2 hours
- Fever, chills, nausea, dizziness, weakness, headache, abdominal pain, and chest pain

Brown recluse spiders (also called hobo, wood, or fiddler spiders) are small, ½– to ⅝–inch long brown, flat spiders with a "violin" shape on their undersides.

Symptoms of a brown recluse spider bite can include:

- Mild, stinging pain at first, but intense pain may develop 8 to 24 hours later
- A blue-gray halo at the site
- Fever, chills, weakness, nausea, vomiting, and joint and muscle pain
- A blister at the site; depending on the severity of the bite, an ulcer may form

Scorpions, yellow to greenish-yellow crab-like insects, are ¾ inch to 3 inches long.

A scorpion delivers a sting with a device (telson) at the end of its tail. The sting may not cause any pain initially, but its symptoms can include rapid heartbeat and breathing, high blood pressure, increased salivation, vision changes, difficulty speaking, and lack of coordination. In general, because of their size, children and small adults are more seriously affected by a dose of insect poison.

Tarantulas are poisonous, and their bites are painful but usually harmless. Still, a tarantula bite should not be ignored, especially in children and small adults.

❏ ❏ ❏

Maryland, in the midwest in Wisconsin and Minnesota, and on the west coast in California and Oregon, although nearly every state has reported cases.

Flu-like symptoms of Lyme disease can develop a few days to a few weeks after you've been bitten.

- Chills and fever
- Head and body aches
- Stiffness
- A red-ring "bull's-eye" rash at the site of the bite

If diagnosed in this early stage, Lyme disease is effectively treated with antibiotics. If not treated early, these symptoms may recur for months or years. "Lyme arthritis"—chronic joint pain and swelling—may occur. Some people with Lyme disease also develop problems in the heart and brain. All of these symptoms can be treated with antibiotics.

Protect Yourself from Tick Bites

Because of its size, you may not realize the pinhead-sized deer tick—which is smaller than the ticks that carry Rocky Mountain spotted fever—has attached itself to you. That's why preventing tick bites is the key to avoiding exposure to Lyme disease.

- ❏ **Dress appropriately.** When walking in woody or grassy areas, wear long pants (tucked in socks), a long-sleeved shirt, shoes, and a hat.
- ❏ **Apply insect repellent.** Use one that contains DEET

(diethyltoluamide) on any exposed skin (except the face) and on clothes. Repellents that contain DEET last four to eight hours.

❏ **Check children, pets, and yourself every few hours for ticks.** Ticks most often attach to humans around the neck, waistline, and sock line. Like fleas, ticks love to use dogs for transport. Check your dogs thoroughly after a romp in wooded areas or areas thick with brush. Bathe them with an antiflea, antitick shampoo.

REMOVING A TICK

So what should you do if a tick does attach itself to you? First, don't panic. In the case of Lyme disease, usually a tick must remain attached to the skin for 24 to 48 hours to transmit the disease.

A tick's mouthparts are barb-shaped, and can remain imbedded if not removed properly, leading to an infection at the bite site.

If you live in or travel to an area with ticks, consider purchasing a tool called a "tick licker," or other similar device. Using tweezers to grasp an imbedded tick is generally not recommended. It takes a great deal of practice to apply just the right amount of pressure not to crush the tick and not to separate the tick's body from its head. Tick lickers are small, lightweight, and easier to use than tweezers. They are available in stores that sell camping, hunting, and sports equipment.

If you must use tweezers, *carefully* grasp the tick as close to the skin as possible, and gently but firmly pull the tick straight up. *Do not use a lighted match or cigarette to try to get the insect to let go and back out. It doesn't work, and it can cause burns.*

Be sure you've removed all of the tick, and flush it down a toilet. Wash the area thoroughly with soap and water. Apply a local antiseptic such as alcohol or an antibiotic cream to the bite. There's no need to see a doctor unless you develop swelling, redness, the bull's-eye rash, a fever, skin rash, or other symptoms. You may, however, want to save the tick's body in a jar for analysis, just in case you develop problems later.

Mosquitoes and More

We all know how pesty mosquitoes can be—buzzing around our ears, sometimes ruining warm summer nights. But we need to be aware of another fact about these annoying insects—some carry disease. Fortunately for us in the United States, only a very few mosquitoes carry disease, but this fact makes it no less important for you to take action to keep mosquitoes away from you and your home.

A small proportion of mosquitoes carry encephalitis, a virus that causes inflammation of the brain. The two types of encephalitis that mosquitoes can transmit are St. Louis and LaCrosse encephalitis. *Note: Mosquitoes do not transmit HIV, the virus that causes AIDS.* The northern house mosquito, the carrier of St. Louis encephalitis, breeds in small, stagnant bodies of water. The tree-hole mosquito, the carrier of LaCrosse encephalitis, got its name because of its practice of breeding in tree holes. Now,

A Small Proportion of Ticks and Mosquitoes Carry Disease

327

however, this mosquito is found most often breeding in discarded tires.

The majority of people bitten by an infected mosquito experience mild or no symptoms of encephalitis. But the symptoms developed by one to two percent of those bitten, generally five to fifteen days after the bite from the infected mosquito, are the same for both types of encephalitis.

Minor symptoms:

- Slight fever
- Headache

Severe infection may cause these symptoms:

- Severe headache
- High fever
- Neck stiffness
- Muscle aches
- Lack of coordination
- Disorientation
- Convulsions
- Coma

Mosquito-borne viruses can affect anyone, but St. Louis encephalitis usually occurs in people aged 55 years and older. Most people recover fully. Symptoms are usually milder in LaCrosse encephalitis, which occurs most often in children.

The key to preventing mosquito-borne disease is eliminating sites where mosquitoes can breed.

❏ Properly discard rubber tires, tin cans, and other items that can hold even small amounts of water.

❏ Look for items or areas in your yard that may hold water: Store buckets and watering cans inside, fill in low spots in the ground, empty water out of ornamental lawn items.

❏ Check for holes in door and window screens through which mosquitoes can enter the house.

❏ Use mosquito repellent. Follow label instructions for application.

Snakebite First Aid

If you live or vacation in an area where poisonous snakes reside, you should keep a snakebite kit on hand. Poisonous snakebites require immediate medical attention, but if you are bitten and can't get help right away, you'll need to know what to do until you can get to the nearest emergency department. Follow these steps.

❏ If possible, have someone catch and kill the snake and take it with you for identification. Do this only if it can be accomplished without excessive danger.

❏ Stay quiet, still, and warm. Try not to panic. Increased heart rate only pumps the venom faster through the body. Take long, slow breaths.

❏ Cleanse the wound with soap and water, if they are available, and cover it with clean gauze or other dressing. Don't apply ice, which may damage swollen tissues.

❏ If you're bitten on a limb, remove rings, shoes, socks, and other potentially restrictive items in case the limb swells. Keep the area still and resting below the heart.

To Prevent Mosquito-borne Disease, Eliminate Sites Where Mosquitoes Can Breed

❏ Do not apply any sort of tourniquet! Contrary to what you've seen in old western movies, a tourniquet is dangerous and not to be used in this circumstance.

❏ If you have a venom extractor available, try applying the suction device until you reach medical help. But do not delay transporting a snake bite victim to medical care because you're using a venom extractor. *Don't suck the venom with your mouth or cut the wound with a knife or other instrument.*

❏ Get to a hospital as quickly as possible. Have someone else drive you. Poisonous snake bites can quickly cause pain and weakness.

Prevent Bites Before They Happen

Bites, including insect bites, are not inevitable. Keep these prevention tips in mind:

❏ **Know the local varmints.** Be informed about the insects, spiders, snakes, and other animals likely to be in the area. For example, if you're in the southwest or the Rockies, become more knowledgeable about the habits of the area's scorpions and rattlesnakes.

❏ **Wear the right clothing.** Choose the appropriate clothing for the area and for the biting critters that live there. For example, if you're hiking in snake country, wear high-topped leather boots. If you're in the swamp lands of the south, consider long sleeves

STOP THE ITCH!

Insect bites are usually more bothersome than harmful. But as you've undoubtedly found each time you've had a run-in with a few mosquitoes, they can itch like crazy. Use these strategies to tone down the itch.

❏ **Use ice or cool compresses for 20 minutes at a time.** Ice decreases itch, inflammation, and pain. Cold works for nonpoisonous spider bites, too.

❏ **Apply Calamine lotion.** This time-tested, inexpensive stand by, available over the counter in pharmacies, is one of the most effective anti-itch compounds made.

❏ **Paint on a paste of baking soda and water.** Three teaspoons baking soda and one teaspoon water make a terrific anti-itch remedy.

❏ **Try over-the-counter antihistamines.** If your itching is severe, try an antihistamine. Be careful, however, as they can cause drowsiness: Don't use them if you need to drive or work, especially if your job involves operating machinery.

❏   ❏   ❏

and a hat with mosquito netting. Wear gloves when gathering firewood.

❏ **Stay away from wild animals.** Animals in the wild are just that—wild. An animal lethargic enough to allow you to touch it may be sick. Even so-called "harmless" animals, such as squirrels or deer, can transmit fleas and ticks that may carry serious illnesses.

❏ **Be wary of animals you don't know.** Too often people are bitten by domestic animals because they don't use common sense. They assume a dog or cat is friendly and it wants to be handled. Don't approach animals you don't know.

❏ **Use insect repellents.** Wear protective clothing and apply an insect repellent that contains DEET (diethyltoluamide).

Do not use insect repellent on infants or very young children. Protect them with clothing and netting. For toddlers and children up to about 8 or 9 years of age, use a low concentration of DEET—no higher than 20 percent. Children older than 12 years of age and adults can use concentrations of 45 to 65 percent. The 95 percent concentrations are becoming more common but they are not really more effective, and their use is associated with more side effects.

❑ **Eliminate mosquito-breeding areas.** These include any kind of standing water in your backyard and your neighborhood. Many communities have city- or county-operated mosquito abatement programs that can help.

❑ **Stay aware.** Be particularly careful in areas likely to house snakes or spiders. For example, use caution when turning over a rock or fallen branch. Don't reach or step into dark places, such as heavy underbrush. Avoid putting your hand into crevices while climbing; the best tip here is to wear gloves when climbing.

Take the Zing Out of Stings

It's part of the ritual of summer. You're walking along enjoying the feeling of fresh grass between your toes, when suddenly you feel a hot, painful sting. You've been stung by a bee or wasp.

Or maybe you're walking along the beach or wading in the shallow ocean waters and feel the sting of a jellyfish, stingray, or other venomous sea creature.

BEE, HORNET, AND WASP STINGS

In most cases, bee, hornet, and wasp stings are painful, but not deadly unless you're highly allergic to them. If you're stung by one of these winged creatures, try these self-care strategies:

❑ **Watch for signs of a severe reaction.** If the person has problems breathing, widespread swelling, severe pain, or loss of consciousness, get *immediate* medical help. (See the sidebar, *Signs of Anaphylactic Shock*, page 331.)

❑ **Scrape out the stinger.** Bees and some yellow jackets can leave a barbed stinger and venom sac in the skin that continues to release venom. (Other stinging insects have

DO YOU NEED A TETANUS SHOT?

Tetanus is a potentially fatal bacterial infection that can develop in wounds. If fang-like teeth cause a deep puncture wound or you step on a nail or a piece of broken glass, your chances of developing this serious infection soar.

The only surefire prevention for tetanus is the tetanus vaccine. Follow these guidelines.

You need a tetanus shot if:

❑ you're bitten and you've never had the three-series tetanus vaccine.

❑ you're bitten and you received your last tetanus booster more than five years ago.

❑ your wound is deep and you haven't had a shot in five years.

❑ your wound is minor and you haven't had a tetanus booster in the last ten years.

❑   ❑   ❑

smooth stingers that stay with the bug, not with you.) Check the sting site. If you see the stinger, remove it immediately by gently scraping it with a knife blade or fingernail. *Do not try to remove it with tweezers and be careful not to squeeze, grab, or press the stinger*, which can cause more venom to be pumped into the sting site.

❑ **Apply meat tenderizer.** Make a paste of a teaspoonful of meat tenderizer and a few drops of water. Apply directly on the sting. The enzyme, papain, in the tenderizer helps dissolve the toxins injected by the insect.

❑ **Try baking soda.** If you don't have meat tenderizer handy, try applying a paste of baking soda and water to relieve itching and swelling.

❑ **Cool the sting with ice.** Rubbing ice over the sting site can help relieve pain and reduce swelling and inflammation.

❑ **Take an antihistamine.** Over-the-counter antihistamines can help relieve itching.

SEA CREATURE STINGS

The stings of some marine critters such as the stonefish, scorpion fish, lion fish, weever fish, Portuguese man-of-war, and jellyfish can be serious. In some cases the pain and rashes from these stinging seafarers can be severe and bodywide and may result in death. If you or someone else has been stung by a sea creature, try these strategies:

❑ **Reassure the person.** Being stung by a jellyfish, stingray, or other venomous sea creature can be scary.

❑ **Remove the tentacle.** If the person has a jellyfish or Portuguese man-o-war tentacle on the skin, cover your hand with a glove, towel, or heavy cloth, and pull (don't rub) it off. *Do not touch the tentacle with an ungloved hand since it may still be capable of stinging. But note: Never remove the barbed spine of a stingray.*

❑ **Watch for signs of a severe reaction.** Call for help immediately if the person experiences any breathing difficulty, severe swelling, extreme pain, or loss of consciousness. (See *Signs of Anaphylactic Shock.*)

SIGNS OF ANAPHYLACTIC SHOCK

A sting can cause some people to have an extreme allergic reaction called *anaphylactic shock*. Anaphylactic shock is an antigen-antibody reaction that can cause complete collapse, and it can be life threatening. This is a medical emergency that requires immediate medical attention. Symptoms typically develop within 30 minutes. Call 911 or rush the person to the nearest hospital if you recognize any of these signs:

• Wheezing or difficulty breathing

• Dizziness

• Rapid heart rate

• Abdominal cramps

• Nausea and vomiting

• Hives

• Agitation

Anyone who has experienced an anaphylactic reaction should always carry an epinephrine (adrenalin) kit, commonly called an "epi" kit. (If you receive a prescription for an epi kit, be sure to have your doctor teach you how to use it.) The kit contains a syringe; the contents must be injected into the thigh. Once the shot is administered, call 911 and get the person to medical attention at once.

❑   ❑   ❑

Stings of Some Marine Critters Can Be Dangerous

❑ **Wash the injury with sea water**. Then apply alcohol. You can also use diluted household ammonia or lemon juice. *Do not use drinking water—fresh water could cause discharge of more venom.* Be careful not to touch the area with an unprotected hand. Then apply a thick paste of baking soda and water. You can also use sand, powder, or flour mixed with water.

❑ **Get medical help.** Stings from certain sea creatures can be deadly. Once first aid has been administered, transport the person to emergency medical help.

STING PREVENTION

The best strategy is to prevent painful stings. Here's how:

❑ **Become familiar with your local area or places you're visiting**. Find out if bees and wasps are common to the area. If you're going to be wading or swimming, find out which stinging sea creatures inhabit the area and learn how to spot them.

❑ **Keep your shoes on.** Whether you're in a meadow or wading on the beach, keep your shoes on to prevent stepping on a stinging insect or sea creature.

❑ **Wear light-colored, smooth-finish cotton clothing**. Studies have shown these fabric types attract fewer bees and yellow jackets. Also, avoid scented hair sprays, creams, and makeup and bright, shiny jewelry that can attract stinging insects. Bathe daily to prevent sweat buildup (yellow jackets love sweat).

❑ **Keep food and drinks covered.** Picnics are perfect places for bees and wasps. Look before you take that drink or a bite.

❑ **Never mess with a hive.** If you see a bee, hornet, or wasp nesting site, leave it alone.

Take the Ouch Out of Blisters

You've decided to dig up that new flower bed in the backyard, but after a couple of hours with the shovel, you find you've developed blisters on your hands. These are friction blisters caused by constant rubbing. To protect the inner structures from excessive friction, the body pads them with a water-containing fluid under the outer skin (epidermis). In a week to ten days, the fluid is reabsorbed by the body and new skin forms beneath the blister.

SHOULD YOU WORRY ABOUT KILLER BEES?

Scientists tell us that Africanized honey bees, called "killer bees" because of their aggressive nature, have travelled up from South America and are now in parts of the United States. Although the sting from these bees is no stronger than from the domestic honey bee, the Africanized bees often attack in greater numbers and the multiple stings can be fatal.

Experts say the killer bees probably won't advance much farther north than the Carolinas because they can't tolerate the cold winters. In areas where these aggressive bees might be, stay aware and don't disturb potential nesting sites. If you're attacked, run quickly into a building or car.

❑   ❑   ❑

Blisters can also be due to burns, allergic reactions, chemical irritations, and other medical problems such as cold sores and athlete's foot. However, the most common type of blister you'll encounter is the friction blister.

In most cases, you can self-treat your friction blister. Follow these tips:

- **Don't pop the blister.** The fluid-filled pad is protective. You can, however, drain a blister in a location where the pressure is causing intense pain. In this case, clean the blister and a needle with alcohol, and prick the blister near its edge. *Don't use a needle "sterilized" with a lighted match, which can introduce soot into the blister.* Gently press on the blister to drain the fluid. Leave the skin in place.

  For draining blisters on thickened skin such as the sole of the foot, you may need to soak the blister in Burow's solution (available over the counter in pharmacies). Soak for 15 minutes, three to four times a day to make draining easier.

- **Use moleskin.** If the blister is on the foot where shoes or boots will rub it, cut a hole in a piece of moleskin (available over the counter at pharmacies) and place it over the blister to relieve the friction.

- **Try over-the-counter pain relievers.** For blisters that cause pain and inflammation, take aspirin or ibuprofen (acetaminophen relieves pain but not inflammation).

- **Wash and use antibiotic ointment.** If your blister does break or if the blister pad can't provide enough protection, wash the blister, apply a thin layer of

A BACKPACKER'S GUIDE TO PREVENTING BLISTERS

There's nothing quite as painful as hiking ten miles or so, developing blisters half way through, and having to complete the trek with shoes or boots rubbing against the blisters. As a result, most backpackers are experts in preventing those painful pads. Try their suggestions:

- **Wear thick, dry socks and thin liner socks next to the skin.** The thick outer sock acts as a cushion and, in the winter, insulation. Many backpackers (and health care professionals) claim that for the best protection, you should wear liner socks made of a synthetic material such as polypropylene or drylene next to the skin. Proponents of these socks say the synthetic fibers "wick" blister-promoting moisture away from the skin. (Cotton, they say, retains moisture in its fibers, and wet cotton socks increase the risk of cold feet as well as blistering.) Still, many others give their support to cotton inside and out. Try both types of socks, and see what works best for you.

- **Carry a spare pair.** If you're hiking several miles, it's not a bad idea to tuck an extra pair of both inner and outer socks in your backpack, especially if you'll be out in hot or inclement weather, so you always have a dry pair.

- **Make sure shoes are well-broken in and fit well.** One of the biggest mistakes novice backpackers make is buying and wearing new boots for a long hike. To "break in" a new pair of shoes or boots, wear them for a few hours everyday before attempting a long hike.

- **Use foot powder.** It helps absorb excess moisture.

- **Keep shoes dry.** If possible, change your shoes at least twice a day if you have trouble with moist feet. Many athletes wear different shoes every other day to allow their shoes to thoroughly dry between wearings.

- **Opt for leather.** New fabrics have made leather hiking shoes and boots almost obsolete, but long-time backpackers say leather is still the best material for blister prevention. Leather contains microscopic pores that allow air to circulate and help keep the feet dry.

antibiotic ointment, such as Bacitracin or Neosporin, and cover it with an adhesive bandage. Change the dressing at least once a day.

❑ **Watch for signs of infection.** If you have increased pain, redness, swelling, or a yellowish-green discharge, notify your doctor.

Coping with Bruises

Most Bruises Aren't Serious

Smack your leg on the coffee table and you'll likely be rewarded with a purplish blue bruise. When our bodies take a blow, blood vessels in the surrounding skin can be damaged and leak blood. This blood causes the purplish color we call a bruise.

Fortunately, most bruises aren't serious, and they'll heal on their own, usually in less than two weeks. *Of course, any unexplained bruises should be checked out by your doctor.* But if you have had a blow that resulted in a large bruise, you can use these ideas while you wait for the body to reabsorb the blood and heal itself.

THIS BURN NEEDS A DOCTOR—QUICKLY!

See a doctor if:

• your hands, face, feet, or genitals are burned.
• you have a large second-degree burn or any third degree burn.
• you have an electrical burn.
• your blisters are one inch or larger across.

❑ ❑ ❑

❑ **Apply an ice pack to stem the spread of the bruise and reduce pain and swelling.** If you use ice immediately, you may be able to reduce the size of the bruise. Hold the ice on for 20 minutes; off for 10.

❑ **Keep it elevated to prevent blood from pooling in the area.** Elevate the area for 30 minutes each hour for the first few hours.

❑ **Use heat.** After the first day, apply moist or dry heat for 30 minutes at a time, three to four times a day, to relax the muscles surrounding the bruise.

❑ **Take acetaminophen.** If your bruise is painful, take acetaminophen. Don't take aspirin or ibuprofen, which interfere with blood clotting and can make the bruise worse.

Is This a Serious Burn?

Burns—ranging from reddened skin to severely painful blistering—can be caused by flames, hot liquids, steam, chemicals, electricity, and even the sun. To know what to do when you get a burn, you need to know how serious it is. Doctors classify burns by severity into first degree, second degree, and third degree.

First degree: The outer layer of the skin (epidermis) is red and tender. These superficial burns cause pain and redness but no blistering, and they can usually be treated at home. Most minor sunburns and household burns are first degree.

Second degree: These burns involve not only the outer epidermis, but also the underlying skin (dermis). Fluid leaks from damaged blood vessels and causes blistering. These moist, mottled, blistered burns are painful but usually aren't serious unless they're large or they become infected.

Third degree: A third degree burn is a medical emergency that requires *immediate* medical attention. These deep burns involve the outer and inner layers of skin and can destroy the hair, nerves, blood vessels, glands, fat, and even muscle and bones. The burns usually appear white or black and are generally painless because the nerves have been destroyed. Third degree burns can be fatal if they cover a large area.

First degree and most second degree burns can be treated at home. However, if the second degree burn is large, or if the burn involves the face, hands, feet, or genitals, see a doctor right away.

BURN SELF-CARE

These tips can ease minor burns:

❏ **Immediately apply cool (not icy) water to the burn.** Continue until the pain subsides. If the burn is caused by a chemical or corrosive, such as drain cleaner, immediately flush the area with water and continue flushing for 15 to 30 minutes.

❏ **Take over-the-counter pain relievers.** Aspirin and ibuprofen can help reduce pain and inflammation. (Acetaminophen relieves pain but not inflammation.)

❏ **Apply aloe vera once pain has subsided.** This medicinal plant helps speed burn healing. Keep a potted aloe vera plant around and simply snip off a leaf when needed and rub the burn with the gelatinous insides. Or buy a bottle of aloe vera gel (at a drug or health food store) and keep it in the refrigerator.

❏ **Don't pop blisters.** If your burn has blistered, leave the blisters intact. If blisters rupture, wash the area gently with soap and water, treat with an antibiotic ointment, and cover with a sterile bandage.

Learn CPR

Cardiopulmonary resuscitation, or CPR, is a set of techniques for treating a person whose heart or breathing has stopped. Learning CPR is easy and something we should all put on the top of our priority list. CPR can't be effectively learned from a book. You'll need a CPR class for that. But we'll give you the CPR basics.

The three elements of CPR are as simple as "A,B,C":

A—Keep the Airways clear.

B—Restore Breathing.

C—Restore Circulation.

❏ **Keep the Airways clear.** In an unconscious person, the tongue can fall back and block the upper part of the airway. Tilt the person's head back (see Fig. 10.1). If the airway is blocked by vomit, mucus, mud, or dentures, use your finger and "hook" out the debris. *If you suspect the person has a back or neck injury, do not reposition the head.* (See Fig. 10.4.)

Take a CPR Class to Learn this Life-Saving Technique

335

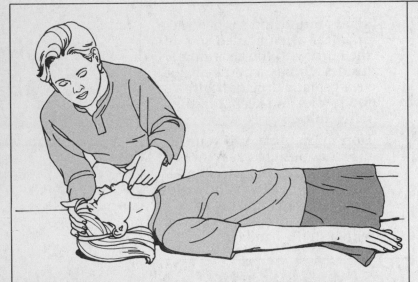

Fig. 10.1 The first step in mouth-to-mouth resuscitation is opening the airway. If you do not suspect a head, neck, or back injury, place one hand on the victim's head and gently lift the chin with the other hand to open the airway.

Fig. 10.2 Look, listen, and feel for breathing for 3 to 5 seconds. Place your ear next to the person's mouth and watch the chest for the rise and fall of breathing.

Fig. 10.3 Pinch the victim's nose closed with your fingers, place your mouth over her mouth, take a deep breath and blow the air into her mouth.

❑ **Restore Breathing.** Once the airway is cleared, place your ear over the person's mouth and nose to check for breathing (see Figure 10.2). If the person still isn't breathing, you need to begin mouth-to-mouth resuscitation. With the person lying on her back, kneel at right angles to her shoulder, place one hand on the forehead, and support the head with the other hand under the neck. Now take a deep breath and immediately blow the air into her mouth. *Be sure to pinch both nostrils of the nose closed so air doesn't escape.* (See Fig. 10.3.) Repeat blowing air into her mouth at a rate of about 12 breaths per minute.

❑ **Restore Circulation.** After the first three or four breaths, if the person still has no pulse, you need to begin cardiac massage, also called external cardiac compression. *Note: Done improperly, this technique can fracture ribs and damage internal organs. Get training before you attempt cardiac massage.*

First Aid for Choking

One minute you're all enjoying a great meal together and the next, you or one of your companions is choking. If you or someone else doesn't react quickly and properly, a tragedy could result.

When a person chokes, food (or an object) becomes tightly stuck in the vocal cords, much like a cork in a bottle. The obstruction prevents the person from gagging, coughing, breathing, or asking for help. Unless the food or other obstruction is removed, the person suffocates. The old technique of slapping the person on the back doesn't work and may, in fact, lodge the food or other object more tightly in the throat (back slapping can be effective for children younger than one year old).

The **Heimlich maneuver** is a choking rescue technique designed to "pop" the obstruction out of the trachea with a squeeze that forces air out of the lungs. *Note*: If the choking victim loses consciousness, call 911 or the local emergency response team.

Here's how to perform the Heimlich maneuver:

1.   Step behind the person and wrap your arms around her waist.

2.   Make a fist with one hand, holding the thumb side against the person (see Figure 10.5), and grasp the fist with the other hand (see Figure 10.6). Thrust your fist forcefully *in and up*.

3.   If one thrust doesn't dislodge the blockage, try the maneuver again.

4.   If the person loses consciousness, lay her down face up, and apply the upper abdominal thrusts with the heel of your hand. Then turn the person's head sideways and use your finger to check for dislodged food.

There may be instances when you may need to modify the basic technique described above:

❑   **For an adult who is pregnant or overweight:** Modify the Heimlich maneuver by grasping the person higher up on the chest. Repeat the same in and up thrust (see Fig. 10.7).

❑   **If you're choking and no one comes to your rescue:** Perform the maneuver on yourself.

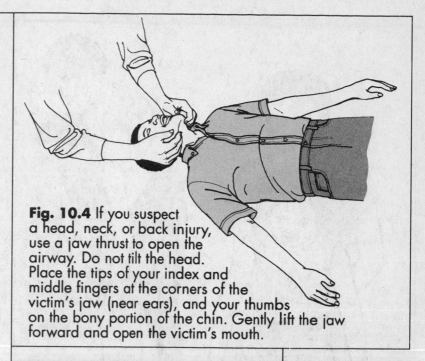

Fig. 10.4 If you suspect a head, neck, or back injury, use a jaw thrust to open the airway. Do not tilt the head. Place the tips of your index and middle fingers at the corners of the victim's jaw (near ears), and your thumbs on the bony portion of the chin. Gently lift the jaw forward and open the victim's mouth.

CPR FOR KIDS

CPR can be effectively used on infants and children. The steps are essentially the same as those for adults; however, you have to make a few modifications to compensate for smaller lung capacity and faster respiration rate.

❑   **Keep the airway clear.** Tip the head back and check with your finger to ensure the airway isn't blocked.

❑   **Restore breathing.** Cover and seal both the child's nose and mouth with your mouth and give four quick, gentle breaths (too much air can cause vomiting). (See illustration.)

❑   **Restore circulation.** If the infant still has no pulse, begin cardiac massage. *Note*: Do not perform cardiac massage unless you have received CPR training.

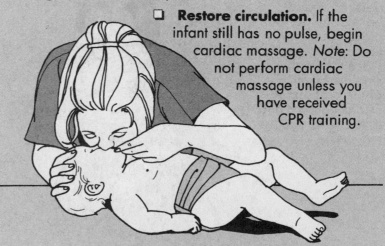

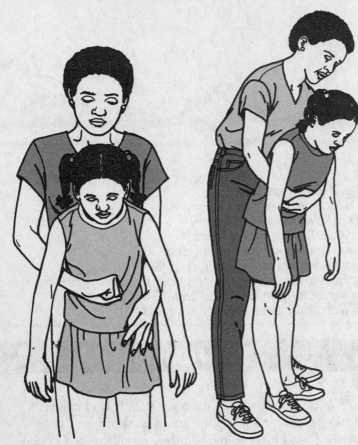

Fig. 10.5, 10.6 Heimlich maneuver. Stand behind person, wrap your arms around her waist. Place fist thumb side against the stomach just above the navel and well below the breastbone. Grasp your fist; press into stomach with quick upward thrusts.

Fig. 10.7 Perform chest thrusts on pregnant or overweight persons. Stand behind the person; place your arms under the armpits. Place the fist thumb side on the middle of the breastbone. Grasp your fist and give thrusts against the chest.

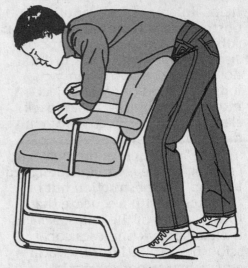

Fig. 10.8 To perform the maneuver on yourself, lean forward and press your abdomen over a firm object.

Lean over the back of a chair, dropping your abdomen onto it (see Fig. 10.8). This should have the same effect as the up-thrusts.

❑ **If the choking victim is an infant:** Follow these steps.

1. Lay the child face down on your forearm with your hand on the child's jaw to support the head. Keep the infant's head lower than the trunk. Support your arm on your thigh (see Fig. 10.9).

2. Use the heel of your other hand to deliver four forceful back blows.

3. If back blows fail to dislodge the object, lay your other forearm on the infant's back. Gently turn the infant over so he rests faceup on that forearm. Support the infant's head with your hand, and keep infant's head lower than the trunk (see Fig. 10.10).

4. Use two or three fingers to deliver four thrusts to the middle of the breastbone between the infant's nipples.

5. Repeat the maneuver until the object is expelled.

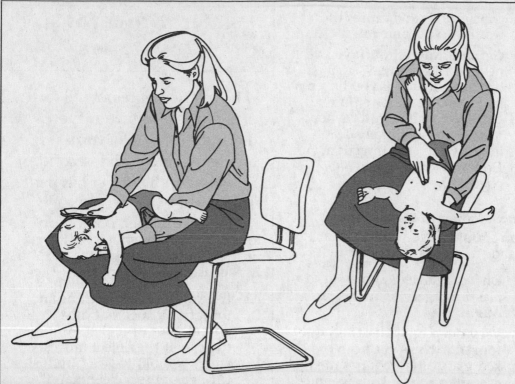

Fig. 10.9, 10.10 Lay a choking infant on your forearm; deliver four back blows. If object remains, turn the infant to rest faceup on your other forearm. With your fingers, deliver four thrusts to the middle of the breastbone.

Care for that Cut or Scrape

Life is full of cuts and scrapes. You probably know from first-hand experience that a scrape, where you horizontally remove skin, exposes a large number of nerves and usually hurts like crazy. A cut, a vertical slice into the skin, involves only a few nerves and, therefore, should hurt less. But if you've just gotten a paper cut, you may be hard to convince that fewer nerves are involved.

Here are the steps to treat minor scrapes and cuts at home:

❏ **Control the bleeding.** Apply firm pressure with a clean cloth or tissue until the bleeding stops. If possible, elevate the area above the heart.

❏ **Wash the wound with soap and water.** You can also use hydrogen peroxide.

❏ **Apply an antibacterial ointment.** Use an over-the-counter antibacterial product, such as Bacitracin or Neosporin, to reduce the risk of infection.

❏ **Close the wound.** If you've got a cut at least one-eighth to one-quarter inch wide, you'll need to close the cut with a butterfly or standard bandage to speed healing and reduce scarring.

❏ **Cover with a coated, gauze-type bandage.** Regular gauze can stick to the wound. Don't make the bandage so tight it

The First Step in Treating a Cut Is to Control the Bleeding

seals out air and causes the wound to become too moist.

❏ **Get a tetanus shot.** If you've never had the three-series tetanus shots or if you haven't had a tetanus booster in five years, get one within 72 hours to avoid a potentially deadly tetanus bacterial infection. (See *Do You Need a Tetanus Shot?*, page 330.)

Know When to See a Doctor

You should have your cut or scrape treated by a doctor if it's:

- **On your face.** You may need plastic surgery to avoid scarring.

- **Very deep or wider than one-fourth inch.** A cut from broken glass often requires medical attention. If your wound requires stitches, don't wait longer than six hours to get them.

- **Too ragged to close.** If you can't easily and neatly close the wound with a butterfly or standard bandage, or if it gapes open, you need medical attention.

- **Very dirty.** When you cut yourself with something dirty, such as a garden tool, there is often hidden dirt and debris in the wound.

- **Very large.** For example, if you scrape your entire arm, see a doctor.

- **Bleeding in spurts.** This indicates you've cut an artery and you may not be able to stop the bleeding. Apply direct, firm pressure with a clean cloth, keep the area above the heart, if possible, and get to a doctor or hospital.

- **Causing a loss of sensation or mobility.**

First Aid for Your Eyes

The method of removing foreign objects from your eye depends, first, on what has entered your eye and, second, on whether the object has penetrated the eye.

Here are first aid tips for various objects. Remember, whatever is in your eye, *don't rub the eye!* You risk causing serious injury.

❏ **If a small object such as an insect or a speck of dust enters your eye:** First examine the eye. If the object moves when you blink, you can flush the eye or use a clean handkerchief or moistened cotton-tipped swab to move it to the corner of the eye. If the object is on the cornea (the center, transparent part of the eyeball), blink a few times to get it into the less sensitive white area before you touch your eye with the fabric or cotton swab.

❏ **To flush the eye:** Tilt your head over a sink with the injured eye lower. Fill a glass with clean, lukewarm water or use the faucet directly (the spray nozzles found on many kitchen sinks are also ideal for flushing). Rinse your open eye for several minutes. *Note:* Flushing should never hurt. If it does or you're not able to flush the object out after several minutes, seek medical help.

❏ **If the object does not move when you blink, or if you cannot see the object but blinking is painful:** Seek immediate help. *Do not try to remove the object or flush the eye.*

When Was Your Last Tetanus Shot?

Patch the eye shut with a sterile pad, clean cloth, or a small paper cup taped to the face and forehead, and get emergency medical assistance.

❑ **If a chemical or other liquid splashes into your eye:** Immediately flush the eye for several minutes. Patch the eye and seek medical treatment from an ophthalmologist or at an emergency department.

Caring for a Black Eye

If you've ever had a black eye, you know how unsightly it can be. Fortunately, in most cases a black eye isn't serious and won't cause lasting damage.

When you receive a blow to the eye area, blood leaks (hemorrhages) underneath the skin, resulting in the purplish appearance. If the swelling around the eye comes down quickly and you don't experience any vision problems, chances are you can treat your shiner at home. But it's a good idea to have a doctor check your black eye to make sure you haven't injured the eye itself. Do see a doctor if you have a black eye that was not caused by a blow to rule out serious illnesses that can cause blackening of the eye.

After the doctor has given the okay, try these tips:

❑ **Cleanse the eye area.** If there are any small cuts around the eye, clean them with soap and water to reduce the chances of infection.

❑ **Apply an ice pack to reduce swelling and pain.** Do so for 20 minutes on; 10 minutes off. Do not press on the eye.

TAKE THESE EYES TO THE DOCTOR

See a doctor immediately if you have any of the following eye problems.

• Bleeding from the eye(s)
• Pain
• Blurred or double vision
• A large cut on or near the eye
• Any debris on or in the eye that does not flush out with water

❑   ❑   ❑

❑ **Prevent recurrence by wearing eye protectors.** Protective eyewear, such as goggles, can reduce your risk of injury.

Dealing with Frostbite

You've been having a great time cross-country skiing. But the day is getting late, you're tired, and suddenly you turn your ankle. Instead of spending the evening sipping hot chocolate by a roaring fire, you spend it hobbling several miles in damp clothes in the cold. To add to your woes, you've developed frostbite on your hands and feet.

Frostbite is freezing of the skin and underlying tissues. When parts of the body such as the extremities get too cold, the body conserves heat for vital areas by shutting off circulation to other areas, and the tissues freeze. Any part of the body can suffer frostbite, but the hands, feet, nose, and ears are the most vulnerable.

Any Part of the Body Can Suffer Frostbite

Do Not Rub or Touch Frostbitten Skin

If you've suffered frostbite, here are some tips to help you cope:

❑ **Take shelter.** Get out of the cold as soon as possible.

❑ **Remove wet clothing.** Damp fabrics chill the body 25 times faster than dry ones.

❑ **Don't thaw and refreeze.** Tissue that has been frozen is very vulnerable to extensive damage. It's critical to not allow frostbitten areas to refreeze. If you can't keep the frozen area warm, put off the warming process until you can get to safety.

❑ **Submerge the area in warm water.** Don't expose frostbitten tissues to intense heat. Instead, submerge the area(s) in warm water (no warmer than 102 to 107 degrees Fahrenheit). Once the area is warm, gently wiggle toes or fingers to increase circulation. *Do not rub or touch the area. And never rub snow on frozen tissue.*

❑ **Thaw the area out as quickly as possible.** One of the most common myths about frostbite is you should warm the area slowly. This simply promotes more tissue damage. Rewarming the area quickly may cause more initial discomfort, but it can prevent more problems later.

❑ **Drink warm beverages.** Not only do warm beverages make you feel warmer, they keep you from becoming dehydrated, which can worsen your frostbite. Do not drink alcohol, which can increase dehydration.

For tips on preventing frostbite and other cold injuries, see *Preventing Cold Injuries*, page 343.

Hypothermia: Deadly Cold

If the body is exposed too long to cold temperatures, the body temperature can drop dangerously low (below 95 degrees Fahrenheit) and cause hypothermia, which can be fatal. Hypothermia is a greater risk in windy, cold conditions when a person has been physically active and has used up stores of energy. Children and the elderly also have a greater risk for experiencing hypothermia.

It's important to note that hypothermia doesn't just occur to someone outdoors. Hypothermia can also develop over time—from a few days to several weeks. The elderly in particular are susceptible to hypothermia because often their bodies do not adjust to changes in temperature, and they don't realize they're gradually getting colder. Indoor temperatures of 60 to 65 degrees can lead to hypothermia.

Signs of hypothermia are a gradual physical and mental slowdown that could lead to coma. Early signs can include the following:

● Clumsiness
● Irritability
● Sleepiness
● Confusion
● Poor judgment
● Slurred speech

Hypothermia is a medical emergency. If the person isn't breathing, administer CPR. Call for help and get the person out of the cold. If possible, put them into warm, dry clothing, cover them with blankets, and administer hot drinks.

Preventing Cold Injuries

Frostbite and hypothermia can be prevented. An awareness of cold weather dangers and a knowledge of cold weather precautions are the keys to protecting yourself and your loved ones. Here are the steps you need to take:

❑ **Dress warmly.** Dress in layers, including extra socks and layered gloves or mittens. A number of thinner, layered garments keeps you warmer than one thick garment because the layers trap insulating air between them. Wool is always a good choice for warmth. Wear waterproof and windproof outerwear made from materials such as Gore-Tex that will keep you dry.

❑ **Wear a hat or other head covering.** A huge amount of body heat is lost through the head. Be sure to protect your vulnerable ears, too.

❑ **Buy boots that are big enough.** Your boots should accommodate extra socks and still allow you to wiggle your toes. Too-tight boots and shoes that restrict circulation are major causes of frostbitten feet.

❑ **Don't get overly fatigued.** Pace yourself. Stop often for rest and food and drink breaks. Carry extra simple sugar foods for quick energy boosts.

❑ **Avoid alcohol.** It can contribute to dehydration and impair your judgment.

❑ **Carry emergency gear.** Plan for emergencies, even if you're only going out for a short drive or hike in cold weather. Carry water, high-energy foods, extra dry clothing, moisture-resistant matches or other fire-starting materials, an emergency "space" blanket, and first aid supplies.

Coping with Heat Exhaustion

Have you ever been in a hot, humid climate and felt tired, headachy, nauseated, or faint? If so, you know the discomfort of heat exhaustion. Overexposure to heat can produce a range of effects from a simple skin rash to potentially deadly heat stroke. Heat exhaustion is one step away from the more serious heatstroke.

When you "feel the heat" try these tips to cool the symptoms:

❑ Get out of the sun.
❑ Lie in a cool spot.
❑ Drink plenty of cool drinks.
❑ Elevate your feet.

First Aid for Heatstroke

Symptoms of heatstroke (sunstroke) include lethargy, confusion, stupor, agitation, rapid

Protect Yourself from Heat and Cold Injuries

You Can Even Suffer Heat Exhaustion Indoors

pulse, hot, dry skin, and sometimes loss of consciousness. Follow these first-aid steps for heatstroke.

❏ Call 911.
❏ Get the person into the shade.
❏ Remove clothing and wrap the person in cold, wet sheets or sponge with cold water.
❏ Fan the person with a fan or with your hands.
❏ Continue fanning and cold water applications until the person's temperature drops to 101 degrees Fahrenheit.
❏ Cover with a dry sheet. If temperature rises again, repeat cooling techniques.

Preventing Heat Injuries

Don't wait for heat exhaustion or heatstroke. Here are a few suggestions to prevent these warm-weather conditions.

❏ **Drink water before, during, and after physical activity.** Don't wait for your thirst to tell you when to drink. The National Institute for Occupational Safety and Health recommends drinking five to eight ounces of water every 15 to 20 minutes during physical exertion.

❏ **For extended activity, include sports drinks.** If your activity lasts longer than 60 minutes, drink one of the sports drinks such as Gatorade that replaces electrolytes. For easier digestion, dilute the drinks with water.

❏ **Let your body get used to the heat and humidity.** It takes about ten days to get acclimated to such changes in temperature. During that time, exercise less vigorously and for shorter periods of time.

❏ **Wear light weight clothing made of fabrics that allow your body to breathe.** Exposing more skin to the sun isn't a cooler solution. Skin soaks up the sun's rays. Loose-fitting cotton clothes are a comfortable choice.

❏ **Wear cool shoes.** Even your choice of shoes can help you stay cool. Choose shoes made of mesh, canvas, or other woven materials that allow your feet to breathe.

❏ **If you're exercising in the heat, warm up and cool down.** Walk slowly for five minutes or so to help "lubricate" your joints and get blood pumping to your muscles. At the end of your exercise period, walk slowly for at least 10 to 15 minutes to cool off. This cool-down period lets your core temperature drop back to normal. Do a few stretches before and after exercising to help prevent heat-induced muscle cramps.

❏ **Avoid alcohol.** It dehydrates the body.

❏ **Listen to your body.** If you begin to feel light-headed, nauseated, fatigued, or headachy, stop, get out of the heat, and cool down. Heat exhaustion can also result from spending too much time *indoors* in an overly hot apartment or house. Seek out a cool spot.

❏ **Take frequent breaks.** The hotter and more humid it is, the more frequently you'll need to take a breather.

Put the Stop on Nosebleeds

A punch in the nose isn't the most frequent cause of nosebleeds. Picking the nose is. You can also develop a nosebleed from nose-blowing due to colds or allergies or from breathing too-dry air. Occasionally, nosebleeds are caused from chronic high blood pressure (hypertension), if the pressure is high enough to cause the nasal capillary walls to rupture.

In most cases, a nosebleed isn't serious. Of course, if you develop chronic nosebleeds or if self-care doesn't stop your nosebleed, see your doctor to rule out serious problems. Otherwise, use these steps to put a fast halt to your bloody nose.

❑ Whether one or both nostrils is bleeding, pinch them firmly together and hold tightly for five to ten minutes. This allows time for the blood to clot.

❑ If the bleeding continues, apply pressure for another ten minutes.

❑ If the bleeding is persistent, rub some over-the-counter antiseptic ointment such as Neosporin on a sterile gauze roll and pack the affected nostril(s): Gently push the gauze in (not up) toward the back of the head with your little finger. Leave some gauze sticking out to make it easy to remove. The ointment helps prevent infection and prevents the gauze from sticking in the nostril when removed.

❑ Avoid blowing your nose after the bleeding has stopped. It takes about 24 hours for broken capillaries to heal. Your nose may start bleeding again for up to a week.

Halt Nosebleeds Before They Start

One of the reasons the nose is so vulnerable to bleeding is that it's one of the most vascular areas of the body. The nasal passages are packed with veins and capillaries, many of them lying just below the thin membranes that line the nostrils.

If a bloody nose is a frequent problem for you, it may indicate a blood clotting disorder or hypertension (high blood pressure). See your doctor for testing. However, if your doctor gives you a clean bill of health, there are plenty of steps you can take to stop a bloody nose before it starts.

❑ **Keep your hands away from your nose.** Nose picking can traumatize delicate capillaries inside the nostrils. Avoid the habit and use tissues instead. Teach children to do the same.

❑ **Moisturize the air.** Air that is too dry is a common cause of nosebleeds, especially in the winter when we're exposed to forced air heat. Use a humidifier, or place pans of water on low heat on the stove or radiators to add moisture.

❑ **Moisten nasal passages.** Apply petroleum or water-based jelly just inside the front portion of the nostrils.

A Punch in the Nose Isn't the Most Frequent Cause of Nosebleeds

Don't Use Aspirin if You're Prone to Bloody Noses

❑ **Use a saltwater nasal spray.** Fill a nasal bottle spray with diluted salt water (one level teaspoon of salt to one quart of water), and spray each nostril three or four times, five to six times a day.

❑ **Don't use aspirin.** It is an anti-coagulant (blood thinner). Aspirin can aggravate sensitive noses and cause bleeding. If you're prone to bloody noses, cut out the aspirin and see if it alleviates your problem. If, however, you use aspirin as part of a treatment for heart disease, do not stop using it without first talking with your doctor.

❑ **Check your medication.** Prescription anticoagulants can also cause frequent nosebleeds. But don't stop taking your medication on your own. Talk with your doctor about alternatives.

❑ **Get plenty of vitamin C and zinc.** Both of these important nutrients help maintain the body's blood vessels. Be sure to eat enough vitamin C-rich foods, such as citrus fruits and fresh vegetables, and zinc-rich foods, such as lean beef, fish, brown rice, and whole wheat products.

❑ **Kick the habit.** Nothing can dry out your nasal passages faster than cigarette smoking. It is also a risk factor in hypertension, another source of nosebleeds.

❑ **Discuss hormone replacement therapy with your doctor.** Many postmenopausal women find they are more subject to nose bleeding. The hormone estrogen plays a role in the production of nasal mucus. As estrogen production falls with menopause, so does nasal mucus. Ask your doctor if you're a candidate for hormone replacement therapy.

Is This Plant Poisonous?

If you've ever encountered poison ivy, oak, or sumac and developed an itchy rash from it, you know how important it is to be able to identify these poisonous weeds. Unfortunately, these hardy plants, all second-cousins of cashew and mango, can be found almost anywhere in the United States, except Alaska, Hawaii, and some parts of Nevada. Use this guide to help you identify these plants and avoid poison ivy, oak, and sumac reactions.

Poison ivy: This plant is generally found east of the Rockies. (California is the only state in the continental United States where it's not found.) Poison ivy is a small plant, vine, or shrub with shiny, pointed leaves that grow in clusters of three. In the fall, leaves turn red and yellow. It often has grayish-white berries (see Fig. 10.11).

Poison oak: This is a native of the west and southwest. It can be tricky to identify, however, because its appearance changes somewhat depending on where you find it. For example, poison oak found in southern California may not look like the variety found in northern California or southern Oregon. Usually it is a small tree or shrub with greenish-white berries and oak-like leaves that grow in groups of three. Other varieties may grow more like a vine and resemble poison ivy or grow as a shrub with clusters of hairy, yellowish berries with leaves that have hairy undersides (see Fig. 10.12).

Poison sumac: This woody shrub or small tree (5 to 25 feet) grows in the eastern United States, especially in moist, swampy, boggy areas. It has smooth-edged leaves, which turn red in the fall, and cream-colored berries that hang from branches in loose clusters. Unlike poison ivy or oak, poison sumac leaves don't grow in threes. Instead, each leaf stalk has 7 to 13 leaflets (see Fig. 10.13).

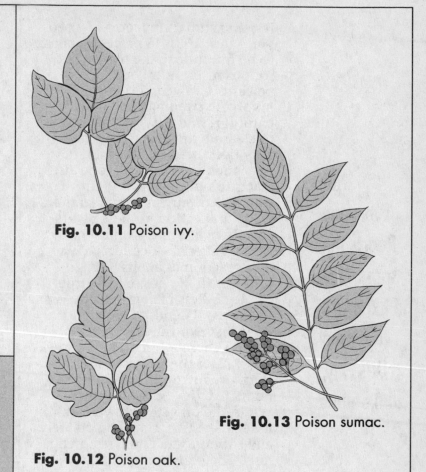

Fig. 10.11 Poison ivy.

Fig. 10.13 Poison sumac.

Fig. 10.12 Poison oak.

What Causes Poison Ivy, Oak, and Sumac Reactions?

Why do beautiful plants like poison ivy, oak, and sumac cause severe itching, a rash, and blisters? When you develop the rash, your body is having an allergic reaction to the plant's oil or sap. A clear or slightly yellowish oily resin, called *urushiol* (uh-Roo-she-all), seeps out from leaves, stems, or roots that are crushed or otherwise damaged.

You are not exposed to urushiol by simply being near the plants. You can develop a reaction if you touch the stems, leaves, or roots of the plants. But unless the plant is oozing the resin, you may get away without a reaction. Your cat or dog can also expose you to the resin. While urushiol doesn't affect these pets, they can bring it home on their fur in small amounts that are enough to produce an outbreak in humans.

Urushiol has a long-lasting shelf life of about five years. You can develop a reaction to it by simply using an old garden tool or touching a shoe that was exposed at some time. If you have urushiol on your hand, you can easily spread it to your face or other parts of your body. One of the most dangerous ways to be exposed to the resin is by breathing it when the plant is burned. If you inhale the poison with the smoke, you can develop an extreme respiratory irritation.

Not everyone reacts the same way to exposure to poison oak,

Not Everyone Reacts the Same Way to Exposure to Poison Oak, Ivy, and Sumac

ivy, and sumac. In fact, a few people, about 10 to 15 percent, appear to be immune to the plants' poisonous resin. Another 10 to 15 percent have very severe reactions involving swelling and large, painful rashes that can take weeks to clear up. (People in this category need medical attention to treat the reaction.) Everyone else reacts to poison oak, ivy, and sumac exposure more moderately.

Your reaction to these plants can change. Some people who weren't allergic as children develop a reaction as adults. Others find just the opposite to be true.

Regardless of your sensitivity to the plants, most people find their first exposure to the resin doesn't cause a reaction for a week or so. After the first exposure, reactions usually occur within a few hours to a day or two at most. When the oil gets onto your skin, it begins to penetrate immediately and soon produces the red, itchy rash. The body's mounting an immune response to the oil causes the symptoms. This reaction is followed by tiny blisters that may be moist and weepy. Eventually, crusts form on the blisters, and within ten days or so, the rash, blisters, and crusts heal.

Self-Care for Poison Ivy, Oak, and Sumac

Staying away from poison oak, ivy, and sumac is obviously the first choice in dealing with these plants. But if you do develop an allergic reaction to these plants, here are some self-care tips for coping with it:

❑ **Flush the rashy area with cool water in a bathtub or shower.** This can help ease irritated nerves and temporarily halt itching. Ice cold compresses help, too.

❑ **Apply Calamine lotion.** The old standby Calamine lotion or Caladryl can help stop the itching and dry up blisters. These are available over the counter at pharmacies.

❑ **Take a soothing bath.** If you've got the all-over itch, try soaking in a bathtub with Aveeno powder (one to two cups per bath), available at pharmacies; baking soda (one-half to one cup per bath); or finely ground oatmeal (one to two cups per bath). Ask your pharmacist for "colloidal oatmeal," or finely grind oatmeal at home in a food processor or coffee grinder.

❑ **Try Burow's solution compresses.** Also ask your pharmacist for over-the-counter Burow's solution (also sold under the name Domeboro). Follow the package directions for the tablets or powder; soak clean cloths in the solution and apply the compresses to the rash.

❑ **Take antihistamines.** If you can't stand the itch, you might get relief with over-the-counter antihistamines. They ease the itch and suppress the body's allergic reaction. However, be aware antihistamines can also cause drowsiness, which is great if you need to sleep, but not so good if you need to work, operate machinery, or drive your car.

❑ **Apply baking soda paste.** Add three teaspoons of baking soda to one teaspoon of water to make a thick paste. Cover the rash with the paste for itch relief. If blisters ooze, apply the baking soda paste and cover blisters with sterile gauze.

❑ **Try hydrocortisone creams.** Over-the-counter hydrocortisone creams aren't strong enough to help extensive rashes, but they may help stop the itch and redness in mild cases.

These Poison Plant Myths Can Harm You

There are plenty of myths about poison oak, ivy, and sumac. Here are just a few.

Myth: Eat a poison ivy leaf to "desensitize" yourself. Not only will this practice not desensitize you, it can make you very sick.

Myth: Rash blisters are filled with urushiol, the plants' poison resin, and breaking them spreads the rash. The blisters are filled with the same watery fluid as all blisters are. Ruptured blisters don't spread the rash to you or anyone else.

Myth: If you hug someone who has a poison ivy (oak, sumac) rash, you'll get it. You can't transmit your rash to someone else unless you still have urushiol on your body or your clothing.

Myth: Urushiol evaporates when exposed to the air. Unfortunately, urushiol doesn't evaporate and can stay potent on clothing, tools, or other objects for up to five years.

Myth: If a plant is dead, it can't cause a reaction. The leaves, stems, and roots of poison ivy, oak, and sumac can remain poisonous for several years after they are dead. Even the charred remains of the plants can cause a reaction.

Myth: Urushiol can't go through fabrics. While heavy fabrics can protect you from this potent resin, lighter-weight fabrics are easily penetrated.

Myth: The plants are only poisonous in the spring and summer. The resin may be more potent during the seasons when the sap is at it highest in the plant. But poison ivy, oak, and sumac are dangerous year-round. During the winter months when the plants are bare of their leaves, the twigs can still cause a powerful reaction.

Keeping Poison Ivy, Oak, and Sumac at Bay

Here are some tips to prevent an allergic reaction to these plants *before* it occurs.

❑ **Learn to identify the plants and avoid them.** Learn which plants are in your own area and in areas in which you're travelling. Find out how to identify them, and then avoid them.

❑ **Dress appropriately.** If you're in an area where these poison plants might be, dress in long pants, long-sleeved shirts, boots, and gloves to prevent contact.

❑ **Wash your clothing.** When you've been in an area that might have poison oak, ivy, or sumac, wash your clothes in detergent and hot water. Be careful removing your clothing so you don't transfer any oil to your hands, rugs, or furniture. Wash your hands thoroughly right after taking off your clothes.

Do You Recognize Poison Ivy When You See it?

- **Clean up tools and other items.** Carefully rinse any items that may have come in contact with the resin.

- **Bathe your pets.** The best idea is not to let your dog or cat romp in areas that have poison plants. However, if they do, wash them right away with a pet shampoo. Then wash the pet towels in hot water and detergent.

- **Carry alcohol.** You may be able to eliminate some of the resin oil and the reaction to it by wiping your skin with rubbing alcohol or alcohol wipes.

- **Wash with detergent or Fels Naphtha soap.** It takes a little while for poison ivy, oak, or sumac resin to soak into your skin. The old-time soap, Fels Naphtha, is a time-tested decontaminant, and it's easy to carry in a backpack. But any good detergent, including liquid dishwashing detergents, works well. Wash thoroughly with the soap and rinse well. Some backpackers soap their bodies first before venturing into the woods. The soap acts like a barrier between the oil and the skin. If you use this technique, be sure to wash off the oil and soap immediately after contact.

Taking the Sting Out of Slivers

You can't avoid them. At some time or another, you're going to get a sliver, a puncture wound with debris in it—wood, glass, metal, or plastic. Do you need to run to the doctor every time you get a sliver? Not unless you can't remove the debris or the wound becomes badly infected. Most slivers aren't serious and you can treat them with these steps:

1. Remove the sliver with one of these three techniques, depending on how deeply it is embedded:

- Sterilize a pair of tweezers with alcohol (not with a lighted match, which contaminates the tweezers with soot). If the sliver is sticking out of the skin, firmly grasp the sliver close to the skin, and pull it out.

- If the sliver isn't sticking out of the skin, you'll need to use a needle to push it out. Sterilize a needle with alcohol and use it to push the sliver out from the *bottom*.

- Deep slivers may have to be removed with an incision.

THIS SLIVER NEEDS PROFESSIONAL HELP

Sometimes a sliver needs to be treated by a medical professional. See a doctor if:

- You can't remove the sliver within 15 or 20 minutes. Excessive probing can cause you to bruise and damage surrounding tissues.

- The sliver breaks up and you can't remove all of the debris.

- You develop signs of infection—increased pain, swelling, redness, tenderness, or discharge of whitish or yellow-green pus.

- It's a minor splinter and you haven't had a tetanus booster in ten years. It's a more major splinter and you haven't had a booster in five years. Or if you've never received the three-shot tetanus series.

- You develop jaw pain or stiffness. See a physician immediately. These are the classic symptoms of tetanus, or "lockjaw."

❏   ❏   ❏

Sterilize a sharp razor blade or knife and make a small incision in the top layer of skin right above and parallel to the sliver. Then spread the incision and remove the debris.

2. Clean the wound thoroughly with soap and water. After cleaning, you can pour a little hydrogen peroxide into the wound to make sure you've gotten out all of the debris.

3. Apply antibacterial ointment and cover with a bandage.

Strain, Sprain, or Fracture?

You're playing a little pick-up basketball with a few friends in the park when suddenly you feel a sharp pain in your ankle and you tumble to the ground. How should you treat your injury? Should you see a doctor? It all depends on whether you've got a strain, a sprain, or a fracture.

Strain

A strain, the least serious of the injuries, is a hyperextension, or "pull," injury. It occurs when muscles, ligaments, or tendons are stretched beyond their limits, causing some of the cellular fibers to become injured. In response, the tissues become irritated and swollen. Pulled muscle tissues bleed.

If you have a strain, you'll probably experience a sharp pain when you try to move the injured area. Some strains, however, cause a dull, throbbing pain. Sometimes muscle strains cause muscle spasms. Over time, a strain may cause discoloration of the area and a gradual stiffening.

A muscle can be hyperextended or pulled to the point where its fibers rupture and cause a muscle tear. This serious injury can cause intense pain and swelling that can last for weeks.

In most cases you can self-treat simple muscle strains. See the next section, *RICE for Relief*.

Sprain

Unlike strains where the tissue is simply overstretched, a sprain is tearing of the tissue. A sprain is an injury to the ligaments, the fibrous, elastic tissue bands that connect bone to bone. Ligaments are like a strong cloth which, when overstretched, can tear. Any ligament around a joint can become sprained, but the most common sprain areas are the ankles, knees, wrists, and fingers.

The severity of the sprain depends on how much of the ligament is torn.

Mild sprain: What doctors call a Type I sprain tears less than 25 percent of the ligament fibers.

Moderate sprain: Type II sprains tear 25 to 75 percent of the ligament fibers.

Severe sprain: These Type III sprains tear more than 75 percent of the ligament fibers.

The symptoms of a sprain include swelling and discoloration of the joint area and pain with movement. Symptoms of a moderate or severe sprain mimic those of a fracture, and an X ray is necessary for a doctor to make an accurate diagnosis.

You can self-treat Type I or mild sprains. For moderate and severe sprains, seek treatment from a doctor.

In Most Cases, You Can Self-Treat Simple Muscle Strains

351

Use the RICE Method to Self-Treat

Fracture

A fracture means a break in a bone. It can be as simple as a crack in the bone (a hairline or stress fracture) or as serious as a compound fracture in which part of the broken bone sticks out through the skin.

Doctors have a number of classifications for fractures:

Partial fracture: This, the least serious of the fractures, involves a hairline crack in the bone. It may or may not be visible on an X ray.

Simple fracture: In this type of break, the bone is broken, but there is minimal damage to the surrounding skin and tissue.

Compound fracture: A more serious injury than a simple fracture, a compound, or "open" fracture, creates tissue damage and the bone protrudes through the skin.

Nondisplaced fracture: Doctors use this term when one or more bones are broken, yet they remain in their original position.

Displaced fracture: Not only are bones broken in this type of fracture, they are also thrown out of alignment.

Dislocation: Doctors use this term to describe a bone out of place from its normal position in a joint. Although a dislocation does not necessarily involve a break in the bone, when administering first aid, you should treat it as a fracture.

Symptoms of a fracture include tenderness, swelling, loss of strength, pain in the injured area that increases with movement, inability to use the injured part, grating noise between the fractured ends of bone, deformity of the area, and muscle spasm during slight movement.

Fractures need to be evaluated and treated by a physician.

RICE for Relief

Strains and mild sprains can be painful, but you can get relief by self-treating with RICE—rest, ice, compression, and elevation.

Rest

❑ Stop using the injured part as much as possible for several days. Immobilize the injury by using crutches or a sling as needed.

❑ Once the pain subsides, begin gentle stretching and movement to keep the area from becoming stiff and weak. Take your time and go slowly. Don't force the area to bear weight if doing so is still painful.

Ice

❑ Apply ice compresses to the injury in the first 24 hours to limit the swelling. Place a bag of ice wrapped in a cloth (to prevent cold injury to the tissues) or an ice gel bag on the injured area for 20 minutes on, 10 minutes off.

❑ When the swelling has gone down, try warm or hot water soaks several times a day to relieve discomfort and help keep the area flexible. You can try a heating pad, hot water bottle, hot compresses, or a hot bath.

Compression

❑ Wrap the injured area in an elastic bandage to help minimize swelling and discomfort while you're healing.

❑ Don't wrap the area so tightly that it impairs circulation. If you experience loss of motion or sensation, tingling, or bluishness in the area, the wrap is too tight.

Elevation

❑ Keep the injured area elevated to limit swelling and pain. If possible, raise the area above your heart.

❑ If you've injured your ankle, prop the leg up with pillows. If you have a wrist or arm injury, raise the arm up with a sling.

In addition to RICE, take aspirin or ibuprofen to reduce pain and swelling. (Acetaminophen helps reduce pain but does nothing for inflammation.)

Fracture First Aid

Fractures—breaks in the bone—require a doctor's care. However, you need to know what to do in case of a fracture until you can get medical help. Follow these steps. Treat dislocations as you would a fracture.

❑ **Never try to set the fracture.** Don't straighten the injured area unless the limb is bent under the person and help is several hours away.

❑ **Immobilize the fractured limb.** Use rolled towels, blankets, or pillows and support the injured areas. (See Figs. 10.14–10.25.)

❑ **If a bone fragment protrudes through the skin, do not try to push it in.** Instead, cover it with a clean cloth or sterile gauze.

❑ **Keep the person warm and comfortable until help arrives.** Have the individual lie

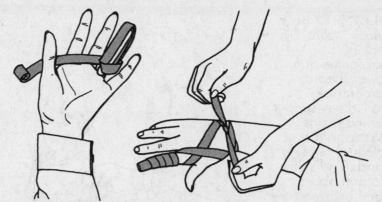

Fig. 10.14-10.15 Finger splint. Apply splint to finger in position found (do not attempt to straighten). Wrap a stick or tongue depressor in gauze or cloth to pad. Tie splint to finger above and below fracture with cloth strips.

Fig. 10.16 Straight elbow splint. Wrap a board, broomstick, or rolled newspaper or magazine with a cloth or towel to pad. Bind splint to arm above and below elbow with a necktie, cloth, belt, or rope.

quietly. Cover him with a blanket (unless the weather is warm and the person's skin doesn't feel cool and clammy).

Fig. 10.17 Bent elbow splint. Do not try to straighten arm. Use a board, broomstick, rolled newspaper or magazine. Wrap with a cloth or towel to pad. Bind splint to arm above and below elbow with a necktie, cloth, belt, or rope.

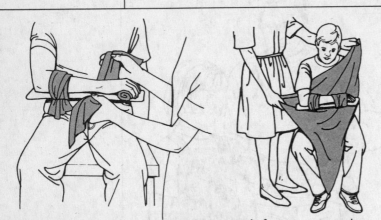

Fig. 10.18, 10.19 Forearm sling. With forearm at right angle to chest, place splint. Have person hold a soft object, such as a gauze roll, to keep hand in natural position. Bind splint above and below fracture. Fold sling into triangle. Thread under injured arm.

Fig. 10.20, 10.21 Bring sling over injured arm and tie at opposite shoulder. It should hold the hand about 4 inches above the elbow. Pin at elbow. Bind the arm to the body with cloth tied around upper arm and chest.

Preventing Strains, Sprains, and Fractures

You can reduce your risk of a strain, sprain, or fracture, especially those that often occur during athletic activities. Follow these strategies:

❑ **Get in shape.** Many strains, sprains, and fractures happen to "weekend warriors," people who exercise infrequently and then go all out physically on weekends or on special occasions and end up injured. These injuries are also more common at the beginning of an athletic season, such as the first weeks of ski season, because people haven't prepared their bodies for the activity. Adopt a regular exercise program to increase flexibility and strengthen muscles, ligaments, and tendons.

❑ **Prepare for your sport.** Each athletic activity has its own stresses and risk of injury. There are specific exercises you can do for each sport to reduce your injury risk. For example, many runners use so-called "runner's stretches" to prepare their bodies for running and reduce injuries. Talk with a coach, a physical therapist, or trainer about the specific exercises for your sport or activity.

❑ **Use protective equipment.** You can often prevent injuries by wearing the right equipment for the sport. For example, you might prevent a sprained ankle or fractured arm with correct taping or padding during a football game.

Fig. 10.22 Leg splint. Thread neckties, belts, cloth, or rope under legs at positions shown.

Fig. 10.23 If splint is not available, place blanket or pillow between legs, and bind ties.

Fig. 10.24 If board, broomstick, or other firm material is available to use as a splint, wrap it in a blanket or towel to pad. Bind splint to leg.

❑ **Warm up.** Pre-exercise warming up, such as walking or slow jogging, dilates blood vessels to prepare the tissues for exercise, and pre-exercise stretching increases muscle, tendon, and ligament flexibility. Warm up for 5 to 10 minutes, then follow with 5 to 10 minutes of stretching. Avoid bouncing or "ballistic" type stretches. Stretch until you feel a pull, breathe out, then stretch a little farther.

❑ **Cool down.** The cool-down period is the reverse of the warm-up. Slow your exercise for 5 to 10 minutes. For example, if you're running, slow to a jog or walk. Then follow with some stretching for about 10 minutes to prevent postexercise tightening up.

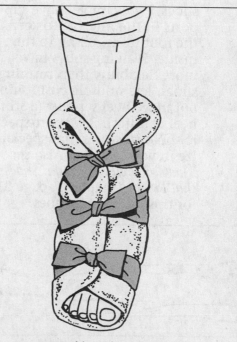

Fig. 10.25 Ankle splint. Remove shoe. Wrap pillow, towels, or blanket around foot, and tie it firmly around the foot.

❑ **If you haven't been exercising for a while, start slowly.** Don't begin running if you haven't even walked regularly. Too often we develop "overuse injuries," such as stress fractures, because we try to do too much too fast before the body is ready. For example, many runners develop stress fractures in their feet from increasing mileage too quickly. Keep in mind an injury will slow your progress much more than building your exercise program slowly. Build your endurance over time.

❑ **Choose shoes carefully.** Getting the right type of shoe for your physical activity and one that fits properly can mean the difference between participating and sitting on the sidelines with an injury. Each sport has shoes specifically designed to withstand the stresses and strains associated with that activity. Running shoes, for example, have supports in the midsole to keep the foot from rolling to the inside. Walking shoes have more flexibility than running shoes, less midsole cushioning but more heel support (a stiffer heel counter). Buy sport-specific shoes in stores that specialize in your activity. Also see *The Cinderella Formula: Shoes that Fit*, in Chapter 7, page 218 for tips on buying shoes.

Don't Do Too Much Too Soon—You Risk Injury

Exercises to Build Strong Feet and Ankles

The feet and ankles are prone to injuries, especially sprains and stress fractures. You can increase your feet and ankle flexibility and strengthen the muscles above the ankle to help reduce these all-too-common injuries.

Try these exercises. Remember, do not perform these, or any, exercises to the point of discomfort. Skip the exercise if you feel any pain. If you've had an injury to the feet or ankles, consult your doctor before undertaking any exercise program.

Achilles tendon stretch. Stand facing a wall about two feet from it. Step forward with the right foot and lean toward the wall, placing your hands and forearms against the wall. Bend the right (front) knee, keeping the back leg straight. Lean forward until you feel a stretch along the back of the rear leg. Hold for 15 seconds. Now straighten your bent leg and feel a stretch in the back of your ankle (Achilles tendon). Hold for 15 seconds. Repeat 5 times with each leg.

Heel raise. Holding on to the back of a chair, stand on one foot. Raise up on your toes, then slowly lower yourself down. Repeat 5 times on each side.

Ankle extend. Lie on your back and point your feet and toes as far as possible. Then flex the ankles and bring toes back up as far as possible (see Fig. 10.26). Repeat 5 times.

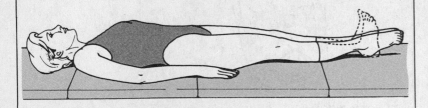

Fig. 10.26 Ankle extend. Extend and flex your feet and toes as far as possible.

Ankle flexes. Attach 1- or 2-pound weights to your ankles and lie on your side. Lift one ankle toward the ceiling, pointing the toe toward the ceiling, then pointing it toward the floor. Repeat, pointing your toes in, out, up, and down. Do 3 sets of 10 repetitions every other day.

Ankle curls. Sit on the edge of a table with a 1- or 2-pound weight attached to each foot. Alternately raise and extend each foot (see Fig. 10.27). Repeat 10 times with each foot.

Alphabet writing. Sit on the edge of a table or in a chair and "write" the letters of the alphabet in the air with your foot. Complete the alphabet with each foot.

Towel curl. With a towel flat on the floor, place your toes on the towel (your heel should be slightly above the floor) and curl your toes, pulling the towel toward you by gathering the towel with your toes (see Fig. 10.28). Repeat 5 times. If this exercise becomes too easy, add weight to the towel.

Pick-up stand. Stand with one hand on a table or back of a chair for balance. Drop a cloth on the floor and pick it up with your toes. Then bend the knee and transfer it to your free hand (see Fig. 10.29). Repeat on each side 10 times.

Golf ball roll. Sit in a chair with a golf ball on the floor at your feet. Put a foot on top of the golf ball and roll it for several minutes all round the bottom of the foot. Repeat with the other foot.

Fig. 10.28 Towel curl. Gather a towel laying flat on the floor with your toes. Be sure to keep your heel off the floor.

Fig. 10.29 Pick-up stand. Use your toes to pick a towel up off the floor and raise it to your hand.

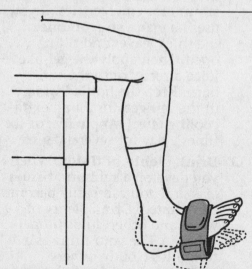

Fig. 10.27 Ankle curls. With a light weight on your foot, raise and extend each foot.

You Need to Rehydrate Sunburned Skin

Easing Sunburn Pain

You've stayed in the sun too long, and now you've got a painful, red sunburn. The pain of a sunburn (or other first degree burn) is the result of loss of skin oil and moisture. The dry skin produced irritates the nerve endings in the skin with every motion you make. To relieve pain, you need to rehydrate your skin. Try these soothing remedies to ease your pain.

❑ **Take a mineral oil bath.** Add one ounce of lanolinated mineral oil (such as Alpha Keri) to a tub full of warm water (about 88 to 90 degrees). Soak for 10 to 15 minutes. The lanolin enters the skin and holds the water in the skin.

❑ **Soak washcloths in cool water and apply them directly on burned areas.** Don't use ice, which can damage the skin. Frequently rewet and reapply the cloths as they warm up. You can increase the soothing power of compresses by adding oatmeal or baking soda to your compress water. Add baking soda directly to the water or fill a cheesecloth or piece of gauze with oatmeal and run water through it. Then toss out the oatmeal and use the water for a soothing compress.

❑ **If your sunburn is bodywide, cool off in a cool tub of water or take a cool shower.** Add baking soda or Aveeno powder (oatmeal powder is available over the counter at pharmacies) for extra soothing. However, avoid soap, washcloths, or bath sponges, which can irritate painful skin. And don't soak too long (no more than 15 to 20 minutes) or you may end up drying out the skin and causing peeling. After a cooling soak, keep your skin moist by patting (not rubbing) your skin damp-dry and applying your favorite moisturizer.

❑ **Stay cool.** When you get a sunburn (or any type of burn), your body literally radiates heat from dilated blood vessels. Keep your body temperature down: Stay out of the sun and stay in a cool spot.

❑ **Apply aloe vera.** One of nature's little miracles, the aloe vera plant produces a thick, gel-like juice that soothes sunburn pain and redness. Aloe vera applied immediately to the burn causes the skin's dilated blood vessels to constrict, making the burn less painful.

You can buy aloe vera gel at drug or health food stores, or keep a live aloe vera plant around for emergencies. If you use the plant, snip off one of the thick leaves and slit it open. Then apply the gel-like juice directly onto the sunburn. Keep the bottled variety in the refrigerator for an extra-cooling effect. Apply five or six times a day for several days.

❑ **Drink plenty of fluids.** When you develop a sunburn, tissues leak and you can easily become dehydrated. Drink plenty of water and other fluids (nonalcoholic). Use your urine as a test: if it's cloudy or very yellow, you need to drink more fluids.

❑ **Take aspirin or ibuprofen.** These over-the-counter pain relievers can cut inflammation and provide pain relief. Take as directed on the bottle. If aspirin upsets your stomach, ask your pharmacist for coated or "enteric" aspirin.

❑ **Try a topical anesthetic and hydrocortisone.** Topical anesthetic products that contain lidocaine can provide some temporary relief from sunburn pain. But before you smear them on the skin, first test a small area to ensure you're not allergic. When sunburns begin to heal, they often itch. Products such as Cortaid, containing 0.5 percent or 1.0 percent hydrocortisone, can also bring temporary relief from pain and itching.

❑ **Prop up your feet.** If your legs are burned and your feet swell, lie down and prop your feet up above your heart. It helps keep the fluid from pooling in your feet and makes you more comfortable.

Protect Your Eyes from the Sun

The sun's ultraviolet (UV) rays can not only damage your skin, they can also harm your eyes. Excessive UV exposure can damage the cornea and retina and lead to cataracts. Wearing the proper sunglasses can prevent problems from the sun.

When choosing sunglasses for UV protection, pay attention to the light transmission factor, which indicates the percent of light that gets through to the eyes.

THIS SUNBURN NEEDS A DOCTOR

You can usually self-treat minor sunburns at home. However, more serious sunburns, particularly if they are widespread, should be treated by a doctor. Call a doctor if you have any of these symptoms with your sunburn:

● Extensive blistering

● Chills, fever, nausea, or fatigue

● Signs of infection (such as swelling, redness, increased pain)

❑   ❑   ❑

Most ophthalmologists say for sun protection, the lenses should allow no more than 30 percent light transmission. In snow, water, or sand glare conditions, it should be no more than 10 to 15 percent. Polarized or mirrored sunglasses are good for cutting glare, too.

Avoid "phototrophic" lenses, the ones that gradually change from lighter to darker depending on the light. They can take up to ten minutes to completely change color and often don't become dark enough to provide protection in bright sunlight.

Be Prepared for Emergencies

Accidental deaths claim more than 150,000 lives each year in the United States. Accidents are the fourth leading cause of death among adults and the number one cause of death among young people. The good news is most accidental deaths can be prevented with preparation and a little common sense.

Accidental Deaths Claim More Than 150,000 Lives Each Year in the United States

Knowing what to do in an emergency is key. So is keeping the right supplies on hand.

❑ **Know how to use 911.** Teach everyone in the family, including young children, to dial 911 in an emergency. When you reach the emergency operator, stay calm, speak clearly, and explain the nature of the emergency and your location. Do not hang up. If you're near a pay phone, 911 calls are free.

❑ **Keep emergency numbers on hand.** Or program your phone with quick dial for emergency phone numbers such as 911, the nearest hospital, the doctor, the fire department, poison control, the veterinarian, and neighbors or friends. If you leave your children alone or with a babysitter, always post a number where you can be reached.

❑ **Learn first aid and CPR.** Your local Red Cross and community college offer classes in basic first aid and cardiopulmonary resuscitation (CPR). If you're already certified in first aid and CPR, be sure to keep your skills updated with refresher courses.

❑ **Keep basic first aid and medical supplies on hand.** See *Your Portable First Aid Kit,* next, and *Your Home Medicine Chest,* Chapter 11, page 384.

❑ **Stock your house for emergencies.** You never know when Mother Nature will send a windstorm, snowstorm, flood, or other natural calamity. See the sidebar, *Emergency Supplies,* for the supplies to keep on hand.

Your Portable First Aid Kit

A first aid kit can come in handy when you get a paper cut at the office; it can be a lifesaver if you're stranded in the wilderness. You can buy prepackaged first aid kits or put your own together for just a few dollars.

Obviously the contents of your portable first aid kit will vary with your activity. For example, an auto or boat first aid kit contains more items than one you put together for a backpack trip. However, all first aid kits should contain some basic items such as the ones listed here:

- Bandages, gauze, adhesive tape
- A disinfectant such as rubbing alcohol

EMERGENCY SUPPLIES

❑ **Fresh water.** Plan for three quarts for each person per day.

❑ **Canned, freeze-dried, and packaged foods.** Stock foods that can be eaten without cooking. Keep some multivitamins on hand to ensure adequate nutrition. Rotate food and supplements once a year to keep them fresh.

❑ **A manually operated can opener, and cooking and eating utensils.** Be sure to include a few pots and pans that can be used with a camp stove.

❑ **Candles, hurricane lamps, matches.**

❑ **Camp stove and fuel or barbecue and briquets.**

❑ **Battery-operated radio and fresh batteries.**

❑ **A change of clothing, rain gear, and sturdy boots or shoes.**

❑ **Blankets or sleeping bags.**

❑ **A backpack or duffle to carry all of the above items, if necessary.**

❑ ❑ ❑

- Cotton balls
- A pain reliever such as aspirin or ibuprofen
- Antibacterial and antifungal ointment (Neosporin, Bacitracin)
- Moleskin or molefoam to treat blisters
- Small scissors
- Tweezers
- Elastic bandage and safety pins
- A "space" blanket

Auto Safety Tips

Nearly 100,000 Americans die in auto accidents every year. You and your loved ones can reduce your risk of an auto accident or injury by following these tips:

❑ **Always wear your seat belt.** Studies have repeatedly shown seat belts save lives when used properly. Unfortunately, many people don't buckle up or they leave the lap belt on automatic seat belts unhooked.

❑ **Use child car seats.** Any child who weighs less than 40 pounds should be properly strapped into a child's car seat. Rear-facing seats should be used for infants from birth to 20 pounds. Never ride with a baby or young child on your lap (in an accident, they are likely to be thrown forward).

❑ **Never drink or use drugs and drive.** More than half of all vehicle accidents involve alcohol or drugs. Even one or two drinks can impair your driving ability. If you or others in your party are going to be drinking, designate a sober driver. Or if you or a friend has had too much to drink, take a bus or cab or call someone to drive you home.

❑ **Don't drive while taking over-the-counter or prescription medications.** They can make you drowsy and impair your judgment. Studies have shown a single antihistamine pill can impair driving ability just as if you've had a couple of alcoholic drinks.

❑ **Drive with your head not with your emotions.** Too often, we allow ourselves to become angry and make poor driving decisions. If someone cuts you off or makes you unhappy, don't use your automobile to express yourself.

❑ **Slow down.** You may save a few minutes by driving fast, but if you have an accident, you may not arrive at all.

❑ **Take a safe driving course.** If you live in areas where there is snow and ice, consider taking one of the many safe driving courses available. They teach how to drive defensively and avoid accidents in inclement conditions.

❑ **Maintain your car.** Don't wait for your car to break down or cause an accident to replace worn out tires, brakes, wiper blades, and lights and other safety equipment.

❑ **Don't drive when you feel tired or sleepy.** Many accidents are caused when drivers fall asleep at the wheel. If you're tired, pull over and take a break.

❑ **Drive defensively.** Keep an eye out for other drivers and don't assume they're going to "do the right thing."

Always Wear Your Seat Belt

Install Smoke Detectors

❏ Look out for pedestrians, cyclists, joggers, and animals.

❏ Carry foul weather equipment. Try not to drive when weather conditions make driving hazardous. If you must drive, equip your car with snow tires and carry other safety equipment such as flares and tire changing tools and equipment.

❏ Keep pets caged.

❏ Keep your view unobstructed by passengers, packages, or other equipment.

Fireproof Your Home

Protect yourself and your loved ones from becoming another fire statistic. Follow these tips:

❏ Place working smoke detectors and fire extinguishers on every floor. Check and change detector batteries regularly.

❏ Develop a fire escape plan and conduct fire drills. Have ladders on the upper stories.

❏ Don't overload electrical outlets.

❏ Have chimneys cleaned and inspected yearly. Use protective spark screens, and place hot ashes in a metal container with a lid.

❏ Keep fire exits free from clutter and other obstacles.

❏ Never smoke in bed.

❏ Use candles with caution, especially around children.

❏ Have your home heating system checked annually.

❏ Store flammable chemicals in metal containers.

What To Do in a Fire Emergency

Fire departments often conduct community and school fire safety and fire prevention classes. Reinforce these fire safety lessons at home by conducting periodic family fire drills so everyone knows what to do in case of a fire.

❏ Get everyone out of the building. Fire can move very quickly. Do not stop to gather valuables.

❏ Get down low. Since smoke rises, you may be overcome with toxic fumes unless you stay close to the ground.

❏ Be careful opening doors. They can act as fire breaks. Feel the door first. If it's hot, don't open it. Close doors as you exit.

❏ Use fire ladders, blankets, or sheets to exit upper floors, if necessary.

❏ Use the stairs, not elevators.

❏ Once everyone is safely out of the structure, call 911. Try to stay calm. Give the operator your name, location, and specific details about the fire.

Prevent Childhood Accidents

Too often, we worry about childhood illnesses hurting our young ones. But what we should be worried about are childhood accidents, the num-

FIRST AID AND SAFETY

ber one killer of children younger than 14 years of age.

In addition to the auto and fire safety strategies outlined in this chapter, you can protect your children with these ideas:

❑ **Prevent accidental poisoning by storing all chemicals, medicines, cleaning solutions, and pesticides out of reach and sight of children.** Place containers out of reach on high shelves and behind childproof latches. Look for containers with safety caps and keep all medicines and chemicals in their original containers. Never tell children medicines are "candy."

❑ **Keep children away from poisonous plants.** Eating plants usually doesn't produce serious harm—just upset stomachs and minor irritations of the mouth and lips. (See the sidebar for a list of common poisonous plants.)

❑ **Have the number of the poison control center handy.**

❑ **Keep syrup of Ipecac, an over-the-counter vomit-inducer, on hand.**

❑ **Teach children to swim.** Even very young children can be taught to swim and be water safe. This may be best done by a skilled teacher. YM-YWCAs, community centers, and municipal pools have water safety and swimming classes. Also, make sure swimming pools and hot tubs have fences and locking gates children cannot climb. Never leave children unattended in the bath, pool, or around water.

❑ **Keep guns unloaded and behind locked doors.** Store ammunition in a separate place from firearms.

COMMON POISONOUS PLANTS

These are some common poisonous plants:

Azalea	Laurels
Bird of paradise	Lily of the valley
Castor bean	Mandrake
Daffodil	Mistletoe
Daphne	Monkshood
Deadly nightshade	Narcissus
Delphinium	Oleander
Dieffenbachia	Philodendron
English ivy	Pokeweed
European bittersweet	Poinsettia
Foxglove	Rhododendron
Hyacinth	Rhubarb leaf
Holly	Rosary pea
Hydrangea	Sweet peas
Iris	Wisteria
Jack-in-the-pulpit	Yellow jessamine
Jerusalem cherry	Yew
Larkspur	

❑   ❑   ❑

❑ **Teach children basic fire safety rules.** Include these tried and true instructions:

"Never play with matches."

"Don't touch electrical outlets or cords."

"Stay away from the stove."

"Stay away from the fireplace."

Also teach them to "Stop, drop, and roll," that is, roll on the ground if their clothing catches on fire.

❑ **Lower the thermostat on your hot water heater to 120 degrees to prevent scalding.**

❑ **Keep small objects that can cause choking away from young children.**

Most Bike Injuries Could Be Prevented with Helmet Use

Be a Safe Cyclist

More and more people are enjoying bicycling for recreation and for transportation. That's great for the environment and terrific for fitness, but bicycling, especially in heavy commuter traffic, can be dangerous. Use these tips to stay cycle safe:

❏ **Wear a helmet.** Bicycling experts say nearly three-quarters of all serious bike injuries could be prevented if bicyclists would wear a helmet. Look for a helmet that meets the standards set by the American National Standards Institute or the Snell Memorial Foundation. Your helmet should fit snugly enough that it won't come off when strapped on. Look for one that provides protection, good visibility and ventilation, and is lightweight.

❏ **Equip your bike with safety equipment.** Make sure your bike has a red rear light and reflector that can be seen for 600 feet and a headlight that can be seen for 500 feet. You can also wear flashing lights on your body. A rear view mirror can help you see traffic behind and to the side of you, and a pump and tire-changing equipment are useful in an emergency.

❏ **Make sure your bike is in good repair.** If your tires, brake pads, or cables are worn or frayed, replace them.

❏ **Ride a bike that fits you.** You should be able to sit comfortably on the seat with your leg extended, knee slightly bent, while your heel is on the pedal at its lowest position. You should be able to straddle the bike and be able to clear the frame's top tube by an inch for touring bikes, as much as five inches for mountain bikes.

❏ **Ride with traffic and follow the rules of the road.** Don't make unexpected moves or weave through traffic. Bicyclists must follow the same rules as autos, which means you shouldn't cycle against traffic or run traffic signals. Be courteous and don't make auto drivers angry. (Remember, the average car weighs two tons!) At turn lights, stay in the middle of the lane.

Tips for Healthy and Safe Travel

Traveling around the United States or to foreign countries can be wonderful and exciting. However, it can also be risky to your health and safety. Here's how to stay healthy and safe on your next trip:

❏ Carry your passport, money, credit cards, and traveler's checks in a hide-a-pouch type wallet.

❏ Don't carry large amounts of money. Use credit cards and traveler's checks that can be easily replaced if lost or stolen.

❏ Carry all your valuables on the plane with you.

❏ Don't overpack. Nothing makes you more vulnerable than being loaded down with suitcases.

❏ Guard your telephone credit card number, especially in airports and hotel lobbies.

❏ Be on the lookout for divert-and-grab scams where one thief, often a child, diverts your attention, while another makes off with your bags.

❏ Be familiar with the currency and normal prices for services and goods.

❏ Never leave valuables in your hotel room.

❏ Use a hotel security door lock, available in travel stores.

❏ Get the proper immunizations for your destination.

❏ Exercise, eat lightly, and avoid alcohol and caffeinated beverages enroute to reduce "jet lag." While flying, drink plenty of water.

❏ Don't drink local tap water. Drink bottled or boiled water. Avoid ice cubes.

❏ Avoid unpasteurized milk products.

❏ Eat fruits and vegetables you can peel yourself.

❏ Read the section *Avoiding Traveler's Diarrhea*, page 250.

Prevent Mugging and Rape

You can't always avoid being the victim of an assault, but you can reduce your risk by developing "street smarts." Here are a few suggestions:

❏ **Move with confidence and stay aware of your surroundings.** Studies have shown that how you carry yourself on the street often determines whether you will be picked out for assault.

❏ **Dress in clothing that won't hinder you if you need to run or escape.** Tight skirts and high-heeled shoes make women much more vulnerable to attack.

❏ **Walk with others.** Whenever possible, use the buddy system, and try to stay in well-lighted, populated areas.

❏ **Stay sober.** Using drugs and alcohol impairs judgment and may cause you to make unsafe decisions about where you are and whom you're with.

❏ **Don't overload yourself with parcels.** Keep your hands free whenever possible.

❏ **Keep your doors and windows locked.** Many intruders don't have to break in because people leave doors and windows unlocked.

❏ **Check your car before you get in.** Take a moment to make sure no one is lurking in your vehicle.

❏ **Trust your instincts.** If you sense a situation or area is unsafe, get away fast.

❏ **Yell.** If you're attacked, yell to draw attention.

❏ **Carry and use a loud alarm.** Many people successfully use a lipstick-sized alarm to ward off attackers.

❏ **Consider taking a self-defense class.** While self-defense training won't guarantee you'll never become a victim of an attack, it can teach you some basic defensive moves to decrease your risk and increase your confidence.

Consider Taking a Self-Defense Class

Be Water- and Boat-Safe

Always Wear Life Jackets When Boating

A beautiful, balmy day. Blue skies and blue water. Sounds like perfect ingredients for a day of swimming and boating, doesn't it?

Keep the day perfect by following commonsense tips for water safety.

❑ **Learn to swim.** Swimming courses are available for little cost at local community recreation centers, health clubs, and community colleges. You're never too old to learn to be water safe.

❑ **Swim with a buddy.** Even expert swimmers can suffer from fatigue or cramping.

❑ **Get out of the water when you're tired.** Learn your limits and go ashore before you're overly tired.

❑ **Don't drink or use drugs around water.** The number of deaths each year involving recreational boating is second only to highway accidents, and an estimated half of all boating accidents involve alcohol.

❑ **Don't swim in the dark.** Especially in the ocean.

❑ **Always wear life jackets when boating.** If your life jacket comes with pockets, equip it with a flare, a mirror, and a whistle.

❑ **Know and follow boating regulations.** Keep to posted speed limits and watch for other craft and swimmers.

❑ **Keep a radio with you, and listen to weather reports.** If there are storm warnings, get out of the water.

M E D I C A L

C A R E

*Y*ou wouldn't buy an appliance, a car, or a home without doing research, asking questions, and becoming an informed consumer. Despite the fact that our health is more important than any appliance, automobile, or house, many of us don't think about being informed consumers when we think of medical care. After all, the doctor knows best, right?

But a big part of a healthy lifestyle is taking responsibility for your health. That means eating right, exercising regularly, and managing stress. It also means knowing how to select the right doctor and medical facility, which tests and immunizations you need, how to avoid medical quackery, and the best way to communicate with your doctors and other health providers. This chapter helps you do just that.

❑   ❑   ❑

If You Don't Have a Primary Care Physician, Now's the Time to Find One

Choosing the Best Doctor for You

Everyone needs a *primary care physician*, a doctor you go to first when you have a health concern. Although a primary care physician may not treat every medical problem, and sometimes may refer you to a specialist, this is the doctor who assumes overall responsibility for your medical care.

Having a primary care physician allows you and the doctor to get to know one another, making it easier to discuss sometimes difficult subjects that impact your health. Over time, he or she will get to know you as a person—your habits, your medical history, your family situation, your occupation, and any accompanying stresses. It is this holistic approach—the knowledge of you as a whole person—that makes care from your primary physician so important to your health care.

Your primary care physician can also recommend specialty care should you have a health problem that requires it. Your physician can also coordinate your care. Busy professionals may not communicate as well as they might with their colleagues. They may also have the tendency to treat only the problem that falls within their specialty area, neglecting other health issues. The primary care physician can help to make sure important health issues don't fall between the cracks.

The type of physician you select is less important than the individual physician. For example, you might choose a family practi-tioner, a pediatrician, or an internist for your primary care. Some women prefer a gynecologist, a specialist in the female reproductive system, as a primary care physician.

If you don't have a primary care physician, now's the time to find one. Don't wait until you're sick. Start looking when you have the time to consider and evaluate different doctors. One of the best places to start is with friends, family, and coworkers. Ask about their experiences with doctors in your community. If you have a nurse or physician friend, ask them for recommendations. In communities with teaching hospitals, medical schools, or local community hospitals, you may be able to get names of doctors who are taking new patients.

Once you have a list of names, go on a fact-finding mission. Call the doctor's office and explain that you're looking for a primary care physician and you'd like to make a brief appointment to talk with the doctor. Read through the following items before your meeting with the doctor. You may also wish to prepare a list of questions to ask the doctor regarding such issues as his or her availability, associates, hospital affiliation, and methods of handling insurance. Then during your meeting consider these aspects:

- **Personality.** Is this a doctor with whom you'd feel comfortable? If gender or age are considerations, does this person fit what you're looking for? Is this person friendly and respectful? Pay close attention to your intuitive, "gut" reactions.

- **Ability to communicate.** Does this doctor take the time to talk with his or her patients? During the interview, did you receive his or her undivided attention? Were you given plenty of time or did you feel rushed? Were your questions answered willingly and thoroughly? Did the physician talk in conversational language or "medic-speak"? Was the doctor concerned about and willing to address your concerns?

- **Emphasis on prevention.** Look for a doctor willing to discuss lifestyle issues such as smoking, exercise, and stress management. Does the doctor set a good example of a healthy lifestyle or does he or she show signs of smoking, overworking, or overeating?

- **Presentation of alternatives.** How does the doctor feel about presenting treatment alternatives? Look for someone who isn't rigid about one approach. Will he or she discuss the risks and benefits involved in all possible treatment options? Is this doctor open to discussing "alternative" practitioners such as acupuncturists and chiropractors? How does he or she feel about options such as massage therapy, nutritional remedies, biofeedback, and other less invasive treatments? And how does he or she support those feelings?

- **Availability.** Is it relatively easy to get an appointment? How does the doctor handle emergencies? Who "covers" for the doctor when he or she is not available?

- **Hospital affiliation.** With which hospitals is the doctor affiliated? Doctors are generally carefully screened before being placed on the staff. What kind of hospitals are in your area? Teaching hospitals, for example, train doctors, so they possess the latest medical equipment and keep up-to-date with

techniques. Many community hospitals also provide excellent care. (See *What Kind of Hospital Should You Choose?* page 372.)

- **Cost.** Was the doctor comfortable discussing charges in advance?

Making Sense Out of Medical Specialties

There are all kinds of physicians and a mind-numbing list of specialties. How do you know which one is right for you? In most cases, your primary care physician acts as the "quarterback" of your health care team. If your primary care provider can't give you an accurate diagnosis or adequate care for a particular health problem, he or she will refer you to a specialist, a doctor with the appropriate training and expertise.

Essentially, medical training is broken into categories of specialization, or specialties. Internal medicine is the largest of the specialties; doctors with this specialty are called internists. These specialties further break down into Certificates of Special Qualifications. (There is also a designation for physicians with Certificates of Added Qualifications; for example, a physician who is board-certified in family practice may also have a certificate of added qualification in geriatric medicine.) See the list of specialties accredited through the American Board of Medical Specialties on page 370.

Your Primary Care Physician Acts as the "Quarterback" of Your Health Care Team

AMERICAN BOARD OF MEDICAL SPECIALTIES CATEGORIES OF CERTIFICATION

*B*oard-certified means a medical doctor has taken and passed a certification examination given by the medical board that governs his or her specialty. After a doctor completes four years at an accredited medical school and passes state exams, he or she goes on to three to seven years of specialty training. Board certification indicates this specialist has been given a "seal of approval" by the medical experts who oversee that specialty.

Allergy and Immunology
Anesthesiology
Colon and Rectal Surgery
Dermatology
Emergency Medicine
Family Practice
Internal Medicine
    Cardiovascular Disease
    Endocrinology, Diabetes, and Metabolism
    Gastroenterology
    Hematology
    Infectious Disease
    Medical Oncology
    Nephrology
    Pulmonary Disease
    Rheumatology
Medical Genetics
Neurological Surgery
Nuclear Medicine
Obstetrics and Gynecology
Ophthalmology
Orthopedic Surgery
Otolaryngology
Pathology
Pediatrics
Physical Medicine and Rehabilitation
Plastic Surgery
Preventive Medicine
Psychiatry and Neurology
Radiology
Surgery
Thoracic Surgery
Urology

❑ ❑ ❑

Choosing the Right Medical Facility

Do you know what to do when you need medical care? Do you know where to go? Matching your medical need with the right facility can save you time and money and ensure you get the best care.

First, if you have an accident or there is a possibility the condition is life-threatening, call 911 or your local emergency response team.

Second, if the condition is not life threatening, and you don't know whether you require emergency treatment, phone your primary care physician. He or she may prefer to treat you at the office or meet you at the hospital emergency department. Your doctor's office should also be your choice for routine care, for conditions that require follow-up care, or for minor emergencies.

But what if you become ill in the middle of the night or when you're away from home? Or what if you don't yet have a primary care physician? Two common sources of medical care are hospital emergency departments and walk-in clinics.

Hospital Emergency Departments. Care in emergency departments is expensive and it can be time-consuming. Unfortunately, because many people don't have a personal physician, they rely on hospital emergency departments when they really just need to see a doctor. This isn't a good idea. These facilities aren't designed to provide continued care. You'll likely see a different

---

doctor every time you visit. The doctor focuses only on your major complaint and cannot provide the kind of thorough examination you may need if your problem is more complicated.

Many people mistakenly believe they'll save time by going to a hospital emergency department. Most emergency waiting rooms are packed with people with nonemergency complaints. When a life-threatening emergency occurs, those waiting with nonemergency problems are pushed further down the waiting list. In many busy emergency departments, it's not uncommon for people with minor illnesses or routine problems to wait several hours for care.

Hospital emergency departments are designed to handle medical emergencies. Routine problems can be handled more easily and more economically in a doctor's office or walk-in clinic. In addition, your medical insurance may not cover care provided in a hospital emergency department if your problem isn't truly an emergency. Choose these facilities only when you have a serious medical emergency.

Walk-in Clinics. Often located in shopping malls or other convenient places, walk-in or so-called "urgent care" clinics provide quick service for those who have non–life-threatening emergencies, such as a fractured finger or a deep cut that needs stitches. These clinics are usually open nights and weekends, and they provide services at a relatively reasonable cost (less expensively than emergency department care). Like hospital emergency departments, these facilities are not usually designed to provide follow-up care. If you need extensive follow-up care, walk-in clinics can become costly.

WHO ARE THESE HEALTH CARE PROFESSIONALS?

Here are a few of the other types of health care providers you may encounter.

Home health aides: These are personal aides who provide personal care and some nursing services to people who are homebound.

Licensed practical nurses (LPNs): They provide hands-on nursing care under the supervision of registered nurses and doctors.

Medical technologists (MTs): These individuals perform diagnostic laboratory testing. The technician who draws your blood for testing or donation is called a phlebotomist.

Nurse practitioners (NPs): Under a doctor's supervision, nurse practitioners provide routine care, including treatment of infections and injuries and follow-up care for such conditions as high blood pressure. In some states, nurse practitioners can order tests and give out medications prescribed by a physician.

Physical therapists (PTs): These are specialists in using exercise, heat, cold, hydrotherapy (water), and massage to restore function to people who have been injured or disabled.

Physician assistants (PAs): Under a doctor's supervision, these health care providers can perform physical exams, provide counseling, and follow treatment protocols and give out medications prescribed by a physician.

Radiologic technicians (RTs): These individuals prepare patients for X rays and obtain and develop X rays.

Registered dietitians (RDs): These are licensed specialists in diet and nutrition.

Respiratory therapists: Under a doctor's orders, respiratory therapists treat breathing disorders and assist in rehabilitation after surgery.

Social workers: Social workers provide individual and group psychotherapy. They may also assist patients with finances, insurance, placement, discharge, housing, and other needs.

❏   ❏   ❏

WHAT KIND OF HOSPITAL SHOULD YOU CHOOSE?

If you've been in a serious accident, the best hospital for you is often the nearest one. However, when you have a choice, it's good to know the types of hospitals available in your area and be able to choose the one that best fits your condition and your preferences.

First, check your medical insurance for any restrictions regarding your choice of hospital. If you have a choice, talk with your physician about which hospital he or she prefers. He or she may feel you need the services of a particular facility. But if your doctor has admitting privileges at more than one hospital, he or she may leave the choice to you. You may wish to be admitted to the hospital closest to your family or your home, or the one that is affiliated with your religion. If you don't know anything about the hospitals in your area, do a little homework. Talk with neighbors about their hospital experiences, then visit the hospitals. Here's some information to get you started with your homework:

Community (private) hospitals. These are the most common type of hospital in the United States. They may be profit or nonprofit. They usually give high-quality, personalized care and can handle most health problems.

Public hospitals. These are county, city, military, and Veteran's Administration-type hospitals. They tend to be larger (400–1,000 beds) than most community hospitals and have staff physicians. They can often offer more services than smaller community hospitals and serve people of all economic means. Because many public hospitals are teaching hospitals, the qualities listed below generally apply. But they can also have greater disorganization, inefficiencies, and limited resources due to budgeting problems.

Teaching hospitals. If you live in an area that has a medical school, you may have a teaching hospital in your community. These facilities typically offer the latest in technological advances. However, because they are teaching hospitals, you may be cared for by interns or residents, "physicians-in-training," who are supervised by teaching doctors. Some people feel the care they receive in teaching hospitals is less personal than in community hospitals.

❏ ❏ ❏

Getting the Most from Your Hospital Stay

A hospital stay can be frightening. When we're hospitalized, we often forget all we've learned about being intelligent medical consumers. With this in mind, you can appoint someone to look out for your best interests while you're in the hospital. And keep these tips in mind next time you're scheduled for a hospital stay:

❏ **Have an advocate.** Ask a close friend or a relative to become your patient advocate. This is the person who can sit in on doctor conferences with you, talk with the staff on your behalf, and help you get the best care available. Be sure to introduce your advocate to all your physicians and the nursing and support staffs. Make this person a list of all your doctors so he or she knows who's who.

❏ **Negotiate your care.** No hospital can perform any test or procedure on you without your consent. Don't automatically agree to everything recommended. Ask about the purpose, risks, and discomfort of any procedure. If you have time, investigate and learn about the pros and cons of recommended tests and procedures.

❏ **Bank your own blood.** In this day of blood-borne diseases such as AIDS and hepatitis, banking your own blood is a good idea if you're undergoing surgery. If possible, begin this procedure, called *autologous donating*, several weeks before you're scheduled for surgery.

❏ **Keep track of your medication schedule and your dietary restrictions.** Errors in medications and food service aren't uncommon in busy hospitals. Food service may send up a meal right before a test or procedure that requires you to have an empty stomach. A nurse might misread a medication order and give you the wrong medication. If you know your dietary restrictions and which medications you're taking, their purpose, and schedule, you can better monitor your own care. If you're too sick, ask your patient advocate to keep track. Ask your nurse to check your plastic wristband and your chart to reconfirm your medication before you take it.

❏ **Personalize your surroundings.** Hospitals can be dehumanizing places. Surround yourself with things you enjoy—a plant, books, a radio, puzzles, games, and other items. Of course, you should obey restrictions related to your illness.

❏ **Keep your sense of humor.** It's easier to negotiate what you want if you're pleasant to others. If you joke around with the staff, they're more apt to see you as a reasonable person who's simply looking out for your best interests rather than as a "difficult patient." In addition, many health authorities believe humor speeds healing.

❏ **Speak up.** If you're not getting the care you want, say so. For example, if the quality of food is very poor, you can't sleep because it's too noisy, or you've been kept waiting for an hour for a bedpan, speak up. You are paying for your care and you deserve a quality experience. If your nurse consistently ignores your reasonable requests, ask to speak to the head floor nurse, the nursing supervisor,

KNOW YOUR PATIENT RIGHTS

You've heard of the Bill of Rights, but did you know there is a Patient's Bill of Rights? Drawn up by the American Hospital Association in 1972, the Patient's Bill of Rights spells out your rights as a hospital patient. Be sure you get a copy of it when you're admitted to the hospital. If you're well enough, read it carefully. If not, have your patient advocate read it.

In addition to other rights, these are several of the most important rights spelled out in the Patient's Bill of Rights:

● You have the right to receive complete and understandable information about your diagnosis, your treatment, and the expected outcome.

● You have the right to know what measures other than the ones proposed by the doctor are available, and what their risks are.

● You have the right to review your medical records. These can be difficult to understand. Ask your doctor about anything contained in your chart or records that you don't understand.

● You have the right to refuse any treatment or test. Unless you're unconscious or it's an extreme emergency, every procedure requires your consent. Major procedures require informed consent, which means your doctor or the hospital staff must explain the risks and benefits to you and answer all of your questions before you agree to sign your consent. In addition, you have the right to change your mind even after you've given consent.

● You have the right to considerate and respectful care.

● You have the right to receive an explanation of all charges on your bill, regardless of whether they are covered by insurance.

❏   ❏   ❏

or your doctor. And by all means, report your symptoms. Many patients receive inadequate pain medication, for example, because they believe they are supposed to tolerate the pain or they're afraid to "bother" the hospital staff.

❑ **Activate your support network.** A hospital stay is not a time to go it alone. Call friends, relatives, coworkers, or anyone else in your life who can become part of your support group. If you need help, ask for it. For example, you can make a list of things you can't do, such as cleaning your fish tank or watering your garden, and ask members of your support group to take care of them for you.

Take the Bite out of Hospital Bills

Let's face it: Hospital stays are expensive. In fact, the average hospital cost per day is about $900! Even if you have health insurance, you may still end up paying for a significant portion of your hospital bill. Here are some ideas to lower your hospital bill.

❑ **Stay out of the hospital.** Talk to your doctor about whether a hospital stay is necessary. Many procedures can now be performed on an outpatient basis. If your physician recommends a hospital stay, ask about less expensive alternatives. Your doctor can treat many non–life-threatening emergencies at the office, or

you can try a walk-in urgent care center instead of the hospital emergency department.

❑ **Compare rates.** Unless your hospital stay is an emergency, you'll probably have time to hospital shop. Call around and check into room rates in advance.

❑ **Go low-tech.** For most health problems, you don't need the latest, most expensive high-tech tests and procedures. You'll find more of these cutting-edge marvels at teaching hospitals.

❑ **Share a room.** A private hospital room is more expensive. Opt for a semiprivate or, better yet, a three- or four-bed room. Ask about discounts for multi-bed rooms.

❑ **Avoid for-profit hospitals.** According to health consumer advocates such as the People's Medical Society, some for-profit hospitals charge as much as 20 percent more than nonprofit hospitals.

❑ **Time your arrival.** The longer you're in the hospital, the more it costs. Whenever possible, avoid being admitted on weekends or during holidays when you're likely to get no treatment.

❑ **Brown bag it.** If it's not in violation of hospital policy and your doctor gives the OK, consider bringing your own food to the hospital. Ask friends and relatives to bring in beverages and meals. Negotiate for a discount and *get it in writing* before your admission. You may eat better and save money.

❑ **Bring your own essentials.** Have you ever looked at a hospital bill and seen how much

Many Procedures Can Be Performed on an Outpatient Basis

they charge for items such as facial tissues? It's outrageous. Let the hospital know you'll be bringing in your own essentials, and you don't want to be charged for things you don't want or use.

❏ **Bring your own T.V., radio, and telephone.** Charges for these items can be high, especially if you have to stay for a long period of time.

❏ **Request generic drugs.** Tell your doctor you want less expensive, generic drugs whenever possible. On average, generic drugs are as much as one-third cheaper than brand names. For some drugs, the savings can be as much as two-thirds.

❏ **Check out ASAP.** Don't hang around. Check out before the new day charges begin. Ask your doctor to let you recuperate at home, when possible.

❏ **Ask for an itemized bill and study it carefully.** It's not uncommon for hospitals to make billing errors. Your best bet is to keep a hospital log while you're there, tracking doctor visits, tests, and medications (if you're too sick, ask a friend or relative to do it). Then compare your log with your hospital bill. If you have questions, take them up with the hospital. Ask your insurance company not to pay items that are in question until there's an audit review.

❏ **Ask your doctor about a day surgery center.** Established a few years ago, day surgery centers (also called short-stay surgery centers) offer minor surgical services for conditions that require a few hours or overnight care at most. They are convenient and less expen-sive than hospitals and can handle minor surgical procedures efficiently.

Avoiding Surgery

Surgery, in many instances, can be lifesaving. However, all surgeries carry risks. As a medical consumer, there are steps you can take to decrease your chances of undergoing surgery.

❏ **Reduce your risk factors.** Many common health problems that result in surgery, such as hernia, hemorrhoids, gallbladder disease, and many bowel problems, are strongly related to lifestyle risk factors. Some risk factors, such as family history, cannot be avoided. But many risk factors, such as cigarette smoking, overweight, poor eating habits, and a sedentary lifestyle, can be prevented. By adopting a healthy lifestyle now and eliminating risk factors, you can avoid many of the most common surgeries in the future.

❏ **Learn about your condition.** Take the time to educate yourself about your health problem and the treatments for it. Many public libraries carry lay health and medical books and magazines that may offer information. If you live near a medical school, use the resources of the medical library for information. Ask the librarian to help. You can also call associations and support groups concerned with your condition.

❏ **Ask questions.** If your doctor recommends surgery, don't automatically agree to it. There

By Adopting a Healthy Lifestyle Now, You May Avoid Some Surgeries in the Future

When Your Doctor Recommends Surgery, Ask for a Referral for a Second Opinion

may be alternative treatments. Ask your doctor: What are the risks and benefits of the surgery? How long will it take to recover from surgery? What are the alternative treatments, if any, to surgery? What will happen if we do nothing?

❑ **Get a second opinion.** When your doctor recommends surgery, especially if your physician is a surgeon, ask for a referral for a second opinion. By doing so, you are not challenging your doctor's authority or competence. You're simply being responsible for your own health and well-being. In addition, many insurance companies require that you get a second opinion before undergoing any major procedure.

Most physicians gladly offer referrals to other doctors for a second opinion. If yours does not, ask your family physician. You can also get referrals from your local hospital or the medical school in your area. Call the head of the appropriate department and ask for names of specialists or subspecialists who have a local practice. Then be sure to check the specialist's qualifications (board certification, hospital affiliations, years of experience, and so on) before making an appointment.

Your Guide to "Alternative" Care

In recent years, interest has grown dramatically in nontraditional forms of medicine and healing, so-called "alternative" medicine. Alternative therapies and remedies have been proposed for problems as minor as the common cold and as serious as cancer. Indeed, individuals suffering from chronic problems for which traditional medicine can offer no cure—such as arthritis, chronic fatigue syndrome, and some types of cancer—are often the most vulnerable to claims from alternative practitioners. Out of desperation, many are willing to try just about anything for relief.

Unfortunately, while some alternative therapists have a genuine interest in helping people, many are simply out to make a buck. And while some alternative therapies have shown some promise for certain conditions, many more have never been scientifically proved to have any benefit at all (often, their practitioners cannot even explain how the therapy works). Some may even cause harm—either directly, through the administration of potentially dangerous substances or treatments, or indirectly, by delaying traditional medical diagnosis and treatment that could provide benefit.

How can you protect yourself from useless or dangerous products and therapies promoted by quacks and hucksters? Here are some tips and guidelines:

❑ **Check out scientific evidence.** Most snake-oil salesmen make liberal use of scientific terms and references in promoting their "miracle" products or services. They may use meaningless, overblown, or vague phrases such as "oxygenate your body" or "cleanse your body of numerous toxins." They may claim credentials or degrees that are fraudulent. Before buying a product or service, find out who endorses it. Is it a national professional association or health organization that has credibility, such as the Arthritis Foundation? Or is it some scientific-sounding group you've never heard of? Find out if recognized experts in the field recommend the product or service.

❏ **Don't be swayed by "testimonials."** It doesn't matter if there are "thousands of satisfied customers." Weight-loss programs are notorious for showing fuzzy "before" and "after" photos of people who presumably lost weight on their plan. Don't be fooled. Testimonials may be totally fabricated. Even if they're true, it doesn't mean the product or service will help you.

❏ **Be careful of "guarantees."** No reputable medical product or service comes with a "100% money back guarantee." In medicine, there are always exceptions.

❏ **Don't fall for "secret" cures, and don't believe claims of "new scientific breakthroughs" that few other professionals know about.** Be suspicious if you're told you are "one of a select few who know about this product" or this is a "secret" treatment that medical doctors don't want you to know about. Any treatment that could help a serious condition would be widely used by medical professionals. There aren't any "secret formulas" or "magic bullets" in the medical community. New products or procedures are put

COMMON ALTERNATIVE THERAPIES

In recent years, consumer interest has grown in these common types of alternative therapies:

Acupuncture: Practiced in China for thousands of years, acupuncture involves inserting long, thin needles into what practitioners call *meridians*, or energy pathways, in order to release any blockage. The acupuncturist then gently rocks or rotates the needles or applies a small electric current to the needles for a short time. The technique stems from a theory that health is based on the free flow of energy, or *qi*, through the body. According to the theory, when a blockage occurs along the energy pathways, disease can occur.

No one really understands how acupuncture works. There have been some reports of its effectiveness in blocking pain, and some surgeons have used acupuncture to perform drug-free surgery. Acupuncture has also gained some popularity as an aid in helping smokers and other addicts kick their habits. Acupuncture is gaining a wider acceptance among some medical doctors, and some medical schools now offer courses in it.

Chiropractic: Doctors of chiropractic (DCs) receive several years of chiropractic training and must pass a state examination to practice legally in that state. The focus of chiropractic is manipulation of the bones of the spine and of the muscles and joints of the body to relieve a variety of health problems. Chiropractic "adjustments" may be accompanied by other techniques—heat treatment, massage, and exercise, for example—that more traditional practitioners such as physical therapists use.

While some studies have shown that chiropractic manipulations of the spine may relieve certain types of lower-back pain, there is yet no solid scientific proof that it works for other ailments. In most states, chiropractors are not allowed to prescribe medications or to recommend or perform surgery.

Homeopathy: The philosophy in homeopathy is that "like cures like." Homeopaths administer a very small quantity of a natural agent that, in larger doses, would *cause* the patient's symptom, in the belief that the minute quantities will actually cure the disease or relieve the symptom. Critics point out that because the agents are so diluted, they could not possibly have any appreciable effect.

❏   ❏   ❏

through years of testing to ensure they're safe and effective. Besides, just think about it: If such a secret cure existed, no doctors and no one in doctors' families would die of cancer or otherwise suffer from disease.

❑ **Be suspicious if the product or practitioner warns you against telling your medical doctor you are using the product or undergoing the treatment.** A responsible practitioner would want you to inform your other practitioners so potentially dangerous interactions or side effects could be prevented.

❑ **Never buy from telephone solicitors or door-to-door salesmen, and be careful of practitioners who sell products out of their office.** It's the job of solicitors to sell their

product or service. Bona fide health products or services don't have to be peddled by high-pressure salesmen. Never give your credit card number or bank account numbers to solicitors no matter how convincing they may be or how honest they seem. In addition, be wary of any practitioner—traditional or alternative—who is clearly and directly profiting from a product, such as one who insists you buy vitamin supplements from his or her office rather than at your local pharmacy.

❑ **Avoid a claim that sounds too good to be true.** It probably is. Outrageous claims are another clue you've encountered medical quackery. If that cream could really enlarge your bust size, why wouldn't plastic surgeons be using it? If tissue from cow fetuses could really make your skin look "years younger," why haven't dermatologists been prescribing it? Ask yourself, do these claims make sense?

If you still plan to try an alternative practitioner or therapy, keep the following guidelines in mind:

❑ **Get an adequate diagnosis.** Even if you decide to have your condition treated with alternative medicine, have your condition diagnosed first by someone with thorough training in clinical diagnosis. If you have any doubts about the diagnosis, don't hesitate to get a second opinion.

❑ **Ask your doctor for his or her opinion about alternative therapies.** And be sure to ask your doctor if he or she believes the alternative therapy could cause you harm, either

PUT THE STOP ON MEDICAL INSURANCE FRAUD

Fraudulent insurance claims are another huge source of medical fraud. You may say, "Why should I care? My insurance company pays for it." Actually, you pay for fraudulent insurance claims in the form of higher insurance premiums. Here are some tips to put the stop on medical insurance fraud:

❑ Review your medical bills carefully. Look at the type, number, and dates of service billed.

❑ Ask questions if you don't understand the charges or you didn't receive the services billed.

❑ Never sign blank insurance forms. Make sure all forms are dated.

❑ Never lend your Medicare or other health insurance card.

❑ Never give your Medicare card number or other health card I.D. out over the phone.

❑ Report suspected insurance abuses to your health insurance provider.

❑   ❑   ❑

alone or if used in conjunction with any conventional therapy or medications you might be using. (You may be willing to risk money on the chance that an alternative therapy could provide some benefit, but are you willing to put your health in further jeopardy?)

❑ **Learn about your condition and about the alternative treatments.** Talk with friends and those in support groups and find out which alternative treatments have been successful for them. Read all you can about your health problem.

❑ **Check out the practitioner's credentials.** Is he or she licensed? (Some states don't require licensing.) Where and for how long did he or she train? What conditions does the practitioner's training and clinical experience qualify him or her to treat? What experience has he or she had with treating your condition?

❑ **Be clear about the treatment plan before you begin.** This item does not just apply to alternative health. When you undergo any form of treatment from *any* health practitioner, ask: What will my treatment entail? How long will it take? What are the possible adverse reactions I might experience? Is there any research to back up this treatment for this condition? How many people with this condition that you treated got better?

❑ **Find out what it will cost.** Alternative health has its share of con artists. Find out the charges beforehand. If the price seems unreasonable, it probably is.

❑ **Don't give up your power.** You're in charge. Stop treat-

ment if you don't feel it's working. You're paying the practitioner. If you don't like the results, fire him or her.

❑ **Trust your "gut" reactions.** It's important to have a good "fit" with any healer. Do you feel comfortable and cared for by this practitioner? How do you feel after a visit?

Compiling Your Medical History

When you first go to your primary care provider, he or she will take your medical history. The information is usually gathered through a combination of a written questionnaire and an interview with your doctor. Your medical history should include the following information.

● **Your chief complaint.** If you're seeing the doctor for a reason other than a routine screening or physical, he or she will ask, "What brings you here today?" Your answer to this question establishes the priorities for the rest of the questions the doctor asks about your medical history. Express your problem clearly. If you have more than one problem, but you're unsure if the symptoms are related, tell the doctor. Above all, be honest and thorough in your description.

● **Your present illness.** This is the story behind your chief complaint. Be prepared to

Do You Have a Complete Record of Your Medical History?

It's a Good Idea to Keep a Medical Log

answer these questions: When did the problem begin? How long has it been going on? How have your symptoms changed? Tell the doctor about your situation in the order it occurred. Making your account well-organized and avoiding unnecessary details or digressions helps. Include any supporting information such as medications you may be taking, reports or X rays from other doctors, and any allergic reactions you may have to drugs.

- **Your past medical history.** Information here provides the doctor with more information about your general health. Be direct and reasonably brief in your answers. Include any operations, hospitalizations, allergies, medications, and childhood as well as adult illnesses. Don't forget to report vitamin and mineral supplements and any over-the-counter medications you may be taking.

  It's a good idea to keep a medical log in which you record dates of any illnesses and hospital stays, prescriptions, immunizations, and so on. The log helps you keep all the information your doctor needs handy and easy to update, and you don't have to worry about trying to remember everything.

- **Your social history.** Here the doctor may ask seemingly personal questions about your habits—your job, family, interpersonal stresses, smoking, drug and alcohol use, and your exposure to toxic substances. Your answers can be vitally important to diagnosing and treating your current illness. Be sure you give the doctor thorough and honest information.

- **Your family medical history.** More than 3,000 ailments can be inherited, including increased risk for cancer, diabetes, arthritis, and heart disease. Letting your doctor know about your family medical history can be one way to help ward off your inherited "fate." Before you visit the doctor, create a family health tree to share with your doctor. Start with your grandparents and list all of your close relatives. If you don't have this information, interview family members to learn as much as you can. Include chronic ailments as well as major surgeries and causes of death. Then talk with your doctor about any obvious inherited health patterns.

How to Talk with Your Doctor

Many of us seem to lose all of our communication and assertive skills when we face a doctor. To get the best care, you need to be a *partner* with your doctor and you need to know how to communicate well. Try these suggestions:

- ❑ **Prepare an agenda.** Before you go to the doctor, make up a list of questions, symptoms, and concerns. Be specific, concise, and direct. Take this list with you so if you do get flustered, you can read directly off your list.

- ❑ **Be sure you understand the doctor's diagnosis.** If your doctor mentions a word or procedure you don't understand, ask him or her to explain it.

There are no stupid questions. Remember, you're not the one who went to medical school; you're not supposed to know all about medicine.

- **Ask about your treatment options.** What are the risks and benefits of each option? What will happen if you do nothing about your condition? What lifestyle changes can you make that might improve the situation?

- **Avoid unnecessary testing.** Ask the doctor to explain exactly why you need each test, what's involved, and how much it will cost.

- **Understand your medications.** Before leaving the doctor's, be sure you understand what the drug is for, its name, how to take it, any possible side effects and risks, precautions necessary while taking the drug, and any special instructions such as food or drug interactions. (See the sidebar, *What Should I Ask My Doctor About My Prescription?*)

- **Find out if you need a follow-up appointment.**

- **Ask about a second opinion.**

Screening Tests

One way to reduce your health risks and your medical costs is to have periodic screening tests. The intervals for testing we suggest here are only guides. Talk with your doctor about a screening schedule appropriate for your age and current health status, among

WHAT SHOULD I ASK MY DOCTOR ABOUT MY PRESCRIPTION?

A wise health consumer asks the following questions about any medications a doctor prescribes.

- What is the name of the drug and what is it supposed to do?

- How much will it cost? Is it a generic or brand name drug? (Generic drugs are less expensive. If your doctor prescribes a brand name drug instead of a generic drug, ask if he or she has a good reason for doing so.)

- How and when should I take this drug?

- Do I need to take this medicine on an empty stomach or with meals?

- Should I take the medicine until it is gone?

- What are the side effects? What should I do if they occur?

- Must I abstain from alcohol or any foods with this medicine?

Also, be sure to tell your doctor about any other medications you may be taking and remind him or her about any medication allergies you may have.

❏   ❏   ❏

other factors. If you have a family history of a particular disease, your doctor might want you to be screened more often.

- **Pap smear.** Women who are sexually active should be regularly screened for cancer of the cervix. Many health experts recommend annual pap smears; others say after three negative tests, a screening can be performed every three to five years.

- **Breast examination and mammogram.** The American Cancer Society (ACS) recommends women older than 20 years of age perform a breast self-examination monthly and

Talk with Your Doctor About a Schedule for Screening Tests

have an annual physician exam. Talk with your health care practitioner about how to perform a breast self-exam; also see *The Breast Self-Examination*, page 271, for a description of the technique.

ACS also suggests women have periodic mammograms—breast X rays—that can detect lumps too small to feel. The ACS suggests women between the ages of 35 and 40 have a "baseline" mammogram. Women aged 40 to 49 should have a mammogram every other year and after aged 50, annually. Other health experts recommend regular mammograms only for women aged 50 and older. But if you have a family history of breast cancer, you may need more frequent exams.

- **Blood pressure screening.** High blood pressure has been called a "silent killer" because it produces no symptoms. To reduce your risk of stroke, have your blood pressure checked annually.

- **Cholesterol screening.** The National Heart, Lung, and Blood Institute's Cholesterol Education Program suggests adults have a total blood cholesterol screening once to determine their level. If the total is below 200, repeat the test every five years. For readings greater than 200, you should undergo, annually, a more detailed test that determines the levels of high-density lipoproteins (HDL), or "good" cholesterol, and low-density lipoproteins (LDL), or "bad" cholesterol (see *Keep Tabs on Your Blood Cholesterol Level*, page 293, for additional information).

Get Immunized

You may think vaccinations are only for children. Think again. The Centers for Disease Control and Prevention recommends the following immunizations for adults:

- **Tetanus.** Initially, you'll need a three-shot series then every ten years a booster to protect against this potentially deadly bacterial infection.

- **German measles (Rubella).** Babies whose mothers develop rubella during pregnancy are at risk for severe birth defects. If you receive this immunization, wait at least three months before getting pregnant.

- **Mumps.** If you never had the mumps as a child, get a vaccination. Mumps in men may impair fertility.

- **Influenza.** Have a flu shot every fall if you're older than aged 65 or if you have a chronic health condition such as respiratory problems.

- **Pneumococcal pneumonia.** People older than aged 65 or those with chronic health problems should have a single vaccination.

- **Hepatitis B.** Anyone who is at high risk for contracting hepatitis B (such as health care workers, injecting drug users, or persons who have sexual contact with an infected person) should be vaccinated.

- **Measles.** Have a measles shot if you were born after 1956 and have never had the disease.

- **Overseas vaccinations.** People who travel overseas need immunizations specific to the area to which they're traveling. Talk with your local health department or call the Centers for Disease Control and Prevention Office of International Health Information (404-639-2573) for the latest vaccination information. In addition to shots, some overseas travelers may also require medicines to prevent other illnesses such as malaria.

How to Take a Temperature

A loved one feels hot and feverish. Before you call the doctor, take the temperature so you can relay this important information to your health care provider. Here's how to do it right:

Using an Oral Thermometer

1. First, be sure the person hasn't had anything cold or hot to eat or drink for the past 30 minutes.

2. If you're using a glass-mercury thermometer, shake it until it reads 96 degrees. If you're using an electronic thermometer, check the batteries (a clear set of black numbers means the batteries are working; faded, partial, or scrambled numbers means it's time to change the batteries).

3. Place the bulb end of the oral thermometer or the probe end of the electronic thermometer under the person's tongue, and have them close their mouth (instruct

READ YOUR PRESCRIPTION RIGHT

As a smart medical consumer, you should know how to read your prescription. If you don't understand what your prescription says, don't be intimidated; ask your doctor or pharmacist. Use this handy list to help you decipher your doctor's R_x (prescription) lingo.

ac	before meals
AD	right ear
AL	left ear
bid	twice a day
c	with
c̄	without
cap	capsule
cc	cubic centimeter
ext	external use, extract
gt, gtt	drop, drops
h	hour
hs	at bedtime
int	between meals
ml	milliliter (1 oz=30 ml; 1 tsp=5 ml)
npo	nothing by mouth
OD	right eye
OS	left eye
OU	each eye
pc	after meals
po	by mouth
pr	by rectum
prn	as needed
qh	every hour
q2h	every two hours
q3h	every three hours
qid	four times a day
sl	under the tongue
sol	solution
susp	suspension
tab	tablet
tid	three times a day
top	apply topically
Ut dict	as directed

Do You
Know the
Proper Way
to Take a
Temperature?

them not to bite down on the thermometer).

4. Leave the thermometer in place for *two minutes*.

5. Read the glass thermometer by slowly rotating it until you can clearly see the line of mercury. The number where the mercury ends is the temperature. Normal oral temperature is 98.6 degrees Fahrenheit.

Using a Rectal Thermometer
To take a young child's temperature accurately, you need a rectal thermometer.

1. Coat the bulb or probe with petroleum jelly. Gently insert the thermometer into the rectum *no more than one inch*.

2. To hold the thermometer in place, gently cup the child's buttocks in the palm of your hand, resting the thermometer between your fingers.

3. Leave the thermometer in place for *two minutes*.

4. Read the thermometer as above. Normal rectal temperature is 99.6 degrees Fahrenheit.

Using an Armpit Thermometer
You can also take a temperature using an armpit or "axillary" thermometer.

1. Place the bulb or probe under the arm, pressing the arm snugly against the body.

2. Wait three or four minutes.

3. Read the temperature as above. Normal axillary temperature is 97.6 degrees Fahrenheit.

After using any type of thermometer, be sure to clean it thoroughly with warm (not hot) water and soap. Then wipe with rubbing alcohol and store in its container.

Your Home Medicine Chest

Take a few minutes and look through your home medicine chest. What did you find? If you're like most people, you found toothpaste, several bottles of expired prescription medications, a few adhesive bandages, makeup, and beauty products. You're not exactly ready for a minor medical emergency. Here's what should be in a well-stocked medicine cabinet.

Medicines (kept in a cool, dry spot, not in the bathroom)

- **Aspirin.** The less expensive generic brands are as effective as brand-name products. Aspirin is terrific for relieving fever, aches and pains, sprains, menstrual cramps, and inflammation (especially from arthritis). However, aspirin can cause an upset stomach. If you're bothered by aspirin stomach upset, try coated (enteric) aspirin. It takes longer to work but is kinder to your tummy.
  Aspirin Warnings: Persons with a history of bleeding disorders should not use aspirin. Pregnant women should not take aspirin unless directed by a physician. Children who take aspirin are at risk for developing Reye syndrome, a rare but potentially fatal illness that affects the brain and the liver.

- **Acetaminophen.** Available as a generic or brand-name pain reliever (such as Tylenol or Datril), acetaminophen is effective in reducing pain and fever, but it does not reduce inflammation. It tends to be easier on the stomach than aspirin and is available in liquid form for children. *Pregnant women should not take acetaminophen unless directed by a physician.*

- **Ibuprofen.** You can buy this pain reliever over the counter (Advil, Nuprin, Motrin) or in larger doses by prescription. Use as you would aspirin. The warnings for ibuprofen are the same as for aspirin. Ibuprofen is especially effective for menstrual cramping. If you're pregnant, have a history of kidney or liver disease, peptic ulcer disease, or bleeding disorders, talk with your doctor before taking ibuprofen. Because it is uncertain whether ibuprofen has a role in Reye syndrome, do not give ibuprofen to a child.

- **Aloe vera gel.** This is burn-relief-in-a-bottle. The gel from the aloe vera plant provides effective relief for minor burns, scalds, cuts, and scrapes. You'll find it in most drug and health food stores.

- **Antacids.** You can buy antacids (such as Tums or Rolaids) or you can simply keep baking soda (bicarbonate of soda) on hand to relieve heartburn or indigestion. Don't overuse baking soda or use it if you're on a salt-restricted diet.

- **Antihistamines.** Over-the-counter antihistamines are good for relieving stuffiness and other symptoms caused from some types of allergies. They are also effective against hive-type reactions. But antihistamines make the user drowsy. *Pregnant women should not take antihistamines.*

- **Antibacterial and antifungal ointments.** These ointments help prevent and treat minor infections and keep bandages from sticking to wounds.

- **Decongestants.** You can buy decongestants in pill or spray form to relieve nasal and chest congestion from colds and flu. Don't use decongestant sprays for more than three days or the medicine itself may actually cause the lining of the nose to become inflamed. When the medication wears off, this inflammation causes more congestion, and a vicious cycle develops.

- **Hydrogen peroxide.** This is a handy cleanser for cleaning wounds.

- **Rubbing alcohol.** Another disinfectant, alcohol is good for cleaning thermometers and other items.

- **Syrup of Ipecac.** If you have children, this is a particularly important addition to your home medicine chest. Syrup of Ipecac induces vomiting in the event of accidental poisoning. Never use this product without consulting your physician or local poison control center. Don't use it to treat corrosive poisons such as lye or acid.

Supplies
In addition to medications, keep these supplies on hand in your home medicine chest.

- Adhesive bandages
- Gauze pads
- Adhesive tape
- Thermometer
- Tweezers
- Scissors
- Elastic ("Ace") bandages

Does Your Medicine Chest Contain What You Need to Handle a Minor Emergency?

INDEX

Blood *(continued)*
  pressure, high. *See*
    Hypertension.
  pressure, low, 42
  sugar, 284, 285
  supply, 260
  transfusions, 262
Body
  composition, 48, 51, 73,
    75
  shape, 48, 280
Botulism, 216
Bowel regularity, 55,
  199–200
Breast
  cancer, 191–192, 240,
    267, 268, 270, 301,
    312
  cysts, 192
  infection, 191
  lumps, 191–192, 269,
    270, 272
  mastitis, 191
  self-examination, 271–272
  size (male), 318
Breast-feeding, 20,
  190–192
  and calcium, 39–40
  and nutrition, 39–42
Breathing
  deep, 165, 174
  Lamaze method, 143
  meditation, 137–138
  mouth, 111
  rapid, 141
  shallow, 141
Bronchospasms, 265
Bronchitis, 192–193, 197,
  277
Bronchodilators, 289
Bruises, 334
Bruxism, 119–120
Bulimia. *See* Eating disorders.
Bunions, 218
Burns, 334–335
  care of, 335

Bursitis, 193, 242
Bypass surgery (coronary
  artery), 281

C

Caffeine, 120, 155, 204,
  207
  and anxiety, 168, 175
  and breast lumps, 192
  and insomnia, 234
  and restless legs
    syndrome, 245
  and stress, 132
  and ulcers, 305
Calcium, 35, 36
  deficiency, 300
  and kidney stones, 297
  and lactose intolerance,
    34–35
  and menopause, 240
  and osteoporosis, 300,
    301
  in pregnancy, 39–40, 42
  supplements, 20, 37–38,
    39, 117
Calculus, 108–109, 110,
  116
Calluses, 218, 219
Calories, 26, 54, 56
  burning, 61
  from carbohydrates, 12
  from fat, 13
  restrictions, 48, 54
  total, 15
Cancer, 267–276. *See also*
    Leukemia.
  bladder, 267
  breast, 190, 191–192,
    240, 267, 268, 270,
    301, 312
  cervical, 270
  colon, 21, 23, 55, 199,
    226, 267, 268
  detection, 269–270
  endometrial, 301
  and fat, 14
  and fiber, 21

Cancer *(continued)*
  lung, 267, 316
  lymph, 271
  and marijuana, 316
  ovarian, 267, 268
  pancreatic, 267
  prostate, 268, 270
  and protein, 12–13
  rectal, 23, 226, 267
  skin, 267
  and smoking, 268, 319
  uterine, 240, 267, 268
Carbohydrates, 12, 16, 25,
  27, 38, 59
  calories from, 12
  types, 12, 27
Carcinoma, 272
Cardiopulmonary resuscitation, 335–336
Cardiovascular
  conditioning, 75–76. *See
    also* Exercise, aerobic.
  endurance, 72, 75, 96
  stress, 76
Carotid bruit, 303
Carpal tunnel syndrome,
  193–195
Car sickness, 224
Cataracts, 286
Centers for Disease Control
  and Prevention, 217–
  218, 256, 258, 261
Central nervous system,
  298, 299, 311, 312,
  317
Cerebral embolism, 302
Cerebral hemorrhage, 302
Cerebral thrombosis, 302
Chalazions, 210
Chemotherapy, 270–271
Chicken pox, 245
Children
  and accidents, 362–363
  arthritis in, 262
  choking in, 338
  conjunctivitis in, 210
  CPR for, 337

Rape, 365
Recommended Dietary
    Allowance, 16–21, 24
    minerals, 16, 18, 19
    vitamins, 16, 17, 19, 20,
        21
Reflexology, 143
Relaxation
    exercises, 174
    progressive, 138–139,
        176
    techniques, 165, 168,
        176, 237
Reproductive system
    and alcohol, 312
    disruptions, 318
    surgery, 232, 238
Reserpine, 158
Restless legs syndrome, 245
Restoril, 158
Retinopathy, diabetic, 286
Reye syndrome, 206, 212,
    224
Rhinitis, 186
Risk factors
    back pain, 188
    cancer, 267–269
    cholesterol, 294
    glaucoma, 291–292
    heart disease, 278–280
    hypertension, 296
    osteoporosis, 300
    skin cancer, 274
    stroke, 302–303
    for suicide, 159
Rocky Mountain spotted
    fever, 325
Rubella, 382

S

SAD. See Seasonal
    affective disorder.
Safety, 323–366
    auto, 361–362
    bicycle, 364
    boat, 366
    from crime, 365

Safety (continued)
    exercise, 98–99
    food, 31–33
    home, 362
    travel, 364–365
    water, 366
Salicylic acid, 183, 255
Saliva, 108
    artificial, 121
    non-production of, 121
Salmonella bacteria, 217
Salt. See Sodium.
Scorpions, 324, 326
Scrapes, 339–340
Seasonal affective disorder,
    153, 154–155
Sedatives, 157
Seizures, 289–291
    in encephalitis, 328
    medication, 158
Self-help groups
    addictions, 321
    for anxiety, 176
Serotonin, 58, 155, 169
Sexual
    abstinence, 260
    dysfunction, 169–170,
        227–229
    impotence, 227–229
    infertility, 231–233
    intercourse, 239, 256
    monogamy, 260
    responsiveness, 230
Sexuality
    mid-life, 239
    teenage, 156
Shiatsu massage, 143
Shingles, 245–246
    and AIDS, 259
Shock, 217
Side effects
    antianxiety medications,
        169, 176
    antidepressants, 161, 164
    chemotherapy, 271
    cholesterol medication,
        295

Side effects (continued)
    diarrhea as, 203
    diet pills, 316
    glaucoma medication, 292
    hypertension medication,
        297
    radiation, 271
    steroids, 318
    vitamins, 19
Simethicone, 214
Sinuses, 197
Sinusitis, 246–247
Skin conditions
    acne, 182–183
    from alcohol, 311
    cancer, 267, 272–275
    chafing, 195
    dermatitis, 201–202
    diaper rash, 202–203
    dry skin, 205
    eczema, 128, 195,
        201–202
    hives, 128, 227
    poisonous plant rashes,
        346–350
    psoriasis, 244–245
    sunburn, 274–275,
        358–359
    tanning, 273–274
    warts, 255
Skinfold-caliper testing, 51
Sleep, 73
    apnea, 247
    deprivation, 247
    improving, 76
    insomnia, 233–235
    pills for, 316–317
    snoring in, 247–248
Slivers, 350–351
Smoking, 207, 258,
    307–322
    addiction, 318–319
    and allergies, 184
    and asthma, 265
    and bronchitis, 192
    and cancer, 268, 319
    and cholesterol, 294

Symptoms *(continued)*
  depression, 153, 154
  diabetes, 169, 284–285
  drug abuse, 320
  ear infection, 206
  encephalitis, 328
  epilepsy, 290
  food poisoning, 216
  fracture, 352
  gum disease, 111
  headaches, 223
  heart disease, 169
  heat stroke, 343–344
  herpes infection, 221
  HIV infection, 259
  hypothermia, 342
  influenza, 215
  irritable bowel syndrome,
    235–236
  kidney stones, 297–298
  Lyme disease, 326
  menopause, 238–239
  multiple sclerosis,
    298–299
  osteoporosis, 300
  pneumonia, 193
  premenstrual syndrome,
    244
  shingles, 246
  sprains, 351
  stroke, 303
  teething, 125
  ulcer, 304–305
  urinary tract infection,
    252
  varicose veins, 254
  yeast infection, 256
Syrup of Ipecac, 363

T
Tae kwan do, 144
T'ai Chi chu'an, 137, 144
Tartar. *See* Calculus.
Teeth, 116–117. *See also*
  Dental health.
  aches in, 119
  brushing, 103, 104, 116

Teeth *(continued)*
  choosing toothbrushes,
    107, 112, 116
  dentin, 102
  disclosing tablets, 112
  enamel, 102, 115
  fillings, 113–114
  flossing, 103, 104–107,
    111, 112
  and fluoride, 102,
    103–104
  grinding, 119–120
  injury to, 126
  permanent, 124
  primary, 124
  sensitive, 118
  staining, 104
  toothpastes, 110, 112
  using toothpicks,
    108–109
  whitening, 118
  wisdom, 116, 126
Teething, 125
Temperature. *See* Fever.
Temporomandibular joint
    disorder, 120
Tendinitis, 242, 249–250
Tennis elbow, 249–250
Tenoretic, 158
Tenormin, 158
Testosterone, 228, 317
Tests
  for allergies, 184
  blood sugar, 284
  cholesterol, 293, 382
  fitness, 73–75
  HIV, 261–262
  hypertension, 382
  infertility, 233
  Karvonen, 77
  mammography, 269–270,
    381–382
  maximum heart-rate,
    77–78
  Pap smear, 221, 270,
    381
  prostate, 270

Tests *(continued)*
  pulmonary function, 266
  screening, 381–382
  skinfold-caliper, 51
  stress, 280
  ulcers, 305
Tetanus, 330, 340, 350,
    382
Therapy
  alternative, 376–379
  anxiety, 176
  behavioral, 112, 160,
    176
  cognitive, 69, 160, 166,
    168, 174, 176
  for depression,
    160–164
  desensitization, 112, 174,
    175
  drug, 168, 176
  electroconvulsive, 160
  finding a therapist,
    161–163
  hormone, 183
  hormone replacement,
    224, 238, 239, 240,
    279, 281, 294, 295,
    301, 346
  interpersonal, 161
  light, 155, 202
  relaxation, 120, 128
  and stress, 129
Thermometers, 383–384
Thrombophlebitis, 254
Thrush, 259
Thyroid
  and anxiety, 168
  disorders, 194
  and perspiration, 208
Ticks, 325–327
  removal, 327
Tinnitus, 207–208
Toenails, ingrown,
    219–220
Tofranil, 161, 231
Toothbrushes, 107,
    116–117